PUCK OF THE DROMS

Puck

OF THE

DROMS

THE LIVES & LITERATURE OF THE IRISH TINKERS

BY ARTELIA COURT

With Folktales, Other Oral Literature, and Biography
Collected by Alen MacWeeney with the Collaboration of
Artelia Court. Literary Notes by Thomas Munnelly and
Others. And Photographs by Alen MacWeeney.

UNIVERSITY OF CALIFORNIA PRES
BERKELEY · LOS ANGELES · LONDO

University of California Press
Berkeley and Los Angeles, California

University of California Press, Ltd.
London, England

Library of Congress Cataloging in Publication Data

Court, Artelia.
  Puck of the droms.

  "With oral literature and biography from the collections of Alen MacWeeney and
Artelia Court, photographs by Alen MacWeeney, and literary notes by Thomas Munnelly
and others."
  Bibliography: p. 281
  Includes index.
  1. Tinkers—Ireland. 2. Tinkers—Ireland—Folklore. 3. Tinkers—Ireland—
Biography. I. Title.
GT5960.T542I733   1985   305.5'68   84-16400
ISBN 0-520-03711-1

Printed in the United States of America

1 2 3 4 5 6 7 8 9

This book is a gift to my mother
Artelia Bowne Court
Who died on the eve of its completion,
And to my quick daughter
India.
Travel on.

CONTENTS

Patrick Stokes
Laborer and Tinsmith / 87

Johnny Cassidy
Storyteller / 181

PREFATORY REMARKS
TO THE READER

I t will assist the reader of *Puck of the Droms* to know, from the beginning, a few of its facts. Its title means "trickster of the roads," an epithet that the Tinkers of Ireland have used to describe themselves. Traveling the roads of Ireland and Britain in family bands, living in Gypsylike fashion, working as tinsmiths, peddlers, fortune-tellers, horse traders, entertainers, confidence artists, farm laborers, factory hands, and at any number of other occupations, these unlettered commercial nomads have long adhered to customs, loyalties, and values that set them apart from Ireland's larger population. Traditionally they have been called either "Tinkers" or "Travelers," and I use the terms synonymously in this book, although both smack of disrespect since the Tinkers are outcastes. The Tinkers' way of life is known as "the Traveling life" and is referred to that way here; thus I use the term *settled* to describe the other, dominant way of life and the Irish and British who subscribe to it.

During the years from 1965 through 1973 Alen MacWeeney and I spent many months with Tinkers in Ireland. In their camps and houses, on roadsides, and in pubs and fields we talked with them of their adventures and recorded their biographies and some of the vast body of literature—including stories, songs, riddles, and charms—which they knew by heart and were fond of recounting. This book is the product of that experience and the thought I have given it since.

In the Introduction I offer some observations on Tinker values and styles of thought. I then summarize the passages of Ireland's history which seem to have relevance to the formation of the Tinker clans and some scholarly attempts that have been made to identify Tinker culture and distinguish it from that of the Gypsies. I conclude with a general description of Tinkers' typical activities and styles of behavior and the way these complemented or conflicted with settled interests, chiefly in the period of our visits.

The central part of the book consists of three Tinker biographies, each with a selection of the stories, verses, and songs that furnished the Traveling inner life. Like most of their fellows, Bridget Murphy, Patrick Stokes, and Johnny Cassidy had grown up in the Irish countryside and had been educated by the precepts inherent to rural nomadism. Each had recently come to live in a city or village and was trying to find an occupational and psychic point of balance between the old, rural habits and the new demands that national urbanization forced upon them. The three brought various talents to the effort, but in many ways Patrick and Johnny seemed less able than Bridget to resolve the precariousness of their position. Thus they can be said to represent here three different adaptive responses to modernity, Bridget's being cooperative submission, Patrick's confusion, and Johnny's refusal.

The first biography is that of Bridget Murphy, who was about thirty-four years old at its telling. She had been born the daughter of a tinsmith in the mountains of County Wicklow. One of her grandparents had come from a settled, farming family, and she spent part of her childhood Traveling and part of it settled in an isolated country house. Bridget was deeply attached to her hard-pressed, energetic mother, and her personal ambition was nurtured by helpless commiseration for her mother's lot as well as by an inquisitive intelligence. Although largely unschooled she learned to read and write—the only one of the three Tinkers here who could—and at sixteen married Mickey, whose poverty equaled her own. The young couple spent their early years Traveling the routes their parents had followed, making tinware and peddling, but they abandoned this in time and went to work in the factories of England. Later they returned to Ireland where they took up horse trading and despite Mickey's predilection for drink and characteristically Tinkerish improvidence they achieved a certain prosperity. At Bridget's insistence they bought a small house in a Wicklow village, and they outmaneuvered their failure to have children—for Tinkers, a shameful one—by raising a nephew, Jerry, as their own.

Attributing her establishment as a village housewife partly to her farmer grandfather's "blood," Bridget had taken up the settled life with relish—and some wistfulness. She told the story of her life in a straightforward, linear way, editing from it most of the conflicts, immaterial fancies, and divided loyalties she must have experienced so that past and present formed a continuum justifying the accomplishments of which she was proud and forecasting a compatible future. Conventionally but sincerely romantic, her simplicity of speech, her taste in songs, her orderliness, and her aspirations all reflect her appetite for the values of the settled culture.

Patrick Stokes was also in his mid-thirties, and when we met him, he, his wife Mary Ellen, and their five little daughters made their home in a tent of sacks pitched beside a factory on the outskirts of Dublin. Later they were granted shelter in one of the Sites, or small housing projects built to facilitate Tinker integration into the settled community. Patrick and Mary Ellen both came from prominent Tinker clans of the west of Ireland, and their appearance and ways were declared "old-fashioned" by the eastern Tinkers among whom they found themselves. Mary Ellen was wrapped in a shawl and her skirts were long; Patrick wore the uniform of the rural poor: a pair of high boots and a dark suit coat and trousers. A tinsmith and the son of a tinsmith, he had practiced his trade little for the past ten years or so, and his search for an adequate livelihood had led him a series of adventures in Ireland and England, working at farm labor and various "rackets." He drank heavily, and his practical difficulties were enlarged by his imaginative ones, for the realm of Irish traditional belief—with its omens, ghosts, prescient animals, spirits, and magical rules of safe conduct—was as real to him as the newly met realm of social workers and child-allowance officers.

Of all the Tinkers we knew Patrick was perhaps most alive with moral sensitivity. His biography, told in numerous meetings spanning two years, reflected a complex awareness of his past and present, his inner and outer lives, in urgent collusion and change. A Tinkerish quicksilver mood that alternated between petulance, feverish disappointment or hope, and wild play informed his speech, which boldly combines both old and new elements of his verbal environment.

Johnny Cassidy, the narrator of the last biography and group of stories, had been raised in County Wexford by a widowed father who shepherded five dependent children from one prosperous farm to another, earning their keep as a farmhand and tinsmith and bedding his family down in the farm's hayloft or barn during each prolonged stay. The family's welcome at the same farms year after year was at least partly ensured by the widower's storytelling, which entertained the neighbors who gathered sociably when a day's work was done. As a young boy Johnny sat listening to his father and was deeply impressed with the power of the storyteller's role and of the stories themselves, "hundreds of 'em." In time he married a woman from a family of musical performers, had five children of his own, and Traveled widely in the east and west of Ireland telling the tales he had learned in childhood, giving recitations in pubs, and buying and selling asses. Although he knew tin work, it was not his chief means of support.

Johnny was in his late forties and thus a Tinker elder when we came upon him, his ailing wife, and several of their teenage children living in a sheet metal shack in a city suburb. A tiny, wiry man with a gravelly voice and a hot temper, his patriarchal dignity could be easily offended by an intractable horse, an unexpected shower of rain, or an impertinent woman or child. Other Tinkers were amused by the contrast between his small person and his large self-importance, but they respected him nonetheless.

The responsibilities that Johnny honored were those of the storyteller to his literature and the patriarch to his family. In fulfilling them he served a nobler reality than the one presented him by modern times. The petty incidents, the ups and downs of his life were, he felt, hardly worthy of mention, but for his tales he showed the reverence that the pious feel for a religious tract. Feet fixed to the floor and hands to his knees, Johnny delivered his stories with an intensity that made him seem to levitate as his voice grew high with excitement. Each tale, its precious form and language intact, made a perfect vehicle by which the gifted teller transcended and ruled his mundane surroundings.

The reader of Johnny's, Patrick's, and Bridget's parts of the book will notice that two different typefaces have been used throughout. The biographical material, or what each narrator represented as his original experience, is in one typeface. The avowedly literary or traditional materials told by the narrator and by his friends, relations, and fellows—stories, verses, and songs—are in another typeface. I have presented biographical and literary materials not in an archival fashion but in a way meant to suggest the flow of these three Travelers' talk and their psychic and social uses of oral literature. As it does for all people, literature shaped, elaborated, and supplanted Travelers' firsthand experiences and their memories of the past. But for Patrick the conventional boundaries between fact and fiction (boundaries that the settled world often claims to recognize and trust) were especially obscure. Events he had physically experienced, for example, could be invaded and substantially changed by a literary tale or legend. Equally, he might appropriate such a tale for part of his personal history. Bridget and Johnny exerted more self-conscious literary control than he. They were both careful to preserve the discrete literary form of a tale or a song and thus, on one level of awareness at least, distinguish between literary and other kinds of experience.

At the back of the book the reader will find notes on the provenance and scholarly classification of the literature herein. A glossary of words, phrases, and peculiarly Tinkerish locutions follows.

ACKNOWLEDGMENTS

I acknowledge here my profound gratitude to all those who buoyed me up, bore me along and advised me in the several arduous stages of making this book. They are: the Irish Travelers themselves—especially Bridget Murphy, Patrick Stokes, and Johnny Cassidy and their families, who gave the work its first cause and content—and Dr. Wall, Henry Shapiro, Carol and Donald Braider, Robert Speer, Paula Weideger, Linda Scoville, Sean O'Haughey, Deedee Moore, Andrew T. Court, Bobbie Bristol, Elizabeth Court, Harry Hughes, Leslie Dobbs, Caroline Court, Barbara Heinzen, Angus Cameron, Cynthia Rice, Desmond MacWeeney, Artelia Bowne Court, Kenneth Goldstein, Ellen Andors, Jon Clark, Elizabeth Conlon, Norman Stone, Mary Pinto, Stephanie Woodbridge, and Evelyn MacWeeney. I also wish to thank Jack Miles of the University of California Press and James Odell both of whom kept persistent faith in this project; Ruth E. Andersen, Robert K. Oermann, Iona Opie, Dáithí Ó hOgáin, and Sean O'Sullivan who contributed to its usefulness; and Thomas Munnelly who checked, corrected, and made suggestions for the manuscript and gave selflessly of his enthusiasm for and erudition in Irish culture. Finally, I thank Alen MacWeeney for introducing me to many Travelers, for his zeal, skill, and collaboration as a collector and for his consent to this use of collected materials without which the book would not be as it is.

A. C.

INTRODUCTION

The Why of It

I reland arrived at the middle of the twentieth century an oddity among the small nations of western Europe. Its geography and ethnic attributes had given it a certain political and cultural originality, much of which had been paradoxically preserved by four centuries of alien colonization, rather as the seed of an antediluvian tree may keep its form and even its vitality while buried under an ages' old accretion of stone. When the independently Irish Free State emerged from the obfuscations of World War II—when the stone was finally removed—this cultural integrity was revealed. Native architecture and agrarian technologies, crafts of many kinds, customs, superstitions, social relationships predating the metropolitan, industrial influence, and a complex, lively oral literature were among the antiquated traditions and artifacts that had vanished elsewhere but which Ireland possessed in abundance. The Irish who had preserved and shaped these traditions by active use had also been shaped by them, thus they were not quite like most of their European contemporaries. And even among these countrymen the Tinkers were conspicuous for remaining doggedly true to themselves.

In the 1950s and 1960s while the rest of the citizenry strove to shed its local peculiarities and by industrial, financial, and educational development to prepare itself for membership in the "global village," the Tinkers still pursued the idiosyncratic, mobile style of life that had been an indispensable—although in ways a proscribed—element of traditional Irish society. Tinkerism embodied many of the dynamics and devices of benighted but ancient Irishness and, in some instances, Europeanness, and its contemplation yields a glimpse of the buds that blossomed into several of the most seductive and thorny concepts of the present day: racism, professionalism, commercialism, mass communications, and the species of individualism that compensates for and yet serves the power of the impersonal state. But the public preoccupation with discovering and evaluating varieties of domestic culture (Afro-American and Amerindian, for example), which so marked Americans in the 1960s, was not shared by the Irish, who wished to expunge Tinkerism, not vindicate it or assess its significance.

A 1961 census count of about 6,000 Tinkers living in Ireland and an estimate of perhaps twice that number scattered around Britain, along with the findings of other investigations, were published in 1963 in the *Report of the Commission on Itinerary*. This controversial government booklet—the first of its kind—outlined Tinker health, educational, employment, and behavioral problems and proposed methods for solving them and converting Tinkers to a settled way of life. The *Report* called its subjects "itinerants," a term that seemed a brilliant neologism, and thus was quickly adopted by journalists, officials, and members of the urban middle classes who were eager to unburden themselves of the past and to enroll the Tinkers, undifferentiated, among the nation's laboring poor. In a sense this renaming betokened a humane desire to divest Tinker clans of their immemorial outcasteness. Still, if Tinkers were to be distinguished from other impoverished Irish only by superficial characteristics, then their immense difficulty in assimilating settled values—the difficulty that had given rise to the *Report*—seemed inexplicable except as wrongheadedness, ignorance, or mere perversity.

The assimilation that the *Report* said could be taught and that the settled public impatiently awaited—the settling down to permanent housing, permanent jobs, and orderly subservience to settled institutions—did not take into account what Tinkers themselves called their "blood": a vital quality of their nature which was unalterable and unique.[1] Whatever the Tinker did, however he lived, his blood—so he believed—would ultimately compel him to return to at least some of his Traveling ways. And he was generally right. The conviction of the settled that Tinkers were disadvantaged, everyday Irish whose eccentricity and miscreance could be easily treated by administrative means would meet many disappointments. Clearly, whatever Tinkerism was—and several of the intriguing cultural possibilities are reviewed in the second part of this Introduction—it was more than just disadvantage. I came to believe that it expressed certain perceptions of time and substance, self and society, very unlike predominant twentieth-century settled perceptions. I felt that this difference of perception or cognition was, to use a Tinkerish phrase, "the why of it"—why Tinkers could not easily be like everyone else.

Perhaps the most convenient emblem of the difference was the Tinkers' alternative name: Travelers. The word *Tinker* was properly an occupational title meaning tinsmith, but in Ireland and Britain the word had long since lost its narrow metallurgical connotation and had come to be applied to all the nomadic Irish outcastes of whom I speak, those who worked tin and those who did not. The apparently less definitive term *Traveler* in fact pointed quite specifically to the more essential, psychological attributes of the Tinker. In common Irish parlance *Traveler* was the counterpoise of *settled*, and the different parts of speech here signified. "Travelers" were never said to be "traveled" folk but always those who were "Traveling" or who lived the "Traveling life." Perpetual movement was intrinsic to their state of being. "Settled" people and "settled life" had by definition achieved in the past a condition of stability which no amount of superficial change could undo.[2] The terms betrayed not only the two groups' obvious, external distinctions but also their elusive, internal ones; and external and internal usages were, of course, indissoluble.

One of the cardinal external realities of Traveling life was the traditional exclusion of its followers from important participation in most of Ireland's governmental, industrial, educational, and financial institutions and their lesser social analogues. Tinkers did not vote, pay taxes, or often seek the help of the police or the teaching, medical, or legal professions. They did not belong to trade unions or common-interest or sociable associations, nor could they freely enter most restaurants, pubs, dance halls, theaters, department stores, or public buildings. The jobs they performed were ones that necessitated or traditionally entailed moving from place to place and jobs that settled people would not do or had not thought of doing because they seemed only marginally profitable, respectable, or legal.

Most Tinkers were skilled at several kinds of remunerative work, and they changed the work they did frequently according to the options offered by different situations. In addition to the perhaps culturally seminal work of cold-metal smithery (forming metals without resort to high-temperature processes), peddling or "hawking," horse trading, fortune telling, music making, and begging, Tinkers had discharged innumerable other tasks, so many that they might have coined the phrase "to have many irons in the fire." Their chief source of income was the settled community, and a Tinker's trade life normally consisted of a multitude of small transactions with settled individuals, such as the sale of two horses or a day's labor to a farmer or some baking tins to his wife, a half an hour's singing for coins in a pub, or the purchase and resale of a few used refrigerators.

Since Tinkers had little experience of wage labor and were in other ways estranged from major settled markets and their institutions, few employed the usual settled tactics for increasing the profits of work and realizing capital goods. These tactics—such as cost-cutting, advertising, and improvement of production techniques—required, in any case, a mode of work consistent enough to be examined and regulated. Typically, a Tinker took only a small profit from each of his various trade transactions, and adequate earnings depended largely on his having many such.[3] Thus success in Traveling trade and life ordained that he be relentlessly observant and quick to recognize opportunity and act on it in such a way as to create work and profitability, both monetary and other kinds. But commercial opportunity was inherent in Travel. The Traveler often found his advantage in the distance between country houses and settlements, the lack of convenient communication and transport, and the resultant "harmlessness"— or innocence and isolation—of country folk. He imported and exported goods and services, such as the mattresses that Patrick Stokes remembers selling and the stories that Johnny Cassidy told. (And storytelling was but one of the verbal services provided by the Tinkers' intermediary network of gossip, news, and entertainment.)

While varieties of entrepreneurial trade as well as the entrepreneurial mandate itself encouraged good memory, an accumulation of incidental knowledge, and, above all, alertness, so did the Tinkers' vulnerability resulting from their out-casteness, their lack of civil rights and protections. Settled people were permanently fixed in architectural and societal defensive formations, such as houses, towns, and government, but the Tinker's chief defense against animosity, injury, or loss lay in his family's solidarity.[4] His relations with the family members with whom he Traveled and with more distant kin who made up the family's clan gave the Tinker many of the practical resources settled folk found elsewhere. The loyal kindred was his safe harbor in a sea of other variables.

The critical Tinkerish perceptions that were reinforced or taught by these exigencies of Traveling life can be succinctly stated. First, since cooperation among family members and kindred was vital, any loyalty to nonfamilial organizations that could contest or disrupt the family's primacy and the individual's responsibilities to it was potentially life threatening. To submit oneself—as settled people did—to pyramidal institutions that bound together disparate, unrelated individuals through structured deference and authority was to entrust to those institutions needs for protection, organization, and succor, which were the proper province of the kindred. The family and clan were the only bodies the Tinker had reason to trust with such needs and within which true deference could be paid and authority claimed, largely on the basis of seniority.

Second, in dealing with the world beyond the family responsiveness, flexibility, and ingenuity were the attributes that made for personal success. The successful Traveler responded with flexibility and ingenuity to knowledge of the world that he obtained from custom, from intense aural, visual, and tactile focus, and from imaginative sympathy—in short, from the projection of his undivided self. Settled people, on the contrary, commonly believed that different emotional and intellectual faculties best comprehended different spheres of life, and that knowledge should be compartmentalized accordingly. A settled tradesman, for example, might well believe that only through sympathy could he understand a friend's feelings and that only through rational processes could he master the complexities of his business. To him the idea that business affairs could be conducted on the basis of sympathy or that friendliness might rely on rational analysis would seem disastrous. In the settled realm, too, certain kinds of knowledge were subject to the abstract laws of figurative systems, such as letters and numbers, which were impervious to human feeling. For the Traveler such compartmentalization of human faculties and knowledge was largely dysfunctional. The Tinker only preserved his knowledge by living memory and only enlarged it by sensitive observation. Therefore, the kinds of knowledge that required dissociation from custom and from sensory and sentimental nuance seemed unreliable and unreal.[5]

Third, rightful property, to a Tinker, was personal property: an extension in the material realm of the undivided self. Ownership was licensed by the customary and active use of such property—consisting largely of essential tools, clothing, bedding, vehicles, animals, and ornaments—which was given respect equal that due its owner. Property that was not put to immediate, customary use or that was greater than that use required, that is, private property, was not necessarily rightfully owned and was not due the same respect. The settled person acquired private property as defined by settled institutions (such as the law and the marketplace) in the belief that these agencies would enlarge his social and economic worth and security. The Traveler, on the contrary, usually invested whatever excess property he came by—and his hope—not in goods coextensive with impersonal institutions but in his own pleasure and his natural allies, his kin. Like certain native American hunters he felt that "the best place to store a surplus is in someone else's stomach because sooner or later the sharing will be reciprocated."[6]

Fourth, for Tinkers generally, each unit of property—even a unit of money—

had its concrete value, a value as concrete as a sheet of tin or a sack of potatoes. This value was not widely negotiable, and so property did not have potential for appreciation through speculative use, that is, through use as capital. The limitation on value was partly ensured by the Traveler's alienation from institutions that instrumented speculation and partly by his perception of time and its effects. Settled folk, in their topical stability, typically thought that their acts were subject to temporal progresssion, that time's inexorable movement carried the energy or initiative of their acts forward into a series of subsequent events. Travelers, however, seemed to assume a kind of temporal free will whereby the meaning of time emanated from the singular pattern of an individual's exertions. One practical evidence of this, for example, was the Traveler's acceptance that the period of time that passed while a certain job was being done was proper to that job; he did not plan the job so it would fit into a predetermined period of time. Events were not ruled by time's separate, impersonal progression but by the Traveler's own sense and use of timeliness. And his freedom from temporal determinism favored his agile changes of work and location and the experimental nature of his trade relationships.

Finally, the Traveler's skepticism about impersonal cumulative effect and his entrepreneurial bent, together with his acceptance of confining custom and outcasteness, gave him a surpassing belief in luck. Luck, the ever-present, glittering possibility of unearned or undeserved benefit, was the natural coefficient of his social and economic limitations. But it was also the good fortune that could not be anticipated or planned but that would nonetheless occur and could be seized. It was the real opportunity that Traveling adventitiousness offered, just as the proverb promising that "the lazy man has no luck" implies the active man's plenty.[7]

Settled folk thought some typical Traveling traits constructive or inoffensive, but they deplored others, such as drunkenness, family violence, dishonesty, economic improvidence, superstitiousness, "illiteracy," and lack of punctuality. Both the apparent strengths and alleged weaknesses of the Traveling personality seemed to me warranted or encouraged by the complex of perceptions I have just described.

Tinkers' commonplace addiction to alcohol doubtless reflected their need for a source of warmth, cheer, and bodily well-being which was cheaper and easier had than, say, food, cozy shelter, or medical attention. But more than this I believe drink was a superior easement for the solitary soul on whom—by the tenets of Travel—so much depended. Drink anesthetized against immobilizing fear, for example, and it enabled a man or woman to face the hostile stares of settled folk and to take responsibility for the lives and deaths of his or her children without institutional support. The various stresses of Traveling independence doubtless also gave rise to many of the brawls and violent quarrels among Tinkers, who were usually drinking when they became bellicose. Such quarrels seemingly had certain positive functions as well. They were an expeditious way to resolve those disagreements, territorial ones for example, which no external authority could adjudicate. And Traveling families who were habitually caught up in disputes with other families (as many were) by this means defined the all important extent and coherence of the family and the Traveling community. After a specific matter was resolved the disputants felt little or no antipathy toward one another and they might well join together a week later against some newfound Traveling antagonist. The pattern of quarreling suggested a style of engagement much more than it did an expression of hostility.[8]

Tinkers' dishonesty very often consisted of failure to acknowledge and respect private property, as when they took firewood or hay from a field or broke its walls to allow their own animals pasturage.[9] Equally often, what settled folk called dishonesty was not a pointed effort at deception but adaptive verbalism. In recounting their own experiences and in answering questions, for example, Tinkers frequently intermingled seeming truths and lies. This kind of verbal liberty expressed the individual Traveler's social creativity outside the family. His broad receptivity to sensory and sentimental information and his trust in its uses often made the Traveler answer to his questioner's tone of voice and implicit wishes as much as or more than he answered to an abstract standard of veracity. The Traveler's corresponding ability to attend with sympathy to the verbal inventions of others, whether or not these inventions made common or literal sense, nourished his literary liberality.

Although unlettered, Tinkers were deeply literate. They commanded a sprawling corpus of verbal and musical literature that served the communal purposes of cultural continuity, order, and entertainment as well as the individual's predilections and momentary necessity. While settled groups were inclined to adopt and enjoy only the particular strata of literature that affirmed respective group indentities—as small farmers favored patriotic or nationalistic songs, say, and city office workers read only recently published romantic novels—Tinker literary enthusiams were not so comparmentalized and self-limiting. Tinkers were equally susceptible to forms as varied as the songs of Johnny Mathis, nineteenth-century ballads containing ornate, unfamiliar language, and traditional folktales telling of strange, inexplicable events. Once these stories and songs were committed to memory they became equivalent to many other experiential realities that informed the undivided self and were used orally in its changing interest without inhibiting reference to external canons of truth, untruth, or social precedent.

Many of the traits most frustrating to the settled community were rooted in Tinker incomprehension of abstract quantitative and temporal systems and the complementary concept of property. Social welfare workers who counseled Tinkers to save some of a day's earnings against future wants went unheeded by their clients, who spent all the money they had at day's end on rounds of drinks in the pub, on sweets, or on movies. Many Tinkers thought of money as existing only in the range of small sums customarily exchanged in day-to-day trade: larger sums seemed to defy description. A man was said to have fifteen pounds, or he was said to be "a millionaire." In short, the abstract scale leading from "small" to "great" was unreal and thus not an example of how "great" could be accumulated by small increments. Other difficulties relating to abstraction arose for employers who tried to hold Tinkers to prearranged schedules or tasks, for many perfectly competent adults could not read a clock face or—like the peddler who measured out the linoleum he sold by his own, prone body length—use simple measuring devices.[10] And settled well-wishers who presented Tinkers with objects calculated to increase their social and financial credit saw those efforts wasted when the credit was not realized. Some Tinkers abandoned serviceable houses—as had Bridget Murphy's parents—or used unneeded furniture for kindling, while others instantly sold or discarded well-made clothing, household implements, and luxuries instead of using these to accouter themselves in the settled fashion. Property did not become personal simply by virtue of its admirable qualities, and impersonal credit and creditability were not germane.

The superstitiousness Tinkers evinced by their dread of ghosts and capricious, otherworldly beings of many types, by their anthropomorphizing of animals, and by their adherence to all manner of traditional customs long since discarded as impractical by most of the settled population again seemed a function of the undivided self and its way of knowing and projecting itself onto the world. Since neither the Traveler nor the external challenges he faced remained constant from day to day, he had little occasion for passivity but must adapt and try his strengths repeatedly against the strength of current environmental conditions. Traveling life had a prevailing atmosphere of force meeting force, of flux and interplay. And, I imagine, the very activity, variability, and cleverness of the Traveler's environment seemed to authenticate the humanlike intentions of even its nonhuman components and develop the feeling that the Traveler was negotiating with other entities like himself or aspects of himself, albeit in the form of a cat or the darkness of night. Threatening manifestations of humanlike force he fended off with the customary formulae of Irish tradition: the rat that was incarnate evil could be killed by a silver bullet, say, and a persistent ghost could be shaken by crossing running water. Helpful manifestations—for example, birds such as magpies whose behavior conveyed preknowledge of certain events—he accepted as reliable helpers in his own enterprise.

Patently, neither superstitiousness, unletteredness, monetary naivete, nor other traits I have described were unique to Ireland's Tinkers. In the 1960s these characteristics were shared by many members of the rural settled population and perhaps only a hundred years earlier by the majority of settled. There is also reason to believe that the perceptions that commissioned these traits may have been widespread before present-day industrial, governmental, and economic modes became well established. Most settled people previously isolated from the modern state, however, were fairly easily inducted into its style of cognition and its systems, while most Travelers—even those seasoned by long residence in and around cities or by employment in factories—were not.

Of course, all Tinkers were not as beholden to these perceptions as, say, Patrick Stokes. Many, apparently grappling with the process of perceptional change, alternately acted on settled values and then balked at them. And a few, like the economic and occupational radical Bridget Murphy, were able to consistently supply the demands of a settled life. Even these last, however, could still be made uncomfortable by the insistence of their Traveling blood.

The single most inevitable complaint of Travelers who had committed themselves to the settled life was of "loneliness." Tinker householders spoke of being lonely even when they lived with gangs of children and other adults and were visited often by itinerant kin. Listening to so many plaintive testaments, I came to ascribe this loneliness to their novel inability to meet the tumultuous world, to contend with its puckish peculiarities, and to prevail. Tied to one place, to one relatively invariable round of duties, and to the kind of regulated social interaction that was the essence of stability, such Tinkers felt lonely for themselves. Before, their personal powers had been principal and had been exuberantly exercised—as many put it—by "the old green roads." With these powers rendered useless, they felt disengaged and they suffered from a terrifying extenuation of inner life.[11]

The stubbornness of Traveling attitudes and the poignant obstinacy of Traveling identity invite one to look—beyond the conspicuous requisites of nomadic trade and outcasteness—to the broader, historical origins of Tinkerism for clues to the intricacies of accultured behavior which likely sustained these attitudes even when traditional Travel ceased. Answering the invitation, however, is a problem.

The Past and
the Problem of History

I f the substantial cognitive differences between settled Irish and Irish Tinkers which I have proposed did exist, they had not been remarked by the 1960s, nor had other cultural aspects of Tinkerism been closely examined. The now acknowledged and debated differences between Tinkers and Gypsies (who followed an equivalent style of life in great numbers in Britain) only came to prominent notice a hundred years ago and are still a source of mystification. In the century preceding that, the settled folk of both North Atlantic islands seem not to have pointedly differentiated Tinkers from other perambulatory Irish or else to have presumed them a species of Gypsy, sprung from the same stock and sharing a common culture.[12] In short, the Tinkers' historical relations with their nearest neighbors in closeness and kind have not to this day been clearly mapped.

While the generalities of twentieth-century Tinker trade described in this book are corroborated in the main by what little can be read in eighteenth- and nineteenth-century writings, the earlier reality is elusive. British and Irish documents are strewn with references to Tinkers, to Gypsies, to smiths, and itinerant bands who may or may not be linked to those we now call by the same names, but older documents yield less and less detail of practical Traveling conduct.[13] Both Tinkers and Gypsies are historically unlettered peoples, thus all writings attesting to their past come from settled hands. And although Tinkers figure in many Irish and British novels, poems, journals, and plays from Shakespeare's day to the present, for the most part they appear as peripheral stock characters whose dramatic and social value is assumed to be well understood and hence goes unexplored.[14]

Mention of Tinkers in chronicles, national and regional histories, and official records may reveal more of their actual lives and enterprises, but often the occasion of mentioning the Tinker at all is his moral or legal offense. The typical chronicler dwells on that and his own abhorrence of it. Scholars who have tried have been unable to spin from these many threads a skein of generation which all can confirm as central, authentic Tinker history. And the oral traditions of Tinkers themselves have so far been of little assistance. Tinkers do not seem to have shared the general Irish addiction to genealogy, and Tinker family memories seldom go back beyond a couple of generations.[15] If in Ireland's remote past there was a cohesive Traveling group of artisans, tricksters, traders, and performers who were the forebears of modern Tinkers, they could have failed to attract their contemporaries' scrutiny for the very reason that they were not nearly the exception to the general style of Irish life their supposed descendants have been. The roads and pathways of Ireland had ever been occupied by travelers of many sorts. The founding pattern of Irish settlement, with its numerous small independencies, licensed several varieties of professional itinerancy and incidentally provided conditions to discourage nonprofessional itinerants from taking root. Irish society into the modern era continued to be distinguished by vestiges of that early pattern as well as by a lack of legal traditions and nationally cohesive political institutions that might better have secured land and landedness against its own growing population and the grasp of foreign invaders. There runs through all Irish history a will to travel and a coincident propensity to homelessness that may have obscured or, may still explain Tinker beginnings.

Like the prehistoric Celts—renowned as Tinkers have been for their metalwork and horsemanship—who moved from the heart of continental Europe to its farthest extremities and hence to the British archipelago, the earliest historic Irish organized themselves into tribes. The tribe was their typical social and political unit. The Celts had conspired in their own displacement (or so scholars conjecture) by failing to join in common defense against waves of subsequent European immigrants. The tribes of Ireland were similarly without widely binding federations, and they were scattered and many. One or more chiefs, kings, or queens led each tribe, and within the three major strata of nobles, freemen, and slaves or serfs, tribe members were united by kinship and corporate self-sufficiency. It is hard to imagine nowadays while admiring Ireland's windy spaces and play of sky light on bare stone, but the island then was heavily forested. Most tribesmen were kept to their native enclaves both by the inhospitable wilderness and the social isolation of the tribe. There was no established network of communication and mutual accommodation codified as intertribal law and no singular external authority to which all would submit. As Irish language scholar David Greene has written, "The [tribal] king . . . was the embodiment of his people, and it was natural, therefore, that he was their sole representative in intertribal matters. Indeed, the ordinary man, whether noble or plebeian, had no legal rights at all outside his own *tuath* [tribe]: if he were injured or killed there was no legal machinery whereby he or his kin could proceed against the aggressor."[16]

Effective law within the tribe, however, was very much felt for it was based on obligations of kinship and ultimately on the bonds between human families and superhuman forces, ancestor heroes, gods, and the larger design of nature. The religious beliefs of archaic Irish society—the personae of divinity, for example, with all their attributes and styles of governance—have not been made explicit by received tradition. But scholars have labored to reconstruct them from the copious fragments of evidence in language, literature, and material remains. Many scholars have agreed that while they do not fully understand the cosmology dictating it, the early Irish ranged themselves in a socioreligious system of caste. Such a system typically assigns to each social level and occupational role moral functions that mimic and are authorized by the particulars of accepted cosmology. The privileges, duties, rights, and limitations of individuals in society are freighted with extrasocial meaning and are as inflexible and stable as, it is reckoned, the natural and supernatural verities from which they take their image. The individual's caste is a circumstance of his birth and generally as unalterable as his biological inheritance.

The importance of genealogical records to such a system is clear, for they give the individual title to social participation, and the hereditary, exclusionary nature of the system tends to forbid participation to those without genetic entitlement. Greene spoke of "the iron curtain which separated the [Irish] tribes from one another."[17] It is known that there was a particular caste or class of people who could pass through this curtain, who were permitted travel between tribal settlements and professional participation in the affairs of different tribal kindreds. We can presume too that there were others who had either lost caste or never acquired it and who were excluded from the central activities of the settled tribes and moved about their fringes.

The professional travelers in those days were "the men of special gifts . . . not only *fili* [poets, genealogists, and seers] but druids, lawyers, doctors, and historians, as well as skilled craftsmen, though these seem to have been considered an inferior category. To this class were later added the ecclesiastics, when Christianity became the official religion."[18] It has been supposed that these gifted men were compelled to travel because the smallness of each separate tribe and its subsistence economy could not support a full complement of professionals whose services were only intermittently needed. Fleeting comparison with other superficially similar tribal societies that have sustained sedentary corps of (sometimes part-time) spiritualists, intellectuals, and literati arouses the suspicion that the early Irish travelers were moved by more complex, cultural causes. All the same, as cultural analysts Alwyn and Brinley Rees stress, "the importance of this learned professional class in early Ireland cannot be over-estimated, for, in the absence of towns or any centralized political system, they were the only national institution."[19] Our twentieth-century experience of the transformative powers of monopolistic communications media makes it possible to suggest that this institution *was* early Ireland's centralized system. Just as tribal integrity was embodied in king or queen, so an intertribal continuity was embodied in the professional travelers. They preserved literary and religious traditions, assisted in the local interpretation of law or custom, provided genealogical justification for local preeminence. In effect, the needs and strengths of disparate tribes and kings met and were integrated in the person of the professional whose accumulated experience became a polity, modifying the services he rendered. The craftsman made finer spears or ornaments for one king than for another, and the poet's satire was dreaded because it could wither or kill its object, and it retained this potency still in eighteenth- and nineteenth-century Ireland.

In addition to the gifted travelers, who were identified with the sacred or priestly caste and with the aristocracy, there were two specific plebeian groups that ought to be mentioned here. Relatively little is known of them since they were not the patrons to whom historian, poet, or genealogist owed his livelihood. The Rees brothers, in developing a description of early Irish society that corresponds to an Indo-European model, have called one of these "a fourth class which comprised a variety of people . . . agricultural serfs . . . folk of vocal and instrumental music . . . jockeys and charioteers and steersmen . . . followers in feasts . . . mummers and jugglers . . . buffoons and clowns" and also certain craftsmen, including some smiths.[20] The writers emphasize the early "association of craftsmen with low-class musicians in Irish and other [Indo-European] societies. Among the 'folk of vocal and instrumental music' in Ireland, only the harpist could aspire to the rank of freeman—and he only on condition that he 'accompanies nobility.'"[21] The members of this subservient fourth class had no "honor price" or effective civil rights independent of their employers or masters. But there was—so the Reeses and others have said—a "fifth class" lower still. It was made up of outcastes, "barbarians" defined chiefly by their total exclusion from the sacramental, legal, and practical structures of the tribes. They were perhaps the descendants of inhabitants of Ireland who predated and came to be dominated by invading Celtic-language speakers sometime before the birth of Christ. Literary references to these fifth-class people—or the passages that have been so interpreted—portray them as physically repugnant and alien, given to criminal or unthinkable habits. They seem to have been held subhuman.

The study of the social and religious constituencies of ancient Ireland is labyrinthine and fraught with ambiguities. It is not my wish to make it seem otherwise or to attempt oversimplification but to note a few fundamental Irish proclivities that may relate to the Tinker issue. First, in the ancient order of things itinerancy was associated with certain occupations that linked scattered and mutually suspicious communities and that thrived by politic use of the secrecy that suspiciousness encouraged. The followers of these occupations, in their freedom of movement and the nature of their works, functioned outside the law of settlement. Or, to put it another way, they were the law, the personification of tradition, and had personal command of some of its superhuman and extrasocial force. Second, the caste system itself expressed the social primacy of kinship and focused on the maintenance of aristocratic prerogatives. Caste demanded its complement of outcaste, and the people most easily reduced to this subhuman level were those farthest from the system's point of focus and without their own vindicating genealogy: the slaves. Third, an aggregation of occupations very like those practiced by later Tinkers was associated with slave status. Finally, to be outcaste was to be characterized by animalism, uncleanness, and criminality.

It can be imagined that the dissolution of the early society, the shattering of its primitive form, and its subsequent growth, saw an evolution of new groupings, and extemporized uses of the ancient attributes and skills that still retained some of the authority of their original associations. When performers, metalworkers, and horsemen of the slave class, for example, became separated from their masters they may have at once assumed the noxious aura of the outcaste and taken to themselves some of the functions and force of "the men of special gifts" with whom they now shared detachment from settlement. Following in the path and learning from the example of the exalted poet, historian, and druid, the lowly singer, mummer, or clown may have enlarged his repertoire with gossip, tales and legends, acts of divination, and deployment of the withering curse. The newly independent metalworker may have invested himself with the wizardry of the master arms maker, and the unemployed charioteer may have become a broker in horses, to which he applied the arts of "doctor." It can be supposed as well that disinherited slaves whose skills had been developed to serve settlement persisted in that service but that their marginal status and de facto connection with the outcaste required them to become mobile. Likely, too, they would have applied the values of the dominant society to their own condition, taking their footlooseness for a divine entitlement, their kinship for divinely entitled caste, and their self-interest for custom or the secret law.

Had this specific reassortment of practical activity and adaptation of early values occurred over hundreds of years of social change, such proposed itinerant slaves would be plausible ancestors of the traveling Tinkers of recent record. In fact, neither this nor any other singular line of descent has been documented. And while the congruence between some dynamics of archetypal Irishness and some aspects of Tinker life is extremely provocative, its meaning is obscured by the palpable influence of those same dynamics on a whole spectrum of Irish institutions, populations, and events.

The Irish Christian church inherited many of the honors and responsibilities borne by the pre-Christian itinerant literati, and from the fifth century it established an organization that can be seen as the reflected image of pagan social configurations. The characteristic institution of the Irish church was the self-ruling monastery, not the hierarchical priesthood. The church resisted nationally unifying structures just as it resisted the centrality of Rome, and individual monks as well as monastic groups enjoyed unique independence. Ireland still remembers nostalgically the time when many a monk lived in his own wilderness cabin and sought the state of grace from isolation. The residue of caste could be found in the generations of kindred who headed some monastic communities and in the role that inheritance often played in religious potency. One satirical story tells of a "hermit-ascetic" churchman being admitted to a sacrosanct religiopoetic gathering only after he proved "that the grandmother of his servant boy's wife was the great-grand-daughter to a poet."[22] The licensed travel of the poet or druid was carried on by the early ecclesiastics, as was the guardianship of the pre-Christian literary tradition, wedded to the literature of Mediterranean Christianity. And travel was not confined to Ireland. From the sixth to the eleventh centuries proselytizing Irish religious went forth in great numbers to Britain and continental Europe where their itinerancy is memorialized by the Irish glosses left on local manuscripts. The privilege of mobility in the execution of sacred and learned duty, the belief that these offices deserved human and divine protection, demonstrated itself in the welcome and shelter traveling priests and poets received from all settled, non-Anglicized Irish through centuries of national change. The learned travelers were persistently supported even as they became the objects of fierce political suppression, culminating in the English threats of torture and banishment at the start of the eighteenth century.

In secular institutions too one can read the long-term effect of Irish geopolitical peculiarities and feel the repercussion of native tribalism. The Irish Christian church, unlike some of its continental equivalents, did not build the kinds of conventual establishments that became nuclei of commercial and urban development. And since nothing else in the economy or society of early Ireland mandated the construction of cities or towns, the island remained townless until ninth-century Viking raiders established coastal camps that supplied the deficiency. Even after Dublin, Waterford, Cork, and other sites came to be inhabited by Irish as well as Vikings and after later Norman and English invasions contributed numerous lesser towns and villages, these places were chiefly the seats of foreign interests and not the axis of native culture. The European city with its powerful markets and political brokerage has historically been the scene in which caste gave way to unmitigated class, where the sanctions of family and kinship modeled on nature's precedents were supplanted by the exigencies of mundane and civic convention, such as money and government. Irish society did not harbor the germ of this particular metamorphosis and so did not invent institutions to foster it (as had the French, for example, whose villages supported the feudal order that made monarchy and administrative nationalism possible). To use historian Edward Whiting Fox's distinction, the native "trade" society of the hinterland remained aloof from the "commerce" society of the invader.[23] And as urbanization and commercialization were progressively forced on Ireland by external sovereignty, the native pattern became more conflicted and covert and the social displacement of native humanity vastly increased. All the same, as late as the 1950s the historian D. A. Binchy was able to state that "down to the present day, the isolated holding remains characteristic of the country districts in Ireland . . . in contrast to the typical group of houses clustered round the parish church in England. It is a contrast which lies at the root of many differences and has had far-reaching consequences."[24]

Resolutely isolated holdings were what the Normans (whose vanguard reached Ireland in the late twelfth century) and the English proper (under the Tudors in the mid-sixteenth century) met on their arrival. They who would make of Ireland a nation unified in subjugation if in nothing else found themselves contending with a monster of internal divisiveness. Ireland was a dragon not with one or seven heads but with too many heads to count and no one of them steadily prominent. The competitive Irish kingdoms, with their endless internal disputes over rights of succession and jurisdiction and their endlessly shifting external alliances, were surrounded by yet other chieftainships and factions, religious and secular, each struggling for its own territorial purchase. Sporadic efforts at broad coalition or the inauguration of an effective monarchy collapsed as quickly as they were mounted. And the Normans, far from inculcating Irish allegiance to a feudal system or imposing hierarchical order in Irish affairs, found themselves isolated in heavily defended homesteads, seduced by the native ways, and converted into the intrigue-ridden rulers of their own embattled, regional "kingdoms."

Among many other feudal institutions, the Normans brought to Ireland the licensed, commercial fair, the primary juncture at which rural trade was to lend itself to the purposes of international commerce. The first such Irish fairs were located in regions under Norman protection or on the boundaries of Norman protectorates, and they were often held on dates associated with local ceremonial feasts or gatherings of ancient Irish origin. One of the features of the fair was the extension of certain legal indemnities to fair-goers; ancient ceremonies had often offered similar truce and the lifting of normal class or caste distinctions. Thus from the start fairs provided a liberal, celebratory ambience, an opportunity for making new, useful connections, and (especially, I should think, on boundary sites) a cross-cultural exchange of goods, services, and information—conditions particularly attractive to performers, artisans, traders, and people of marginal social or political status. These last had proliferated in numbers, kinds, and mobility. The dominant social structure was changing, but it had not subscribed its human supernumeraries or occupational specialists to the process of urbanization. And those Irish who were evicted from their lands by Normans and who had not returned as serfs had no place to go but the roads or the wilderness.

While Ireland's rural parochialism remained essential and fitful colonization elaborated the possibility of all kinds of occupational itinerancy, the invaders labored to turn all Irish out of house and home. The consuming interest of Normans and later English alike was control of the land and its potential wealth and the removal of Irish claims to it. From the twelfth-century seizure of Leinster (Ireland's most fertile province) to the sixteenth-century conquest of Munster (her most musical) to Cromwell's seventeenth-century plantation of Ulster (her most warlike), the invaders' depredations read like a series of bloody homilies on the fragility of settlement.[25] Apart from the signal dispossessions of Irish by military might, a succession of laws was written for the main purposes of discouraging mutual Irish-invader interests and of making the Irish tenure on land unstable. Beginning with the fourteenth-century Statute of Kilkenny, which proscribed cultural and domestic fraternization, and proceeding to the infamous Penal Laws, written in the seventeenth century and enforced until the nineteenth expressly to destroy Irish Catholicism, these laws forbad and worried the structures and customs that had maintained Irish property and the landed community. Marriage, rights and duties of inheritance, schooling and the practice of religion, the common language, and all manner of other cultural continua including hairstyle, style of dress, and literary and musical traditions were affected. Irish who could not be displaced bodily were disinherited by laws they could not obey while remaining culturally Irish. And by this conclusive means the indigenous aristocrats and their allies of the gifted professional class were finally completely estranged from their territorial base and divested of open social authority. Their ruin and alienation contributed to the ruin of the lower ranks, which followed quickly after.

By the eighteenth century England's military incursions on Irish soil had largely ceased and the feudal system of land management had been replaced by a landlord-tenant system that was rapaciously commercial. In the early society tribal lands had been held in common. Aristocratic groups had retained control of animal stock, and by lending stock to free tribal farmers and receiving from them tributes of stock and foodstuffs the early aristocrats had cemented corporate dependency and supported the elite activities that were of general social value. Through Ireland's feudal period this system underwent major modifications and the agricultural as opposed to pastoral use of land spread. But the rise of eighteenth-century landlordism and a final cultural barrier between workers and managers of land accomplished the most wrenching systemic transformation. In place of the tribal aristocrat or feudal lord, the landlord now demanded money rents (as his alien church did tithes) from those who farmed land that he totally controlled. With no inhibiting cultural or legal responsibilities to his tenants the landlord set rent levels and evicted unprofitable tenants at will. A prospering agriculture and relative peace had resulted in explosive growth of the farming population, so the number of aspiring tenants far exceeded available tenancies. This disproportion was heightened by the decreasing need for farmhands in some regions where landlords began to convert land from tillage back to pasturage, which promised steadier profit. With the successful imposition of English culture as the official one, landlords and the surviving aristocrats (by now a mingling of Norman, English, and Irish strains) increasingly gave their allegiance to the central institutions of that culture. They spent their time and wealth in its cities, severed their sympathetic ties to the larger Irish population, and became careless, indeed ignorant, of its concerns. As the folklorist Maire MacNeill has written, "there is historical justice in the view that the representative Irishman of the period from 1690 to 1900 was the peasant. All other ranks of Irishmen depended on him."[26]

The Irish peasantry was composed of people historically of various ranks—not only the descendants of serfs and freemen but also those of land-managing aristocrats and professionals—and in terms of practical daily life it was virtually a slave labor force that knew no benefit from servitude beyond the barest subsistence. The regional, commercial fairs gained perilously great importance. They were the markets where tenants must raise rent monies by selling what produce their miniscule holdings could spare or by contracting themselves to temporary employers. And the fairs were the conduits of wealth from the rural interior to the Anglo-Irish cities and to England. Should money be lacking and a farming family be evicted, it had no recourse but to take to the roads in search of another farmstead. The sufferings of the precariously stationary Irish and the homeless wanderers were equally intense. In the 1730s, George Berkeley, the Bishop of Cloyne, wrote, "The house of the Irish peasant is the cave of poverty. . . . In every road the ragged ensigns of poverty are displayed; you often meet caravans of the poor, whole families in a drove, without clothes to cover, or bread to feed them. . . . They are encouraged in this vagabond life by the miserable hospitality they meet with in every cottage, whose inhabitants expect the same kind reception in turn when they become beggars themselves."[27] Early slaves or serfs and free farmers alike had shared with their superiors a common culture. The eighteenth- and nineteenth-century peasants did not. In effect, almost the whole non-Anglicized citizenry of Ireland had been reduced to the role of outcaste and was often described in the very terms that had been used for the outcaste of antiquity: animal-like, barbaric, dirty, and criminal.

In the 1740s the social and economic imbalances promoted by the landlord system were disastrously tipped by crop failures and the hardships that followed them. The ensuing famines and landlordly attempts to cut losses resulted in cataclysmic homelessness. Hundreds of thousands of former farming folk roamed the country, foraging for food on meadow and seashore, pleading for charity in towns, and dying in droves when they found neither. No substantial amelioration of conditions occurred in the hundred years that passed before the famines of the 1840s cast adrift another, larger tide of wanderers, many of whom fled Ireland altogether and forever. These final, convulsive crises decimated the native population, which had been so avidly exploited, destroyed the fount of Irish commercial wealth, and fomented the spirit of rebellion and reform among Ireland's partisans who fought for and ultimately achieved her independence.

From the 1890s onward the desire to assert independence and the assurance of its success depended to a degree on the reclamation of Ireland's right to be culturally Irish and on the national coherence which that culture could inspire. Economic and political revitalization was nourished by the study of native traditions that lived largely in the memory and habits of the all-inclusive peasantry. And restoration of nobleness to specifically Irish traditions recommended the reconstitution and democratization of the Irish aristocratic inheritance. The links between modern-day Irish people and the early aristocrat-focused Celtic society were assiduously unearthed by patriots and tested by nationalists. Where genealogy could not be supposed and foundational cultural integrity could not be proposed, justification was not sought. What I have called the Irish will to travel and propensity to homelessness not only hid the Tinker presence in complex effects but benumbed Irish sensitivity to the Tinkers' historical value.

It is one of the acknowledged weaknesses of written and official history that it supports its drama on the monumental personae of the great men and women of an age and makes fairly anonymous stuff of the eventful web connecting them. The Tinker was a stock character of historical Irish life, but he was not destined to be appointed a principal role when that history was restored. There were other Irish travelers—the fugitive priest, the hedge-school master, the "Gaelic poet," the storyteller, and the itinerant harpist—whose clearer lineage and attachment to ancient ascendancies boosted them, in the Tinker's stead, to prominence. These others could represent at the same time the survival of an ideology and its high arts, mobility that was a privilege not an affliction, and the individual's defiance of hideous oppression. The Tinker, it would seem, represented the survival of self, the lower arts, mobility that was flight, and the degradation oppression had wrought. And perhaps, after all, the Tinker was not even Irish. This possibility held considerable attraction, for he clung to his outcaste status with every semblance of loyalty and seemed unperturbed by the rally to national pride. It was wondered if he weren't a Gypsy.

The terms *Gypsy* and *Tinker* were used almost interchangeably by disinterested settled folk in Britain and English-speaking Ireland in the eighteenth, nineteenth, and early twentieth century. Irish Tinkers appear to have traveled frequently and lingered indefinitely in Britain, especially in Scotland and Wales, and general British opinion lumped together Gypsies, Irish Tinkers, tramps, peddlers, and a great variety of other disreputable road folk as more or less uniform in kind. In parts of Ireland, the English word *Gypsy* seemed as good as any other to tell what Tinkers did and how they lived. Thus a confusion, or commonality, between Tinkers and Gypsies was well established in popular usage when the late nineteenth-century flowering of Irish historical, linguistic, and literary studies turned attention to Ireland's other saintly and scholarly travelers. Dismissed or postponed by pro-Irish investigators, the question of who precisely the Tinkers were was first forcefully addressed by students of Gypsy life in Britain. And just as the problem of Tinker history had been eclipsed by pressing Irish concerns, so in time it was slighted by the Gypsy mania of its British advocates.

Gypsies were first recorded in western Europe in the thirteenth, fourteenth, and fifteenth centuries when they entered Germany and France from Bohemia. By the sixteenth century they had become fixtures of local life as far west and north as Scotland and Wales. Exactly where Gypsies had come from in the first place, why they left, and how they made their way to Europe were controversies then and continue so. But most scholars now agree that some local upheaval or rout caused the first Gypsy tribes to leave their native northern India around A.D. 1000 and that other tribes emigrated thence and moved irresistibly westward up into the modern era. That Gypsies made a great impression on Europeans from the start is not in doubt. Their manners, speech, dress, and customs were startlingly foreign. Often hundreds together, dark-skinned men, women, and children traveling in riotous bands with horses, asses, and wagons, they argued persuasively and were given to pilfering, begging, and magic. They were horse traders, cold-metal smiths, dancers, singers, fortune-tellers, and counterfeiters. They were adept at gambling games, confidence games, and other diversions and wore gaudy finery. The women were considered indecent for their bold behavior; the children were said to be wild and the men perfect heathens. At first regarded with uneasy tolerance and fascination the Gypsies soon inspired only fear and loathing. In eastern Europe thousands were enslaved as agricultural serfs by aristocratic landowners. In the west they were left to their own wanderings and pastimes until their presence became unbearable and then they were shunted on to the next town or province or across a state's border. In Britain particularly they were reviled. Many sixteenth- and seventeenth-century records attest to formal execution, torture, and imprisonment of Gypsies, sometimes for specific crimes, sometimes for reason of their race. There too banishment was a common antidote. A 1665 record, for example, describes the transportation of Gypsies from Scotland to Jamaica, Barbados, and Virginia as "it was proposed to convert them to a field where there was a pressing want of labor."[28]

The patterns of dispersal and continuity marking Gypsy history have been traced largely by such records and by linguistic study. The chief language by which European Gypsies have been recognized is Romany, which originated in India and is related to a number of dialects still spoken there, one of them Hindi. Gypsies speaking this tongue, including the Gypsies of Britain, are also known as Rom or Romanichels. And the discovery at the end of the nineteenth century that Irish Tinkers and some Tinkler-Gypsies (a name given certain Travelers in Scotland) spoke a different language entirely startled scholars into contemplation of the Tinkers as a separable people. In scholarly circles the language is called *Shelta*, a term supplied by one of its earliest informants but unfamiliar to the majority of Tinkers then as now. Most Travelers and settled folk who were aware of the language called it "Tinkers' Cant," "true cant," "gammon," "the poverty language," or (in the language itself) *minkers' torri*, which means "Tinkers' talk."[29]

It was an American journalist, Charles Leland, who first publicly announced the existence of Shelta. Leland had conversed with an itinerant knife-grinder in Bath, England, a man selling ferns in Aberystwyth, Wales, and subsequently an Irish "tramp" in his home state of Pennsylvania. Each of these contacts used strange words that Leland, who knew Romany, did not recognize, and each attested to an "Old Irish" from which the words came. Leland amassed a small vocabulary, guessed that this hitherto undocumented speech was indeed derived from a Celtic or Irish antecedent, and went on to lecture about and publish his finding. His announcement was the magnet that started the engine, attracting reports of earlier and ongoing interest in the subject in England, Scotland, and Ireland. Amateur collectors had noted down Shelta from traveling Irish Tinkers on the Scottish sea islands of Tiree, Barra, and Arran, in County Wexford, and elsewhere. By 1891 a number of vocabularies of transcribed Shelta emerged, various in size and quality and reflecting regional diversity and the assorted phonetic skills of collectors and their preceptors. At about this time John Sampson, a librarian and a participant in England's newly formed Gypsy Lore Society, undertook the first systematic investigation of Shelta in the slums of Liverpool, with its teeming population of immigrant Irish, Central European Jews, Italians, indigent English, and poor of every stripe.[30]

The Gypsy Lore Society had been convened "to gather new materials, to re-arrange the old, and to formulate results, so as little by little to approach the goal—the final solution of the Gypsy problem."[31] Sampson had a broad knowledge of Romany and had made long study as well of many kinds of English slang and underworld cant. (The term *cant* had never applied exclusively to Shelta and is still widely used to mean "deceptive or misleading speech," particularly as spoken among the lowest or criminal classes.)[32] Sampson's background and linguistic acumen enabled him to sort out examples of Shelta from the slum "Babylonish." He agreed with Leland that Shelta sprang from a Celtic source, but he himself had no command of the Irish language. Ultimately the inquiry passed into the hands of Kuno Meyer, a German linguist and eminent interpreter of ancient Irish language and literature then resident in Britain. By analysis of Shelta materials Meyer demonstrated the linear relation of Shelta to the Irish language: the one was an intricately contrived transformation of the other. Particles of Irish-language words had been variously transposed, removed, and/or substituted for by other phonemes, and the distorting techniques of back-slang (best known to Americans as it is worked in pig Latin) and rhyming-slang had been employed.[33]

Shelta proved to be not a new language but Irish so disguised that it was inscrutable to the contemporary Irish-speaker though not, finally, to the Irish scholar. It was classified with the other secret languages of Ireland fashioned by aboriginal linguists to encode and perpetuate the privileged, secret knowledge of certain occupational groups (for example, that of the druid or that of the mason) and for general communication by people whose style of life was repudiated by the dominant social forces, as may have been true of Tinkers.

Leland, Sampson, and Meyer all believed that Shelta dated from Irish antiquity—one of Sampson's informants said it had been spoken for "800 years"—but this has been disputed by later investigators. R. A. S. Macalister, who published in 1937 what remains the most comprehensive work on the Irish secret languages, stressed that much of the grammar and syntax of Shelta was based on the English-language, not the Irish-language, model. He conjectured that "Shelta is a language concocted for purposes of secrecy by a community living parasitically in the midst of Irish speakers. When these people began . . . Shelta, they may possibly have been primarily Irish speakers; but they gradually adopted English from other wanderers with whom they joined forces. A sufficient number of the Irish-speaking hosts knew enough English to make English alone insufficient as a disguise. But they were not well enough acquainted with it to enable them to follow a conversation in English when it was freely interspersed with jargon words. These being adapted from Irish had to be sufficiently modified to prevent eavesdroppers from analysing them. . . . This is the reason for the anomaly that English words are used without modification, while all but a microscopic proportion of the Irish words suffer alteration of one kind or another."[34]

In the late nineteenth century and equally in recent decades Shelta has incorporated standard English and English slang words and phrases. Many Shelta-speakers have had as well a significant component of Romany words in their speech. It is usually concluded that Tinkers acquired these in their meetings with Gypsies in the roadways and slums of Britain, just as Gypsies had enlarged Romany with words borrowed from the languages spoken in countries where they sojourned on their westward exodus. Greek words, for example, are plentiful in standard Romany, leading scholars to believe that certain tribes spent long periods in Greece before moving on. A good example of the polyglot road cant compounded from these and other sources is offered by the epithetic title of this book. The expression *puck of the droms* contains no true Shelta words although it was regarded as a Shelta phrase and uttered by Patrick Stokes, Tinker and Shelta-speaker. *Puck* derives from either an Old English or Celtic word for "demon" or "trickster," and *droms* from the Greek word for "road" as used by Romany-speakers throughout Britain.[35]

Shelta does reveal the use of some Irish words in their ancient forms. But the undeniable primacy of English structure to Shelta argues that the language originated either in Ireland's modern era (for English was widely spoken by high-ranking Irish only at the close of the sixteenth century and by most other Irish later) or with those who knew English from travel, special education, or other precondition. Macalister and others have insisted that Shelta's complex linguistic trickery would have been beyond the inventive powers of Tinkers themselves and was likely thought up by traveling monks expelled from their monasteries or by lay masters of the verbal arts forced to join company with itinerants of lesser status. Irish monastics had a long and unique tradition of study and composition in the vernacular (Irish) language and, presuming a familiarity with English, would seem to have been well prepared for the task. Although I have no capacity to independently assess the linguistic investigation of Shelta, the coincidence of an overbearing Rom presence in Britain in the late sixteenth and seventeenth century and the possible emergence of Shelta at about that time is suggestive. Perhaps this particular English-based, secret Irish jargon was developed by a contingent of English-speaking Gypsies who fled, were transported, or were pressed into military service to Ireland and stayed there.[36] Apart from enriching their own tongue with loanwords, historically many Rom have been able enough in the several languages of settled nations they have Traveled. And for all his belief in the inadequacy of Tinker inventiveness, Macalister pointed out that Shelta was in important respects primitive. Its verbal constructions, for example, show "helplessness" wherein "roots are strung together with few . . . inflexions . . . and only the context, or the tone of voice, can indicate the exact meaning."[37]

To this day no conclusive proof either of the circumstances and date of the origin of Shelta or of its bearing on genetic or other nuclear sources of Tinker identity has been uncovered. While this situation invites many speculations, it inclines, too, to give them all an air of whimsy. Nonetheless, the revelation of Shelta's existence made a turning point in speculative trends. The notion that Tinkers were a motley flock bred by the promiscuous intermarriage of Gypsies with assorted vagabonds of the Irish and British roads (though it was well known that the Rom were stubbornly endogamous) now required serious reconsideration. The shock of discovery and the perception of Shelta as a cultural artifact of great antiquity exclusive to Tinkers at last animated the search for a discrete Irish source of Tinker nature and culture.[38] Leland wrote in 1899, "It is one of the awfully mysterious arcana of human stupidity that there should have existed for a thousand years in Great Britain a cryptic language—the lost language of the bards—which no scholar ever heard of . . . that I should have discovered it . . . the most curious linguistic discovery of the century . . . the fifth British Celtic tongue!"[39] Although later study modified that interpretation of Shelta and its age, the consequent belief that Tinkers must be entirely Irish has not altered.

Twentieth-century scholars for the most part have discounted the idea that Tinkers are the heirs of any significant element of Gypsy blood or culture. The consensus is that present day Tinkers are a people of varied but uniformly Irish background: descendants of several kinds of traveling or homeless Irish brought together by shared adversity.[40] Chiefly, these travelers are thought to have been some of the Irish tenant-farmers and landowners unsettled by English colonization, vestigial clans of artisans and performers whose itinerancy was loosely enfranchised by their occupations, and individual Irish (such as political criminals) who were denied the settled community by strictures of English rule.

The turbulent social and political history of Ireland gives ample circumstantial reason for this reading. And some efforts have been made to find traces of these separate origins in the organization of modern-day Tinker families. For example, the families of Traveling "musicianers" who have stated themselves socially superior to tinsmithing families have been supposed the descendants of itinerant musicians attached to the exclusionary aristocracy. Similarly, it has been said that in the veins of certain tinsmithing families may flow the blood of ancient metalworkers, not master smiths but makers of lesser military furniture—spear rivets and the like—who traveled from one tribal stronghold to another to supply the incessant warfare of antiquity. The possibility of a congruence between historically distinct vocations, classes, and castes and latter-day occupational preferences and social stratification among Tinkers is enhanced by what has been observed of Tinker marriage in the last hundred years or so. For Tinkers too incline toward endogamy, and particular families have been bound together by new marital alliances with each generation. Nonetheless, this popular view of Tinkers as a thoroughly agglomerate people characterized by historically defensive reaction rather than active social purpose does not seem to speak to many of the most salient aspects of Tinker life, including the actual variety of a family's occupations whatever its nominal vocation, the Tinker solidarity that supersedes family rank or status, and the positive refusal to assimilate.

Language has been the single most important index of culture for modern social scientists, and so far Tinker speech has betrayed no deep Romany influence. Another argument against a Rom heritage is the Tinkers' apparently complete lack of the more diffuse cultural attributes displayed by acknowledged Gypsies. For centuries the Rom have obligingly adopted the religions and much of the oral, customary, and musical tradition of their host nations, often with a zeal disconcerting to settled folk. Liszt maintained that all Hungarian music was the invention of Gypsies, and the Gypsy devotion to important Catholic shrines such as Lourdes has at times overwhelmed settled worshipers. Under cover of local acculturation, however, the Gypsies have continued their own, well-secreted customs and superstitious practices, presumably relating to an original cosmology. Settled investigators have found these difficult of access. The material gathered has been extremely diverse and does not indicate the persistence of what might be called a coherent, founding Romish religion, although some points of correspondence with Indian religions have been discovered. Still, there are a number of folktales and legends, ceremonies attached to the vital passages of life, regulations of everyday conduct, magical and medical practices, dietary proscriptions and preferences that are nigh universal among Romany Gypsies. It has never been clearly demonstrated that Tinkers share in these. Instead, such inquiry as has been made into Tinker oral traditions and active customs has shown them to be generally consistent with those of the dominating Irish culture. Finally, there is no record, in memory or writing, of a Rom invasion of Ireland. Even supposing that a migration of Rom to the westernmost island might have preceded or eluded the notice of British or continental chroniclers, we could expect that the Irish would have marked a Gypsy arrival. Neither oral nor manuscript sources, with their vigorous historical interests, did so.[41]

It would seem difficult to challenge circumstantial evidence that Irish Tinkers are not a Gypsy people or that they sustain no Gypsy inheritance. Yet in my opinion there are grounds for such a challenge, the greatest of these provided by the very neglect the matter has suffered. Arguments in favor of the Tinkers' non-Gypsy origins are compromised by the profound scarcity of information about Tinkers themselves. Not only past but recent observation by scholars and enthusiasts of Tinkers' active lives, personalities, imaginative biases, and styles of intelligence has been desultory and often superficial. For example, the avid communal focus on Shelta dissipated within thirty years of its beginning, and individuals pursuing Shelta's truth thereafter did so in isolation and without institutional support. The relation between Gypsy life and Tinker life has never been subjected to comprehensive, exacting study.

For every writer or scholar who has dismissed the Tinkers as half-castes of little cultural interest or insisted on their unexceptional Irishness, there have been others unable to deny the palpable correspondences between Gypsy and Tinker lives and equally unable to elucidate a vital, integrating connection. The state of heightened but equivocal curiosity felt by those who have observed both peoples closely was expressed by the British writer Brian Vesey-Fitzgerald in 1944: "The wandering folk of Ireland are tinkers, and they are quite distinct from Gypsies. Quite distinct: and yet obviously closely allied, so closely allied, in fact, that it has been suggested that they are a branch of the Romanies. . . . They are not just Irishmen who have taken to the road. They are a race."[42] Of course, ideas about how race can be measured or whether it is a concept deserving any attention at all have changed radically since 1944, but some startling Gypsy-Tinker unities have remained.

Horse trading, cold-metal smithery, fortune-telling, begging or soliciting, confidence artistry, and entertaining—the same pivotal occupations identified Tinkers as well as many British, continental, and American Gypsies in the 1880s, the 1940s, and the 1960s. Furthermore, the occupational adaptations Tinkers and diverse Gypsies have made to progressively industrial and urban environments seem remarkably consistent, even in distant localities presenting vastly different opportunities. Thousands of Gypsies in western Europe and America, like the Tinkers I knew in Ireland, have resisted any enticement to attach themselves to central industrial trades or commit themselves to lifetime wage labor. Both groups have continued to prefer marginal, entrepreneurial undertakings. An example of this adaptive bias can be seen in recent uses of the traditional skills of the itinerant artisan and his old habits of trade. When, in a period of industry prosperity and growth, the attractive wages of auto workers drew thousands of so-called unskilled and semiskilled American workers of low socioeconomic status to the factories of Detroit, the proportion of Gypsies was insignificant.[43] And yet, like Ireland's Tinkers, America's Gypsies have thrived as traders in automotive scrap and as street-corner auto-body repairmen.[44] Some Irish Tinkers from horse-trading families found prosperity in the 1960s and 1970s as operators of traveling tar-spreaders. And in the late 1950s Gypsies in New England were conducting similar businesses—sandblasting, for instance—while camping on wooded back roads.

In addition to the occupations and modes of adaptation shared by Tinkers and many Gypsies there are several other essential likenesses between the two groups: their principle of movement or (to put it another way) their lack of sentimental investiture of house and land, community-as-construction; their principle of secrecy and the unassimilable clan; and their principle of oral record and communication or resistance to writing. None of these principles has been slavishly served by all Tinkers or Gypsies. The exceptions are many and well known. There have been for centuries established Gypsy villages in eastern Europe, in Spain, and elsewhere.[45] The great seventeenth-century allegory *Pilgrim's Progress* was written by a Tinker born, and this century has produced Gypsy novelists and memoirists who have flouted secrecy and Tinker businessmen and musicians who have ventured integration into settled life with great success.[46] Nonetheless, the Tinker and Gypsy aversion to landedness, candor, assimilation, and alphabet is still strongly manifest. To ascribe this behavioral complex entirely to social and economic conditions in given times and places—mere moments in the span of Gypsy and Tinker history—seems like a myopic rationalization. Information about the interaction of Gypsies and Tinkers with their immediate environments always has great value, but it may never yield a satisfying explanation of why the two groups are so much the same and why they do as they have done so persistently in situations as remote from one another as first-century India, eighteenth-century Ireland, and twentieth-century California. Illumination of the matter will, I suspect, increase if inquirers respectfully admit the possibility that Tinker culture has positive, independent dynamics founded in the unconscious secrets of family, personality, and the social past. But for Tinkers and Gypsies the attentive and sensible respect of settled folk, including scholars, has not been easily gained.

The study called Gypsiology was established in the late nineteenth century by British enthusiasts for whom the Gypsy Lore Society became a chief instrument of collaboration, but quickening interest in Gypsy life was not confined to Britain. The society attracted other Europeans and Americans seeking confirmation and elaboration of their independent researches into local Gypsy matters. And the period saw many seminal discoveries (such as that of the India homeland) which have motivated subsequent Gypsy studies. In fact, Britain's social and intellectual climate fostered a whole spectrum of similar activities bent on unveiling the unofficial, unlettered history of British and other peoples. Folklorist Richard Dorson has written of "the golden century from 1813 to 1914" inventing the concept of folklore, "when diverse intellectual pursuits flourished during the Pax Britannica and the physical scope of Empire afforded special bonuses to the folklorists of Britain . . . until the dislocation of the Great War, coincident with the passing of a brilliant generation."[47]

Gypsiology was not the only expression of Gypsy mania. There was a British fad for going Gypsy which compared with the well-established vogue for Gypsy diversions among wealthy Russians.[48] An item in the London *Morning Leader* in 1912, for example, announced: "The latest of London Clubs is the Gypsy and Folk-Lore Club, opened last evening by Mrs. Elizabeth Robins Pennell, the novelist. The club has its habitation in a suite of quaint and old-fashioned rooms . . . decorated in what is stated to be the most approved Gypsy fashion."[49] And a magazine called *The Gypsy and Folk-Lore Gazette* ran ads for tents and camping equipment suggesting that readers with leisure take up the Traveling life, "learn to Rokker Romany" [speak Romany], and follow the chic example of "his Majesty King George [who] took with him on his recent voyage to India . . . [George] Borrow's *Lavengro* and *The Romany Rye*," popular novels of Gypsy life.[50]

For wistful settled admirers Gypsy culture represented a survival of long lost, premodern values of human high spirits, racial purity, and individual liberty. This perspective inspired the work of some scholars who propounded the "prehistoric theory" of Gypsy dispersal in Europe "for more than 2000 years . . . by which Europe or a great portion of Europe owes to the gypsies its knowledge of metallurgy"[51] and a theory that gave Gypsies credit for composing and disseminating many of the most widespread, Indo-European folktales.[52] The peculiar nature and justness of Gypsy fascination, however, demanded a cautionary attitude to the seemingly impure Irish Tinker. Even so sophisticated an observer as John Sampson was able to write—with considerable humor—in the *Journal of the Gypsy Lore Society*:

"The Tinker has already been introduced to us by Mr. MacRitchie [the society's president] and as he is undoubtedly a good fellow, and worth knowing, there can be no impropriety in further cultivating his acquaintance. Although his less reputable . . . connections . . . may perhaps cause him to be somewhat coldly received by the more exclusive of our members . . . yet he still comes of a good old stock, rich, if in nought else, in hereditary and developed characteristics . . . an inviting field for the labors of the missionary and social reformer."[53]

This discriminatory attitude among scholars was reinforced by the antipathy the coveted British Gypsies themselves showed for Tinkers, particularly conspicuously Irish Tinkers as opposed to tinsmithing Gypsies or Tinkers who had become "Scottish" and were slightly more acceptable. Brian Vesey-Fitzgerald later guessed that "the Gypsy dislike of the tinker springs very largely from the similarity between the two in the way they live and the way they earn a living, and because wherever the two meet the Gypsy is blamed for sins that more often than not are the tinker's."[54] And it does not seem improbable that the Gypsies of Britain, whose experience has been much more insular than almost any other western Gypsy group, were infected by the settled British enmity to all things Irish.

The result of this general wariness was that even when Gypsiology flourished it spent little ingenuity or energy investigating Tinker matters, the Shelta excitement being the single, short-lived exception. Early volumes of the *Journal of the Gypsy Lore Society* which logged the first major concerns of Gypsy study admitted an interest in Tinkers, but it was incidental. For the most part, when the subject was not Shelta, *Journal* contributors contented themselves with worrying the Tinker-Gypsy connection or with slight descriptions of fleeting encounters with Tinkers. From the 1840s to the 1860s the aforementioned George Borrow, a journalist and amateur linguist, had published several widely read books of fictionalized autobiography recounting adventures with Gypsies and other outcastes in Britain and Spain. Later authors, such as the acute Francis Hindes Groome, developed the genre with their own books of Gypsying travel, some of which are reliable compendia of contemporary Gypsy life. No writer, however idiosyncratic, set out to capture the atmosphere of Irish Tinker life. And I know of no observer who eagerly sought Tinker companions so as to report their affairs from an intimate point of view.[55]

The demise of Britain's "brilliant generation" and its Gypsiologists was not the demise of Gypsy studies, which have been carried forward since the 1920s by a range of scholarly specialists worldwide, the Gypsy Lore Society remaining one major nexus. The field has continued to be enriched by the contributions of amateurs, an exceptional liberality in the context of modern scholarship and a consequence of the discipline's political and social status. Like its subjects, Gypsy study has been refused the protection of settled social institutions. To this day no American, British, or Irish university has a department of Gypsy studies, and geographers, sociologists, archaeologists, linguists, psychologists, and others who have turned their academic skills to Gypsy inquiries have done so in the certainty that their progress, however great, would not advance their institutional standing; their researches thus involved a measure of professional self-sacrifice. Even those who have devoted long labor to Gypsy matters have remained without wide professional recognition. And because the perimeter of the field has not been jealously defined by institutional interests, nonacademic scholars and observers have been permitted a place within it. While the advantages of this uniquely democratic colloquy are plain (happy amateurism was one of the most productive characteristics of the "golden century"), its expansion has been cramped by its ignominious status. Money for research and public receptivity to its results have been lacking, and the methods of modern social and physical sciences have only fitfully been brought to bear on Gypsy matters. It is not difficult to attribute this state of affairs to the political impotence of Gypsies themselves.

Though Gypsies have played a highly visible part in European and American life since their arrival, have sustained their externally well-defined "subculture" through thick and thin, and have found themselves from time to time a focus of settled politics, they have generally declined to organize themselves to long-term political purpose or to show allegiance to settled political processes.[56] Thus, in every host nation, Gypsies' interests have been deemed an intellectual diversion, their problems a social annoyance, their history an anomaly, and their very presence inessential. Public indifference to the half million or more Gypsies killed by Nazi hands is often cited as a case in point by Gypsy advocates. The "science of folklore" (the study of customary, technological, and verbal or literary practices not intrinsic to the avowed structures of dominant institutions) has joined linguistics as one of the most fruitful approaches to Gypsy culture. But folklore study, with its promise of the revelation of primary cultural identity and national character, has so readily lent itself to the political and nationalist objects from which Gypsies are categorically excluded that it has often neglected the subject that was its birth-mate. Tinker matter, only grudgingly accepted as a branch of Gypsy matter and, from the pan-Irish perspective, representing only the flotsam of the great tides of national history, has been obscured by a redoubled fog of pro-Irish feeling and Gypsy disregard.

Although Irish scholarly and popular journals published in the first half of this century disclose considerable public curiosity about Tinkers and the indefatigable activity of a few local investigators (such as Padraig MacGreine of County Longford who forged ahead in the 1930s with the language issue), there was no concerted effort to grasp the totality of Tinkerism. The Irish Folklore Commission, established in 1935 and later transformed into the Department of Irish Folklore of University College, Dublin, was the agency of government responsible for the documentation and archival preservation of Irish oral and social traditions. But from its inception until the mid-1960s the Commission made no systematic survey of Tinker lives or any attempt to collect folklore from a group of Tinkers. The oversight seemed especially untoward since the Folklore Commission was one of the most effective such agencies in western Europe, renowned for its well-organized, intensive study of many spheres of national life. The Commission's archives contained Tinker material gathered by fieldworkers in the course of explorations of the settled community, but this material had not been isolated, collated, or interpreted nor had Tinkers been approached as a community in themselves. The sole endeavor specific to Tinkers had been a questionnaire circulated among fieldworkers querying the attitudes of settled people toward Tinkers; there were no questions that Tinkers themselves were wanted to answer.[57] As for archaeological, anthropological, sociological, literary, or other Irish studies of Tinker life at the time, I know of none. This is not to impugn the zeal and effectiveness of the Irish scholarly and academic institutions then. The Folklore Commission, making do with bitterly inadequate monies and facilities, had justifiably trained its energy on the task of gathering Irish-language material that was vanishing as surely as native speakers were trooping to their graves. And it was believed that few Tinkers spoke Irish. But the equal inevitability that the unlettered Tinkers' adherence to obscure and preindustrial custom made them prominent candidates for scholarly tenderness was not countenanced. As much as it represented careful husbanding of national resources, the Irish institutional lack of interest in Tinkers was a political decision.

When in 1965, Alen and I began keeping company with Tinkers and seeking their testimony, we laid our plans before a celebrated Dublin folklorist and official under whose direction I had previously studied. He discouraged our work and urged instead that we devote ourselves to tracing the development of the Irish racehorse. This was a subject (not as hollow as it may seem to some readers) which could be relied upon to comfort national identity and assist the nation's economic and political purpose. And indeed it might have been an easier one.

Trade and the Traveling Life

The discouragement of our interest by people in high places was more than compensated by the generosity of the Tinkers themselves who, until the end of the 1960s at least, conducted trade and the Traveling life much as their forebears had for three or four generations.

Tinkers were to be found camping beside Irish country roads, in waste fields bordering Irish cities, or in greater congregations in the slums of English industrial towns such as Manchester, Birmingham, and Liverpool. Urban Ireland had neither slums capacious enough nor temporary work opportunities adequate to absorb them. Although a rural campsite might be inhabited only by an elderly husband and wife whose caravan had been so long parked that its wheels were laced with well-grown vines or a young couple and their children who had pitched a tent beside their open cart, for the most part Tinkers Traveled and "stopped" in family bands composed of several generations and sometimes those allied to them by friendship. A typical band we met in the country might include two married couples, their dependent children, a grandmother and grandfather, the children's unmarried aunt, and the grandmother's widowed cousin.

Rural camps displayed great variation in appearance. One might be tidily arranged, another an exuberant convocation of rag and scrap heaps, upturned crates, basins, and derelict perambulators encircling assorted caravans and tents. Tinkers' tents were not the airy pavilions of some continental nomads but low tubular or peaked structures for sleeping in and sheltering from the rain.[58] Most of their caravans were horse-drawn, wooden "Gypsy wagons," although a prosperous few owned house trailers with chrome stripping and windowboxes blossoming with plastic flora.[59] In every well-populated camp there would also be several two-wheeled carts standing on their shafts. This light cart was the ubiquitous vehicle of all Irish travel and probably the only one used by Tinkers in earlier days when Ireland's narrow tracks would have been impassable by any more cumbersome conveyance. Keeping the immemorial pattern, dogs foraged for morsels of food and young children cried for comfort or played seriously with a bucket, a board, or a piece of twine while laundry flapped on nearby hedges.

The camps around cities were much the same as the country ones, but for the fact that they usually accommodated several bands crowded together and the propensity to disorder increased. In the city camps, too, shacks improvised of scrap timber and sheet metal sprang up among the wagons, and existence seemed bleaker, unsoftened by country verdure. Often we saw signs of a camp along the road a mile or so before the campsite itself came into view. Piebald horses—which some farmers shunned as "Gypsy horses"—grazed the road's verge untethered. A splash of bright rags colored the pavement. Or a child in high rubber boots pushed a pram laden with broken kettles toward home. Closer to the camp, especially in the evening, we smelled the smoke of supper fires and heard the pained voice of metal being forced from one shape into another, harmonious with the voices of calling women, argumentative children, and shouting men.

None of these people, it would emerge, had "Tinker" or its Irish-language equivalent for a surname.[60] The assuming of family names from occupations (as in our Shepherd, Taylor, or Collier) was not the invariable practice in Ireland. Until the late eighteenth century the Irish-speaking majority had often taken their family names from locality, legend, descent (the Fitzs, the Os, and the Macs), or from personal attributes such as hair color or temperament. The unexceptional Tinkers bore a like assortment of names, all shared by the settled; besides Stokes, Murphy, and Cassidy, for example, we encountered Sheridan, Cash, Wall, Ward, O'Connor, MacMahon, and Donohue. Tinker given names were common ones such as Joseph, Martin, Sara, and Mary. Outside the regional context where a particular name was known only as that of a local Tinker clan—as was Sherlock in County Clare—a Tinker could not be told by name alone.

Tinker physique was as varied as Tinker nomenclature, and if stripped of the marks of their itinerant life, many Tinkers would have appeared like any other Irish. Two groups, or extended clans, however, were physically distinctive. The members of one of these, most of whom lived west of the Shannon River, were exceptionally big and broad-boned with copious wiry, wavy red or gold hair and fair skins ruddy and freckled from the weather. The people of the other group, who were scattered east and west, had the fine, dark hair and often dark eyes, the deeply tanned skins and lissome bodies that recall traditional images of Gypsy grace. Some settled observers of these distinctions have speculated that the first, robust group might be of ancient Irish lineage while the second group could represent an infusion of Romany blood arrived from the Continent in the more recent past. Generally, however, Tinkers' coloring and stature spanned the northern European spectrum, and although a Tinker could almost invariably be spotted by look alone, that look did not reside in his build, hair type, or cranial index. It was an admixture of the effects of sun, wind, and cold—which aged some faces beyond their years—of habits of work and health, and of style of dress.[61] The Tinkerish mannerisms of precociously independent children, of women who strode purposefully through the streets but might address a shop-keeper with studious deference, of men alternately stiff with shyness or bombastic and swaggering were distinctive. But most of all the Traveling look consisted of a unique kinetic energy. Perhaps only the bright, responsive eyes in a Tinker's otherwise resolutely impassive face expressed his readiness for opportunity or adversity. But settled folk seldom failed to recognize such allusions to his otherness, to "wildness."

Although Tinkers were identified with a number of traditional and innovative occupations, their nominating trade seems to have been that of the tinsmith, manufacturer and repairer of tin vessels—buckets, scoops, mugs, milk cans, basins, and others of every shape and size—for use in household, farm, and small business.[62] What was called tin in the 1960s was in fact light sheet steel coated with a tin plating or wash, also known as "white iron."[63] The Irish tinsmith usually chose a spot where fuel and water were near at hand and built his fire on the bare earth and stones,[64] at the roadside or sometimes in a farm-yard, when a big farm offered him a good deal of work. With shears or metal snips he cut the patterns of vessels out of the flat sheet he had purchased from a settled dealer and then bent the flat patterns into voluminous forms using hand, hammers, and assorted wooden sticks and rods—simple forming tools—on a light anvil mounted in the ground by its pointed stake. The seams of the vessels were then soldered and their sharp edges filed smooth. When the seams of a bucket or pot would have to sustain heavy weight or rough treatment, the Tinker often secured them with rivets. He then fabricated handles either of wire or folded, crimped strips of tin attached to the vessel by rivets or by threading the handle ends through loops, flanges, or holes.

This process (described here only broadly) and its standard products by no means exhausted the tinsmith's repertoire, for Traveling craftsmen were pre-pared to take up almost any kind of cold-metal work that could be assayed with light tools and a wood or turf fire. The improvisatory readiness that typified many aspects of Irish Traveling life extended to the application of metal-working skills, and it was a point of pride for many that they could puzzle out all problems presented them. As a result the array of objects made or modified by Tinker tinsmiths was huge, for in their peregrinations they met all kinds of want to respond to, sometimes with ingenuity and sometimes with a half-satirical spirit, as when Patrick Stokes's brother made their mother a tin pipe. I have seen a tin cradle, a gargantuan baby rattle filled with rivets, and a tin grave marker in the shape of a cross. Tin lanterns and sconces meant to hold candles—some with elaborate perforations either to emit light or to embellish its pattern—were once very popular. Umbrella fittings, buttons, nails, jewelry, and rudimentary forks and spoons were commonly produced, as were straps, patches, corners, and handles of tin to repair or improve the usefulness of glass jars, wooden containers, wood, cloth, or leather trunks and cases.[65] Tin fiddles, each with the leg bone of a heron for a sound post, had been made for Tinkers' personal use. And there were those smiths—active until the early 1960s—who repaired silver-plated dishes, flatware, and decorative objects and possessed the special tools and light touch this work required. Some who did so found customers in the higher ranks of settled society and perhaps as a consequence styled them-selves "whitesmiths." Since, from all I heard, these smiths usually continued to work tin and probably spent the greater part of their effort on it, the title variation likely reflected social challenges rather than technical ones. "White-smith" seemed to carry none of the social derogation of "Tinker" or "tinsmith" and as the complement of "blacksmith" it lent dignity to its bearer. From the beginning Irish society had conferred on the blacksmith awesome wisdom and power drawn, scholars have suggested, from the apparent magic of early metallurgy. By the 1960s, however, "whitesmith" was rarely heard in Ireland, and when Tinkers uttered the word, harking back to fathers or grandfathers, they did so in vindication of a family pride that their current circumstances seemed to belie.

While historically most Irish tinsmiths have been traveling Tinkers, itinerancy is neither an unvarying nor necessarily an optimum condition of the craft. From its first development until the advent of cheap, industrially mass-produced vessels of less corrosive metals and ultimately of plastic, the craft of the tinsmith was indispensable to European and American communities. Itinerant cold-metal craftsmen plied the roads of many nations, but sedentary tinsmiths also prospered, for example, in England and New England, France, and Spain, and even in Ireland. Like their fellow artisans in leather, wood, cloth, or clay, these smiths kept workshops in town and village and for the most part did not display Gypsy-like social unorthodoxy. The sedentary tinsmiths of Ireland and Britain, in their proximity to so many enterprising itinerant counterparts, have often been at pains to state that they are not Tinkers and have none of the behavioral traits that title implies. An English industrialist and historian of metal crafts emphasized the difference not long ago when he wrote that, "the tinker's name is a byword for shoddiness, for lack of social respectability. . . . The tinker is a repairer, especially an itinerant repairer, of such domestic products of the coppersmith, whitesmith or tin-plate worker as kettles, pots, and jugs. The whitesmith himself is a highly skilled worker."[66]

In fact, as we observed, until quite recently the Irish Tinker tinsmiths were active manufacturers of metal objects, not just repairers, though in their travels in Britain they may have manufactured significantly less than they did at home, perhaps as a result of the domination of that market by sedentary rivals.[67] A more important distinction between Tinker and sedentary craftsmen than the quality of workmanship may have lain in the differing professional attitudes of the two groups. Early in the industrial development of their crafts the settled English smiths and metal workers marshaled themselves into trade associations to regulate the quality and kinds of wares their members produced and to cultivate and protect their market. Tinkers seem to have abstained from organizing themselves into similar political and professional bodies with self-regulating and self-interested purposes. An incident in 1694 in which England's "Worshipful Company of Tin Plate Workers alias Wire Workers" fined one of its number for "offering for sale . . . two candle boxes badly wrought and not 'tacked' with solder" calls to mind Patrick Stokes's account of how as an unseasoned youth he tried to make "soft money" by turning out cans that had not been soldered properly but only caulked.[68] While the English tinsmith was officially penalized by his fellows for betraying their standards of corporate professionalism, Tinkers like Patrick learned their error when people stopped buying their wares. The professionalism that Tinkers possessed developed spontaneously out of family solidarity, individual conscience, and ambition, providing the Traveling tinsmith ample liberty for his own failures and follies and ample exercise for the talents he had in the field. The trade associations' concern with delimiting and protecting market rights effectively discouraged improvisation and opportunism where it overstepped established limits. The above-mentioned Worshipful Company had "a Fleet Street undertaker taken to task for making coffin-plates and furniture of tin-plate, contrary to the Company's regulations."[69] In comparison, the products of a Tinker's work and the range of his working skills were potentially limitless.

Many settled urbanites who have had little contact with Tinkers have called their metal-working abilities rude and unreliable. In truth, though the work of some tinsmiths was bad or haphazard, there were many more who year after year turned out quantities of serviceable, hard-wearing goods adapted to subtle changes in market and finished neatly, even elegantly. Some Traveling tinsmiths, whether on their own initiative or in imitation of the hallmarks licensed to settled artisans by their guilds, had the habit of engraving their work with a proprietary device that expressed pride of workmanship. Exuberant with accomplishment, some decorated their best vessels and other objects with punchwork, appliqués of soldered-on brass or tin, and indented patterns. Clearly, the making of a tin fiddle that could give lively dance music to several generations—like one I heard boasted of in Donegal—took no small measure of engineering skill. The achievements of expert Tinker craftsmen were a source of satisfaction to their families as well. Once, some years after his father had died, Patrick was crossing a field in Roscommon and stumbled over a rusting can. When he plucked it from the grass and saw how well built it was he turned it over and found his father's insignia, an S encircled. Patrick stood rooted to the spot, weeping in loneliness and admiration.

Dealing with the housewives, publicans, and farmers who would put his cans, buckets, and other wares to immediate, everyday use, the Tinker tinsmith was directly accountable for the value he had given. Although some smiths sold tins in bulk to retailing shopkeepers, in the general trade there was no middleman to deflect the dissatisfied customer's complaints. These had to be met by the craftsman himself if he hoped to continue a profitable relationship. He would be returning perhaps several times a year to the same roads and the same households. If his bucket had not served well or the handle of his saucepan had fallen off, he was obliged to make good on it without extra charge, for the customer's confidence must be restored if he or she were not to shift favor to the next promising smith who happened by. Although many Tinkers with their families in train had made the occasional long journey to a distant part of Ireland or to Britain, supporting themselves by piecework done along the way, the majority spent most of their lives circuiting within given, small regions of Ireland.

Typically, during spring and summer months a family band would remain at a campsite for two or three weeks, prevailing on nearby settled folk to buy its goods and service. Then the band would pack up and move fifteen to fifty miles farther along its accustomed route to another site and fresh opportunity. In the winter months Travel largely ceased and one family might keep camp in the lee of a familiar village, another spend the season in the barn of a friendly farmer, while others camped indoors in village houses borrowed, rented, or bought for that sole purpose. This winter sojourn under the eaves of settlement was a vestige of older custom. A hundred years earlier most Tinkers probably Traveled exclusively on foot with an ass or pony to carry their gear and had neither tents nor caravans. Apart from natural shelters such as caves, they may have made year-round use of barns, outbuildings, abandoned limekilns, empty houses, and the like, as Johnny Cassidy describes his father doing.[70] This continuous reliance on the hospitality of the settled would have reinforced good trade practices.

The constancy of regional trade routes, like the one described by Bridget Murphy, was for many Tinkers an index of economic and social security. A particular route and the territory it defined were usually shared by several branches of one family, which would combine to defend it against other Travelers' incursions. Territorial defense frequently took the form of pitched battle between all members of two or more competing clans in the streets of a convenient village. Among Tinkers, few disputes, even over such issues as personal debt or sexual jealousy, were considered the individual business of those who initiated them. Most became contests between family-based factions. This was emphatically true of territorial matters. In the past and still in the 1960s, fair days, when scattered Tinkers converged on the towns for trade and entertainment, were so notorious as the scene of Tinker hostilities as to make some settled folk wary of participation.[71] For though a Tinker conflict might begin as a two-man fistfight with onlooking mothers, brothers, and wives shouting out cautions and insults, it soon became a brawl, women specializing in ferocious verbal abuse, assault from the rear, and the flinging of rocks and bottles, men in hand-to-hand combat.[72] Costly damage to the town often resulted as shop windows were broken and doors, gates, and pub interiors torn asunder until one faction retreated, leaving the other victorious.

Changes in territories and their constituencies could be brought about from time to time by nonviolent events, such as the intermarriage of families with bordering territories, or defection to death, city life, or emigration. But this division of the market and the right to defend the clan's or individual's share of it constituted the Tinkers' only effort at cooperative trade regulation. And although the arrangement had features in common with regulatory activities of settled artisans, it had greater differences. The only mercantile goal of the Tinkers' market division was to protect one group of craftsmen from others practicing the same craft, and then by slender means. Trade inevitably went to the ablest and most aggressive in any case. Excepting perhaps the mysterious Tinker "kings," tinsmithing clans elected no trade leaders and had no way of mediating, planning, or guiding craftsmen's destinies as they were molded by the trends and institutions of the larger society.

Like the sundry kings and queens of various American and European Gypsy groups, the existence of Irish Tinker kings has come to the attention of the general population chiefly on the dates of royal coronations or burials when exceptionally large Tinker gatherings and unusual ceremonies have been reported by the press.[73] All the same, practically nothing has been reported of the nature of the office in question. Those who have held it seem to have lived ordinary lives without special privilege. The means of royal selection and succession are obscure, the governing powers of the monarch seem few, if any, and often his preeminence has been acknowledged only by the members of his own clan. Nonetheless, the sheer number of Tinkers who have borne witness to their kings, whether by naming them that, by contesting their authenticity, or by attending their funerals, shows that the office has a significance, perhaps one that can be explained by comparison with (in writer Pearl Binder's phrase) the "dustmen Dukes and coster Kings and Queens" of other outcastes.

In the 1960s the most widely acknowledged Tinker king was a certain Lawrence Ward of County Galway, a middle-aged man whose clan had produced at least two other kings within living memory. Ward seemed free of administrative or ritual duties and he explained that once he had gained the kingship by besting all challengers in hand-to-hand fight (a feat also attributed in the 1946 press to one of his kingly forebears), his royal function was to "give advice" to those who asked it.[74] Conversations with other Travelers about Ward's role in assorted Tinker business deals and problems with officialdom seemed to recommend him as an arbiter and negotiator: one who was able to marshal and dispense important information, to act as a go-between in some trade arrangements between Tinkers and as their advocate with the settled establishment. This was also the role of the kings that nineteenth-century London's legions of street peddlers, or costers, chose for their "physical strength and courage, quick-wittedness and strong personality." A coster king's fighting strength was a symbolic deterrent to rival coster factions and to "bullies" attempting to harass or exploit the costers who, like the Tinkers, were an unlettered people, unlicensed in their trade and unable to "invoke the law to protect themselves." Coster kingship like Tinker kingship might descend in one family so long as that family produced younger men suited to the office, although family membership apparently did not secure the title.[75] Seen in this light, the Tinker king emerges as a species of trade union leader: eminent for his usefulness when he is useful but invested with no greater executive right or luster.

If a king was able on occasion to ease relations between his clan, its allies, and the local officials, then he was an undeniable asset. For although Tinker families within their respective territories did not prohibit competition between members—indeed they encouraged the opportunism of each man, woman, and child seeking to gain a few coins, the fixings for a supper, or the steady custom of a householder—they made considerable cooperative effort to ensure the goodwill of the territory's merchants, clergy, farmers, and police.

Tinkers seldom sought or were offered remedy for their dilemmas in the courts. They usually resorted to hospitals and doctors only when an illness was far advanced and serious. And, like Gypsies, they had always been considered ineligible for all manner of state-administered programs and activities for reason of their unsettledness and, essentially, their race and culture. (Bridget Murphy's account of being refused help by the English Labor Exchange because she had no fixed address was typical.) Thus friends in the settled community were greatly prized, not only as anchors for the economic base but as a source of informal assistance in case of want, sickness, accident, or trouble with Traveling or settled antagonists. For example, many a police sergeant who expected a work-aday deference from local Tinkers would come to their aid if a brawl with a clan of interlopers broke out in town. Although both sides might be equally culpable, such a sergeant would find some pretext to banish the "foreign" band from the area.[76] Bridget, Patrick, and Johnny all spoke proudly of the trust and familiarity that they or their parents had established in their home territories. And other Travelers told of bringing family pressure to bear on members who had carelessly imperiled family reputation and common welfare by dishonest trade, say, pugnacity, or other acts that might erode local goodwill. These external considerations, too, urged the practicing craftsman to as high a level of competence and responsibility as he could attain.

Furthermore, many Tinkers took a certain glory in craft mastery itself, glory that helped motivate the impromptu tinsmithing competitions commonplace through the 1950s. When two or more tinsmiths camped in the same vicinity they would meet and compete to see who could turn out the greatest number of vessels in an hour or the smallest saucepan or the finest churn. Though settled folk doubtless got wind of these competitions, they apparently were not intended to advertise the superiority of one smith over another. Rather, such trials probably stimulated Tinkers' sense of shared enterprise and gave the participants a setting in which they could display their arts to appreciative rivals, developing a scale of craftsmanship that nourished personal aspirations. Contests of this kind were popular among sedentary Irish as well, but, like the trials of agricultural skill still featured at American country fairs, these were often in the nature of public events with the result that the nimblest tailor or strongest blacksmith gained the esteem of other community members as well as the approbation of his fellows. Whatever renown for resourcefulness, reliability, and skill the Tinker had with his "houses" he won by his traffic with them over the years and by his membership in a family that had shown itself worthy in preceding generations. He was not patronized and respected because he was licensed by guild, school, or any agency accountable to the public or because of his singular exhibitions of metallurgy.

Just as the Traveling tinsmith's success in trade was wrought by his own aptness, so his wife's prosperity depended largely on her ability for the traditional enterprises of a Traveling woman. In work and in money matters her family responsibility, and her autonomy, often exceeded those of her settled counterpart.

Tinker girls married when they were fourteen or sixteen and boys when they were two or so years older. Although romantic infatuation between young people doubtless occurred, it was not the accepted basis for a lifelong match. Marriages were frequently arranged by older relations and were made with a view to achieving complementary working skills, age, physical stature, and, within the Traveling ranks, social stature of husband and wife, who were often near cousins. The notion that personal beauty, harmonious character, or some other ineffable charm could supplant these values or bridge a vast social gulf was alien. The occasional and always locally shocking union of a Traveler with a settled person—such as the match Bridget's grandmother made—was the exception that proved the rule. And, as Bridget explains, settled blood in a family line could account for peculiar behavior even unto the second or third generation. Casual dalliance between settled and Traveler was even rarer, for, like many Gypsy groups, the Tinkers were sexually conservative, perhaps far more so than their settled neighbors.

The venerable Irish and British popular tradition of the sexual promiscuity of Gypsies and Tinkers flies in the face of all reliable accounts of their actual practices.[77] The tradition, attested by story and song, probably grew partly from evidence that in the past both British Gypsies and Irish Tinkers permitted themselves divorce and serial marriages, unthinkable alternatives until quite recently for most settled Britons and impracticable ones still for law-abiding, settled Irish.[78] The wheedling and manipulative posturing of female Gypsy and Tinker beggars and solicitors, the obscenities they often spewed forth when frustrated, and the undisguised zest of Tinkers of all ages and sexes for ribald conversation have doubtless fed the settled misapprehension. In fact, the words of one veteran British Gypsiologist who found "Gypsy girls to be modest and chaste in their bearing [but] this does not apply to their speech" describe most of the Tinkers of our acquaintance.[79] Unmarried Tinker girls clutched their skirts down around their knees and were often stiff with modesty. The courtship of such a girl and her intended bridegroom was brief and restrained, consisting of a little self-conscious talk, a passage of silent sitting together at a parent's fireside, and perhaps a few excursions into town "to the pictures" with several brothers and sisters in tow. A perfunctory church wedding was quickly arranged after which all parties repaired to a pub for the rest of the day to celebrate with drink.[80] The young couple then commenced producing a family—and the Tinkers we knew used the word *family* to mean, just, children.

According to the 1961 Irish census, the average Traveling family had about twice as many children as the average settled one. Large broods of children, though often terribly difficult to support, had long been favored by all Irish, who in any case were prevented by the Catholic church and the state from using birth control devices. By the mid-sixties, however, many settled Irish had begun to regulate their fertility, even when it took illegal or irreligious acts. But Tinkers resisted the trend. A high infant mortality rate owing to the health hazards of their way of life and their medical naiveté justified their high birthrate. But for Tinkers numerous children also remained a proof of sexual potency—which they did not express, as was the settled wont, by flirtations, seductive appearance, or pair dancing—and an assurance of the social importance of the clan. Since Tinkers were sensitive to the disadvantages that minority added to their already low social rank, they drew solace from contemplation of their growing numbers. And members of particularly populous clans exulted in the distinction, as does Patrick, rather obliquely, when he jokes about the number of his wife's people, the Wards of Galway.[81] Finally, the situation of a prolific Tinker parent was unlike that of, say, a city clerk whose several daughters would be entirely financially dependent through their mid-teens or a farmer who did not own enough acreage to offer all his sons lifelong occupation. From a tender age Tinker children were essential helpers in the work of the camp and the enterprises of the road, and as they grew older the entrepreneurial, mobile nature of Traveling life gave them at least the illusion of a boundless field of endeavor. Up until the age of twelve or so much of the productive work of both boys and girls was supervised by their mothers, grandmothers, aunts, and, as Patrick ruefully recalls, even their older sisters, who were thereby assisted to the womanly autonomy I have mentioned.

> A man may care and still be bare,
> If his wife be nought;
> A man may spend and still may mend,
> If his wife be ought.

So pronounced a queen of the Scottish Gypsies in 1865.[82] Her maxim mirrored the custom of the many Tinker families who relied on the wife's earnings and gathering for basic sustenance, for food, clothing, and fuel, while the husband invested his earnings largely in his trade—in materials if he were a craftsman, in animals if he were a dealer—and in drink. By the early 1970s the wife's supportive role was exaggerated, for tinsmithing and some other traditional men's work had become futile, and women had greater scope for gain. But women may have had this fundamental responsibility in Queen Esther Faa-Blyth's time and before. To them and their childish helpers fell much of the work of domestic routine: preparation of food and clothing, tending of fires, ministration to the sick and those who could not mind themselves. But women were also the most numerous "hawkers," the vendors of men's tinware and countless other small items, some made or gathered by the family, others bought by a woman with her own money from a town merchant or a wholesaling peddler.

Once a campsite was chosen, the horse unhitched and water and fuel fetched from nearby woodlot and stream, then those women and children able for it took to the surrounding roads. Most often on foot though sometimes in comparative splendor on an ass or horse-drawn cart, they sallied forth with strings of tin vessels and baskets full of the requisites of rural work, play, and vanity. Reels of lace, pins, combs, hand mirrors, buttons, cord, needles and thread, bootlaces, clothes pegs, small toys and artificial flowers fashioned of wood shavings, paper, or dried rush tops were among the goods that Tinker women carried into the countryside and villages: an inventory comparable to that of a well-stocked Woolworth's.

While hawking as much tinware as she could shoulder the craftsman's wife also managed his trade's peripheral business. She and her children would carry a vessel needing repair or an order for new tins back to the camp. They would frequently deliver finished tins, collect payment for work done, and relay messages between the smith and his customers. Some women too had the talent, learning, or earnings to develop substantial sales specialities of their own, such as the crockery that Bridget bought with her wages from a flurry of factory work.[83] Two specialized hawkers who had vanished from the Irish scene before our arrival were the balladeer and the herbalist. The first was a well-known figure in town and village streets, particularly on days of community gathering when she sang aloud the songs of the printed ballad sheets that she purveyed for a few pennies each. This was a job often undertaken independently by children, who in the 1960s could still be seen singing for coins although without any texts to sell. To the activities of Tinker herbalists I have found little written testimony, but they may well have been as sophisticated in their gathering and marketing of plants as were the Gypsy herbalists of Britain. Records of the early study of Shelta mention Tinker hawkers in England selling groundsel, a plant used as a dressing for wounds and as a women's tonic, and ferns, different types of which can be infused as a tea substitute or employed in deworming. Traveling women I knew spoke of selling lavender (useful against fainting, vomiting, and moths), mosses (for stanching wounds and curing jaundice), shamrock, and other plants: common or garden remnants of what was probably once a flourishing trade in specifics for household, superstitious, and medicinal use.[84]

While passing through village streets, up country lanes, and across gardens and farmyards in their daily round, Traveling women and children kept watch for useful things that might not go amiss: some nice dry sticks for the fire perhaps, or lumps of turf fallen off the back of a cart, or a few apples from the orchard's farthest tree. In the houses and shops they approached in trade they looked also for gifts, sometimes by asking outright, sometimes simply accepting what a merchant or householder would customarily give when Tinkers presented themselves: a handful of potatoes, a loaf of bread, old shoes, some eggs, or a slab of bacon. The reliance of certain Traveling families on the generosity of certain settled ones created bonds that could last the lifetime of adults and be inherited by their young. For example, one Traveling woman would know which autumn week she ought to turn up at a given housewife's door to receive her yearly share of a recent harvest or slaughter and would pass the knowledge on to her daughter. And although most pubs would not admit Tinkers (who did some of their heaviest drinking from bottles bought to take away) the local pub that did and that they frequented would serve a free round of drinks to a familiar Traveling band on the evening it first returned to its local campsite.

Regular gift giving seems to have been both a charitable gesture toward Tinkers to whom householders felt well disposed and a reassertion of the social fabric of traditional rural life, dictated as much by integrating custom as by personal preference. Whereas it was common for regular gifts to elicit regular services from Tinkers—particularly Tinker women and children to whom the gifts of food and clothing were most often presented—such services were not interpreted strictly as payment for the gifts but as the Travelers' independent contribution to mutual pacification. Typical services included carrying oral messages from one household to another, spreading news of local or distant events, making small purchases on behalf of a farmer and his wife, and assisting settled folk with difficult jobs or errands. One Tinker, a teenager, and her younger sisters regularly visited an elderly woman and ate a hot dinner at her table after they had scoured her kitchen. Another, a middle-aged hawker, unfailingly accompanied an ailing woman to the doctor's office for her weekly examination. Traveling men performed similar functions (as when Patrick's cousin shared expensive cigarettes with a needy farmwife) and were also likely to lend a farmer a hand with a heavy task or an emergency, to keep him apprised of gossip about his neighbor's crops, fair-day prices, and other topics of interest, and perhaps to act as beaters when he wanted to hunt.

Some Traveler-settled relationships, particularly those between older women, achieved the level of personal intimacy that each party might normally enjoy only among his or her own kind. Usually, however, even relationships of long standing had a tenor of restraint, of patronage and supplication, which also characterized casual dealings between settled and Traveling folk. Underlying the pattern of commonsensical mutual aid was the stressful, mutual understanding that the Tinker's outcaste status entailed both privilege and danger. However familiar an individual Traveler might be to the inhabitants of a certain settlement, Tinkers remained categorical strangers and mendicants within Irish society. As such they elicited from the settled uneasiness, fear, and the impulse to placate the divine will that could be visited on earth, perhaps in Tinker flesh.

The custom of welcoming or at least treating circumspectly any traveling stranger in deference to his potentially blessed or superhuman identity was widespread in Ireland and the rest of Christian Europe, and there is evidence that it originated in pre-Christian belief.[85] The first canny bands of Gypsies to appear in western Europe had ingratiated themselves with the natives by claiming divine connections.[86] And although twentieth-century Tinkers were not so outspoken, their reputation for possessing magical powers as well as the magical acts they performed—in horse-dealing, confidence games, and fortune telling, for example—conveyed the same information. Perhaps unselfconscious of this extrasocial privilege, Tinkers nonetheless expressed it by behavior that was neither passive nor selfless, like that associated with saintly exemplars of the Christian way, but authoritative, presupposing a divine connection superior to pietism. For instance, while Tinkers harbored both the anticlericalism and superstitious awe of clerics that were general in Catholic Ireland, they also seemed to perceive a unique likeness between their own position and that of the religious.[87] It whetted their acuity and enabled them to regard priests, nuns, and other clergy as equivalent human beings, which settled Irish usually could not do. In particular, certain Traveling men took the religious for confidence artists licensed by sanctity to manipulate lay folk with impunity and thus for rivals and equals. When Patrick tells of the many deceptions he worked on priests and of the nuns who outmaneuvered him in a contest of exploitation, he is free of the terrible guilt another good Catholic would have suffered in his stead.

In dealing with the general settled population Tinkers played on its piety and its dread of their magical powers. Traveling women invoked God and His deputies in soliciting trade and support from the settled ("in the name of Mary, missus, give us some help"), and when they were thwarted or angered they invited supernatural beings to wreak disaster on their opponents. Ireland, where ordinary folk would not use lightly such expletives as "the Devil take it," still believed in the power of curses, and Tinker curses were held to have special efficacy.

If the outcaste were privileged on some planes of interaction, however, they were disadvantaged on others. Their negligible rank allowed settled folk to complacently ignore their importuning as well as their real needs and, less frequently, to resort to violence against them in a dispute or simply out of abhorrence. Such violence usually seemed justified to the settled community, which only prosecuted the settled offender when his act was grave, like that of the settled man who shot and killed a Tinker youth in the heat of a petty argument in 1966. The threats inherent in the deep alienation of settled and Traveler were constant. And perhaps it was because Tinker men were the primary personification of Tinkerish threat that Tinker women and children bore a chief responsibility for maintaining contacts between the Traveling community and the settled one.

Besides performing the duties I have mentioned, Tinker females and young also served as expeditionary scouts and diplomats. Customarily they were the first to assess the trade potential and receptivity of a settlement, converse with householders, and initiate interdependencies that promoted the welfare of the whole Traveling band. Tinker women, too, could be relied on to intercede with settled authorities and detractors on behalf of Tinker men, providing alibis, distractions, and appeals for mercy to cover their men's real or imagined offenses. That Tinker men disparaged this aspect of women's work just as they failed to acknowledge women's vital contribution to family economy did not lessen the importance of either. For example, Tinker men's public wife beating, their pilfering, drunken brawls, and illicit trespass (of horses and vehicles in planted fields), were the commonest inspiration for settled complaint to the police. For each situation Tinker women had a repertoire of protective dodges, many representing themselves as helpless, ignorant, or lacking in self-interest. As one Tinker woman explained to a settled complainant: "Who has a better right to beat me than my husband?"[88] Being in the first line of advance and the last line of defense gave Tinker women a greater command of varieties of public behavior than men had. They were adept at the small talk, whispered confidences, and relaxed pleasantries that men found difficult. Settled folk often felt that Tinker women were easier to get along with, but in some quarters they were also thought more wily and lacking in candor than their men.[89]

Wile and supplication were not the only means Tinker women used to obtain their families' daily provender. Basic items such as milk and meal, if they were not forthcoming as gifts, might be purchased from farms or shops with payments of trade goods or cash. The diet of Tinker families was substantially the same as that of the rural poor, and I encountered none of the eccentric appetites, such as that for roasted hedgehog, which had distinguished British and continental Gypsies.[90] Bread and butter, milk, tea with sugar, beer and ale, root vegetables, green vegetables such as leeks and cabbage, and cooked cereals were the constants, garnished now and again with a chunk of bacon or preserved fish, or another animal morsel. Meals made on large cuts of pork, mutton, or beef were rare, as they were for impecunious farming folk, and few Tinkers kept hens, so they probably seldom enjoyed eggs. Like Gypsies, Tinkers had a reputation for abducting barnyard fowl, and in recent decades they seem to have foraged more widely for wild fruits and greens and to have poached (hunted or fished without license) more zealously than their landed neighbors. Those who were skilled in these pursuits may often have tasted foods many farmers and villagers had not, such as game birds. For a hundred years or more Irish settled people, the less than rich, had been rather parochial in their gustatory attitudes, and in the 1960s most were wary of even indigenous foods that were outside their usual experience. Wild plants, for example, were seldom put to nutritional use. Tinkers appeared to be of a more experimental disposition and availed themselves especially of small game animals, wild fowl, and fresh-water fish, which, though not strictly theirs for the taking, were easy to find and seldom missed. Normally men were the hunters and fishers while women gathered berries, duck eggs, and all.

The illegality of some of these activites, carried out on private property which Tinkers did not respect, as well as Tinker methodology, aroused the ire of settled sportsmen, conservationists, and landowners. While some Tinker hunters were artful, others were crude, and it was typical of all that they made no concession to the idea of fair play so cherished by their settled critics. There were those who detonated charges in streams, killing every swimming thing, in order to acquire a few edible fish, although explosives and firearms were scarce and tightly controlled by the state. The ordinary tools of the hunt were hooks and lines, dogs, sticks, and snares. And the usual canine companions of Traveling families were not imposing beasts but small, quick-witted terriers that could follow a wild creature into its burrow or snag a hen from her coop without undue fuss. To complement the terrier some kept as well a larger, houndlike dog and the pair worked together, one chasing and the other unearthing and harrying the prey. Few Tinkers owned the full-blooded greyhounds preferred in Ireland for chasing the country's most abundant game, hares, although apparently in the 1940s and 1950s Tinkers had held their own coursing matches in which greyhounds competed for speed and agility in the field. The lurcher, a hunting dog of legendary cleverness bred from greyhound and farm collie (or sheepdog) stock and identified with Britain's Gypsies, was not well known in Ireland, and Tinkers seemed to have no tradition of selective dog breeding.[91] They were not insensible, however, to canine charm, even when it served no particular purpose. They kept some dogs as pets and valued any dog of exceptional size, appearance or behavior, such as a bulldog, as a family ornament.[92] These pets were destined to be sold after a time or abandoned. They were hard to feed and, since Tinkers did not purchase licenses for their dogs as the law required, the police were fond of checking the camps and assessing higher penalties due the greater the number of dogs present. Those dogs that stayed with a family repaid their keep by guarding the camp and by taking game.

Illicit game and other, legal, meat would be cleaned by the camp's women and children, who might boil it—as they did greens and cereals—in a pot slung from a pothook (an iron bar with one end crooked and the other pointed and driven into the earth) or resting on a grate over the fire. Breads were baked in pans placed directly on the coals, and potatoes and turnips were tasty boiled, eaten raw, or roasted in their skins beneath the ashes. Tinkers consumed little store-bought food before the 1950s but by the mid-sixties the families camped on the fringes of cities began to depend heavily on bakery bread and factory jam.

Those Tinkers who had relinquished their rural routes found their culinary and dietary habits changing, but perhaps the most radical transformation of women's domestic work and their trade related to the uses of clothing. Before World War II few Irish householders possessed clothing in excess of their own needs, and the equally few castoffs Tinkers received they put to immediate, personal use. After the war factory-made garments became plentiful and Traveling women began to collect and deal in secondhand clothes. Many housewives in the early 1960s still practiced clothing conservation since the factory products available were neither cheap nor of good quality. These women still commonly "turned" collars, cuffs, and whole garments, reconstructing the thing inside out so the fresh surface of the cloth replaced the well-worn one. But most Tinker women, who remembered their mothers' and grandmothers' busy needlework, eschewed like tasks and sewed only temporary repairs, say, on a favorite jacket or skirt. When clothes became insupportable they were discarded. Except for a few women, such as several in Galway who did decorative embroideries, Tinkers of the sixties had given up ambitious sewing in compliance with industrial trends and also perhaps because they had no tradition of unique or ceremonial dress.

In the last century and the first decades of this one observers described the vestiges of a style of costume that had once identified British Gypsies. Gypsies, they said, loved red and yellow and particular conceits, such as many metal buttons on a man's coat, draped scarves around a woman's head, and masses of jewelry.[93] No mention was made of the tastes of Tinkers, who seem then and later to have worn nothing remarkable or exotic. Nonetheless, the Tinkers we met created a singular appearance by their use of ordinary clothing and their grooming. The first thing that set them apart was the hair on their heads. Boys and men had their hair cropped short in agreement with the general settled fashion; girls and women usually let theirs grow long. But while mature settled women with long hair bound it up or back, Traveling women were inclined to let their "streeling locks" fly free, and the majority of heads of both sexes were often disheveled to the point of wildness. Such hairdressing as Tinkers practiced was conspicuous both in contrast to their own norm and in its deviation from settled styles. There were those men and women who daily drenched their hair with oil and certain families that had a fondness for setting long corkscrew curls on a female of any age.[94]

Practically no Tinker wore masses of jewelry, but the few pieces most Tinkers owned they preferred to be made of precious metals. Women fancied gold earrings in their pierced ears, wedding rings of gold, silver, or silver plate, and other rings mounted with old coins, especially British sovereigns and half-sovereigns.[95] Men did not wear wedding rings but favored other talismans, including gold Claddagh rings depicting two hands holding a crowned heart, and the occasional tattoo, such as that international favorite "love" spelled out on the knuckles of the right hand and "hate" on the left. The ears of little girls were often pierced and fitted with small earrings, but it was not self decoration that characterized the Tinker style so much as a certain pastiche combined with disregard for the rules of costume harmony, modesty, and cleanliness followed by the settled.

Women, children, and assorted young, unmarried men were the most striking proponents of this style. While Tinker babies and men and women were usually dressed in garments approximately the right size, children between infancy and adolescence were often haphazardly outfitted in too-small clothes or voluminous adult ones, as if their intermediate human status were ill defined and unacknowledged. There was a universal fondness for bold plaids and optimistic colors. And the flouting of harmony and modesty consisted not in a show of skin (like other Irish, Tinkers kept skin well covered) but in the brilliant blue or pink sweater encasing the stout Tinker matron (whose settled sisters went shrouded in dull grays and greens) or in the American faux-leopard jacket of her twenty-year-old son. Clothes, fancy or plain, were worn sportively even when they were tattered and soiled—a girl in a ragged, colorless cardigan might tie a yellow silk ribbon around her neck—and some settled folk found this expressiveness unseemly, even audacious, since it did not speak of wealth. Tinkers who could muster the funds made their greatest show at family weddings and baptisms when the children normally so ill accommodated appeared in gowns of net and lace, hair ribbons, new shoes, jackets, and neckties and women put on bright print dresses and flower-laden hats. That these articles were often cheerfully augmented by the perennial ragged cardigan or frayed stockings indicated that their purpose was largely ceremonial rather than tributary to the settled aesthetic. And gala store-bought clothes frequently disappeared after the occasion, never to be worn again.

Cleanliness and dirtiness, of clothes, camp, children, and personal possessions, were the domain of the Tinker woman, whose person often exemplified this aspect of family life. There were neat women and unkempt women, and from the appearance of each the condition of her camp and her children could be divined, sight unseen. The appearance of men was far less revealing, for they seemed to hew to an undifferentiated, middle way of grooming obligatory to their sex. Dirtiness has been the Tinker trait that Irish, English, Gypsy, and American commentators in the past have singled out as most offensive and inevitable. Nineteenth-century Gypsies sneered at the "dirty Crinks" (rhyming slang for Tinkers, or Tinks). Twentieth-century journalists decried the smeared faces of Tinker children and the quantity of refuse generated by Tinker camps. The dirtiness of women has often been particularly cited. Some Traveling men's occupations such as tinsmithing, scrap dealing, and chimney sweeping were naturally associated with grime and soot, but to many settled folk that dirt was more acceptable than the dirt of the women's realm.[96] The tacit expectation that the right-thinking Tinker woman, because she was a woman, could overcome circumstantial disorder and dirt was shared to a degree by the Tinkers. Whatever the evils of a Traveling man's character they were not laid to "dirt," but one campwife would righteously condemn another as a "dirty woman." The epithet did not always reflect actuality, and among Tinkers the "dirty woman" was often one whose uncooperative behavior or clan status denied her the sympathy of her judge. In reality, immaculate tidiness was not practicable in

Traveling life, and even "clean women" and their families did not try to achieve it. The settled poor of small farms and city tenements took much the same attitude, and perhaps the chief difference between the two groups was the greater visibility of some Travelers' squalor.

The nation's climate, its paucity of indoor facilities, and a prudish avoidance of nudity had long discouraged all Irish from frequent bathing, and Tinkers still followed age-old ways. The large washtub carried by any well-appointed caravan would be set out on the ground and filled with water heated over fire or by adding hot stones. In this tub or a convenient stream—fair weather permitting—infants were bathed, laundry was scrubbed, and children and adults washed their hands, feet and heads. Although Tinkers occasionally patronized the public bathhouses found in some cities, most renounced bodily immersion after early childhood. Many settled town dwellers felt that these Tinker measures were inadequate. Their acquisition, in the 1950s and 1960s, of household water heaters and bathtubs and a new canon of delicacy distanced them from the Travelers, distance they attributed to moral rather than residential differences. In fact, they were not entirely mistaken, for the word *dirty* as applied to Tinkers referred as much to their outcaste status as to their physical habits or appearance.

The terms *dirty* and *clean* and alternately *black* and *white* have been used in many social contexts, including this Irish one, to designate outsiders and insiders. Tinkers, for example, have frequently been called *black* by Gypsies as well as by settled Irish, two peoples who were themselves named *black* and *dirty* by the English.[97] The *black* or *dirty* person in these instances is one who is not entitled to full participation in the institutions that embody the vital, moral structures of the given society, one who is denied its membership and protection. Tinker women especially invited charges of *dirt* because settled and nonsettled communities alike believed that women had a more tenuous link to institutions such as the genealogical family, the professional establishment, the church, and the state than did men. Women had greater potentiality for *dirtiness* or for violating given institutions and being disenfranchised of their social rights and privileges. Everyday and ceremonial practices devised by preindustrial societies worldwide to preserve their men and institutions from the ritual uncleanness of their women (practices often revolving around women's sexual functions) were still followed by Britain's Gypsies in the late 1940s.[98] Tinkers seemed to have no comparable customs, and it is probably not coincidental that Tinker *dirt* and the nature of Tinker men's relations with their women were often fastened on by Gypsies as important proofs of Gypsy superiority.[99]

The two conventional labors of Tinker women which I have yet to describe were fortune-telling and begging. Women's prior right to these activities equaled men's right to metal work, but both exposed women categorically to settled social and legal censure as no man's art did. Fortune-telling, like all other forms of divination that either rivaled or suborned Christian scriptural ones, was illegal in Ireland; begging was considered a public nuisance and a betrayal of self-respect. Women often practiced both arts as an adjunct to hawking and with the aid of children of both sexes between the ages of four and about twelve, when boys no longer took part.

Tinker women told fortunes when visiting houses and whenever chance encounter gave opportunity: at fairs or markets and in pubs. Most of their clients were settled women who paid them with coins of silver, a metal thought to give the process magical assist. Playing cards, the palm of the fortunate's hand, and tea leaves were the usual tables on which destiny was written. The Tinker woman consulted these, however, noticeably less than she scrutinized her client's face, clothing, and other outward signs of personality and condition. If the client was under the age of thirty or so she was almost always advised to expect marriage or a new baby plus an inheritance or some other windfall. Older women were promised an end to illness and an increase in creature comforts.

Early writings make little mention of Tinker, as opposed to Gypsy, fortune-telling, and perhaps its inappropriateness to the Irish Catholic setting or its fairly recent adoption as a Tinker specialty prevented it from becoming a steadier trade.[100] Nonetheless, in the forties and fifties it seems to have flourished more than it did in the sixties. Middle-aged Irish remembered Traveling soothsayers so able that they attracted flocks of local women to their roadside camps for readings. And the housewives on many a wise hawker's route routinely sought her word on personal problems at their own kitchen tables or hobs. The custom was still kept by some Tinkers who clung to their rural territories, but the hit-and-run method of fortune-telling in public places had become more common and doubtless more lucrative.

The only fortune-teller I met whose clients traveled to her was about forty-four years old and settled into a Dublin house after spending her youth on the Irish roads. Although her husband was a Traveler, her broad hints and scattering of Romany words suggested that she was a Gypsy, perhaps attached to one of the six Gypsy families officially counted resident in Ireland in 1963.[101] She did a brisk trade as a seer. Rising every so often to answer a muffled knock at her street door, she excused herself from company, carefully closed an interior door behind her, and admitted the client to a front room, where she would spend half an hour or more. To my inquiries she rather vaguely replied that the visitor had "come to see my globe," which I took to mean a crystal ball. On the matter of the visit's price, however, she was explicit: she had received a good fifteen shillings. Her operation was covert, whereas casual fortune-telling in crowded pubs and fair grounds was relatively open. Probably her fixed address and sizable income made this woman exceptionally vulnerable. Self-doubt and denial, however, were endemic. It was not difficult to see fortune-tellers at work, but it was nigh impossible to find a Tinker woman who would not disparage the immorality of the practice and additionally state (as does Bridget) that it was almost unknown to her. Begging was discussed with equal discretion.

To beg meant to ask for money, either door to door or on the street corner, from settled strangers. Most Tinkers made a clear distinction between begging and their regular traffic with their "houses," which had diverse purposes. They saw the first as a low act, the second as the fulfillment of a social role sanctioned by tradition. Success in either pursuit required, of course, that Tinker women indulge in cajolery and supplication. But those who begged demanded money whereas others, though they might have preferred cash, seldom asked for anything more specific than "help" and stood prepared to accept what they were offered. The beggar only flourished where she could make contact with a rapid succession of settled strangers, and thus she relied on the tumult of large towns or populous occasions. She who solicited help and trade house to house, on the contrary, counted on personal familiarity and the certainty of her arrival to develop the householder's charity. By the mid-1960s numerous women who had been raised as hawkers and who spoke of begging with derision nonetheless engaged in it from time to time, but those who begged daily seemed to be as few as those who abjured it entirely.

Nineteenth- and early twentieth-century writers described being besieged by begging women and children when injudiciously entering a Gypsy or Tinker camp, but we did not witness like behavior. Although several beggars might approach a settled camp visitor, they did so with extreme tact. On the whole, beggars selected their stations some distance away from the home camp and seemed to make an effort to protect the camp and its immediate neighborhood from the unflattering imputations their particular activity could attract.[102] To be known as a beggar was probably to be compromised, at least in the eyes of the settled. For example, one woman grew visibly confused when she asked us for money on a city street and then recognized us as acquaintances from her own camp; her relations with us were strained ever after that.

Committed, veteran beggars were probably less sensitive. And they were distinguished from the average amateur by their histrionic style. They fixed themselves in the shopping sectors of the big towns and assailed potential benefactors with either well-rehearsed pathos or boisterous aggression. A young child or two or a baby slung in a blanket against one hip—sometimes a friend's baby borrowed for the purpose—made good props for such women. Some men accompanied their wives to their begging stations and then hung around in front of a pub a block away, apparently unconscious of the business being transacted. Only when one saw a beggar and her man together later in the day talking over her receipts—he often with express dissatisfaction—did his interest in her work become clear. Young children seen begging alone, usually in pairs, were often actually supervised by a mother or older sister who collected the beggars' earnings every hour or so in a nearby doorway. Older children took to the streets on their own, for even mothers who did not beg tolerated or urged it in their children. Settled adults who scolded, chided, threatened, or commiserated with Tinker children for begging, or for pilfering, scavenging, or trespassing, had little effect. Outside the circle of the family and its friends, children were not easily deterred from their purposes by adult authority or public shaming. Indeed, they had been prepared to disregard these reproaches or to face them down.

The manner in which Tinkers raised children capable of such initiative and generally suited to the demands of the Traveling life varied in some basic respects from conventional settled child-rearing in the 1960s. Once weanlings had found their feet they were meant to fend for themselves in almost everything beyond food and shelter, and by the time they were seven or eight years old they were held accountable for a good portion of the family work. There was no notable difference in the way Tinkers handled boys and girls, though each kept to the kinds of jobs considered proper to his or her sex. Both boys and girls acted as caretakers of their younger brothers, sisters, and cousins. The fact that children were constitutionally incapable of many of the judgments their hazardous environment required did not seem to influence Tinker parents to give the instruction and protection that settled parents felt a natural obligation, even though Tinker parents were equally broken if accident befell one of their young. Children of two and four freely roamed the camps and adjoining fields and roads, learning by experience to keep out of the way of hooves, wheels, and irascible dogs. Older children worked on scrap heaps, with horses, or at farm chores without much adult intervention. At night children might be put to sleep in a canvas tent where a candle was left burning—so tent fires took the lives of quite a few—or in wet weather they might lie down under a cart which could unexpectedly roll. Children's special nutritional needs were not recognized unless the child was ailing, and school was generally avoided. Few families sent their children daily to the local school during any extended stay in a given area; most children attended settled community schools only for a week or so now and again. And although the government officially deplored this state of affairs, teachers and settled pupils often mistreated the young Tinkers, who were innocent of schoolroom proprieties and who seemed strange.

The half-clothed two-year-old standing defenseless in a field, the long-haired girls of six crouched under a hedge in a rainstorm, talking absorbedly, and the ten-year-old boys whose serious faces were furrowed with worry gave evidence that the object of Tinker children's lives was to make adults who had been tested by adversity and found strong or lucky enough to endure. Like the fictional heroes of many of Patrick's and Johnny's tales who leave home to enter a world that is hostile, that cannot be understood, and that sets them seemingly impossible tasks, the Tinker child's success would depend not on careful initiation into the world's ways but in large part on a quality of selfish ingenuity uninhibited by altruism, personal fear, understanding of natural or physical probability, or social correctness. At home the child was to show unwavering submission to his parents while outside he was to act with remarkable independence.

And some aspects of typical parent-child relations seemed to forcefully impart these precepts. While Tinker parents could be tenderly patient with a child under five, they often treated the rest summarily. Orders to do their chores or to be silent were issued without explanation and reinforced with a cuff or a shove if necessary. At the same time parents would not interfere with children's squabbles unless it was to egg them on in their rivalries, as when Patrick's father pitted his nephew against his son. Neither would a parent attempt to woo or reason a recalcitrant child into an agreeable frame of mind. Tinker children, meantime, often mocked and taunted their parents with a boldness that settled parents would not have tolerated without striking back.[103] The kind of autonomy parents granted their children and the Tinker concept of parental authority were both subtly illustrated in parents' handling of children who seemed to offer competition. When a child as young as six or seven attracted praise or attention, his parent was often quick with a retort that shattered the compliment. Parental supremacy in an art or trade was especially jealously guarded. For example, Johnny, a masterly storyteller, routinely disparaged his sons when they had the temerity to retell his stories in his presence or to try to help when he stumbled over a phrase or passage. The excellence of a son's rendering did nothing to lessen Johnny's ferocity, for it was his family leadership—most fully realized in occupational mastery—that he defended. But when his sons were not around to hear him and misconstrue his remarks as an invitation to rebellion, Johnny could speak proudly of their storytelling abilities.

Children were told what *not* to do, not what to do. As Johnny says, they had to be "kept under correction"—and this applied equally to the learning of the social and vocational skills they would practice in the outside world. Boys and girls received little or no expository instruction in such skills, for it was assumed that by keeping adult company and by native acumen and sharp observation they would acquire the knowledge they needed. Shielding themselves against parental jibes, children would make their first attempts at, say, fortune-telling or metal work alone or with the assistance of other children. And they would develop their skills secretly until opportunity allowed them to reveal their competence as working adults. I saw no sign that children were discouraged by this arrangement. On the contrary, Patrick, who appropriated his father's materials and customers to "learn the tin" on the sly, and Johnny's children, who knew most of his stories and songs to perfection, were examples of Tinker children's eagerness to seize their occupational birthright.

Whatever the self-preserving cynicism of children and the apparent callousness of parents, the integrity of the Tinker family remained inviolable. The love parents and children shared, besides being the love of person for person and the love of progenitor and young, was love of the Tinkers' primary societal unit, the family. Parents were its only founders and lawgivers, children were its only future; it had no other apparatus. Even teenagers spent much of their leisure with their "Mammy" and "Daddy," visiting the pub, hunting or fishing perhaps, or talking. And young married couples commonly lived and Traveled with one set of parents or the other for some years—as had Bridget and Patrick—before setting out on their own. The occasional teenager who sought autonomy of a kind that Traveling society could not customarily afford, the youth who ignored parental demands, or dissociated himself from family life and work, created conflict with his parents which seemed never to be resolved but which hardened into lifelong alienation, as Bridget tells of her sister.

For the majority of children who kept their good family standing into adulthood the figure of the chief parent—mother or father—as an absolute judge and maker of punishments and liberties remained a vivid presence. Such grown-up children as Bridget, Patrick, and Johnny felt a conscious responsibility to the implicit lessons of the parent's behavior, a responsibility that was neither lightened by that parent's death nor qualified by the child's own adult experience. Bridget, for example, still condemned the sister who had fallen out with their mother, and Johnny would not tell stories in the secret language, Shelta, because "me father might hear me and I wouldn't like that." Each testified to the struggle the chief parent had had to raise his or her children to the point of critical independence, and this great enterprise, each reckoned, justified whatever violence or sense of desolation the children themselves had experienced. Travelers commonly rationalized a parent's failures and elevated his or her survival efforts or "trying" to a good greater than kindliness or fairness. And this revealed the imaginative means by which Traveling children bore the emotional costs of their upbringing and by which, as adults, they faced the relentless uncertainty of their lives.

These then are some of the principal occupations and styles of conduct by which Tinker men, women, and children could be recognized. But even so broad a description as I have given distorts actuality, for the imperative condition of all successful Traveling life and trade was that the family and the individual be capable of occupational innovation and that skills and behavior offset the deprivations and exploit the opportunities of their outcaste rank. Thus the diverse twists and turnings of Tinker work lives were great in proportion to the energies of each person and each band.

I have mentioned two other occupations that identified certain families in the 1960s: horse trading and music making. Although most Tinker horse traders and musicians were men, women were not invariably barred from these occupations as they were from tinsmithing. Like the Gypsy dealers of Europe, Tinker "horse copers" or traders functioned as purchasing agents for settled farmers and breeders and also legitimately in their own interests, often deploying a repertoire of devious techniques. Tinkers sometimes stole, concealed, and furtively exchanged superficially similar animals and more commonly applied deceptive remedies to deficient animals to ensure their sale. The Tinker reputation for expert, seemingly magical, management and doctoring of horses may have depended on secret use of herbal nostrums and exploitation of the equine sensitivity to certain odors.[104] But Tinkers spoke too of an understanding of animals that sprang from their broader sympathy for the natural world—as when Patrick warmly describes the feelings of hares and foxes—and of a more mysterious kind of human-animal communication. Many a family, for example, had one personal horse that was kept to do the essential work of pulling cart or caravan and maintained even when no equine labor was needed and other horses came and went in trade. This personal horse, we were often told, had been acquired for little or no money because nobody could handle it until it met the Traveler who was its destined master or mistress. The animal kicked at his cart and rampaged down the road when someone else tried to drive him, one woman said of her favorite, but he followed her like a pet and came from the far field when she shook his bridle. The sense of the horse as an ally and not a commodity was implicit in this unique meeting of minds.[105] Besides horses, some Tinkers—including Johnny Cassidy and Bridget's husband Mickey—dealt in asses or goats. But any animal with which Tinkers were occupationally involved had to be a nimble traveler itself and this excluded most of the cloven-hooved tribe.[106]

Tinker "musicianers," as they called themselves, often belonged to families whose members, as far back as they could recall, had been players of the traditional musical literature of Ireland's most popular instruments: the bagpipe, the *bodhrán* (a single-headed drum), the fiddle, the banjo, the mandolin, the accordion, the wooden flute, the tin whistle, and the bones or spoons (rattled together in the fingers of one hand). Historically, Irish singers (apart from singers of art song and similar forms, some adopted from continental European culture) sang unaccompanied but for the rhythmic percussion of drum, bones, or spoons. The term *musicianer* itself was usually reserved for instrumentalists, who in the 1960s were mostly men. Tinkers who made their way as singers were not necessarily members of "musicianer" families and could be either men or women. Their repertoires included a wide range of materials, from Irish and English ballads, bawdy music hall songs, and "jigging"—in which nonsense syllables imitating an instrument's sound were sung to accompany dancing—to American commercial love songs and country and western. Musicianers and singers alike performed at home for themselves and friends as well as at pubs, fairs, and markets and at a kind of music festival, called a *fleadh ceoil*, which was held for several days and nights in given towns and villages. Traveling musicians in the thirties, forties, and fifties seem to have worked for the most part as soloists or in pairs, a fiddler, say, with a spoon player. Johnny mentions that an accordionist and a singer in his wife's family made their rounds together, and sometimes several related musicians would disperse through a town, each choosing a separate pub or sidewalk for his stage. There seems to have been no tradition of Tinker orchestral performances like the ones that made certain European Gypsies famous in the eighteenth and nineteenth centuries. Nonetheless, great musicianship, especially instrumental virtuosity, was a proven path to eminence in the settled world for Travelers, and this possibility of stardom shone its ennobling light on certain families.

We knew a few musicianer families in the 1960s and 1970s. The father who headed each was a virtuoso of at least one instrument and proficient with others. In each instance he had raised several sons with instrumental specialties of their own. These fathers, in contrast to others I have described, straightforwardly tutored their sons, who also benefited from the guidance of other male musicians who were older and unrelated. As the sons matured, musically and personally, the father retained active, sometimes dictatorial, influence over their occupational decisions, performing with them not only in the usual settings but also at prominent regional and national music competitions and concerts. Such groups received much public attention and often good pay.

Although these families each had a Traveling past, they looked down on the ordinary run of Travelers still occupied with camps and carts. On the whole the musicianer fathers would not speak of their own less prosperous years. It was their wives and children who told us of the families' earlier road life, their hawking, horse dealing, and performing, one woman adding nostalgically that her instrument then had been an ivy leaf, hummed over like a kazoo. These accounts suggested that among the musical Tinkers the unified family ensemble was an innovation of the fifties and sixties and that the glowing esteem with which the settled world had received such ensembles had, for the fathers at least, eclipsed less creditable passages of family history. The higher stratum of Traveling society that musicianers, and some horse traders, felt they occupied might also have taken definition from ancient custom, from the social pattern established by Ireland's "men of gifts."

Writers of the 1800s often referred to the animal trading activities of itinerant tinsmiths, and in the horse-trading and performing families we knew there was memory of cold-metal and other typical Travelers' work as well. In sum, if families specializing in music, horse coping, and metal work derived from isolable occupational groups in the past, as some scholars have proposed, these families probably had not observed such occupational exclusivity for a hundred years or more. It is true that twentieth-century Tinkers treasured a sense of family vocation, but that did not prevent their involvement in other businesses that in fact often provided their livelihood and took most of their time.

Throughout written record, for example, Tinkers have been named as occasional or seasonal farm laborers. Ireland's *spalpeens,* the sons of cash- or land-poor families who hired themselves out to more prosperous farmers from May to October of each year, composed an important migrant labor force in the eighteenth and nineteenth centuries and doubtless counted many Travelers in their number.[107] The spalpeenage system lost its usefulness for most settled folk at the close of the last century. In the mid-1960s, however, Tinkers still sought seasonal employment on farms in Ireland, Scotland, and England. The farm tasks undertaken by Tinker men and boys, in different times and places, included almost every imaginable kind. Girls and women served chiefly as harvesters of berries and hops, fruit and potatoes. A few women found more profitable work as laundresses, cooks, and cleaners in settled households. Fair and market novelties were another immemorial interest for Tinkers of both sexes. Besides peddling, fortune-telling, begging, trading, and performing, they operated games of chance and marksmanship and wheels of fortune at these events. Many Tinker men we knew and their fathers before them had done stints as itinerant chimney sweeps and thatchers. A number had peddled heavy household furnishings such as linoleum, mattresses, chairs, and stools while others trafficked in raw horsehair, rabbit pelts, and feathers. Several women spoke of fresh-water pearl fishing, saying that the place where a "crane" (heron) paused while wading an Irish or Scottish stream marked the spot where pearls could be found. We heard of one man who had kept a fox cub and exhibited it for a shilling, boys who had trapped wild songbirds and sold them before that market vanished, and certain men who seemed to be involved in a clandestine badger-baiting operation attended by settled and Traveling spectators who wagered on the winning dog. Coin counterfeiting was a popular nineteenth-century pastime and more recently some Tinkers had fenced stolen goods and others had run *poteen* (unlicensed liquor) and smuggled between British soil and the Republic, especially in time of war or closed borders.[108] We met many Tinkers like Bridget and Patrick whose male antecedents had volunteered for the British army. Perhaps the sole, and remarkable, instance of meaningful Tinker participation in any settled institution, this volunteerism was doubtless inspired by the need for bread rather than by nationalist zeal.[109] Finally, one exceptionally wealthy Traveler of late middle age who was courted by ranking settled folk was said to have made his fortune marketing Irish horseflesh to the abattoirs of France for human consumption.

In the mid-1960s and early 1970s many Tinkers were still engaged in some of these and still other occupations enfranchised by the traditional round of rural and village life, its work, ceremonies, and amusements. A great number, however, were striving to follow the precedents of Ireland's most recent demographic and economic transformation. Whole families and bands turned to conserving and recycling the products of post-World War II industrialization and consumption. Men collected and traded secondhand appliances, engine parts, and scrap metal and wood scavenged or purchased as bulk junk from manufacturing and construction sites and outlying farms. The feverish demolition and rebuilding of Irish country towns and old quarters of cities presented new opportunities to adaptive tradesmen. Large camps near towns were now characterized by heaps of packing crates, disabled autos and vans, slabs of corrugated iron, and other goods in process of being picked over and sorted for resale. Women engrossed in similar trade in cast-off clothing and household objects now cultivated in the towns and suburbs networks of relationships superficially comparable to the rural trade routes. They regularly visited those houses, shops, and institutional establishments, such as convents and hospitals, which could be counted upon to have copious discards or susceptibility to the artful solicitation. They gathered a great array of objects, from broken alarm clocks to carpet trimmings, cracked teapots, and outgrown gym suits. Some things were promptly dumped, often a few yards from the donor's doorway, where they were seen and gave offense. The rest were sold in street markets or to settled dealers who licensed stalls in the covered markets of the big cities.

When prosperity and the alienation from traditional housekeeping habits among certain groups of settled Irish progressed to the point where it prompted a longing for relics of those habits, some Travelers sensitive to the trend developed an appropriate sophistication and reserved selected discards to be sold as "antiques." Others aggressively pursued this new line, purchasing wagonloads of apparently derelict furniture, farm tools, and cutlery from "innocent" countryfolk and transporting their gains to the high-toned Dublin shops patronized by urbane Irish and dealers from Frankfurt and New York. The surfacing of private roads and driveways with tar (macadam) became another well-remunerated Tinker trade, practiced chiefly in Britain. Rumor of emigrants who had bought their own tar-spreaders and vans and rambled round collecting a big fee for each afternoon's work flew through the Irish camps exciting hope and envy.

Tinkers showed quick resourcefulness in adapting the products, the wastes, the processes, and tastes of the new industrial realm to their own uses, but those uses remained characteristically marginal. Few sought integration at the productive center of the evolving economic order. By the late 1960s many Traveling men and women had spent some time in Manchester, Liverpool, Birmingham, Coventry, or other English industrial towns working in factories or on construction lots. Wages were higher, provisional acceptance more easily come by, and temporary jobs more numerous there. Some had stayed on as permanent factory hands housed in subsidized estates, making a new life with the peculiar stabilities and aspirations of the settled.[110] For the majority of Tinkers, however, the English adventure was not a first step toward cultural or caste conversion but an act of sensible opportunism like others they had always practiced. When their contracts were up or they tired of the work, they had tried something else or returned home. They did not expect to become accustomed to rote work for wages or to become "settled" by simply, for a time, staying still.[111]

This, the Tinkers' perceived freedom from impersonal cumulative effect and failure to see or choose their actions as a source of that effect (what I called above their assumption of temporal free will) was essential to Tinker ocupational flexibility. But it was also the foundation of the duplicity with which Tinkers as workers were often charged and which some developed into an avocation and finally into the consummate Travelers' trade, confidence artistry.

Certainly, conscious duplicity was not a component of every Tinker enterprise or personality. While there were many for whom falsification, theft, and evasion were the reliable means to any objective, many others were deeply offended at having to share this reputation undeservedly. Nonetheless, the Traveling life prompted in all its followers the entrepreneurial bent and an appreciation of the uses of secrecy. Sedentary society's relatively fixed institutions and structures gave the apparent assurance that a life's trajectory could be planned or antici-pated to proceed from stable point to stable point and, barring accidental interference, follow a candid, narrative line from proper start to necessary conclusion. But the Traveling experience did not. It urged instead the efficacy of playing both ends against the middle. The only stable point of developmental reference was the unity of kindred and kind, and the conclusion of effort lay not in the future but in the collusion of possibilities immediately present.

The confidence game can be seen as an unmitigated expression of this Travel-ing perspective, for with little more than wit he who was willing could make out of air, out of coinciding psychologies, something of concrete value. And besides those Tinkers who were simply resourceful and guarded and those others who habitually minimized giving and maximized takings in work (by short measures, slipshod products, or misrepresentation), there were some who en-gaged in confidence games. The most famous game (popular also among Gypsies, some of whom called it the *hokkano baro,* or "big trick") depended simply on the pet settled idea that a future objective could be assured by predictable, linear development: the right acts now would in time yield the distant, desired result.[112] In all the variations of this game the Tinker told the settled "mark" that his private property—usually money—would "grow" (silver coins would turn to gold or paper notes would multiply) if the Tinker put it through a certain ceremony (wrapping it in paper, immersing it in water, or burying it, often with incanta-tions) and then held onto it or deposited it in some secret place (a hole in the ground or under a mattress) for a particular period of time. All was done. But when, after the number of days or weeks specified for change, the mark retrieved the precious package or jar from a prearranged place he discovered, of course, that there had been a switch. Far from becoming gold, the cash he invested had turned to old newspaper, rusty nails, or stones. And while the gullible farmer willingly postponed gratification believing that in good time, surpassing gratification could be his, the Tinker triumphed by his ability to be satisfied with the moment—and went off cash in hand.

Where It Was Going

I n the mid-1960s the precipitate displacement of Travelers from their traditional ways and the consequent uneasiness of their settled countrymen culminated in a spate of little conflicts, public pronouncements, and hopeful experiments that gave new direction to settled-Traveler relations. These were the years that signaled where it (the confluence of Traveling and settled differences) was going, and the course those relations would take to the present day.

Tinkers troubled the peace and tried the prosperity of both town and countryside. Their crowded suburban encampments had grown in size, number, and fixity as they followed the migration of extraneous settled folk from the land to the enclosures of industry and commerce and, as it were, clustered round the walls clamoring for sustenance, all unable or unwilling to convert to the nine-to-five style of work. In place of the complicated interdependencies that settled and Traveler had cultivated in the recent past, contacts between the two in the sixties took on narrowly specialized purposes. Tinkers bought in one place, sold in another, and solicited in yet a third. Few had anything to offer to "the houses," for the wares they had made and hawked were now easily available in nearby shops. And what they used to tell, teach, perform, and report was being replaced by the unanswerable voice of a radio, television, or phonograph.[113] The attraction of mutual personal support had lessened as Tinkers' opportunities to give to the settled vanished and the Traveler seemed fit only to receive. The growing reliance of Tinker families on the dole (income subsidy from the state) and charitable agencies of the town only seemed to confirm the town dweller's growing belief in Tinker rapacity and social selfishness.

In the country, particularly the east, modernization of farm and land management and mechanization of many procedures had eliminated the need for Tinkers' day labor and other services. Throughout, the waning of small productive farms and the new agribusiness attitudes of big farmers and landowners shrank the geographical and social tolerances by which Tinkers had lived. Traditional public rights-of-way through fields and lanes were blocked; pastures were fenced to their edges; conscientious police "shifted" Tinkers along to where they would not discountenance local economic growth or disrupt auto traffic.

The 1963 *Report of the Commission on Itineracy* had been but the first open acknowledgment that accustomed modes of Tinker-settled interaction were ill suited to the new era. While private citizens grew ever more vocal and indignant over Tinkerism's impositions, representatives of the state and the press publicly argued the most socially constructive defense against the threat to the body politic latent in the Tinker presence. The chief arguments, like arguments about Gypsies and Tinkers a century earlier, were distinguished by a tendency to either romance or realism. And two agencies of the Irish government can be said to have represented these apparently opposing attitudes.

The Irish Tourist Board touted "caravan holidays" wherein visitors would rent brightly painted Tinker-style wagons for leisurely trekking along back-country roads. At the same time board members worried about whether actual, visibly ragged and importunate Tinkers might be a tourist attraction or deterrent. A romantic wish to celebrate the colorful, adventuresome aspects of Traveling life and to efface or ignore that life's true complexity was implicit in the board's dilemma. Meantime, the determinedly realistic Committee for Itinerant Settlement, having sent emissaries to Holland to study provision made there for Gypsies, advocated local action that "should always have as its aim the eventual absorption of the itinerants into the general community."[114] Two specific recommendations were that permanent housing be made available for Tinkers who would take it and (anticipating that that would not be easily accomplished) that a string of permanent camps be established for the rest. These "Sites," as they came to be called, were to be places where Tinkers could legitimately stop, park their wagons and carts, corral their horses, and have the use of specially constructed shelters and indoor sanitary facilities, unmolested by and acceptable to settled folk. Mutually protective boundaries, fences and shedlike "storage accommodation" could be thrown around the traditional sprawl, and itinerants could be overseen, visited, and improved upon by health and social workers, educators, and religionists. In time, Travelers could be confined to the route from Site to Site and Tinker children (thought to be more impressionable than their elders) could go to school.[115]

The partisans of various romantic and realistic schemes had, by 1967, achieved some reconciliation and some practical implementation of their proposals. The government approved the Committee's reported plan for a factory where Tinker workers could apply their anomalous skills to making souvenirs for the very tourists they had been importuning, and several small private businesses with the same purpose were launched. The first Sites had been designated and in a few cases the promised facilities built. But the optimism of the fair-minded individuals who thus assayed a solution to "the Itinerant problem" was not infectious. The businesses developed slowly, and the design and situation of the Sites, with their thin-walled rectangular houses in tight rows, was as misguided as the assumption that Tinkers could live in them as if born and bred to such a life. Families with traditional enmity or with incompatible ideas of rank found themselves assigned to be neighbors, and regulations against drunkenness, the sharing of a single house by more than one family, and use of the houses for sleeping invited disregard.[116] For example, a social worker overseeing the Site where Patrick stayed for a time admonished him for fighting with his neighbors and told him to avoid the problem by staying inside his house and keeping its door closed. To the settled mind the closed door stood for protection against the unforeseen. To the Traveler, who had spent little or none of his life housebound, safety lay in the very openness of his tent, caravan, or hut, which permitted him to see and to know what was going on outside, to anticipate and deal with its effect. Shut in, he was ignorant and hence powerless.[117]

It was not only the carefully selected Tinkers living in the Sites who were unhappy. The exclusivity of the facilities whetted the opportunism of those who could not share them. Rejected and disgruntled Tinkers made camps round Site perimeters, fueling the already strident protests of settled Site neighbors. These extramural camps became the focus of rancor symptomatic of growing class or caste hostility. Along with many other town-associated camps, the extramural camps were periodically evacuated by civil or private authorities. As abandoned shacks and debris were bulldozed and carted off, Tinker campers limped to another patch of ground in another suburb where they planted themselves with renewed determination. The tourists continued to complain.

If racist or classist romance was expressed in the treatment of Tinkers and Tinkerism by promoters of tourism and the assorted academics, scholars, patriots, and organization officials who were disarmed intellectually by their emotional responses to Tinker issues, then to the roll of disciples of realism—the philanthropists and innovators of health, integration, and settlement schemes—must be added Grattan Puxon. A political organizer and founder of Britain's Gypsy Council, he put himself forward as the first and only advocate of Tinker politicization.

Puxon's participation in Tinker affairs in the 1960s was brief but stellar. He rallied embattled bands of town camp dwellers to mass marches and passive resistance of bulldozers, and he fascinated the Dublin press. He strove to interest Tinkers in rights formally granted citizens by the state and in the pursuit of its active protection. Some of those who were close to him took to singing "We Shall Overcome" and tacking self-assertive notices to their wagons and shacks. Though Puxon followed noble precedents and his intention was sincerely constructive, he was shunned by other, Irish, realists and allegedly harassed by a venerable Irish republican organization as well as by the police. Soon after his return to England it became evident that the Tinkers remained largely unmoved by his hopes for them and remembered his visit as a curious, deliquescent adventure.[118] It is fair to say that for most the very idea of subscription to a state—within which a stable constituency could be formed and to which demands could be addressed—was meaningless. It had little pertinence to the Traveling lexicon of ways to get things done.

Puxon's voluble leadership had alerted the general public to some of the Travelers' practical difficulties and had helped invest the political issue of Tinkerism with humanitarian significance. Patently, though, it was neither the Tinkers' political potential, their colorful eccentricities, nor their personal sufferings that accounted for the notoriety they acquired in this period. What their issue attested to most poignantly was the final unraveling of the social and cultural fabric that had clothed essential Ireland and kept it alive for ages past. As one of the last, stoutest components of that fabric, Tinkers were the carriers and custodians of its sympathetic pattern. But for many of the settled, Tinkerism—parochial, superstitious, and divisive—was also a shameful me-

mento of Ireland's historical disunity and incapacity for national self-determination. What was perhaps worse, Tinkerism seemed to suggest Ireland's inadequacy to international equity in the future. Since such equity demanded of the nation habits of industry, regimentation, and capitalistic self-improvement which the Tinkers, who represented a certain immutable Irishness, could not learn, then these habits might be beyond the reach of all Irish.

Whatever freedoms Ireland's earliest itinerants had bequeathed them, historical Tinkers had inhabited a social place warranted by its utility. In a society still mindful of ancient, caste values they had had the natural rights and indemnity proffered by the divine plan thought to be the source of human organization. As objects of exclusion in an exclusionary system their existence was justified. And although their place—the lowest in a land brought low—was doubtless aggrieved, it had also been familiar and socially secure. It ensured the conditional but reliable acceptance of other Irish and left individual Travelers to their personal misfortunes and characteristic liberties. Socioeconomic and ideological changes following World War II brought the Tinkers from this to another position where their integrity and usefulness as a people were widely questioned and found to have no basis in the ascendant moral and economic order. The finding, with all its difficult implications for Irish culture and character, naturally aroused passion and confusion.

The attitudes of the settled folk whom I have named romantics and realists were, of course, not so neatly discrete as the titles imply. There was utopian romance aplenty in political, educational, and integrational plans that took little account of Tinker dignity and customs and a realistic respect for Tinker independence implicit in the standoffishness of scholars and the glamorizing of commercial promoters. Among those settled who were actively concerned with Tinkers, unities of the settled style of perception were greater than differences of opinion. Virtually all shielded themselves from the confusion surrounding the Tinker issue, or sought to penetrate that confusion, by means of their own occupational ethics and methodologies. In the end, the professional identities of these settled activists appeared to prevent them from recognizing the kind of preindustrial professionalism, "commercial nomadism," or Gypsyism, with its dynamic ethos and symptomatic ideas, that lay at the heart of the Tinker variance. It was as if the seven blind wise men of fable were to examine not an elephant but an eighth blind man and were to discover many truths about him except that one that shaped his life: he was as astigmatic as they.

Despite the controversy that surrounded the Travelers, our engagement with them often seemed lonely and unique. The strategic intricacies of getting acquainted with people who were purposefully secretive, radically unlike ourselves, and political objects closely watched by the police were many. What is more, we did not ally ourselves with any of the prevailing settled advocacies, and we had no interest in applying to Tinkers any established scholarly or social methodology.

That is not to say that Alen and I lacked occupational identities of our own. Photography was his life; I was a writer and a student of folklore and of children. But we were guided by the hope of aesthetic probity and personal sensitivity, not by principles of professionalism or the desire to limit our engagement to the purposes of professional self-interest. We met the Tinkers as amateurs, in friendship. And although this probably made our interrelation more complex, like all friendships that start from feelings of curiosity, attraction, and the promise of attachment, it also kept us mindful of their separate reality, a part of which I set before you here.

Their adopted son Jerry with Mickey and Bridget Murphy and, in the background, a friend.

Bridget Murphy

HAWKER AND HOUSEWIFE[1]

Oh, and, Sullivan John to the road is gone,
Far away from his native home,
Gone away with a Tinker's daughter,
Aye, along the roads to Rome.
Oh, Sullivan John he won't stick it too long
'Til his belly will soon get slack.
He'll be roaming the roads with an almighty load,
And a tool box on his back.

Oh, it was heavy she'd be with a neat baby,
Behind on her back, strapped on,
And a hazel wattle all in her hand
To drive her donkey on.
She inquired in every farmer's house
Along the road that she pass,
Oh, where would she get a pot to mend,
Or where would she swap an ass.

Oh, there's a big asses fair in the County Clare,
In a place they call Spancil Hill,

Where my brother James got a rap of a hames,
And poor Paddy did long to kill.
They moved them off in an ass's car
Where Kate and Mary did stand.
Oh, for he may curse, he may rue the day
That he joined with the Tinkers' van.

He won't get his supper at six o'clock,
Nor his tea or nought at three.
He'll be roaming the roads with an almighty load,
And a tool box on his back. [2]

Yes, my father's father he was a farmer, and he come from farmers. They were very big farmers, and they were reared in a place in Ballingarry. They were all Protestants. His grandmother was a woman by the name of Biddy Dray.

Then my grandfather, Lord have mercy on him, married this Traveling woman, and he turned a Catholic with her. All belonging to him was Protestants and they cut him out. He stuck with the Traveling people and he turned a Catholic.

He was a little small man and she was a huge big woman, blonde and very good-lookin', I believe. Oh yes, she was only very young when she was married to me grandfather. She was only seventeen and she was noted for her singing, was a beautiful singer. She sang all the old songs, that me father remembered. And I suppose I got a lot of those songs from her, indirectly you could say.

Oh, it's early, early all in the Spring,
While the small birds whistle, and they warbly sing,
And they change their notes from each tree to tree,
And the sun rises over a green valley.

Oh, there is an alehouse all in the town,
Where my love goes and he do sit down.
He do take this fair girl all on his knee,
And it's then that he cares no more for me.

Sure, I wish, I wish, Love, I wish in vain,
I do wish to God I was in love again,
But that's a sign it can never now be,
Ah, while apples grow on an ivy tree.

Right well he knows I can wash and wring.
Right well he knows I can card and spin.
I can change all his linens from coarse to fine.
For the want of money, sure, I'm left behind. [3]

They went off then, and sometimes they Traveled and other times they stayed in a house. My grandmother, she had four daughters, that'd be four sisters of my father's, and three more brothers along with himself. There was seven childer altogether. But two of the daughters died during the Black Flu then. You often heard tell of it, it was a ragin' flu at the time. Two daughters survived and they married two Traveling people, Connorses of Wexford.

Well, it probably could have been that my grandfather just fell in love with me grandmother, even though they were from different people, like. It must have been, because it lasted. They lived to be very, very old and they were very happy, even though they drank.

They were both very fond of drink. I must tell you what they had for their breakfast, 'cause my mother often told me. They'd send down for a little can of porter, and they'd break up a loaf of bread and stick it down in it and eat it. That's true. That time drink was very cheap, and that was their breakfast. She loved drink, I believe. I never remember them, because I was too young before they were gone, but I believe she was a nice old lady. Me mother often told me.

The sisters went Traveling, but all of my father's brothers didn't take to the road. He had a brother, Johnny Wall, lived in Athy, County Kildare, and had a big family. They're all settled now in Athy. In fact one of them had a barbershop and he's died recently, and you'd never believe to look at him that there were any connection with Traveling people.

My grandfather and my grandmother, they had this little house in Athy also, and the childer was sent to the Christian Brothers' school, and they were very happy. All of them children didn't take to the road. But eventually, me father, of course, was reared up in the Traveling type, and he married a Traveling woman.

> For my name is Paddy MacInerny,
> And an old County Down man am I,
> In the search of a wife I started Traveling
> Around the main streets of old Carramee.
>
> The first man I met was Red Danny,
> And a good welcome he had it there for me.
> He invited me out to the wagon,
> And good comfort there was there for me.
>
> Was the first he drew down about Ellen,
> And the next he drew down about me,
> And the next I flung me eye upon Julia,
> Saying, "You'll make a hawker for me."
>
> Such a boasting and bragging out of Julia,
> You'd swear she'd sailed all the storms of the road:
> Selling lino, buying horses or feathers,
> In the old streets of old Carramee.
>
> I went to a village outside it,
> Where I always was used for to be,

> She was selling her tiepins and hairpins
> In the main streets of old Carramee.
>
> For the first month me and Julia lived happy,
> And the second we could not agree,
> And the third month Julia wore the trousers,
> And she wore the black bottle on me.
>
> Well, whenever you want to get buckled,
> Sure, inquire then for old Carramee,
> And it's there you'll find another like Julia
> Around the main streets of old Carramee. [4]

Yes, my mother was a real Traveling woman. Connor, O'Connors, it's famous among the Traveling people. She's one of the very old stock. She had the old language, we call it gammon, and me father knew it too. They'd talk to us like that, or they'd speak it together if they didn't want anyone else, could be standing by, to know what they were saying. So, just as you'd expect it, my father and mother moved about for a while then, and they raised their own family on the road. I was born in Baltinglass, County Wicklow. Nineteen and thirty-two I was born, and there was seven brothers and three sisters along with meself, eleven of us altogether. I can remember back as far as me Holy Communion stage, and times were terrible poor then. Me mother and father, they got cruel hardship.

I often look back and think how much they suffered, because them years there was no employment. Me mother used to have to go out selling things, and she'd no transport, only to walk. Hardware she done, a lot of hardware. She used to sell buckets and saucepans and mugs and delft and things like that. Me father made some of it, the tin buckets and things, and me mother used to buy a lot more, delft and things, from a dealer. She used to carry big, huge basketfuls miles. She'd think nothing of going out ten, twelve miles a day to sell those things, to provide for us, house to house. Everybody admired her, because she wanted to educate us and, although we were poor, we were reared well. And then it came back to my father that he wanted to see his children educated too, and so we came to live with this old man by the name of Paddy Keegan.

> I went into a shiney's house and asked to borrow bread.
> They wrapped me up in a tablecloth and put me into bed.
> They put me into the kettle, the kettle begin to sing,
> "Get out, get out, you little dear thing, and fill the kettle again." [5]

Now, I don't remember it, when we came to live with him, but me brother Luke'd remember, he'd be about eight or nine then, I suppose. And when they settled in with this old man he told them they could have the cottage, his cottage, as long as they wished. So, after some time then, the old man died, and we were left the cottage, and we all went to school and was educated there, in a National School, of course. We lived in a very remote place then. It's in Merginstown, three miles from Dunlavin, west Wicklow. School was right beside us, but we'd no shops sooner than about three miles away. I remember my childhood. We used to love school, of course.

We'd one room and a kitchen, that's all we had in the cottage. I remember waiting in the room. I didn't know the time then, but, say now, it'd be about one o'clock in the night. I'd see the light under the door and I'd creep up, and there me mother'd be baking bread, or sewing, or maybe washing to get things prepared for the next day, the way she'd get out. She used to be going out selling each and every day. And in the family, well, I was the youngest, and there was eleven of us in it. She had a very big family and there's two years between every one of us, and it must have been horrible, and it must have gone on forever. I often look back and see the hardship she got, but if she seen it was hardship she never spoke of it. She didn't tell us her troubles.

They say this is true, about this man one time and he fought a mermaid. This man was a farmer and every morning he used to see this mermaid abroad in the grass field. Every morning she come, you know, eating grass or combing her hair, and he seen her there. And he fell in love with her. "I'll get you," says he, "longer nor shorter." She was a lovely looking girl.

One day he come along, anyway, and he went down behind the deal ditch and he started to steal and steal and steal down a-through the field, 'til he got to the turn in the river that run through the field. She seen him then and she run to the river, but he grabbed her. Into it with the two of them, they fell in the water, and they fought, but he bested her. And, begad, he brings her up to the house. He takes the cloak of scale off her then. Her feet was only stuck into this cloak like a fish's tail, but she was a plain woman within. He takes the cloak and he hides it above in the thatch, and she never knew where he hid it.

He gets the girl anyways, and he loved her. She had a family then, three in number, and she lived happy. It was about ten years after, and one day the little girl, the youngest, come to her and says, "Oh Mammy, do you know what I seen today? I was atop," says she, "up in the loft and I seen a remarkable sort of thing with scales on it, something, now, like a fish."

"Where'd you see it?" says the mother.

"Up in the loft," says the child.

Up the woman goes and she gets it. It was in a little loft in this thatched house, where only just the man was used to go. Well, you see, she had to get it, and once she got it she was enchanted again, as soon as she got the cloak of scale. She had to go back to the sea then, and the roaring of her and the crying of her as she didn't want to go! She brought the three childer with her down to the strand, and she took them into the water.

Well, your man was above ploughing the field, and he seen them going down. Ah, he left ploughing and helter-skelter with him to the river, but he wasn't fast enough. Just when he got there they were turned into mermaids, all four of 'em!

The woman didn't want to ever find this cloak, you know. When she got into the sea she calls back to him, "For all those years I'm married to you, and you never did away with me cloak! Why didn't ya burn it? Now, sure, we're separated same as the first day."

Then she went away out in the sea and sat on top of a big rock and started combing her hair and, sure, singing. "Come in," she says. "Come in to me." And she kept calling to him to come.

He'd see her every morning on this rock, but if he'd ha' go in to her she'd have drownded him, you see. And it'd be a couple of mile out to sea anyway, and he couldn't get to her.[6]

Well, I'd love me mother to be alive, to give her some bit of comfort now. I really would, because I'm just thinking this now, and I'm sure it's quite true: she was often pregnant and carrying another baby and this big basket of stuff and she'd think nothing of walking miles. She told me one incident of this, that happened in her life. She bought an ass and car one time, and she thought she was really well off. And she went out that day, we'll say, about ten miles. At the end of the day she'd all her provision in this car, anything she needed, like her grocery, after doing her day's selling, and she'd two small children with her, Luke, now, and me other sister Mary, she was the baby. And then some farmer give her a big carload of turf, and she put that in the car too. Now, didn't the ass get tired and she couldn't get it to go home, and what did she do? She unyoked the ass and she wheeled the car with the childer, turf and everything she had, home to Merginstown, that'd be about twelve miles. So, you can well depend, it was really dreadful, really was.

Me father, now, he done the tinsmithing business, and then he was a bit fond of drink as well. He loved to drink, definitely, but he was kind to us and he was good. And he cared for us as he could, but in them years, like, there was nothing, and he couldn't help it by being idle. He couldn't turn the world around.

> *I wish I lived in Carrickfergus,*
> *Only four miles from Ballygrand,*
> *I'd swim right over the deepest ocean,*
> *Only four miles from Ballygrand.*
>
> *But the sea is deep, I cannot swim over,*
> *And neither have I wings to fly,*
> *I'd have to get me a handsome boatman*
> *To ferry over my love and I.*
>
> *Oh, in Kilkenny, it is reported,*
> *They have marble stones there as black as ink.*
> *With gold and silver I did support her,*
> *But I'll sing no more 'til I get a drink.*
>
> *I'm drunk today, but I'm seldom sober.*
> *I am a rover, I go from town to town.*

And so I'll sit here, in grief and sorrow,
And when I die, won't you lay me down. [7]

The people always respected us because they knew, like, that even though we were very, very poor, me mother and father seen that we were very honestly reared, and they wouldn't allow us to do anything wrong. The sort me father was, now, he wouldn't allow the lads to touch a bit of a stick, he'd think it was an awful crime to do a thing like that, and she felt the same. And the people were so good to us; when they'd kill pigs or anything in the district I think we got the best part of it. It was through the people that really we were reared, you know what I mean. Only for them we'd have never got on.

For our breakfast, now, we usually had bacon and homemade bread. As I told you, we lived in a very remote place, but there was big farmers' houses around, and they used to kill their own bacon. And at nighttime me mother made a big pan of oatmeal porridge, that'd be boiling for hours. It's not like the processed stuff now, it just came out of the mill and she kept boiling it and boiling it. All the farmers lived on it too, then, and we got this from different farmers when they'd bring it from the mill, and it was beautiful. We'd always a big plate of that and a big tin of new milk, going to bed. And for supper then she'd always have bacon and cabbage, and lots of potatoes. She was a great woman for food; we never knew what it was to be in want.

Me mother'd nearly made all our clothes that we wore as well. In fact, I've several little things here she made herself. She was a very good woman for sewing and she used to make nearly all our quilts, patchwork quilts. She made them beautiful. Anyone'd give her old clothes, well, if they weren't good she'd cut them up and make patchwork quilts out of them. And she was marvelous, she was a very clean woman. Then our underwear consisted of flour bags. Yes, that's true. The people'd keep her the flour bags. She'd wash them and boil them and take the brand out of them and make beautiful sheets and pillowcovers and our little vests and little shimmies, she used to call it. It'd be snow-white the way she'd have it done out, and nicely done. That's the way we were dressed, and then she'd have old things, she'd cut them up and make other clothes out of them for us.

And she was a very good quack. In fact, when all my brothers now'd get married, there was seven of them, and when the women'd be pregnant she was always there at hand.

Where have you been all the day, Billy Boy, Billy Boy?
Where have you been all the day, my Billy Boy?
"I've been walking all the day with my charming Nancy Day,
And my Nancy diddle-my-tancy," Oh my charming Billy Boy.

Can she cook a bit of steak, Billy Boy, Billy Boy?
Can she cook a bit of steak, my Billy Boy?
"She can cook a bit of steak, as a fork is to a plate,
And my Nancy diddle-my-tancy." Oh my charming Billy Boy.

Is she fit to be your wife, Billy Boy, Billy Boy?
Is she fit to be your wife, my Billy Boy?
"She is fit to be my wife, as the fork unto the knife,
And my Nancy diddle-my-tancy." Oh my charming Billy Boy.[8]

Sure, she never was afraid. She was as good as a nurse. I had one brother and he had double pneumonia and he was dying. He was just a little lad then, and the doctor gave him up as dead. "He's not going to die, Doctor," she said.

"Mrs. Wall," he says, "I don't want to build up your hopes. The child is very ill and I think he will die."

Well, she brought him home, she often told me about it. I don't remember it because he'd a good bit older nor I am. The child was smothering, sort of gasping. So she took a new pair of blankets and she had a big coal fire, and she heated the blankets 'til they were red hot, 'til she roasted the wool off of them. And she lapped the baby up in it tight as tuppence. When she was done that, she went out and looked for a feather. She came back in then and she dipped the feather in either olive oil or castor oil, I can't say which for definite, and she run it up the child's nostrils and kept pulling down the stuff out of it. She'd do it and do it again. Just an ordinary feather, probably out of a crow or something. And she sweated the child. When the doctor came the next morning, he said, "The child's temperature is down!"

"Ah yes, Doctor," she says, "but I cured him meself."

"How did you do it?" he says.

"I done it," she says, "I relieved the child. He was dyin'."

And then if a child was chesty, she believed in brown paper and a blessed candle. Later, when they were Traveling together, me brother Johnny and his family and me mother with them, they all looked to her to cure 'em. Johnny's daughter, Nanny, for instance, she'd a very bad chest and of course Johnny's wife'd come and say, "Oh, Auld Mammy, baby has an awful bad chest."

"Ah, she'll be alright," me mother'd say. "Tonight bring her up to me and I'll do something with her." She'd cut out a sheet of paper exactly like the shimmies she used to make for us. And she melted this blessed candle, and put it all over the paper, and put it on the child. And then she says, "Put on her clothes and let her wear it. She'll be alright." And Nanny never looked back, she never had any bad chest after that. It really worked. She was marvelous, poor woman.

She used to be singing all the time, and me father sang too, and he used to tell stories 'round the fire at night. He was a great storyteller. In fact, I never can recall any of the stories now, but he was great for telling them. And I'll tell you our luxury now, the one we had when we were living in the house. Every Friday or Saturday night himself and me mother'd go into the town of Dunlavin and he'd buy a book, a Western story, and they'd come home and that book was gave to one of the brothers, the eldest brother. We'd have a good fire in the grate and we'd all sit around and me brother started to read this story, and I can picture him to this day. He'd try and talk like a Western and we'd be all intrigued listening to this.

May I sleep in your barn tonight, Mister?
It's so cold lying out on the ground,
And the north, north wind is a-whistling,
And I have no place to lie down.

Now, I have no tobacco nor matches,
And I'm sure I can cause you no harm
I will tell you my story, kind Mister,
For it runs through my head like a storm.

It is three years ago just last summer,
I shall never forget that sad day,
When a stranger came out from the city,
And said that he wanted to stay.

Now, this stranger was fair, tall and handsome,
And he looked like a man who had wealth.
Said he wanted to stop in the country,
He wanted to stop for his health.

Now, one night as I came from my workshop
I was whistling and singing with joy.
I expected a kind hearty welcome
From my fond loving wife and my boy.

Now, but what did I find but a letter,
It was placed in my room on a stand,
And the moment my eyes fell upon it
I picked it right up in my hand.

Now, this note said my wife and the stranger
Have left and have taken my son.
I wonder if God up in heaven
Only know what the stranger has done.

May I sleep in your barn tonight, Mister?
It's so cold lying out on the ground,
And the north, north wind is a-whistling,
And I have no place to lie down. [9]

He'd read about six pages, and then the little bit was turnt down and 'twas put up 'til the next night. That was the only luxury we had, and we were all contented and happy with it.

Well, even in them poor times, we were all born in hospital, all of me mother's family. She always went in. And she often told me herself that before there'd be a baby she'd be always preparing, and she'd have food stored away that we wouldn't be short while she was gone. She must have been strong as a bull to stick it. But something else I want to tell you about me mother: One of my brothers was born in at Rathdrum, in the Home. The ambulance came for her to Merginstown, now that'd be about twenty miles across the Gap. I'm sure it would be twenty miles from where we lived. He was born in Rathdrum and the baby was seven days old when she got up out of her bed. And the nurses said, "Oh, you can't get up, Mrs. Wall! Your baby's too young."

"Oh," me mother says, "I'm going home. I have me childer to think of."

"Well," said the nurse, "the ambulance is out. You can't go home."

"But," she says, "I am going home." She wrapped her baby up in a shawl and she started walking the twenty miles to home.

When she came to the top of the Gap she was kind of getting weak, and she was sitting down for a bit of a rest, and a lady and a gentleman in an auto overtook her. They stopped the car and they said, "What's wrong?" And she up and explained to them that she was after coming home from the hospital and that she was weary.

"Oh, my God," the man said, "that's horrible." And they took her into the car.

They opened a flask, they had whiskey in it, and they gave her a drop of it, and then the lady took the baby on her knee. She said to my mother, "Would you sell me the baby?"

"Oh, no!" me mother says. "I wouldn't part me baby!"

"Sell me the baby," the lady says, "and he'd have a good home, and he'll never want for anything. We've no family of our own," she says.

"I'm living in poverty," me mother says, "but I wouldn't part me child for nobody."

So they left her home and they gave her the address to write to 'em, just to be friendly, like. But me mother was terrible superstitious and she wouldn't write to the lady then, because she thought she was overlooking the baby. This old woman only wanted to help her, but she felt the woman'd overlook her baby and something'd happen to it.[10]

> Wallflowers, wallflowers, growing up so high,
> All pretty maidens do not like to die,
> Especially little Mary, she is the youngest child,
> So turn your back against the game.
> Yes, turn your back to Salty Jack and say no more to me.[11]

Often she said to Tom, that was that baby, as he grew up to be a big man, and he's a very big man now, often she said, "I should ha' sold you, I'd ha' got a good price for ya that day and I walking across the Gap." Joking him, but wasn't it horrible?

Yes, me mother was very superstitious. If she seen a magpie in the morning she'd imagine there was something 'twas going to happen. And me father was superstitious too about magpies. I remember one time they were coming from Donard in an old ass and car, and a magpie lit on the car. They said, "Something is going to happen now! Please God nothing'll happen." And when they went home there was a telegram waiting for them that me father's father had died in Athy. So, they believed it and it happened. And the childer did have some of this too. I remember quite well when I was about the age of nine and Luke, he was about eleven. When me mother'd be late at night and not come home, we'd go to meet her and we'd be crying. There was this little crossroads past our house and we used to stand at this crossroads and expect her to come some way. And Luke'd say, "I wonder if I'd go this road and you'd go that road, would we meet her?" We were terrified that something'd done her harm.

Other things she was superstitious about: if she felt her face itchy some of the childer was coming to see her, and it always happened. "Oh," she said, "some of the lads is coming today," and her jaw was itchy. But she never told fortunes, she thought that was a horrible thing. She believed in people, you see, and she believed that things happened.

Now, I had a fashion of cutting the cards, because an old woman learnt me how to do it. To cut the cards for somebody, you know, tell fortunes out of them, out of ordinary playing cards, and me mother used to be horribly against it. She'd say, "You shouldn't do it, Biddy." She'd say, "You might put somebody on the wrong road." She always believed that, do you see. She was a very good little woman.

Now, I can see by the straight line of your hand, Dear, that is your line of life. Your line of life runs wide and deep; you've got a long life to live. You're a person is not fond of rows or arguments, but you've got a hasty temper when your temper's risen. You're fond of brightness and bright surroundings, Dear, but you're a peculiar person, it's very hard to please you at times, isn't that so?

Your past life wasn't all sunshine for you, isn't that so? You have worked and toiled hard in the past, and you haven't gained much riches or prosperity through your past life. But there is brightness ahead of you, that you do not least expect.

You're a straightforward person, Dear, and you're fond of amusements. You're well liked, not for your appearances alone, but for your trustworthy and your honesty. Where you show your face once, you can always show it a second time, isn't that so?

Now, Dear, you had a little darkness in your past. You parted with one in your family that caused a drawback in your own life, isn't that so? You're a person that's fainthearted, you shed tears over slight matters that don't concern you at times. It's easy to worry you, if you can understand me plainer. But you don't have to worry, Dear. There is nothing to worry you. Your darkness will come, Dear, even that you worry. Otherwise, there is brightness.

You are mostly interested, and you're very anxious, that you'll have the pleasure of rocking a cradle, isn't that so? Well, you will have that pleasure, Dear, in the space of three. Your firstborn will be a baby boy, which will cause a lot of happiness between you and your husband both. More of your time will be taken up rocking a cradle than it will to go outdoors.

Now I'm going to ask you a very serious question. You did have a relative abroad that you haven't been in close contact with for a number of years, isn't that so? Well, in a very short time you are to receive news from that particular person. Well, it is going to be hasty. I'm sorry to have to tell you the truth: you'll come in contact with this particular person through a death, Love. But through it you're going to gain a piece of money. Now you tell me the truth, there is a relative in your relationship bear a J in his initial, a gentleman? You'll have to sign large government forms and you'll make arrangements to divide this money with four. The first of the four is this particular gentleman. The money doesn't trouble you much. You're not anxious for money, but you are going to gain it through a death, Love. Outside that you don't have to be upset as you usually do be.

You don't have to take life seriously, Dear, it's only just come and go, as we call it. You're interested in the gentleman you changed your life for and he's interested in you, Dear, and that's all that counts in this life. Well, wish on something good anyhow.

Now, I want you to be straightforward and truthful in what I repeat to you. When you took that wish you didn't wish for eatables, drinkables, wearables, or money, isn't that so? No, you did not. Your particular wish is to be lucky and successful, to have luck with yourself, luck with your fiancé in life, and you do wish to rock that cradle, Dear, isn't that so? Isn't that particularly your wish?

You'll be very lucky, happy, and successful in the near future, Dear. You'll rock a cradle that will make both you and your fiancé very lucky.

Now are you quite satisfied to part with this bit of silver here? You're quite happy about this bit of silver? Good enough, and I'm very thankful to you. [12]

Then when I was ten we had our Confirmation, and me father got a caravan and we started back on the road. And I think me mother got it a bit easier then, although she always regretted leaving the cottage. That's what I wanted to tell you about.

In the beginning, do you see, Mary was the eldest of us and she went away and she got married to a Traveling fella, Tom Doran was his name, and she went off to England. And then Paddy, me brother, went off on his own, Traveling around. He'd be selling things and he bought a pony and car. He thought he was rich to have such a thing, luxury we'd call it now. And then Johnny went, and, by degrees, Luke left then and went away. And one by one, you see, them all drifted, until we were down to me and Tom and Allie. There was only three of us childer left in the house, and I think me father and mother got a bit lonely for the rest of them. They wanted to take up and to go with them, you see. They were lonely for each other. So we started on the road.

I think we always regretted leaving the house. In fact, me mother never was the same really from that time, although she was a Traveling woman. That was the unfortunate part of it. We never sold the house or nothing. We just left it, abandoned it, and it's standing there still. We never bothered to look it up or anything. I suppose, really and truly, it should be some of ours, but it's falling now. I went to see it a couple of years ago, and it looks dilapidated looking. And there's a tree that Luke sowed in it. I remember he plaited it. It was an ash tree and as the little tree grew up he plaited all the leaves and they grew into a big plaited knot. It's growing up there still, huge and big.

When we did start in to Traveling again we used always Travel with Johnny, 'cause he always adored me father and mother and, like, he was fairly good, and he got well-off. Like, he never seen them shook. It was through him that they bought this caravan and went on the road and I can remember the first night we slept in the caravan; I thought I'd smother. I was used to the big spacy room and I had to go into this little press-bed, me and my sister, to sleep in it. It was a round-topped caravan, I'll never forget it. I was ten years of age and I had dreams about the room and everything at night.

> Oh, Blessed Virgin, grant me your ear,
> No midnight spirit to tend me here,
> Whilst I am relating on my sad tale
> Of my love was drownded in Avondale.
>
> Oh, Brian Barr was my true love's name,
> His heart, his soul I had freely gained.
> His charmy features my heart it won.
> Now he is drownded and I'm all alone.
>
> The night before the dreadful day,
> When I asleep on my pillow lay,
> I dreamt I saw my true love pass by.
> Pale was his cheeks and dim was his eye.
>
> But when I awoke and found it a dream,
> Tears of relief down my cheeks did stream.
> But to my grief, sure, I heard the tale:
> My love was drownded in sweet Avondale.
>
> All along those banks where my love fell in
> A flowery garden I'll build for him.
> No midnight spirit shall it prevail
> Of my own true darling, lies in Avondale. [13]

We traveled mostly County Wicklow and parts of Kildare, and then me sister married down in Tipperary to a Traveling man and we used to go down there to see her. I had to leave the school. We'll say I went to school at about five and I left at ten, that's all the education I got. I didn't know how to read or write. So then we used to play at school when we were on the road. Me eldest sister, that was the eldest left, Alice, she was fourteen. I was ten and Tom was twelve. Allie was the schoolmistress and we played with our school books. So eventually I learned to read and write through her. I picked it up.

When we were out in the country, stopped by the roadside maybe, we were always roused very early, 'cause me father never slept longer nor six. You see, he was a soldier in the early part of his life. He was in the Curragh, and then he was in the Connack Rangers. He got pneumonia then and had to be sent back to the Curragh, or something like that. Well, he was very proud of the fact that he was a Connack Ranger, because if anybody was impident to 'im, or maybe someone wouldn't know him and they'd maybe give him cheek, he said, "Do you know who you're talking to? I was in the Connack Rangers!" And he was a huge big man.

So, we riz very early in the morning, and then he always retired early. I don't think we used to like to go to bed early, but we used to. I suppose ten o'clock'd be very late for us to bed. We weren't like the ordinary Traveling people now that'd lie on in the bed half the day. We'd have to get out of it, because he'd be roaring around the road like a bull if we didn't. And we were reared up to think our father was right, and we must obey his wishes.

> *I been scarcely nineteen year of age*
> *When to join the army, sure I first engage,*
> *But I left the factory with a good intent,*
> *And I joined the forty-second regiment.*
>
> *As I was stationed down on guard one day*
> *Some soldiers' children all came there to play.*
> *The officer Quarter Captain Hamill came,*
> *And he ordered me to take their parents in.*
>
> *I took but one, let the others go free,*
> *On the neglect of duty, sure, he did charge me.*
> *But out of trouble, sure, I never will be,*
> *Since Captain Hamill took a dislike to me.*
>
> *With a loaded rifle I did appear*
> *To shoot my Captain on the barracks square.*
> *I done the deed and I shed his blood.*
> *At the Lipperpool 'sylum, sure, my trial I stood.*
>
> *I've got no father for to take my part,*
> *Or yet no mother for to break her heart,*
> *But I've got a friend, and a girl is she,*
> *And she'd lose her life for old McCaffery.*[14]

In the morning, outside the wagon, me mother, she had a big fire lit, and she had her pan and lid, a bake pan. I have it still, out there. She'd put her lid on the fire and she had a pole stuck in the ditch. She put on her pan. She'd mix up her cake and it was put into the pan. She'd put the lid on then, and put some greeshuck on top, some of the hot fire, and she'd leave it for about twenty minutes, and we'd a beautiful lovely cake. In fact, she learnt us all how to do that, and a lovely bread it is.

From the time I was ten, when we left the house, I used to always be washing and she learnt me how to bake. I'd bake the bread again she'd come home, and I'd have a big washing done. And if there was any soiled thing in it, I'd be made to take them clothes in off the ditch and do 'em all over again. We used to have a big churn for carrying the water in the caravan, or two buckets and lids. And then, I always had the caravan clean and the evening meal prepared when she come back from selling. She'd never have a dinner in the daytime then, we always had it in the night because she'd be moving during the day. About twelve o'clock we'd maybe have cold meat and tea and bread and butter, lots of it. We never was hungry, that's one thing sure. In the evening, then, she was terrible fond of cabbage, and she'd have a big pot of meat and cabbage. Or, if she didn't have that, she'd have maybe soup and a big pot of potatoes. She would get that food, but I would cook it, like. And, before we'd go to bed me father never had anything, but she'd always make a cup of tea for us.

When we started Traveling we sort of got well-off. 'Twas during the war and me father made plenty of money out of those cans and things. He was able to get horses and then he was able to have lots of money to drink. Well, in the beginning of me mother's life they had no horses; they'd nothing. But when we started back on the road we always had two horses then. In west Wicklow he sort of supplied everybody with their buckets and pans and all that they needed, and he was a very good tradesman. He made the work and me mother sold it, that's how they made their living. Yes, me father had his own district, and he'd be very annoyed if anybody else tried to sell across his territory, like. Bally-knockin, a very big townsland, and Valleymount, and Blessington, all around there. Knocknatruss and Dunlavin area, Laminstown and all, they had all that. And them years they were needed. The tinsmith was needed and the hawking was needed, because there was none of this modernized enamelware or anything like that. Even farmers couldn't afford it in them years, so my mother supplied 'em with tin. The big boys, then, they was always out foraging for theirselves. Them years, there was no linoleum or anything like that, so they'd be out selling this tinware too and looking for horsehair. They used to sell it raw to a Jew-man, and rabbit skins and whatever they could get to turn money on. And then they saved their own money.

Now, yous all know young Tom Murphy,
And 'tis plainly yous can see:
He's the best-liked man ever made a can
Round the Burns of Askakeagh.

Sure, he have a great big wagon,
And he pulls it with his jin,
And he have no food nor feeding but
The auld furze of Ballinaglen.

And if you see that mule in the wintertime,
Don't mind him for being thin,
For he expects him to fatten
On the furze in Ballinaglen.

Sure, he have no straw or hay for him,
Nor a house to put him in,
Ah, 'tis rain and snow, sure, out must go
To the furze in Ballinaglen.

He was coming home one frosty night,
But he slipped and cut his knee
And old Mag and all the childer
Had to walk to Askakeagh.

If you see poor Tom that winter's night,
I'm sure you'd pity him,
For it was very far and he wheeling the old car
To get back to Ballinaglen.

But late that night, old Tom got home
With his box and a half of tin,
And he had no stout and the lights was out
When he went to Ballinaglen.

Ah, from Aughrim Town to Hackettstown
For a box and a half of tin,
He'll come there and working for
The shops round Ballinaglen.

And in that country in the wintertime
I couldn't get one rabbit skin,
For they keeps 'em all for my brother Tom
That lives around Ballinaglen. [15]

Begging, we was never allowed to do that. My father was very strict on such things. He felt that he'd feel terrible ashamed if we done it. In fact, some days I'd go off with me mother in the pony and trap, where she'd be selling those wares. Everybody 'round those parts knew her of course, and they'd say, "Come in, Mrs. Wall, and I'll give you a cup of tea." And I'd feel that dreadful, for I never was used to going into the houses. Me mother often called me to go in with her, and I wouldn't go. She'd have to bring the tea out to me then and she'd say, "That's a disgrace for you, Biddy, and the woman have it ready and all!" I'd sit outside and the horrible shame'd come over me. I wouldn't know what way I'd feel. I'd feel terrible small. Of course, then, as the years come on I overcome all that.

I met me husband when I was fifteen. Michael Murphy was his name and me brother and him went off gathering goats together, and that's how I met him. So we went together for nine months and then we got married, and I needn't tell you we'd no nice reception. We went with sixpence to the priest. We had to put silver on the plate and Mickey'd sixpence. That's quite true. It was in a

Catholic church, because, except for the Gypsies, all Traveling people is Catholics. There's none of them Protestants or any other religion.

One time there came this fella to a priest, and, oh, he was a terrible innocent fella. He was a harmless fella. All the people in them days was so harmless. The fella axed the priest could he help him and the priest gave this fella a thrupenny bit. The fella looked at it and he says, "Ah Father, this is a poor little bit. It's so small, and its color is bad. Poor little bit!" And the priest said then to the fella that he should put it in some moss so it could grow. So, the fella put it down in some moss, near there to the priest's door. And the priest says he's to come back in some days to see how it's getting on.

So, when the fella was gone, the priest took out the thrupenny bit and put sixpence in the moss. And some days after the fella come back and feels around in the moss and pulls out the sixpence. "Oh, Father," he says, "how my little bit is better! What a good color it's got! But it's still so small, poor little bit." And the priest says to put it back in the moss again so it can grow.

So, after some days more the fella comes back again and the priest has put a shilling in the moss, and he says, "Oh, Father, see how my little bit has grown! And it's such a lovely color. Isn't it wonderful? I'll put it back in the moss so's maybe it can grow more."

And then the priest put a two-shilling piece in the moss, and when the fella came back he was ever so pleased. Says he, "Oh, Father, my little bit is getting a proper size now, and I'll put it back in the moss once more to see won't it grow even bigger." So he did. And this time the priest changed the two shillings for a half-crown. When the fella come back and he saw that, he told the priest, and he said he'd leave the bit in the moss for a few more days.

Now, the priest couldn't find anything to put in the moss this time but a golden sovereign. So when the fella came back he felt around in the moss and pulled out the golden sovereign. "Oh, Father," says he, "my bit has grown well in this here moss. But now look, it's gone an awful sickly color again, and I think maybe the moss is not right for it after all. And I'll just put it in my pocket and keep it there now." And so he did. [16]

I was married in Dublin in Francis Street, with a priest by the name of Father Kelly. The day we got married, in fact, we were only going in to go to church. We were to be married the following day, but the priest, I suppose, wanted to hurry it up. We were only poor, and he said, "Oh, I'll marry yous now." We had to call a woman out of the chapel, some person we didn't know, to witness it, and me brother was there. We put the sixpence on the plate and the priest give it back to us. He knew we had nothing more. It was tuppence each on the bus, and we came back on our sixpence, up to Captain's Lane. We had to climb a great big wall then, to get over to where the caravans was, and Mickey pulled me across. We were married then.

So, I was married at sixteen and dreadful hardship we got after that, because, as I told you, times were poor for us too and very difficult. Mickey was at the tinware, and then he was getting some scrap and selling it. But he had no money, and he had only a few sheets of tin, that was to keep us, to survive, like. We'd no place to sleep, so I stayed in me own bed and he stayed with my brother, sleeping, for about a week 'til he got this barrage-balloon cover. They used to call them barrage-balloon covers, what do you call them things that comes down out of the air? A parachute! We made a tent out of that, and that was our home, and then we went off on our honeymoon. I remember waking one night and I was feeling dreadful cold, and I looked up. This thing had blew off us and I was left with the stars for a shelter!

We came back then and we were with my father for about two months after being married, Traveling around together. And, as I told you, my mother always provided for us, and I didn't know much about going out to look for anything for meself. I didn't know what to do, to tell you the truth. She hoped, you see, that we might never have to do it, and she'd say, "You be time enough doing it, you don't want to do it now."

But we left me father and mother then and came out to a place called Ballinaglen. It was during the end of the war and this tinware racket was very good at the time. So Mickey made a lot of tinware and, of course, I was no good to sell it. "Now," says he, "you just have to go! I can't make it and sell it at the one time. So you'll just have to go out!" He'd a very bad old horse, so he yoked up this old mare and car for me and away I goes in it.

I remember distinctly the place I went, a place called Askanagap. I was terribly young, and every place I went I'm sure the people must ha' took pity on me, 'cause I looked so shy going to the door asking them to buy these cans off me. So I sold every one of them, and I came back and got on right then. After that first time I was just fine. We used to sell the cans maybe for eight or nine shillings each, and them half-gallons, what we'd have for dipping down into a churn of buttermilk, making the bread, or for hot water and things like that, them'd run about three and sixpence, or, lucky enough, maybe you'd get four bob. If you met someone to peddle with you, that was nice company, but you'd have to sell them a lot cheaper, of course. So then, we got on. Mickey used to take us up for a drink then, when he'd get his money for his cans.

I was reared west Wicklow and Mickey's people was east Wicklow. This was their area and we had the other side. But when we got married, Mickey and me, we Traveled east Wicklow now. It was our territory now, for our business, where Mickey's parents was before him; we'll say from Arklow to Newtownmountkennedy, and up around Roundwood, and out as far as Tinahely and Hackettstown. So eventually everybody got to know me and I sort of was accepted among the people, and they'd wait on me to come with those cans and things.

When we were about two years married we got that man down there, Tommy Murphy, he built us our first caravan, and we bought an old pony that kicked the sun, moon, and stars. She let no one drive her, only me or Mickey. Then she had a foal, and we sold her and the foal in Dublin for ten pound. That'll tell you how cheap horses was then. And then we bought another one, we bought Queenie. I'd be about twenty years of age then, and Queenie sort of built us up since. We have her still. She's sixteen now and every year she bred a foal for us, and the horses became dear. And then when Mickey sold his first couple of horses, and was after dealing horses, well, he made plenty of money.

There was a Galtee farmer and he had a balty mare.
He brought her out to sell her, oh, unto Kilkenny Fair.
The big son, he went with him saying, "Father, I'll do me best,
For I'll engage this mare to all work, no trial will be request."

Up comes a Dublin buyer and he bid him well inclined,
"I'll give you twenty guineas, and the auld mare she shall be mine."
He paid him for this little mare, and he then took her away
To a stable in Kilkenny he had taken for the day.

He clips this mare all over and he trimmed her tail and mane,
But inside of one auld half hour she been on the fair again.
With a saddle and a bridle and a jockey on her back,
You'd swear she was a racer that you would see on the track.

And says the father to the son, "There is a mare I'll buy,
She looks so styled and handsome she's great action in my eye."
He asked the jock the price of her, the jockey looked around
Saying, "The price is sixty guineas, and for luck I'll give a pound."

He paid him for this little mare, sure Mick Murphy could tell
That he would not take no pound for luck, he liked the auld mare so well.

He gave her into the big son's hand, saying, "I'd like to see her going."
But the big son could not hold her, she got on the road for home.
This poor mare she felt very cold and the auld day come spilling rain,
He never got one pull on her 'til she come to her own auld lane.

He never got one pull on her 'til she come to her own auld lane.
Ah, but who run out to meet him but the youngest daughter, Jane,
Saying, "Mammy, here's my Daddy, but the auld mare he did not sell.
Sure, you'd hardly know her the way she'd clipped, but I'd know her old walk well."

"What made you get the poor mare clipped, don't you know she'll catch the cold?
For how can she escape it, for she's got so thin and old."
"You may thank the almighty God, what luck that brought me there.
I got twenty guineas for my own and this mare she's nearly clear."

"Now I'll sit down upon the chair, and I'll let me temper cool,
For I'm married to you this fifty year and you are a born fool.
If you had to go out, do a little work, and not go to that fair!
Sure you're out about seventy guineas, lad, and still, you've your own auld mare!"[17]

77

Yes, Mickey made lots of money, but as he'd make this big money he'd maybe go on big bouts of beer. In the beginning of our life if I got a pound a day I thought I was rich, and then suddenly we were able to have four or five hundred pound and we thought we were very well-to-do. I mean, that was an awful amount of money to us, coming up from nothing. So he'd go on big bouts of drinking and this'd be gone down the Swanee again: he'd drink it. Then when I came to twenty-two we had six horses, plenty of money, a lovely caravan, and lovely harness. Everything we needed, everything was new. We'd gorgeous delft and everything the way I wanted it, and he said to me this time, "Do you know what I think? We'll go to England, that's what we'll do!"

So we sold all our things and we went to Dublin and we said, "Where will we go to?"

I seen "Manchester" writ up on a big board, so, says I, "Let's go to Manchester!"

But before we went, Mickey drank all his money. We were in Dublin, you see, and we drank a lot. We bought a case, and he bought me a new coat and himself a new suit, and after paying our fare the money deteriorated down to ten pounds. We'd only this ten pound and we were complete strangers going to England, and we were happy!

So we arrived in Manchester and he said, "Come on you, we'll get a drink." So we got a few drinks, and now we'd no place to go, and what did we do? We went to the Exchange to look for a job, instead of going to look for a flat or somewhere to live!

At the exchange this woman come up and said to me, "Where do you live?" and I couldn't give any address. She said, "You'll have to have an address before you can get a job." So we went off looking for this, and our heels was blisters.

We could find no place that would give us a room. We went around and around and we went into this cafe, and the money was just going all the time. Suddenly we found ourself with only three pounds, so Mickey gave it to his sister that was there, to hold for us, to pay for the room what we got. We did get a room then, an old dirty room, and we were to pay three pounds a week for it. But when he went back to the sister and she put her hand in her pocket the three pounds was gone! Lucky enough, the man that had the place was an Indian and he let us in anyway. We had to go to Subsistence to get our money to live on for the week. So we got a job.

> As I went out walking one fine summer's morning,
> The birds in the bushes did warble and sing,
> Those lads and those lassies together were sporting,
> Going down to the factory, their work to begin.
>
> I spied one amongst them more fairer than any,
> She had cheeks like the rosies, they're none to exile.
> She had skin like a lily that grows in yon valley,
> And beside she's a hard-working poor factory girl.

I stepped up beside her, most closely to view her,
And me she captured in one glimpse of her eye,
Saying, "Young man, have manners, and do not come near me,
I'm only a hard-working factory girl."

"I have land, I have houses, all stored with green ivy.
I had gold in me pocket and silver as well,
And if you come with me, a lady I'll make you.
No more need ya sound on your factory bell."

These last words she've turned on and last I have left her.
All for her sake I'll go wander away
Into some lonely valleys where no one will find me,
And I'll mourn for the sake of my factory girl. [18]

Mickey got a job on the buildings and I got a job in Dunlops. He was earning good money, about twenty pounds a week, and I was earning six pound ten a week. He'd get his money on a Friday night, and I'd never see him 'til about Friday midnight when it'd be all gone. That's true. Friday I'd get me wages and I'd spend half of it buying things. I always have a crave for buying delft and I'd loads of delft and nice things and nowhere to go with 'em.

That was in August that we went to England and he was drinking good-o. He worked hard but he drank hard. And then he said to me, a few nights before Christmas, "I'm going home out of this place."

And, says I, "You're going home now we've nowhere to go and nowhere to live!"

"I don't care," says he, "I'm going home."

"Well," said I, "alright, we'll go home."

I had got a double weeks' pay for the Christmas, and we come home to Dublin with thirteen pounds, my wages. We bought a cover for six pound ten, that's just to make a little hut. Now, we were after having a beautiful caravan before we went to England, six good horses, and plenty of money, and we were back down to this cover. It was just the month of Christmas and we'd no place to go. So we got the train to Newcastle from Dublin, pitched the tent in Newcastle, and I had to go around selling me delft for thirty shillings to get our Christmas dinner.

The wren, the wren, the king of the birds,
St. Stephens's Day she was caught in the furze.
Though she was little, her honor was great.
Rise up, my lady, and give us the treat.

Lawnies, lawnies, wee-gernesse
Is in the bush that I love best,

'Tween the holly and ivy tree
Where all the boys'll follow me.

We chased him up, we chased him down,
We chased him into a bottle of wine.
We dipped his head in a bottle of beer
And wish ye all a Happy New Year.

Come out, old woman, and shake your feathers,
Do not think that we are beggars.
The man of the house, a decent man,
Through the house he carried the wren.

That's Saint Bridget dressed in white.
Give us a penny at the hour of the night.
I don't want copper, I don't want brass,
I want a bit of silver to get up a glass.

Up with the kettle and down with the pan
Give me some money to bury the wren.[19]

Of course, we had Queenie then. I didn't tell you, but we'd always kept Queenie. We put her on grass before we left, and we always had her to turn on. So we took her out, yoked our pony and car again, and we were three months going around again, and sticking the hardship in the winter, house to house. At the end of this three months Mickey said, "Come on, we'll go back to England, and get me own back in England."

So we went back to England. He got a job and I got a job. We went to Manchester again and we stayed six weeks and we saved a hundred pounds. The minute we got the hundred pounds we came home. He bought another horse and he bought an old caravan off me brother for thirty pounds, and we kept building up. Of course, he used to go on bouts of drink still and spend all his money and leave us down to hardship again.

The last big do was about three years ago when Mickey had an awful amount of money saved. You see, before me mother died I always wanted to get a house. I wanted her to come and live with me. She lived with Luke in Dublin, and I wanted her more nor anyone, 'cause I knew I'd no childer and I could give her. I could let her sit back. So then I said to her, "If we got a house somewhere, maybe you'd leave that?"

And she says, "Maybe I would."

We had seventeen horses and Mickey sold them one be one, that we'd have a good amount of money to buy a house. And then me mother, Lord have mercy on her, got bad, and she was dying. Me mother went, then, and Mickey, he drank the money of it, until we found ourselves with only four horses. Thank God almighty, he'd always build himself up again though. It got so bad, then, that he took the pledge, two years ago, and he hasn't taken a drink for two years.

> At the Gate of Jerusalem, all alone,
> St. Peter sat on a marble stone.
> Jesus came to him all alone,
> "Peter, Peter, what makes thee ache?"
> "Our Lord and Savior, the toothache."
> "Get up, Peter, and follow me,
> And keep those words in right memory:
> And whoever do fall for me sake
> Shall be redeemed of the toothache."[20]

We have saved lots of money again in that two years. We've earned every penny of it, by horse dealing, and I work hard meself. I do the cooking for Barry's hotel here in the town. Now they're closed down, in the winter, but I do the cooking for the mistress and her husband, and she compliments me on it. I'm very good, and I earn five pounds ten a week meself. Well, it keeps us. He doesn't earn anything in the winter, but when it comes into summertime he'll go out and he'll buy horses and sell them, and he makes a lot of money. He really does.

What I wanted more nor anything else in all me life was to settle down. I always had a crave in the back of me mind, even when I was young and carefree and happy, and when he was drinking I didn't care a hoot what he done. And yet when I'd come into somebody's house and see the lovely comfort they'd have I said, "Please God, someday I'll be like that." I didn't mind how much he spent, or I didn't care if I hadn't me supper. I was happy, but yet I wanted to settle down more nor anything in the world. We were up there at a place called Carthy's Corner, living in a caravan, and a very remote place it is too. When a stormy night'd come I'd look out and I said, "Please God, I hope soon we'll get a house."

And Mickey said, "House you want! You wouldn't be half as well-off."

But by degrees I kept saying, "I want a house. I'm going to look for a house."

There was a little piece of ground going up there that time, four acres of ground, and he said, "Do you know, I think I'll buy that four acres."

"Mickey," says I, "you're foolish to buy four acres of ground. Why don't you buy a house?"

He said, "Where would I get a house to buy? You're always the same, you want to settle down."

Says I, "Lookit, there's a house down in 'Clash and it's going for sale."

Says he, "That house is falling."

Says I, "I'd sooner have the falling house than four acres. What good'd four acres be to us? We'd still be living in the caravan."

He said, "I'd get a house built on it."

Says I, "You wouldn't have enough of money, Mickey, to build a house. It costs an awful amount of money." Says I, "Buy the little house."

So anyway, we got in contact with the person that owned it, Lord Meath. He said it was going up for auction. When the auction came there was a lot of people outside the door and when they found out that we wanted to buy it nobody'd bid. The people there wanted us to settle down, they wanted us to have the house, and nobody ever bid.

So Mickey put three hundred pounds on it, and the reserve price was four hundred. We went home that night and I was disappointed and I wasn't. Even though I was mad to settle down, I was wondering would I be happy. Then Mickey said this night, "I think I'll take that house." We went in to Mr. Mac Carlow, Solicitor, and paid him the four hundred pounds down, and we got the house.

Oh, here's a health to all true lovers,
And here's a health to where e'er she'll be,
For this very night, oh, wouldn't I be with her,
Although she is many miles from me.

Ara, when I landed to her bedroom window,
'Twas there I rested down on a stone,
And I whispered slowly all through the window,
"Hello, old girl, are you lying alone?"

But now she's rose from her soft down pillow,
Her lily white fingers is on her snow white breast
Saying, "Who is there at me bedroom window
Disturbing me of my long night's rest?"

She rose again from her soft down pillow,
"Who is that voice? Sure, I'd long to know."
"My lovely Mary, Mary, loyal-hearted Mary,
Ain't I a ghost of your Willy-O."

She ran downstairs in her morning dressing
To open the door for to let me in
Saying, "I am after a long night's working,
Besides I am drownded all to the skin."

They both went in and had discoursing
Until the old cocks they began to crow.
Sure they both shook hands, it was then they parted.
They kissed each other and away he go.

Saying, "I've to cross o'er the burning mountains
And I must go without dread or fear.
But one joy to me going without a pilot:
It's all for the love of my Mary Dear. [21]

When we came into it we'd no furniture. We'd nothing. We pulled the caravan out at the back in the yard. There was a huge big grate there, it'd give you the creeps to look at it, and I'd an old oil drum sitting on the grate. We used to light a fire in it and, says Mickey, says he, "Do you know what? Ya were mad to buy this house. Look at it!"

Says I, "By degrees I will get it done up. Don't worry." So by degrees we started buying bits of furniture and such and now our money was going away, dindling away.

Says Mickey, "I'll call in a tradesman," he says, "and get it done up properly. And we'll get it done once and for all." So he called in a tradesman and paid him four hundred and five pound for doing it up. We bought furniture and we bought paper and paint. Mickey planned it himself, and he's done it as you can see. Yes, now he has, and he's very happy I think. I think he never was as contented.

> Oh, I married a girl for better or worse,
> But she married me for the good of me purse,
> Oh, to shell out me money it being her intent.
> She wanted for nothing while I was her friend.
>
> I bought her the tables, I bought her the chairs,
> And likewise the carpet to fit on the stairs.
> I bought the old clothes for to fit other ways,
> But still she bawls out for the cradle.
>
> I bought her the cradle, she says it won't do,
> "I'm sure to have one, but I think I'll have two."
> It's a curse to get married, I'm going to tell you
> "But you'll have to go back with the cradle."
>
> I went back with the cradle and here's what was said,
> "When we have no bigger you must get one made."
> And thirty-five shillings was the money I paid,
> And I bought her a blooming big cradle.
>
> The cradle came home and it lay be the wall
> For seven long years it never got to call,
> And she says it's my fault, I say it's her own,
> She's nothing to stir in the cradle.
>
> One day a man came to visit, he wanted to stay.
> I give him the bed, but she didn't agree,
> And she says it's not big enough for all three,
> And she lent him the blooming big cradle.
>
> In a few months after she had a young son.
> The neighbors cried out it was bloody well done.
> But now she's neither weeping nor wailing nor sitting alone,
> She won't get ready me tea, only stirring the cradle. [22]

No, I don't believe I'd ever like to Travel again. There's an awful lot of hardship attached to it. I mean, you have a carefree life, and I wasn't discontented Traveling. But yet I wanted to settle down, more or less, I think for the sake of the child, Jerry. We only have the one child and he is seven years of age. He's only a little adopted boy; my brother Tom is Jerry's father. He's not my own child, do you see, but to me he's like my own. I don't think I'd be as fond of him maybe if he was me own, and he's very fond of us. I love him, really and truly, I really do.

You see, for a year before we settled down Jerry went to school from the caravan. That was four miles of ground and I walked the four miles to school every morning with him. Then I come and collected him and I was here at the school at three o'clock. It was difficult. But I go to work in the morning now. In the summer I go every day, but I'm on short time, only two days a week, for the winter. And in the morning, before I go, I give them their breakfast and I wash the dishes up. Then Jerry can go to the school with the other childer. It's only nearby. And it comes into me mind day after day when I'm working at Barry's now, about me mother walking with Tom across the Gap. Mrs. Barry has continually told me about the big parties she had then, in nineteen and twenty-eight, nineteen and thirty, and that was about the time my brother was born. She often do tell me about the parties and all the food at 'em. Probably the people in this town was living in luxury, and there was my poor mother, struggling out of the hospital to walk that twenty miles home to us. She thought we'd be hungry. And me father had no idea that she'd chanced the road.

When I come home in the evening I find lots of things to do. I clean up all me place, and if I've washing to do, I wash in the nighttime, or I bake bread, or I do a bit of mending, and so on like that. I haven't time to be lonely, really and truly. I know you'll wonder at that, because there's only three of us in it, but I never sit down. I like doing things right and keeping meself right. I never want to see caravan life again.

I wouldn't mind going away in the summer, we'll say, for a short period when Jerry'd get his holidays. In fact, I think I'd like it. But I wouldn't ever like to start all over again on the road. I'd never live, it'd kill me. No, no, I feel very contented.

> In the stable of Bethlehem our Savior was first born.
> In the River Jordan he was first washed.
> The River Jordan was so pure and good,
> In the name of Jesus, stop the blood. [23]

Well, we are lucky I suppose, that everything came out alright. And, please God, it will still go on so. When we were growing up me mother always wanted us to mind ourselves. She was very strict about morals. Years ago people was reared very innocent and knew nothing. Me mother didn't tell us in so many words, but she'd always warn you to mind yourself. About wearing short clothes or a thing like that, she said it was disgraceful. You had to have your clothes well down around your knees. And about smoking, well, she smoked herself, and them all smoked, every one of the brothers and sisters, except me. I often said, "Mammy, give us a cigarette."

And she'd say to me, "If I ever catch one in your mouth, Biddy!" She never wanted me to smoke.

Oh, she was great, poor woman, and through all the hardship she done her best for us. In fact, my eldest sister Mary, she went away. She was married at eighteen and she came back when she was twenty and she'd one baby. Then she went away again and she never came back to see me mother. Me mother thought that was a dreadful thing, to go away and never come back to see her parents, because she suffered so much rearing her and looking after her. She thought it was a disgraceful thing for a child to do. And I often said to her now, when she got on, "Mammy, would you like to see Mary?"

And she'd say, "Oh, God, only leave me eyesight that I'd never see her, because I wouldn't be sure of what I'd say or do to her." Me mother never wished to see her after. And she used to say, "Have respect for yourself. If you don't have respect for yourself, well, nobody will."

It was me mother that held us together through all those growing up years.

Me sister now, she's in England, and if you see her you'd never think that she was any connection with the Traveling people. It sort of comes back, do you know what I mean, the settled blood in you. It just comes back like that. But I suppose that's just one of those things. We're all happy and have a happy end.

> There's a dear little cottage by the wayside,
> There's a dear little home standing by.
> There's a tombstone I'm gonna decorate with roses.
> Byneath the willow lies my gentle mother's grave.
>
> Shall I ever see you more gentle mother,
> Byneath the green fields where the wild roses blow?
> I feel lonesome for the loss I'll ne'er recover,
> Byneath the willow lies my gentle mother's grave.
>
> Or how will I forget the day of childhood,
> When I strayed byneath my gentle mother's side,
> To pick the primrose and the thistles from the woodside?
> Oh, at long last my childish days are o'er. [24]

Patrick Stokes.

Patrick Stokes

LABORER AND TINSMITH[1]

My life story now, it's just very hard to think of it.

If you have the name of being an early riser you can sleep forever. I often told a man the truth and he wouldn't believe me, and I often told a man a lie and he believed me. For one start, I often said to a person, "Give me something and I'll give it back to ya tomorrow." And I would have, though he wouldn't believe me. But I often went in to plan a lie, "Give me something and I'll give it back to ya in an hour's time." I'd know, now, that I was going to tell this lie, but he'd give it to me just the same. So, I'm a liar, I'm a rogue, and I'm a thief. I'm one of each.

Well, really we weren't Tinkers. We shouldn't ha' been called Tinkers, 'cause the right man is a Tinker is a blacksmith. But we were tinsmiths, sure.

Some of them calls us Travelers, Gypsies, or mumpers. Maybe, itinerants, tramps, or wasters. I heard them say no-goods, scoundrels, and *nackers*. But I'd say we're *minkers*, puck o' the droms. But you are what you are.

Sure, I don't think the Travelers'll ever die off the road, 'cause you're bred, born, and reared to it. You have to go back, haven't ya? So, like, it's surprising as it cannot be helped.

Well, a Tinker is a man does every class of job, and he's tinking on every job, tinking on every job. It comes along that that's how we got the title. Just the same as the story of how Our Lord was getting crucified to the cross.

The Jews come along one time to the carpenter and they said, "Would you make us a cross?"

"Oh, begod," said the carpenter, "I'll not make no cross. What do you want a cross for?"

"We have to crucify the Lord," they says.

"Well, if you do," says he, "you'll go to some other carpenter, but I'll make you no one."

So they went to the blacksmith. "Hi," they said, "will you make a few spears?"

"For what?" says the blacksmith.

"Will you make us a few spears, we want to crucify this Good Lord, as he's supposed to be, to the cross."

"Ah, topping!" says the blacksmith. "I will, of course." He thrown out the job he was doing and started to make the spears, but the blacksmith couldn't make the nails now.

So, begod, they came to the Tinker then. The Tinker was making a can. "Tell me, Sir," they said, "could you make us a lock of nails?"

"I will," he said.

"We want to crucify Our Lord, the Christ," they said.

"I don't care," says he, "what you want to do with him. How many do you want?"

"We want a good deal," they said.

"Oh, I'm very thankful to you," he said, and he thrown the can out of his hand anyway and started to make the nails.

Well, they didn't have the cross still, so then the Jews comes to this other carpenter and said, "Will you make us a cross?"

"Well, I don't make no crosses," he said. "Why don't you go to the stonecutter?"

"I don't want a stone one at all," says this Jew fella. "I want a good big timber one."

"For what do ye want it?" the carpenter said.

"Ah, to crucify the Lord to it."

"If ye do," he said, "you'll go to some other man. I'd rather me son'd get crucified," he said, "than Our Lord."

So back they goes, begad, to the blacksmith, and they said, "Are you any good to make a cross?"

"Well, I'm not too much good," he said, "but I'd try. And I'd want a man to give me help, but no man'd give me help with this job."

Helter-skelter with the Jews again for the Tinker. "Would you earn yourself a few quid?" they said.

"Begad, I could do with it very badly," the Tinker said. "You know I'm badly stuck. The auld horse is after getting drownded and I have neither wheels nor meals to get in the money."

"The blacksmith," they said, "is going to try and make a cross for to crucify Our Lord, and he wants help."

"I'll be very thankful to you to give me the job," said the Tinker, and away with him to the blacksmith.

So the blacksmith and the Tinker they went and cut down a big tree. Now they got an awful job, you see, to split it. They said they'd work their brains and they'd go to the carpenter for to saw it out, and they did.

"Good day," says the blacksmith, 'cause he knew him.

"Good day," says the carpenter.

"You know, I'm going to make a little bit of a mill-wheel," says the blacksmith, "and would you saw the tree for me, to make a decent job of it?"

"What do you want a mill-wheel for?" says the carpenter.

"Ah, well, I'd want it," he says, "for drawing the water into the air from the river. It's very handy." He didn't want to tell the carpenter, of course, what he was doing.

"Maybe you want to try and make a cross of it?" says the carpenter.

"Ara, not at all!" he says. "What's putting stupid things into your head like that?"

"Ah, you can believe him," says the Tinker. "He wants to make a mill-wheel, and if you're going to do it, do it!"

"Well, this is one job," says the carpenter, "I won't do. I'm busy today."

"Well, if it isn't done today, it's no good tomorrow," says the blacksmith. So they did go off.

Begad, when the Tinker got him gone didn't he go back and steal the carpenter's saw, and they started at it, the two of them. And they lost so much sweat as they nearly dropped dead, that's the truth! But they kept at it, sawing, and they made the cross. Oh, it was a fine, big cross now. And when they'd it all cut out and all, along come the Jews. And what did the Jews do? They said that cross wouldn't be big enough!

"'Twouldn't be big enough for the Lord," says the Jews.

"Ah, it would," said the blacksmith.

"Well, as true as I'm looking at you, it's big enough," said the Tinker.

"Well, I don't know," says this Jew-man, "but we'll try you on it, to see if it is."

They gets the nails and they puts the Tinker onto the cross. They made the blacksmith drive the nails in him, and the blacksmith was in a bad state. Ahhh, sure, the Tinker got an awful death. The roars of him!

"If he didn't work, you will," the Jews said to the blacksmith.

"Oh, good God," said the blacksmith, "is this the respect we've got after cutting the tree and all! The best of luck to the carpenter anyway, that wouldn't do anything."

They unstuck the nails in the Tinker then, and they took him down again. Said the Jews, "You're alright anyway. You won't be looking for a horse where you're going to!"

So then they brought the Lord, and he was very poorly and sick.

And, said the Lord, "As long as a blacksmith lives he'll have the curse of God, and as long as a Tinker lives he's never right, and you'll have wandering 'til the Day of Judgment. But," says the Lord, "the carpenter'll have the height of luck everywhere he goes."

Well, therefore, you'll never see no rich blacksmith and you never seen a rich Tinker, and you'll always see a rich carpenter. And, sure, the Travelers is always moving around. They never can settle down. [2]

Well, you learn your trade from a kid, you see. I seen me father, he'd be all the time, you know, at the tinware, and my brothers too. We used to go a week here and a week there, maybe a fortnight some places and maybe three weeks of work, if the guards didn't come along and move us or shift us. And I'll tell you what we made now, starting from a half-pint saucepan up to a boiler. We made half-pint saucepans, pint saucepans, three-half-pint saucepans, quart saucepans, three-quart cans, five-quart cans, and an eight-quart can. I made some milking tins and half-gallons and buckets, some lamps and leaden hoops, a boiler, and them little things we call a churn, and the nails, of course.

Me father'd make some tins and he'd send the family out with them, to sell 'em. And me father was an awful man for going out jobbing from house to house, bottoming cans, buckets, saucepans, and such on as that.

I was borned in Roscommon and I was baptized in Galway. Now, that's a bit curious like, but there was only two miles atweenst the two places. It was Roscommon we Traveled, and Galway and Cavan, when I was a kid. We're stopping here in Dublin now, but this isn't my own country.

I made this hut, you could say, on the outskirts of Dublin. But this is but a poor place for me now, with the wife and four kids. It does get very wet here, and the kids, they've always a cold. The roof is a-falling. The wind is playing the harp.

It's alright, stopping in the one place, for the childer for to get a education, but yet you get lonesome. The wife does go out to the same houses here every Saturday, do you know, to get them old clothes and things. The people knows her and tells her to call back every Saturday. But I do go to the town but seldom. And, here now, when I'm doing nothing with meself in the day, I'd love to do working, to be working me trade. And I feel if I lost the budget I was destroyed altogether. But it might be very hard for to get the tin that'd make those cans today. I wonder, do they sell it in Dublin?

My grandfather, he used to work the tin and he used to work the plate too and he died in the old workhouse in Roscommon. I knew one of my grandfathers and my grandmother. They were all Traveling. I remember, like, that I seen my grandfather making tins, and his father before him made them. That's my grandfather's clips there, but that isn't the oldest. That little anvil, they call that a handstick, that's the oldest. That'd be belonging to my great-grandfather.

All me own people, back as far as I'd remember, they was all in Roscommon, and me father grown up there. Me father, he had six or seven brothers and four of them boys was in the 1914 war. Two of them was shot in the war, but the only brother me father was ever fond of, Pat was his name, he come home with me father. My father and his brother got married to the two sisters when they came back from the war, and me father wore a big black moustache. He never lost the moustache. It's a awful country in the County Roscommon, and all his people wore all big moustaches so. Came along that I think they were a horrible thing for any man to wear.

Then me uncle was killed. I wasn't born at the time, but I heard the story of it. A cart went over his body. There was five or six people working the cart and the weight of the cart across his body, that burst his blood vessel, you know, Lord have mercy on him. He was a man of thirteen stone weight that day and the next morning he was only two stone. He lost ten and a half stone for one night and he only lived about three hours the following day. He had a son only twelve months old.

> Oh, the trees are getting higher, the grass is growing green,
> And many's the cold and bitter night alone that I have been,
> For it's a cruel winter's night and I must lie alone.
> Oh, my bonny boy is young and still growing.
>
> "Oh, Father, dear Father, why did you do me wrong,
> To go and get me married to a man who is so young?
> For he is but sixteen years, and I am twenty-one,
> Oh, my bonny boy is young and still growing."
>
> "Oh, Daughter, dear Daughter, I did not do you wrong,
> To go and get you married to a man who is so young,
> For he will be a match for you when I am dead and gone."
> Oh, my bonny boy is young and still growing.
>
> Well, at the age of sixteen he was a married man,
> And at the age of seventeen the father of a son,
> And at the age of eighteen the grass grew o'er his grave.
> Cruel death put an end to his growing.
>
> Oh, I'll build my love a shroud of the ornamental brown,
> And whilst they are building it the tears they will flow down,
> For onct I had a true love, but now he's dead and gone.
> Oh, I'll nurse his darling son while still growing.[3]

Pat was the name of me uncle that was killed and Pat was the name of the son, my cousin. Him and me, we both had the one name, Patrick Stokes, and it came to the time the two of us grew up together. He was twelve months older than me, I'd be seven and he'd be eight, and my father looked after him better'n he looked after us. He couldn't bear me to say, "Well, Pat's a liar." If I did, he'd whip me to death, you know, not to insult this gossoon, 'twas the only son she had. Me father'd give him two shillings and give me a penny, and we'd fight over it. We'd be always fighting, him and me. Life is funny, isn't it?

My father is dead six years now, and you can say it was nine years back since he was on the move. There was thirteen in it: me father and mother, the Lord have mercy, and there was seven girls and four boys. That was a big population, and we used to go here and there and were very happy together. And me father, when he had the big family gathered, he never would hardly Travel with nobody, only himself, you understand. My mother reared a lovely family of us, that's the truth. She reared eleven of us and she reared us all that we were never sick nor sore nor never give one minute's trouble to a doctor. And then, she got all of her family married and the rest of 'em is dead.

Me father was happy. Me father was a different type of man than me. He wouldn't go to a town until he'd have some business. Say, for one start, he wouldn't go 'til he'd have to buy some tin. But when he'd go, me mother'd go with him. Me mother used to drink a pint of stout. She was a very frail woman, you know, but she'd drink sixteen, seventeen pints on the one day. She used to wear a black shawl and a brown shawl, Lord have mercy on her, and every pint me father'd drink, me mother'd drink one.

I know me father, one time, he went about sixteen or twenty miles to a town. Me mother, she used to always go with him, until this night when they had a bit of a falling out.

"I'm going off now," he says, "and getting drunk." (He never would ha' argued with me mother, you know. It'd be me mother that'd do the arguing, he never would say a word.) But he went off anyway and here he come through a wood called Black's Wood. Well, if you go into a wood there, now, with yourself, you'll always find something breaking or cracking, won't ya?

There was a pub up before he came to Black's Wood called Wards'. So he stopped in Wards' 'till about half eleven, twelve o'clock, 'cause he'd only about five miles to go home then. He gets up then and head for home, and he had about three dozen of stout in the back of the car. He was going through the lonesome wood, going, going, and he crossed this little bridge. And a ghost come up from out the bridge and got stuck to the side of the car. "Goodnight," said the ghost and smiled in a-top him.

Well, this is the truth. My father he was an ex-soldier. All through the war, English army and Irish army, nothing could frighten him. But now he got nervous as he couldn't put back his hand to take a bottle of stout. He was getting weak. That's when he hoped for me mother, then. If my mother was with him he'd have his courage, you know.

Begod, anyway, he kept at it, kept going and going, 'til he came to another river, and at that river the ghost parted him. He gone away. Me father never would go without me mother after that.

Here last night I received the letter of an old hag's death.
Every tear that fell from the bottom of my heart would turn a mill.
I run at the rate of eighteen mile a minute, while I was sitting down to rest meself.
I met John Javis, the coachman, driving fourteen dead donkies under an empty steamcoach, and two old women and they roasting bugs and apples and throwing them to one another.
I asked 'em, "Did you hear tell of the shower of the old hag's death?"
"No, but if ye go up to John Mankam he'll tell you all about it."
"Where does he live?"
"He lives up a long, wide, narrow street. It's a great big tall square house standing only be itself."
But when I went up to the great big tall square house standing only be itself, there were fifteen or sixteen cabins be the side of it.
When I went up, his two sons were thrashing tobacco into peas.

*One of those peas lept out through a stone wall and kilt a dead dog was
barking at a pockmarked cat.
I put me hand in his mouth and I turned him inside out.
I was followed by two eye-glass pensioners, had lost heads, legs, arms,
bodies and all in the Battle of Waterloo.
I run 'til I stepped over a stone wall.
So easy I might, the stone wall was turned into a cabbage leaf.
The cabbage leaf was only the length from St. Patrick's Day to America.
Cattie Patrick, she was the cleanest cook that ever was known.
She could scour scaws through her middle finger, me lord.
She lay in the day 'til the ditch broke on her.
A little bark come out and dogged at her.
She took out her tail and cut his knife across.* [4]

Me mother smoked the clay pipe and me father smoked the clay pipe and
they used to smoke the one pipe together. He'd smoke some cigarettes, but she
never used to smoke cigarettes. So he'd fill the pipe and light it and smoke it
and give it to her until the pipe'd be gone. They used to smoke an ounce of
tabaccy and he used to smoke twenty fags a day, and if me mother had no
tabaccy there was no sleep. If she lost her pipe there'd be no such thing as
peace. She wouldn't sit down, the roars of her, crying about her pipe! I often
seen her, if the shank'd break to the pipe, putting the little shank into her
mouth to smoke it.

Well, I seen me mother losing her pipe one time, the Lord have mercy on
her, and me brother made one out of tin! Now that's the truth! It nearly roasted
her, but he put a very long stem out of it. He had to do it, for ease, 'cause he
was a married man and she'd be up and down the road, crying, crying, crying,
like a baby for a bottle, and there was no town in miles.

When we'd go to Roscommon the first thing me mother'd say "Ohhh, where're
you going? Bring me a dozen of pipes." They're only thrupence a pipe. Then
she'd put them into the bag and put them into water. When she'd buy a clay
pipe in a pub she'd call for a pint of stout and she'd stick her clay pipe into her
pint, that made the pipe hard. Or what me father'd do, he'd stick the clay pipe
into the fire and throw it into water then, which made the pipe as hard as flint.

Then, at the time of the war, there was no tabaccy to be got, only when
you'd draw your rations you'd get one ounce for a week. And my father and
mother'd smoke that in one day. They'd stick the ounce of tabaccy into the
water where it'd swell twice as big and it wouldn't burn so quick. Then they'd
get the briar leaves, all the old women and men down in the country did it.
They'd hang them over the fire 'til they got real dry and they'd break them up
and fill the pipe with it and smoke it. And they'd smoke the tea. Tea was very
hard to be got, but whatever grain of tea we got anyway, me mother'd have it
in the pipe. Me father used to get a bit of tea with the farmers, and he'd give
a can, now, for a quarter ounce of tabaccy.

But it came along that didn't the war stop all in a clap, and everything came
in, in full bloom, into the country: plenty of tabaccy, fags, anything. We went

down, that time, to a dump pit outside Ballygar, where we used to stay around, and six times me father filled the car with half-ounces of tabaccy that the shopkeeper had to throw out there. 'Twas gone hard, you know, while he was holding it for the customers and a whole batch of new stuff come in, so they couldn't sell the old. My mother, Lord, I needn't tell ya what tabaccy she took then! She took loads of it and she never stopped smoking! That was how the old folks lived one time.

I did start to smoke the cigarettes then, when I was fourteen or fifteen years, and I am smoking still. And what made drunkards of the men that time was cigarettes. 'Twas shocking, you see, in them days. If I was seventeen years of age and I was smoking and you were the barman in the shop, well, you wouldn't give me five cigarettes if I didn't buy two pints from you. I had to buy two pints or there're no five cigarettes. But we had a fair good time 'cause me father was a man, like, that was never fond of drink. And he was an awful hard trier. He tried very hard for us, and when me two eldest brothers grew up, they always, you know, helped us up as good as they could.

That time 'twas very seldom you'd see a person too well dressed, 'cause it was rough and ready and things was very hard got. But money was plentier than it is now. Like, when a woman in a house'd send for me father to bottom a kettle, well, he could say, "That'll be a pound."

And she'd say, "Oh, for God's sake, do it, do it for a pound!"

I used to sell for my father then; he'd put a price on a thing and I'd sell. Well, we never used to keep the money but bring it back to him. Any extra you'd give him, me mother'd make a cash-box and put it in for you. My mother had to guard it for you. And when it come that you had the price of a pair of boots or something like that, she'd buy it for ya.

Then, when I was kid of, say, ten years I used to go around with my sisters in the country, from house to house. Now, I'll tell you the truth, it was begging, see. Me sisters'd go out begging and I'd be going out with a bag or something for carrying potatoes maybe. They'd make me do it because they were older than me. Until I was fourteen I'd have to do it, 'til I was able to stand up for meself. They'd come along and they'd make me look for potatoes and milk and money for them, and give me an odd kick and a clout if I didn't. I couldn't tell me father about them. If ever I did they'd give me twice more tomorrow, you understand.

Oh, I am a little beggarman, oh, begging I will be.
Three score or more are little, I'd agree.
Sure, I'll beg for my supper, I'll have nothing else to do
Only jog 'round the corner with me old rigadoo.

Oh, of all the trades going, sure, begging is the best,
When a poor man is tired he can sit down and rest.
Sure, he may touch for his dinner, he'll have nothing else to do,
Only cut round the corner with me old rigadoo.

Well, I'm over the road with my bag on my back,
Down through the land with my big heavy sack,
There is holes in my boots and me toes are coming through,
Then it's skin 'em a wink-a-doodle with me old rigadoo.

Sure, I slept in a barn, down the Curragh-bawn,
A wet night in August and I slept 'til the dawn.
Sure, there was holes in the roof and the rain coming through
Sure, the rats and the mice they were playing big-a-boo.

Oh, who laid awaking but the buer *of the house.*
She had a white spotted apron, a calico blouse.
Oh, she began to frighten and I says, "Boo!
Don't be afraid, Mum, of old Johnny Doo!"

Oh, I've met a little flaxy-haired girl one day.
"Good morning, little beggarman." "Good morning," I did say.
"Oh, good morning, little beggarman, and how do you do,
With your rags and your bags and your old rigadoo?"

Oh, I'll buy a pair of stockings and a collar and a tie,
A nice young lady I will meet bye and bye.
I'll buy a pair of stockings and I'll color them blue,
And an old-fashioned lady you will make her do.

Oh well, I must be going to bed. It's getting late at night.
Sure, my fire it is rigged, and out went the light.
So, now you've heard the story of me old rigadoo.
So, good night, and God be with you, from old Johnny Doo. [5]

But I done other things too, that I did enjoy 'em. I done eel fishing, you
know, poking in the holes of walls and in the river banks. I like the eels. Eel's
skin is the best ever you made a wristband out of, now, for a rheumatism or
anything like that, sciatica, now. There's a cure in it. But if you want to take
the skin off, now, you'll split it in the back of the eel instead of in the belly,
straight down like that, and just catch and pull it down. And you know the
fret, the meat of the eel'd come up then, it come out straight and true.

I used to catch the birds by the tail. I'd follow to catch a blackbird and a
thrush and a snipe, 'til I'd want to get a goldfrinch. I'd sell a goldfrinch then,
you know, in the houses along.

And my brother used to catch a pheasant sometime. He'd be going into a
new demesne, where there was a new forestry, and there was all runs going
along. Well, half of them wasn't hares' runs, they was pheasant runs. Me
brother, he'd set a snare for the hare but the pheasant'd come along and he'd
stick his head in. The snare'd be stuck inside the feathers. He caught two
pheasants that way; he had a surprise.

And we did often snare a trout. They're very easy snares, you know, the trout. You see, when you put a copper wire in water it's the same color as the water. You make that in a knot and you put it on the top of a fish-rod, and you put it down in the water. It is before the trout you put the snare, and a trout stays sort of harmless and he waits there. He wouldn't see the snare. Then you just cut it back 'til it come over him, and you'd give him a good pull, and he's yours.

I'll tell you how they catch trout too. We'd come along to a river and we'd dam it and we'd put a bag at that dam. Then we'd walk up along the river and throw muck and clobber in, to rise the mud. We'd run all the fish into the sack, and you wouldn't know what you could get.

The trouts and the eels, they are a good food, but when I was a lad, while we kept the two hounds and a terrier, I never got sick of eating hares. I wouldn't chase them, it's just when I'd feel like one. I'd go off on a Friday, let's say, and I'd kill a hare for Sunday. Might kill two. But as soon as I'd kill two, I'd finish. I'd have to get them two no matter if I Traveled twenty miles, but where we used to stop you wouldn't have to Travel no journey, because the big farms of land was all around and everything was going on well. I often seen us catching the hares, killing them, and leaving them after us or else giving them to the dogs. A dog likes a hare too, when he follows them.

And the little terriers, oh, they were decent! The terrier, she'd rob a hen for ya. Or if ya wanted her to go into a gap in a wall, she'd catch the hen be the neck and bring him out to you. And the hounds'd do the same thing. But the little terrier, mind you, she wouldn't run straight for you with the hen. If she done that, then the farmer'd know whether ya were down the field. No, across the field she'd run with that hen, you know, to knock the despicions off the farmer. She'd come around after ya then. Oh, the dogs were very 'cute.

Rabbits is nicer to eat than the hare. I'd prefer them before a chicken or a turkey and they were healthy. But in a snare a hare he kills himself quicker than a rabbit. I'll tell you one thing hares are: they'll run fair for their life anyway. A rabbit gets into a burrow now, a hole or a bush, and it's very hard to get him out. But for the last eight years I never et rabbits, since the disease started with them, because I wouldn't know one from the other. I'd be often afraid in case I'd get this myxomatosis.

I did see a fella catch a fox. A fox is easy enough snared, and I think they're very nice. They don't kill that much fowl, sure they don't. It was their own fault anyway, the farmers and all, for their fowl to be taken, because the fox did live on rabbits and hares. But when the rabbits got the disease and were all kilt the fox had no food to eat. He had to do something else. I was only grew up when the fox didn't leave a farmer in the country one sheep, or left him at bigger losses than the rabbits ever done.

Since the rabbits was taken from the country there was never a decent crop for a farmer. Well, that's the truth, because, somehow or another they never had the right weather since. You've seen crops and I've seen crops that couldn't be saved, and a rabbit never left his mouth in it, nor also a hare. And they kilt the poor man's dinner, like the likes of us, on the quest. I know people that made a living on rabbits, selling them and also eating them. They were a nice breakfast for anyone to have.

A bloke came down to the Aran Island that time. Well, I won't say was it from Dublin or where he came from, but he come along and he was getting five pound apiece for the rabbits as had this disease. You'd put one sick rabbit into your land to kill all the others was in it. Begad, he came into Connemara anyway, and 'twas all fish they ate most back in Connemara, and the rabbits. They had great belief in it. Used to get the rabbits ourself in Connemara. So he came to this house and he said, "Would ye buy a rabbit?"

"Oh," the man said, "why don't you go in to the Aran Island, and you'll sell all the rabbits that you have."

"How will I get in?" says the bloke.

"You can go in on the boat," says the Conny.

Alright. He had about seven hundred pounds worth of rabbits in a lorry and his partner there with him. So about twenty Connemara fishermen, you know they're all big men, they brings him and the lorry in the boat. And when they come to the middle of the sea, "Now," they said, "where'd you come from?"

"Came back from England," he said, "with those rabbits."

"You mean to say," they said, "you came from England back to Connemara to leave us without our supper and breakfast?"

And do you know what they done? They thrown the rabbits and van into the middle of the sea and made the two fellas swim it back to the land. They said, "You'll either swim back and you're free, and if you don't you'll drownd." Your men got back anyway and they were never seen in the County Galway after that with a rabbit. "You'll die," the Connies said, "or you're free. You have two choices."

They were killing a lot of diseases in the country themself was rabbits, 'cause for one start, in hospitals they allowed rabbits too. Sure, it left the country unhealthy I think since the rabbits left us. I think it wasn't right at all, because the rabbits was in the world since the world was made, and it came to the time that people thought to take them out of it.

Sure, the world is getting older, and I think the older a man is getting, or anybody, is the worst thing. The happiest time in a man's life is from ten to twenty years. That's the time he's learning how. He didn't understand at first: he'll do a thing that maybe shouldn't be done at all.

There was this boy one time and he was fond of a joke, you know.

One night this boy was coming home from the céilí house on his bike and who was sitting beside the road but the banshee. Now a banshee wears a steel rack, you know, a comb, and she does love to comb her hair. This night she had the comb in her hand, like, and was combing her hair, and didn't the boy grab the comb as he was passing.

"Oh, give me back the comb," she said. "Give me back the comb! Give me back the comb!"

"You'll follow me to the house for it if ya want it," says he, and off he goes on the bike.

So here comes the banshee, after him for about seven mile, to the door of the house.

In he goes to his father. "A banshee! A banshee!" he said.

"Couldn't be a banshee," said the father.

They heard her without. "I want me comb. I want me comb," she said, and she was crying, crying.

"Did you take anything from that woman?" said the father.

"Well, I took her comb, Daddy, for a joke," says the boy.

"That was no joke," says he, "to do that. Give me that comb." So that father gets the comb and puts it out under the door where there was a good high vacancy.

"Oh, thanks very much," said the banshee. "Now, put out the hand and I'll shake hands with ya."

"Don't put out your hand!" says the father to the son. And he stuck the socket of a plough, that digs up the ground, out under the door instead. And the banshee put the track of her four fingers down through it. She tore the iron of it. So, she was going to give him a quare going anyway, you see.

Then, one day, the boy comes along and there he seen the banshee again sitting in the side of the road.

"Oh," she said, "you're the fella that stole me comb."

"I am," he said, "and I'm very, very sorry."

"Well," she said, "you won't be no longer sorry." And she give him a clout. "Now," she said, "you'll be sick from this out. You'll be sick as long as you'll ever live, until you answer my question at twelve o'clock in the night, in the place where you stole my comb."

The boy went for home then and he tells the father about what the banshee done to him, that she struck him and cursed him.

"Well," says the father, "you picked at the banshee first."

So it came that the boy started getting sick, sick, sick. But he hadn't the guts of going to the banshee, so he went to the priest and told him what happened.

"Well," said the priest, "you'll have to get a white cock with not a dark feather on 'im. Make a ring of holy water in the road tonight," he said, "in the place where you took her comb, and stand in the middle of the ring. When she comes to you," he said, "she'll come in a blaze of fire out of her mouth. Throw the white cock at her, and the white cock'll fight her until four o'clock in the morning. Then," said the priest, "she'll go from you and you've got your request back."

"Fair enough," said the boy.

The boy got the cock, made the ring, and at twelve o'clock there she comes, like the red roaring Devil, blaze of fire out of her mouth. He thrown the cock at her.

He stood there then for the whole night watching, 'til he fell asleep where he stood, and the cock bet the banshee the length of the night 'til he came four o'clock in the morning, and then the boy was free. He got his health back and was living happy forever after.[6]

When I come up to about twelve years of age I started to work with the farmers, meself and a brother of mine two years younger than me. We came to a place called Ballinagar and the first farmer ever we worked with. He took us on for about two months at thirty bob a week, thirty bob to me, was older, and a pound to me brother. That time that was good money, and we done anything and everything for him. Then the farmer started to go slack on work to keep on with us. We were two months apiece working there and had to leave. He wanted to keep me for bringing in the cattle and for sweeping up the yard and let the brother go. But I was the strongest of the two for to wheel turf. So I said I'd leave the brother to do that job and I'd go wheel turf with some other man. Then I went to a man called Kelly and I stayed with him for two months again: wheeling turf, spread the turf, and saved the turf, until we brought home the turf.

The while I was doing that me brother left the first farmer and he went to work for a rich priest in that country. Me brother was always calling around there anyway, since he was a little gossoon, and the priest knew him. He had his own race horses, but he wasn't a man to pay for nothing. He kept my brother one day, the whole day, catching his horses and bringing them in, and he give him nothing, a bit of brown bread. And ya know what he done another day? He said to me brother, "John, when it gets dark by and by," he said, "knock a bit of that wall and put my race horses into it." Into another man's field! Would you think that was right, for a priest to say that?

"Oh, I might be seen," says the brother.

"I can always say," says the priest, "that they jumped the wall." 'Cause they were jumpers. But me brother wouldn't do it.

The next, then, I left the man Kelly and I went to a farmer called Mairn-Hester, and I stood with him for a month, sowing cabbage plants.

Now, every plant that ever Mairn-Hester sowed for seven years before, them all died. And twelve months before that I'd sowed plants for a man that was in the same hard luck as he was. That man sent me to Roscommon with his bicycle, about seventeen miles, for to buy him blue cabbage plants. I did buy them, and he said, "Would ya sow them?" But I didn't know what he meant be it. I never had plants in me hands before. "Just sow them," he said, and he went to another bit of the field and he sowed one. "Sow them in drills as I sowed that one," he said. So I did, and they came up lovely heads of cabbage. The whole garden was full!

So the next year when I come back Mairn-Hester said to me, "When you finished with the man wheeling turf, will you come with me?" And the first job ever he gave me was to go to Roscommon for plants; he put me the same as the other man did. So I did it, and the plants they came up lovely.

Then, when I finished with those farmers, I thatched houses for to try and keep going. In those times we had all to help ourself as best we could. Me father, he was sweeping chimbleys then. He did them when he wasn't at the tin. And when I'd be up to fourteen years of age it comes along that I started working in a milk dairy.

I went in to a man called Mr. Love. He was a big farmer there, all for dairy. This man he had about seven hundred acres of land and he had about three hundred head of cattle, and as many men was working for him as there was cattle. But I used to come in with cans and throw the milk for the calfs into the pig troughs.

One day, now, my father was there with some other of our people, and they were beating the hares up of the fields. It was, you know, for all the big farmers. That day they all come there, to Mr. Love, and they were hunting with about twenty greyhounds. But here I comes this day, bad luckful enough, doing me job. I was walking across this yard of cattle, taking me milk into it, with two cans full. I had no other ways to get to the calfs, and then all the cattle seen me.

There'd be about seven hundred head of them, to their deadly cost of me. They seen me and they run at me and they liked to kill me. Here comes bullocks and everything! Now this is the truth. I run from 'em but I couldn't get to me father or no one, and nothing'd stop 'em, guns wouldn't stop them. They were going mad: mooing, mooing, mooing. I run and I run and I came to an earth then and I had to drop, to lie down. And over seven head of cattle jump over me then, and wasn't it a marvelous thing that never one lept upon me! I must never mean to be kilt when this could happen to me!

They jumped like that, and me father seen them and he like died. I was fifteen or sixteen at the time and me father got blind, 'cause he was that tender. "Aw, he's kilt now," he said. Because a horse won't stand on a man, but cattle will, will walk on ya.

Well, I left that, the milk dairy, when I came to sixteen years of age. I looked and I started thinking about myself, and I started working at the tin trade.

Oh, the first time I rolled down to Cardin
I hired with Big Pat in Eltomb.
He told me he wouldn't hard work me;
He'd give me good butter at noon.

Oh, when we arose in the morning,
Saying, "Boys, are yous getting up now?
Let yous go and tackle the horses,
I'll put 'em under the plough."

Oh, we worked very hard in the lowland.
Old Goodham he whistled a tune.
Oh, he said, "We'll go home to our dinner.
We'll hoist the big flag in Eltomb."

When I come in to me dinner,
'Twas Goodham and Black Mary Hore,
Likewise, boys, a small bit of butter
She swore on her soul to do four.

I took up a bit on me knife, boys,
In order to make it hold out,
But before I have the last of it swallowed
Old Goodham had it all in his mouth.

I made a slap and a box at Old Goodham,
And Pat made a lep on the floor.
The cat got away with the butter,
And left her hind leg in the door.

Oh, the shanty he put me to sleep in,
'Twas there I got damn little lay.
The flesh was tore off of me body
With Goodham damnation's buck fleas.

If any of yous are wanting a job, boys,
I'm sure yous are wanting good pay,
Make sure and don't hire with no farmer
He's worse than a bull-terrier dog.[7]

No father ever learned a son the trade, to say, "Sit down and look at me." He never would learn ya. But I'd be looking at him and I tried out meself. Same as if you, now, were twelve months looking at me and I'd give you the tools, then you'd know what tool to take up and I wouldn't never have to speak with ya. It runs in ya.

People was bringing buckets to my father to bottom, and cans and saucepans. And I started to do them meself, instead of me father, the Lord have mercy, and hiding 'em when he'll come back, until the next day. He'd be gone next day then and the people'd come back and say, "Oh, did your father do the jobs?"

"Oh, yes," I'd say, "he did." I'd have a big ball of black pitch and I'd tar them and they wouldn't leak, ya know? And I'd have them cans all plastered up, very bad job. I'd give them to the people and I'd say, "Yes, he done a great job with them now, Missus, and he told me if they were leaking the next day he'd call and he'd do them again, free, for ya." I was getting very soft money.

And then I started making cans. I started to use me father's tin when he wouldn't be there. I'd rob his tin and try and learn. I was getting very interested myself and my father seen me then and said to me, "Begod, you made a good job of that! Try another one."

Well, you learn the trade when you're anything up to ten to sixteen years of age. And me brother and me cousin, they learned it the same ways I done. Then you'd be coming along to start doing things yourself, and, we'll say, you'll spoil five tins to mend one. Comes along that you start to work up to eighteen years of age and you have it properly learned. But it's the trying. I was trying there that I could best me father, like, that if I got an order for to make tins, now, in the line of good tins, I'd make them a lot tastier than him.

But he'd make them stauncher than me. If he put a lug, a loub, in a can he'd put two tin rivets, real big thick ones as thick as your finger, big bolts, to hold it. There was no such thing as them rivets coming out on their own. When you'd be taking out them loubs you'd have to take out a piece of the can and all before they'd come out. Well, when I'd be taking out mine, I could just drive the little rivet down a-through the tin again, and put two new ones up and it was a grand job again. When me father, he'd be wanting a loub in his can he'd get it out of a barrel hoop, a Guinness barrel for one start, that you couldn't cut or anything hardly, but he'd keep at it with the hammer and chisel and borna, borna. I wouldn't do that. I'd cut galvanize, sheet iron, easy. Well, I'd sell my can for a price, but he'd sell his can for six bob dearer. But I'll admit the truth, his can was a pound better. My can'd only last two years. His'd last fifty. But his can'd be very rough-looking. The same as there's two houses built there together and, say, I built mine very rough and ugly altogether, and you built very neat with yours. People'd say, "Oh, there's a lovely house." Still mine was a warmer house, and when yours'd be knocked and gone the ugly one'd be standing. 'Twas that way.

I'll tell you the ways that you gets the tools too. Well, say my brother give me such things as a hammer and snips, and my father give me an anvil, and me other brother, older than me, give me other things. How and ever, when I was about eighteen years of age I was lucky enough. There was a man in Ballygar called Paddy Ward, and he was an old tinsmith, for about sixty years. He was thirty when he learned the trade but he was nearly ninety years of age when he died, and he always said that he'd will me father the tools when he'd die. He had a son, a postboy.

Well, the old man died and one day I went into Ballygar for some tin for my father. So, on the ways out the old man's son called me and he said, "You Stokes?"

"I am," says I.

"I have me father's tools here," he said, "and take them out to your father."

Fair enough," I said. There was hammers, clipses, pliarses, punches, soldering irons, nail tools for making nails, and some timber, they call them scutches, for making cans. There was rivets, roldering, and soldering and all. A full kit of tools, and he give me some tin that the father left after him.

So, on my ways home I was so proud, I was that delighted with it, as I started to pick out me own kit of tools, going back along the road. "I'll hide those," I said, "that I have picked for myself." But in my ways, before I got home again, I changed me mind again, that I wouldn't. I'd tell me father about them, because he'd always find out from the son anyways.

When I did went back home, then, I said to me father, "I got old Paddy Ward's tools, the Lord have mercy on him."

"Oh did ya?" says he. "Well, he always promised me them," he said. Then he picked all the best out of it. "Well, I'll give all the best, now, to you," he said. "They'll always be your own. Look after 'em."

So I did.

I thought I was very happy in them days. Well, you wouldn't notice ups and downs in the country, and we had all them belonging to us, they was all together. But if I was back the same age again, now, I'd prefer that I'd start a different life. I never would learn the trade for one start. If I was back to fourteen again I'd be hoping that either me father or mother did send me to Letterfrack to school. I often thought it was very stupid for my father and mother to never give me education, that I could take me chances in the world and I'd know what was coming my road.

There was a man one time outside Athleague in the County Roscommon. He was a fisherman and Pat Lohan was his name, and he'd be about ninety years of age. And he had the one son.

So there was a pike in the Suck River and every bait that ever a man thrown in, this pike swallowed it and broke the bait. The pike was thirty feet in length. The shallowest part of the Suck was ten feet deep, and the pike never could cross that ten feet to get to the other side. He was so big he could only keep in the deep part of the river, and everytime he'd come, he'd show three foot of his back out of the water.

So, Pat said to his son, "Will we go down and have a try at this pike?"

"I don't mind," says the son, "but won't he break every bait that ever I give him?"

"Well, anyway," Pat said, "I'll get that pike. We'll go down."

"How'll we catch him?" the son says.

"I'll catch him," says Pat.

So Pat gets terrible bull-wire, and he puts bait on it, that nothing could break it, the house couldn't break it. And he ties the bull-wire with the bait on behind his boat, an oar-boat. So, into the boat, and himself and the son went up the river. When they came to the real deep water they seen the pike. The pike passed 'em by, like that, and it took the bait and with the throw the pike give, it turned the boat on the side.

Now, when the pike took that bait 'twas no such thing as getting out! He went up the river with the boat backwards, doing fifty miles an hour, and the father and son in it! The son said to the father, "I'm jumping off, Daddy!"

"Don't jump off, Son," he said. "Stay on the boat, ya can't swim! Don't jump off." And they had nothing on them but tights.

Flying along, and they come to a little bit of a lake and the pike went to it, trying could he drown them, but he couldn't bring the boat down. He turned again then and he come down the river, and then back up the river. Down the river, up the river. Down the river, up the river, until in the end the boat kilt the pike. He couldn't break the bait and, evident, the boat was playing on him. When he died the pike came to the top of the water.

When he kilt the pike he was ever so happy, the fisherman. The pike weighed over seven hundred pounds weight. They got over twenty-five men to put spears into him and they pulls him up the bank. They brings a horse-car. You don't believe this, I suppose, but it's the truth. They brings a horse-car and they brings him up across a field, and, we'll say, there was fourteen good yard of him hanging along the ground. Oh, yes!

Then they opens him up and they got out three hundred baits, et in him, what he took from people. There was a fifty pound pike in him, as big as a nice pig, and rats in him and everything. Everything the pike was getting he was eating it, like a whale.

Well, anyway, Pat sent to the zoo of Dublin and they came and seen the pike. They give Pat two hundred pound reward and the fishing tackle for life, to take the pike to the zoo. He couldn't be et: he was carrion, he was rank.

Well, with the fishing and the pike and all Pat was tired, but he had to go to a big card game this night. There was big money in it and he must go, but now he was a *couple of hours late. So helter-skelter with him for the game.*

He was going up the hill to Athleague and he seen about two hundred cats coming down the hill, and they were in an awful state. The cats were crying and gabbing and talking to one another, and Pat stops to watch 'em.

"Well," one cat says to the other, "that's Pat Lohan going up the hill, you know."

"Sure, he's listening to us," says the other cat, "tell him then."

"Right," says the first cat. "Pat Lohan, Pat Lohan, are ya listening? When you go home, tell Sally that her true love is dead."

"I'm hearing things," Pat said, and off he goes to the party and started card playing. There was four or five lads within, along with his son, card playing too. So they played and played and when they had their game over the father and son goes home.

When they come home their own cat was lying there on the hob as usual and the son said, "Oh, there's tea there, Daddy. Have some." And he did.

Well, do you know, after Pat was about two hours back at home he said to his son, "Ah, I forgot to tell you. I was going up Castlestrange hill tonight and I seen about two hundred cats coming down it, crying and talking and gibbering. And one said after me, 'Tell him, tell him.' So then the other one shout out, 'Pat Lohan, Pat Lohan, when you go home tell Sally that her true love is dead.'"

And with this his own cat sat up. "It took long enough to tell me, Pat," says she. "And I'm late for the funeral now," she said. "So good night for life and for ever, and I'm finished with you as long as ever you live."

And she went off then and never was seen again. [8]

Well, when it came to the time for the lads to be going on their own, 'twas harder for me father then, and I wasn't so happy with the life as when I was a little kid. It came to the time that the first sister of ours got married, and, of course, it was scattering the family and I missed 'em. She got married to a bloke called Reilly, he was from the same county as ourself. It came along that they parted the two: she went to her husband, and we stepped as one less.

Me sister got married when she was sixteen years of age, the first in our family. Her husband was about nineteen. So it came that me brother got married the next, he'd be roughly about twenty. And he'd be about three months married when me other brother got married at about nineteen. So it rolled on that we went to the North of Ireland.

When me two brothers got married they were their own boss then and they'd cars of their own, so they said they'd go to the North. "Ara," they said, "we'll go straight down through the North and out to Donegal." 'Twas a great country that time for tins. You'd treble the money in the North of Ireland that you would get in the Free State. And, that time, they used to make lovely grand cars in the North of Ireland, and some wagons, caravans. They used to make lovely new harness in the North, which was nicer than you'd get in the Free State. They said they'd go to the North from March until October, and they said to my father, "Would ya come?"

"Well, begod," said my father, "sure, if I don't know my way down, I'll be sure to God I'll know me way back. I'll go down with ya anyways."

Ara, I'd be about fourteen years at the time. So we went down to the North of Ireland and it was a lovely, lovely country. When we went inside the border it came a day like today: falling and falling with rain. A B-man, he halted us at the border and he searched the carts to see was there anything smuggling. He searched them and left the things to get wet with the rain. Me father didn't like that, of course. That wouldn't be done where he come from.

We done about five miles then and we were stopped the second time. "Where'd ya come from?" the policeman said.

"We came in from the Free State."

"So," he said, "I'll have to make a raid."

Me father said, "I'm after being searched about an hour ago."

"Ah, that doesn't make any difference," said the policeman. "I'll have to search you again." So he did. Ohhh, me father got real sick-up anyway. He thought he'd rather be dead. The brothers, they'd only the two women with them. 'Twas just throw off and pack up and be out again for them, and they had a great laugh about what was happening to me father. We were going, going along until we went to a place near Belfast. But twenty-one times anyway he turned off his cart, kept on being searched by the police, and he cursed them and effed them and everything. He was afraid to curse them, he didn't know them, but he did it in his own mind. And he said, "I'd rather be dead. Me sons'll never have an hour's luck for bringing me to this place."

"Ahhh, nevermind," says the boys, "we'll find the right place yet."

Well, me father had about fifty quid in cash coming into the North, but we were never left a night in a place, we were constantly going. We had to buy everything and anything and got no leave to earn no money, only spending the whole time. Then we were moved everytime, as me father hadn't fifty ha'pence. He said, "I'm done." He forgot his ways home out of it and the boys wouldn't go with him now.

"Oh," he said, "if I met some boy at all that was going back, I wouldn't rest happy 'til I went with him."

Well, we came on anyway 'til we got to this grand quiet place and we stopped for the night. I'll never forget it. This policeman came along. "Where did ya come from?" he said.

"Oh, I'm about three weeks in the North of Ireland," me father said. And that time you'd have to have a entering card with your photo on it to prove where ya come from. The policeman axed us for it.

"Oh, begod," said me father, "I haven't it. I didn't know I was coming at all."

"Oh, well," the policeman said, "if you didn't, you'll know where you're going to now. Them kids, how many kids have you?"

He told him. I was about fourteen years, my sister was about fifteen, and I had a brother twelve, a sister about nine, and a sister about seven. I had a sister seventeen and a sister eighteen.

"Them kids," he said, "is them going to school?"

"They're not," said me father, "but they used to go in the Free State."

I used to go in the Free State, and that time I could read and write me name.

We'd move every week from camp to camp, or every two weeks maybe, cause we'd have the country done. Supply the cans and we'd go on to a fresh place. Say, every place we'd go I'd go to the school that'd be nearest to me.

"Well," the policeman said, "if they canna read and write their name now I'll have to take them." This place 'twas very, very bad for schooling.

> *I'm a rambler, I'm a gambler, I'm a long way from home,*
> *For if you don't like me, please leave me alone.*
> *I eat when I'm hungry, I drink when I'm dry,*
> *And if sunshine don't kill me, I'll live 'til I die.*
>
> *Oh sunshine for dinner, oh sunshine for tea,*
> *Oh sunshine for supper, it's sunshine for me.*
> *I eat when I'm hungry, I drink when I'm dry,*
> *And if sunshine don't kill me, I'll live 'til I die.* [9]

Anyway, I had my two little dogs and the little dogs saved them three that was younger than me. Them little dogs was in the back and me brother and me two sisters was hiding in the back of the camp too. And the policeman said, "I have to check everybody that's here," when the two little dogs run out. "Oh," he says, "you have dogs! Can I see the license?"

So with the argument going over the license he forgot about the schooling. He went into the town and he came back in about an hour after and served us with a summons for the dogs.

The next morning we looked down the road and there we seen a wagon coming.

"So, who in the name of God," said me father, "would this man be? Maybe he's a friend." (At that time we'd be maybe two hundred miles down from the Free State.) "Oh," said me father, and he seen it was an uncle of mine on the wagon. "How are ya doing?"

"Oh, begad, great!" says the uncle. "How're you doing?"

"I'm doing very bad," says me father. "I never was worse."

"Well," said the uncle, "isn't that a cure for sore eyes to see you in the North."

"Tothan," me father says, "ya never will see me again if I get out of it this time. Where are ya going?"

"I'm heading straight for Roscommon," says he.

"Are ya?" says me father. "Well, you'll have a mate with ya!" He tackles the pony and he puts the camps up.

"How far will we go tonight?" says the uncle.

"Oh," me father said, "you name it and I'll go. Ye can keep going through the night too if ya like."

Begod, anyway, it took us about four or five days to get to the border and when me father got to the border he knew that he didn't give a damn then. He was sound.

We came along anyway and me father never stopped or stood until he got back to Roscommon. You could say it was three hundred and fifty mile from where he started 'til he got to it. When he got home, anyways, he started to talk to the neighbors and he said, you know, that he was a new man altogether and that we enjoyed the North, the bit we were in.

Then I said to my father, "'Bout ready to go down again?"

"Oh," he said, "the curse of Jesus on you, you'll never get me again six miles from Roscommon. I am a-living here all me life and I'll lay me here, now, too."

You'd have to be a man for it, what could happen to ya on the road in some of them places.

Like, one time ago we were stopped outside a place in the County Galway. Me brother, he used to make buckets, so he went to this house and he got an order to make three buckets for this man. When he made them, anyway, and took them back up, the man said, "I have got no change."

"Oh, that's alright," says the brother, "sure, I'll send up the young fella tomorrow morning for the fifteen shillings."

"Very well," said the farmer, "when he comes tomorrow I'll pay him."

So the next morning the brother says to me, "You know Mr. So-and-so, at the house in the auld boreen at the bog? He owes me fifteen bob for three buckets and you'll get it for me today."

"Fair enough," says I.

"Cross that field," he said, "it's the nearest ways to the house. It's about two and a half miles across that field. You get the money, and when you're coming back," he said, "I'll be moving camp. So you come back across the field and come up the road and you'll pass two public houses, and you'll meet me abroad at such a crossroads. I'll be there with the wagon and I'll wait for ya."

"Right," says I. So I crossed the field and I came to the bog and I went up to the house and the man give me the fifteen bob. It was in the short winter's days and when I got there it'd be around half past one. So when I come back and I passed the two public houses and I got along as far as the crossroads, it came to around half past three or four o'clock, and it was getting very late and I was getting very uneasy. It was falling dark, but I could not find the brother there. "He won't come this way today," I said, and I started to walk back for the camp, where we were stopping, and when I went there he was gone.

I started to walk again, and I walked about fifteen miles and I made an inquiry to people, did they see any caravan, and a pony and car. So they told me that it went on before, on this road.

I was getting very, very tired, that it was falling off to eleven o'clock in the night, and I came along to a woody road and I seen this lone house. I walked in as far as the house and I knocked at the door and a man came out.

"Good night," says I.

"Good night," says the man.

I said, "Did ya see any caravan going on this road today any time?"

"Yes," he said, "one went on around four o'clock. So," he said, "it's going a bit late, would you like to stay here tonight?"

I said, "Begod, I'd be very thankful to you if you'd leave me," as I was very tired and I was also very hungry. "And I'd be very thankful to you if you'd make me a drop of tea and give me a sangwich," says I.

"I will," he said, "come in."

So he did, and when I had the tea drank, he said, "You'll come with me now."

He reaches over the door and he takes down a torch, a mackintosh coat, his hat, keys, and a gun, and we walked out the door and down to the road. We crossed the road to a big gate. Through the gate and we walked down a very, very lonesome avenue until we came to a very big house. It was a very big building. He got the keys and he opened the door.

Right before me there was a stairs and to the right there was a fireplace with a crow's nest knocked down into it, and to the left there was a bed.

"Now," he said, "there's your bed, and there's a fireplace, of course. And at seven o'clock in the morning, I'll rap you up and I'll let you out. Until that," he said, "you cannot get out."

"O.K., Sir," says I. "Thank you very much." And when I get him gone, of course, I takes out me matches and I lights the crow's nest and made an awful big blaze.

But with the heat of the fire, as I walked so much, I was very tired and sleepy. I said, "I'll go to bed." So I took off me clothes and I went to bed and I was just lying down, on the point of going asleep, when this step came down the stairs.

I said, "Who could that be now? Sure, there's nobody in this place only myself." Oh, I didn't get afraid, because I thought that this was really a live man.

So then a man walked into the room. He had a hat, glasses, and a coat and a briefcase. So when he came, he takes off his hat, glasses, and his mac and he hung them up. He opened his case and in his case there was all different sorts of razors. He went to the tap and he got some water and he washed his hands, and he looked at me. He said, "Get up until I shave you."

'Course, I was only sixteen years of age, and I never shaved.

He said, "Get up until I shave ya."

"But, Sir," says I to him, "I never shaved in my life, and I have got no beard."

"It doesn't make any difference," he said, "get up until I shave ya."

So I got up and he lathered me and scrubbed me, but, begad, he shaved me. He dried his hands. He puts on his coat, hat, and glasses and close his briefcase, and up the stairs he went.

He wasn't up the stairs until he was down again.

In he comes. He takes off his glasses, coat, and hat. Takes out the water and washes his hands and he looked at me. "Get up," he said, "until I shave ya."

"Begod, Sir," said I to him, "you're after shaving me this minute."

He said, "Get up until I shave ya."

I says, "You shaved me."

"It doesn't make any difference," he said, "I'll shave ya again." So he did. He dried his hands, closed his case and put on his coat and he walked upstairs.

"Well," I said, "who must that be at all?"

He wasn't upstairs again until the step came down along and in he comes. Takes off his coat and hat and glasses, washed his hands and looked at me. "Get up," he said, "'til I shave ya."

Says I, "You shaved me twice, Sir."

He said, "Get up 'til I shave ya."

"Well," says I, "ya shaved me twice and what's the good of shaving me the third time?"

"Get up 'til I shave ya," he said.

Well, he shaved me and he shaved me and he kept shaving me. And that's the why that the beard today is so strong on me.[10]

Begad, anyway, as I was telling ya, it was in about October after the two brothers came back from the North, and they had plenty of everything: value in caravans and harness and plenty of horses. Sure, as I said, if you had no family with you you could get at least, like, twenty quid a day. That was a lot of money. So we came back up to Roscommon, worked from Roscommon over to Ballygar, from Ballygar over to Newbridge, Creggs, Moybalea, and a place called Ballinamore, Athleague, until we landed back into Roscommon again. So that was the finishing up of me father's Traveling that year.

That was the time of the war now, and there was no such thing as tin selling at the time of the war. You'd have to go and cut up old motorcars and me father used to cut up the scrap cars to make the buckets. Me father made buckets the time of the war, that's about twenty-five years ago, and they're still working yet. They were that strong of stuff, steel, you know. And I put some handles on half-pint jam jars, the time of the war, long ago, when there was no tin to be got. Put two straps of tin outside the jar and I'd solder a handle onto it. And people'd get them for to use them in the bog or out in the meadows or something.

Well, a lot of the fellas that used to do the tin work at the time of the war, when the war stopped they stopped theirself, you know. They started to deal in horses then and feathers. It was just about back to fifteen years ago, sixteen years, where 'twas fellas'd give fifteen pound for feather ticks that was in the beds, same as a feather mattress now. A good feather, they were worth up to five pounds ten a stone that time. You'd get some ticks that was four stone of feathers in it, maybe more.

The best feather buyers of the country was such as the O'Briens, the Quilligans, and the Sheridans. Those people had vans and lorries. They'd go in to Galway, now, or Dublin to the big stores, and they'd buy some mattresses, new ones. They'd buy, say, fifty cheap ones and one dear one with cold-hair or fiber and the springs. One Odearest mattress, for one start, that'd be, say, sixteen pound, but the other mattresses they'd only run into about two pound.

Well, now listen: one of those fellas he'd come along to you, to your house. He'd say, "Your old mattress is no good." And he could turn it to bad health be lying on this old feather bed. "I'm giving you a new Odearest mattress that cost twenty-five pounds, and it's after coming off 'n Dublin."

He'd make you believe and swally everything if he could, cause twenty years ago people was harmless, you know. They weren't the same as they are today. And the people out in the country was the most harmlessest and innocent of all. Sure, they thought they was smart theirself to be making the bargain.

Oh, for I've been an old widower, I'm fed up with life,
Four years I've been out in the search of a wife.

For I married an old widow, I'm now settled down,
I'll do me endeavors to make a half-crown.

The population of Eireann is now getting small,
When young De Valera steps in from the Dail,
And the laws that he spoke and he now left them down,
"For every child born I'll give a half-crown."

For the first night I started I was nearly dead.
The next night I started I broke every spring in the bed.
"Sure, bedad 'n," says she, "for I am sixty-three."
"Sure, begod 'n," says I, "it's no half-crown for me."

I awoke the other night between midnight and dream,
Saying, "What did I hear but a young baby scream."
And me wife she shouts out, "Get a bottle you clown!
It's the cause of me death, that old lousy half-crown!"

Sure, now I dissembles a half-hungry goose,
Every bone in me body and joints they are loose.
And the neighbors all laughs and they calls me a clown.
Wouldn't I rather go beg that lousy half-crown![11]

So this fella'd swap with you, and maybe you'd give him a couple of feather ticks and a fiver for the Odearest. Then he'd say, "Can I have this?" And he'd take his label, you know, the receipt that was stuck onto your Odearest mattress. He'd stick it onto a fifty shilling mattress, a cheaper one, and he'd go on to the next house.

"Sork, would you be interested in a good Odearest mattress? 'Tis a good one!" And so on, from house to house.

So that's how it might be, going around. He'd give you the good one, but he might give ten bad ones in the same parish. So it started to come along that people made plenty of money in that, 'cause, as I said before, the worst mattress with feathers then going was worth seven and eight pound, and you could buy that for maybe ten bob. Matter of fact, I often got one to take away that I'd get a tenner for. They're no good now. You wouldn't get five shillings now for the best feather bed going. Well, you see the why: there's no war now.

Well, I knew a man that found over thirty thousand pound in a feather bed. That's the truth, he was one of the Mahons. He bought this old feather bed and it was belonging to Yanks and they stuck all their money into it when they died. But all he didn't drink, he bought things out of, and after a while they were as poor as ourself. They got it too easy and they spend it soft. Money is like that, there's no saving it. A lot less than that now'd do me.

That time, feathers out of a swan was going for a pound a pound. There was three pounds of feathers in a swan and it takes three geese to make one pound. So that'll let you know how much feathers is in a swan!

Well, one day we were stopped in a place outside Balintubber and the name of the place was Curraghstonich. There was a big river up again Hulls where the lords were fishing, and you get trout, salmon, or perch or eels there. So this day I was going fishing and I seen two lovely swans. Oh, two big ones. So I looked across at the swans.

Now, one man isn't able to kill no swan. No matter how good a man is, the swan'll kill him. If a swan and a man meets in the river together, she'll drown him. And for killing a swan you get seven years in prison, because, after all, swans was gentry one time. They was gentlemen and gentleladies. So, says I, "I'll go for it with the hound."

We'd a big hound called Chert belonging to me father, and if ya'd throw a stone into a river he'd go into the middle after it. Just set him after a goose and a minute it'll last until he gets her. I said, "I'll tell nobody. I'll do it all on the quiet myself." Back I goes along and I was very happy. Says I, "That's six pound worth in the river anyway."

Says I, "Here, Chert, come on." Brings my rod and my line and my hooks to go fishing in the meantime. Went down to the river 'til I see the swan again. Well, when I came to the bank I threw out the hook everyways in the world to catch her, and she wouldn't go, only just flashing her wings at me. So I thrown a stone in after her. I says, "Go on, Chert."

The hound went in the water and, as quick as the swan was, Chert caught her. He caught her be the neck. So he kept at the swan and at the swan in the water. I was trying to keep everything quiet until she flattened out.

When it was done, I thrown my hook and I pulled the swan into the weeds. I kilt the swan and then I looks and I sees the other one, come swimming for me. Up she come and, believe me, that swan talked to the one that was dead. That's the gospel truth. She looked at her and she started talking, talking, talking, and calling it out, felt real lonesome and sad. And the swan in the river looked at me, and she clapped her wings at me.

I called the dog up to me. "You'll be dead tonight too," I said to her, "and you won't be doing too much talking either. You won't clap them tonight," I said. Right. I was going now. But the swan kept talking and never took over from the other one, nipping at her.

Back I goes over to a brother-in-law of mine. He was a very religious sort of fella, and if he seen a swan he'd fair throw her a bit of bread instead of killing her. He wouldn't let a kid throw a stone at her. "We're not so bad tonight," I said to him. "We've three quids' worth of feathers anyway."

"Oh," he said, "that's very good."

"If you come with me now," says I, "we'll have three quids' worth more to get."

"Oh," he said, "why wouldn't I? What house are they in?"

"They're out of no house at all," says I. "Myself and the dog kilt a swan."

He said, "You'll never have an hour of luck for killing a swan."

Says I, "An hour's luck? They're only a plain bird, the same as everything else." I said, "And they have to die sometime."

Around three hours after, eight o'clock of a summer's evening, he gets his rod, line, hooks, and baits to go fishing. I get mine too, 'cause I wants to show him where it was. We walks down. So I said to the brother-in-law, "Are you not going to give me a hand to pluck her?"

"You can pluck her and keep the money," says he, "and the best of luck to ya."

I comes along and I looks in the same place as I pulled in the swan and when I looked the swan was gone. And then I looks up and I see two swimming in the river.

Now, there was only two swans in this river, not another swan. And I knew the swan that I'd kilt as I'd plucked some feathers out of the back of her head, and there she was now, swimming. Says I to your man, "That swan was talking to the other swan a while ago, and whatever she was saying, she sent for her mate. I kilt that swan and I pult her out."

"Is she kilt now?" says the brother-in-law. "What did I tell you," says he, "when you do anything to a swan. Do you know," he said, "that swan could be a near friend of yourn, that you're after killing. They were people one time," he said, "that was turned into swans. People," says he, "was turned into a dog, into a rabbit, or into a fox or into a bird. And," he said, "them was two birds that should be left alone."

So I left, and I comes along to where there's a farmer by the name of Mr. Farley living in a slated house up again the river. I walked along there for a bundle of straw to make a bed, for to ground us this night. "Well, Sir," I said to him, "isn't them two lovely swans down there in that river! I'd say," says I, "they'd be two young ones."

"Well," he said, "I'm forty-seven years of age now, and they were big swans, as big as they are now, when I was borned. They've sixty years apiece, them swans."

"Now then," says I, "what'd happen if you kilt one of them?"

"You'd either have a leg broke or your neck broke," he said.

"Well," I said, "I did kill one, and the same swan as I kilt is swimming in the river today, with her mate."

"That's because," says Mr. Farley, "the other one offered her life to get him back, so the two is there. So Pat," he said, "as long ever you live, never bother a swan."

But I did bother her, I tried to kill her, and that's the why I'm so fond of drink today.[12]

> Come all you young fowlers that follow the bawn,
> Be aware of late shooting by the lakes at evensong.
> Be aware of an accident such as happened to me.
> When I shot my own heart's darling beneath a greenwood tree.
>
> She was going to her uncle when a shower it came on,
> She went underneath a green bush the shower for to shun.
> With her white apron about her, I took her for a swan.
> I raised my gun and fired and I killed poor Molly Bawn.

I ran over to the greenwood, all for to catch my swan,
But, alas, to my sorrow, I found 'twas Molly Bawn.
Oh, I kissed her brows and temples when I found that she was dead,
And a fountain of salt tears for my own true love I shed.

I ran then unto her uncle, in great haste and fear,
"Oh, Uncle, dear Uncle, I have killed my Molly dear.
I have killed the fairest creature, I've taken her young life,
And I always had intended for to make her my own wife.

"I'll go to some far country, far off beyond the sea,
And there in some dark valley I will mourn my sweet Molly."
"Don't leave your own country, wait til your trial comes on,
You could never be convicted for the shooting of a swan."

Now the night of Molly's funeral, her ghost it did appear,
Crying, "Mother, dearest Mother, young Jimmy must go clear.
I was going to my uncle when a shower it came on,
And young Jimmy he mistook me and he shot me for a swan."

All the girls of this country, they surely will be glad,
When they hear the sad story that young Molly Bawn is dead.
Take the girls of this country and place them in a row,
Molly Bawn shines above them like a mountain of snow.[13]

There's ups and downs in the world, sure, I wouldn't like to think about them. When I was just a lad I wasn't too fond of the drink, as I'd only take a pint when we'd be in the shop. I was never going drunk. And I done what was expected of me.

I worked for me father for two years, then, after learning me trade. Me father used make some tins and send you out with them, to sell them. But it came the time now that I'd make some of them tins for him. If I'd make the tins for meself I'd still have to give him the money, do you know, to keep the fire going. The family was big. But then, after this for a while, he told me, "You work for yourself now." And I did.

When I started to work for meself I was about twenty years of age and I was happy of it. But it came then that I seen the fire dying, that it was fading away. The big family was soon gone, and things was going on too sudden.

I was twenty years when I got married, and I'll tell you one thing: it's big changes since then. Seems there is always changes, since. Life isn't as good now as it was when I was single. When it comes along to getting married and you has a family, you're buggered. You know everything is gone wrong then, because you're tied up everytime.

How it can happen is just like this time about fifteen years ago, before I got married, and I walked into the town of Roscommon. I had a first cousin there, and meself and himself was very great mates. So, the two of us comes along and we meets a woman about twenty-four years of age, and we brings her into the pub and we give her a drink.

So, we sat drinking until we drank the whole day together, and she said, "You'll have to take me home with yous tonight now, 'cause you know you can't leave me on me own."

"Begod," I said to her, "I canna take you with me tonight. My father nor mother won't like it."

"But," she said, "you're with me the whole day, and you canna leave me now."

"Begad," says your man, "go on. Take her and try and do something with her."

"Begod," said I, "What can I do?"

"Well," says she, "you can take me out to the County Home. And," she said, "when we get there I'll tell you what to do."

"Well," I said, "fair enough."

We get a taxi from the square in Roscommon out the County Home. And she said to me, "You have to say, now, that you're my husband, before you can get me in here."

"Well," I said, "wouldn't that be telling lies, be doing that?"

"Well," she said, "otherways, it's I won't get in. You axe for the headman," she said, "and when he comes out say that your wife is expecting a baby, and that she wants to go in the Home."

"Begod," I said, "Right. I'll do that. Sure, no one'll know it anyway, only ourself."

So I did, and here comes along the headman. I said, "This is my wife and she has to go to hospital tonight, matter of fact she's expecting a baby."

"Oh," they said, "very well. Ye's can come in."

Begod, I was very drunk as I went in, but so was she. And they give me a place to sleep when they takes her to the ward.

Well, I get up in the morning thinking I was at home. Said I, "Where am I? What did I do that I am in here?"

"Begod, your wife had a baby last night," they said.

"Well, I'm going out," I said.

But the headman said, "You canna get out that easy. You must pay for her." And misfortune enough, I'd no money.

"You'll work three hard days breaking stones," he said, "when you have no money to pay for her."

So I did. I had to work three days abroad in the back yard of the County Home for the woman that I never seen her before in me life. She had me then. Wasn't that a hard thing to happen?

So, a woman you didn't know can tie you up as good as your own.[14]

When I did come to get married, the wife she was Mary Ward. She come from the County Galway, and I think the Wards is the plentifullest name in Galway anyway. I was talking to a man here the other day and he said to me, "What county in Ireland is the most Wards in?"

I said, "Galway."

"No," he said, "you've lost. It's Dublin. There's the most hospitals in the world in Dublin, and in every hospital there is a ward."

Anyways, the wife lived there one time ago, in the city of Galway, when they were small kids, nine brothers and four sisters. Their father was a tinsmith, and when they got older they started Traveling. Her father done the plate too, like my grandfather, and she has a silver ring her father made that was made out of the handle of a spoon. That's our marriage ring.

I got married then, and I am married still. Sure, all of us does it. If it's hard for the men I think it's worse for the women, but she doesn't know it at the start.

In Oxford City there dwelled a fair maid,
The truth to yous I am going to tell
She was daily courted by a handsome young man,
Who oftimes told her he loved her well.

He oftimes told her he would never leave her,
While walking home hand in hand.
And he oftimes told her he would ne'er deceive her,
When walking home on a lonely strand.

It was to a dance house they were invited,
And to the dance house they both did go,
'Til another young man, sure, followed after,
And proved this young girl's overthrow.

While she was dancing with the other young man,
Jealousy struck his wicked mind.
To take the life of the charming young girl,
This wretched young man felt well inclined.

He then went on and prepared the poison,
Mixed it up in a glass of wine,
Gave it all to his own true lover,
She drink it off with a winning smile.

She had not long this liquid taken
When, "Take me home, my love," cried she.
"That glass of wine you lately gave me,
It makes me feel quite ill indeed."

"Some of the same, Love, that myself has taken,
Some of the same, Love, I gave to thee."
And they died together in each other's arms.
Young man be aware of the cruel jealousy. [15]

Me father died then, when I was only nine months married, the Lord have mercy on him, and he left me sister. Me youngest sister wasn't married.

All me other sisters was married now but me youngest, and me brother John was single. I was left alone to look sharp for 'em. I was the man. So I took over with me mother and me sister, and I'd a sister a widow woman and she'd a little girl, and me own wife, that's five. There was five women and only one man now. So I sort of got afraid then, going in through the places with meself and nobody to protect them, only I had to protect them. I was afraid something'd happen to 'em, or to meself, and I'd no help for it.

One time there was a big row. There was over twenty-five lads of Travelers stopped about a mile away from Hulls, and they had come into Hulls where there was a row with other people. All fighting in the town. The sergeant there and about twenty guards come to where we was stopped, to get information who was causing the row. Then the sergeant seen my pony in his field, where there was no gate. So he said to me, "You own that horse? Get out that pony, you bastard!" My mother was standing there and he called me a bastard! I wished I was dead now, I seen myself dying.

"Well," I said to him, "if I am, you're another one."

He got mad now. So, anyway, this sergeant's wife had died about a month before, and he had one son a priest and the other one a schoolmaster. I knew 'em. Says I, "Have you a son a priest?"

"I have," he said.

"Well," says I to him, "if you had respect yourself for your son is a priest you wouldn't call me them names."

I knew this man for six, seven years, and no matter what could come I never could fall out with him, 'til this night, 'til he got mad over my pony being let in the field. But now I got afraid that it was the end of the two of us.

So here come the priest, the son, down the road to see what was going on. Said I, "Father, are you lonesome for your mother?"

"I am," he said, "I'm very lonesome, Pat."

"Well," I said, "your old so-and-so of a father called me a effing bastard in front of my mother, and my father dead. I know my father," I said, "but do you know yours? Go back," says I, "and tell him to apologize to me for it, or if he don't I'll tell you more about your father than you want to know."

Back he goes to where them guards was and told him. And the sergeant, then, he come down to me mother.

"I'm sorry, Mrs. Stokes," he said. "I was all of me temper. I'm sorry I said them things."

There was about twenty guards with him and only the guards of Roscommon knew me, and me father before, I'd be kilt with 'em.

Anyway, that sergeant, he has a private house of his own now, and when we pass by on the road, the two of us don't look at one another. And I feel sorry for him. I'd love to make up friends to him, do you know. But still I wouldn't give it to him, that I spake to him first. And he wouldn't give it to me.

His other son, the schoolmaster, still give me the jobs when I'm in that country.

In a while after, anyway, I got me sister married to a lad called Ward, and I felt very happy then. I said, "That's all my care and trouble over me. I'm not afraid any more." And when I gone to the church with 'em I felt free, like.

Travelers' weddings, they is always in the churches, just the same as the likes of you. You'd have to go to a priest and the priest he'd write away to the bishop and the bishop'd write to the pope. Your certificates has to be gone away about a month before, and if the bishop and pope send them back to the priest, then everything is alright, that you're not too near in kindred, such as first cousins. If you're too near, you wouldn't be married.

But all that a Traveler does have, they don't have no fortunes. The girl doesn't get no fortune and she being married. Some of the rich Gypsies, they do that, but the poor class of Gypsies couldn't afford it, or their families is too big. For the *dididreas*, the old Travelers, it was the old ways of getting married and they never changed it. Even if the father or mother was worth thousands, 'twas up to the man that's getting the girl to be able to support her. The father and mother, they'd say they'd done it enough for her. And 'twas just the same with me sister, my father being dead, Lord have mercy on him.

Oh, a pretty young boy come from the North Strand,
He came a-wooin' to me.
He promised he'd bring me down to the North Strand,
And there he'd marry me.

"Oh, get some of your Mother's fee for me,
And more of your Daddy's gold,
And two of the best horses he have in the stables
Where there're thirty-three."

So she got up on her milk-white steed,
And he on the dapple grey.
They rode along unto the North Strand,
Was three long hours before day.

"Oh, get down, get down, pretty maiden," he said,
"Get down and get down to me.
'Tis six little girls that I drownded here,
And you are the seventh to be.

"Oh, your silks and your satins, you must take them off,
And reliver them up unto me.
I think they're too rich and too grand," says he,
"To roll in the bright rocky waves."

"Oh, my silks and my satins, I must take 'em off.
Please turn your back to me.

I think you're too big of a ruffian," says she,
"To see naked woman like me."

He turned his back on for the North Strand,
To watch all the waves a-going by.
She gripped him around the middle so high,
And flung him right into the deep.

"Oh, stop where you are, my cruel-hearted lad.
Stop where you are," says she.
"'Tis six little girls that you drownded here,
And you are the seventh shall be."

Oh, she got up on her milk-white steed,
And she leaded her dapple grey.
She rode along to her father's hall door,
Was one long hour before day.

"For the parrot is up in the window so high,
I'm a-feared he'll tell tales upon me.
Hold your tongue, hold your tongue, pretty Polly," she said,
"And I'll have your cage of the glittering gold
And your door of the best ivory."

"Who's that? Who's that?" the father did cry,
"That's plattering so long before day?"

"It's no laughing matter," the parrot did say,
"It's no laughing matter for me.
For the cats are up in the window so high,
I'm a-feared they'll come down upon me.
And I'll have my cage of the glittering gold, and my door of the best ivory."[16]

Ara, one time ago the country was very soft, and the people'd say to the Travelers, "Well, how did you get married?"

And we'd say, "Ah, musha, I jumped-over-the budget."

We call that a budget, a kit of tools, same as them tools that I'm working here. Well, we'd think when they'd be soft enough to axe us how did we get married, then they'd take me to be something stupid, that I wasn't good enough to go to a Catholic church, or, aye, even any church. The best thing is to say, "Well, I jumped-the-budget," and don't make them nothing the wiser.

Well, be jumping-the-budget was running away, that's what they mean by jumping-the-budget. See, there's a boy and girl fond of one another, and the parents didn't like to get them married. Well, they'd run away then, and they'd come back next morning. Then the parents'd have to agree to get them married. It does happen with some people.

A cousin of me own done that, as I'll tell ya. I'd two first cousins. One was the same name as meself, Pat Stokes, and the other was called Martin. They were only about eighteen years of age, but those two lads were both in love with the one girl. But the girl never knew they were in love with her: she wasn't bothered. They liked her but they hadn't the guts of axing her, you know? So they come into this little town one day and Martin said to Pat, "Well, you know, I'd axe that girl only I'm ashamed."

"Fair enough," said Pat.

"Well, you go in," says Martin, "and axe her for me, and I'd be very thankful to ya. Ahhh, I'll give ya a couple of pints when ya come out."

"Begod," said Pat, "I will. I'll go in and tell your man that you want his daughter."

So when Pat went into the shop he said, "Give us a bottle of stout." He drinks the bottle of stout and he said to himself, "Well, now wouldn't it be as easy for me to axe that girl for meself as to axe her for another? Where's the difference? If the father's going to hit me, he'll hit me for axing her for your man." He takes another bottle of stout and he said to that man that had the daughter, "Will ya drink a pint or will ya have whiskey?"

"Ara," says the father, "I don't know. Sure, a young fella like you mightn't have too much money."

"Oh," said Pat, "don't be calling me young fella. I'm no young fella at all," he says. "I'm a man."

"Right," says the old man. "I'll have a pint."

"Well, you know the why I give you the pint?" says Pat.

"Begod, I don't," says he, "only to drink it."

"Will you give me the daughter?" says Pat.

"The daughter! Well, begod," he said, "when you're a man to axe her, you're a man to get her. But," he says, "a-would your father be satisfied?"

"Oh," says Pat, "as I said a while ago, I'm the boss."

"Well, if your father is satisfied, I'm satisfied, as long as you're satisfied, if the girl is satisfied," says the old man.

Pat went out to Martin. He was nicely jarred, had about three bottles of stout and he wasn't used to taking it. And Martin was freezed in the cold and rain, waiting for the news.

"How did ya get on?" says he.

"Good," says Pat.

"Ahhh, that's good. Good man!" says Martin. "Come in 'til I give ya a pint."

In they goes to the pub across the road and says Martin, "What're you having?"

"Oh, I'll have what you're having."

"Well," says Martin, "as you have the good news for me, I'll have a half a whiskey."

"Well, I'll have another half a whiskey," says Pat.

So they collared two halfs of whiskeys. Martin said, "You'll have the same again?" And he got him the same again.

"Ah, you're too decent," says Pat. "I'll have a pint this time."

Now every time Martin'd axe him to tell him the good news your man'd say,

"Now you have to wait 'til I get my nerves cooled. This is important." So Pat, he got well jarred.

"Well, how did you get on?" says Martin. "What did you say, and what did he say, when you said that I wanted the daughter?"

"Well, that isn't the ways I said it at all," says Pat. "I axed her for myself."

"What!" he said.

"Yes," says Pat, "wasn't it as handy to axe her for myself as to axe her for you?"

"Fair enough," says Martin, "now that you have her, the best of luck to her. What's the good of us arguing with her now." But in his own mind he said, "You haven't her, not 'til ya have the ring on her."

Pat, like, got a bit of false courage anyway, and he went back into the pub again. But the man that was ashamed, he headed for the caravan. And on his ways he meets the girl. "Oh," he said. "Hello, Kate!"

"Oh, hello, Martin," she said. First time they ever talked.

"Funny talking going on in there," he says, "with your father and my father."

"Oh, what is it?" she says.

"Well, there's a match throwed down for me and you," he says. "And your father'll give you to me but my father didn't want to give me to you, so I've an idee."

"What is it?" says she.

"Me and you'll run away," says he.

"Fair enough," says Kate.

Hell for leather all over, the two of them ran away. And here comes your man Pat, singing down the road, and he was saying to himself, "Well, I'm very sorry for what I done to you, Cousin. But there's as good a fish in the sea as was ever caught."

He comes along anyway and the cousin's camp was the first he'd pass. "Are you there, Martin?" says he. Out comes Martin's mother.

"No, sure, he's gone this three hours," says she.

"Where has he gone, back into town again?"

"No," she says, "he's gone off with Kate."

"What!" says Pat, and he nearly went stone mad. "Get me the pony," he said. He gets on the pony and he was on her back, going galloping, when the pony tripped. He falls again a rock and breaks three of his ribs and he was three months in hospital. Again he was three months in hospital your man Martin was ten weeks married. That's the honest truth.

Well, you see the whole auld country when there's a wedding.

I was at a wedding there the other day, about six months ago, in Athleague, where a brother's-son of mine got married, and a brother's-daughter. You know, a brother and sister got married to the brother and sister. There was fifty ponies and cars in it, and there was from eight to nine people in every car. There was no such things as coats, you know, like the women up here wear, but it was all plaid shawls, and the bride and groom, they do be dressed nice, and their sponsors. They draw nice sceneries, all dressed white. There was a photo of that wedding in the paper and it was the best ever. It was the whole length of the page. I had it here, but I lost it; I lost my coat and all. Long as the man didn't lose his head, that's the main thing. And you could lose your head, getting married.

Well, there was those two brothers the one time, Jack and Tom, you know. But, misfortune enough, Tom was a great man to make love to a girl. No matter what girl he'd see he could make love. But no matter what girl Jack'd see, she'd walk away from him, now. He was in an awful state, Jack was. And Tom said, "What's the cause you don't try and get yourself a girl?"

"I cannot," Jack said.

"Well, I'll tell you what to do," Tom said. "When I'm going with a girl tonight I'll stop at such a bush, and you go behind the bush. Listen to everything I say, and from everything I say, you say it to your girl when you meet her the next time."

"Right," says Jack.

So Tom came to the bush this night and he said to the girl, "Goodnight, my dear."

"Oh, goodnight, Tom," she says.

"Well," says he, "you have a head like a goose and a neck like a swan and you stick to me heart like a dewdrop."

Jack was listening behind the bush. "Ara, very good," says Jack.

But he forgot the story now, Jack did, and it comes along the next night and he meets his own girl.

"Goodnight, me lad," said Jack. "You've a head like a dog and a neck like a bull and you stick to me arse like a jam pot."

'Course the girl, you know, she run from him twice further then. "Oh," she said, "my goodness!" [17]

But, fair enough, you must like a woman, that you do marry 'em. I've got two first cousins married to Protestant people in England and they call it, like, a mixed marriage. Sure, what difference does that make? I was at church last Sunday and the priest was giving out about mixed marriage, and I think that a very stupid thing altogether. But it's only stupid going to a priest or anyone, anyways. This new pope that's come out, he's all those things changed. The next pope that'll come out after him there'll be no such things as Catholics and Protestants. For one start, I know Catholics that didn't go to church, chapel, or meeting, Catholics that never went to Mass. There's a thousand of 'em today in your own city here, in Dublin. Where's the differs there? Them has no religion anyway.

Just the same as the Protestants and the Catholics, different Travelers has different talk and action and all, but they're all the one people. But still they do fall out with theirself.

One time there was a wedding going on in Drumshanbo, a MacDonagh was marrying a Stokes. And the MacDonaghs and the Stokeses they were fifty-fifty, you know, great friends, for that time anyway. So there was great sport this day. Two young fellas, Bernie MacDonagh and another Stokes, was coming along in the road and they meets an old man, Old Cauley. Them Cauleys was stopped a-near the town. And the lads, they was that high in spirits, they blackguarded the old man, started giving him all back-cheek. So the old man said, "I'll get my sons, and you get all ye can, for you'll need 'em."

Now Old Cauley'd only the use of one leg, and he had one cripple leg, so when he'd go to fight he'd go on a horse's back. He had about eleven sons and the heaviest of the eleven sons would be only about seven stone weight. About five foot two was the biggest.

"Ah," said the Stokeses and the MacDonaghs, "they haven't a hope. Them Cauleys won't come in to town again, and if they do we'll make jam of them."

"So," Old Cauley says to his sons, "come on, boys. I'm giving the orders and ye take them."

"Yes," they said. Whatever the father'd say they'd agree to it.

"Now," he said, "I'll ride the horse and you fill the cart with stones."

So, clever enough were the Cauleys! They all queued up again the biggest shop windy in Drumshanbo, if it was broke it cost two hundred pound to fix it. "Stand at the windy," said the father, "and if they peg a stone at us and it go in a-through the windy, 'tis them that broke it and they must pay."

The Stokeses and MacDonaghs get their men and they went up this hill where there was no windows and that left the Cauleys could peg at them. The Cauleys started to peg the stones until they put them going from it. But everytime Stokeses or MacDonaghs'd peg a stone, Old Cauley, he'd say, "Oh, mind the windy! If you break it ya get seven years!" So it comes along that Stokeses and MacDonaghs had to give it to them. They couldn't fire their stones and the Cauleys was cutting the daylights out of them.

So, 'twas Stokes and MacDonagh (this fella, now, that was getting married) had caused the whole lot of it, and Young Bernie he was arrested. He was put on remand to Sligo Jail, and, the next, he got another week in it. The father done his best to get the son out because he was getting married. He axed the sergeant, "Please give him a chance." But 'twas no good.

'Twas in the twelfth of January, all in Drumshanbo Town,
The Stokeses, Cauleys, MacDonaghs they came there to fight around.
The Cauleys was only gossoons, as that they were put down,
All when they run Stokeses, MacDonaghs out of sweet Drumshanbo Town.

Well, the row was settled and over. Sergeant Joyce he walked around,
Saying, "Where are you Long MacDonagh, that you're bound for Sligo Town."
Sure, over walks Old Bernie, with a tear all from his frown
"I beg-a from you, dear Sergeant Joyce, don't put Young Bernie down."

Well, the first week they lived happy, when they were on remand,
The second week in the timber yard with a hatchet in his hand.
The dinner it was ready and they callt in all their men,
Saying, "Where is Long MacDonagh? To the lavat'ry again?"

"What's wrong with you, MacDonagh, that you're not chewing your cud?"
"It's alright for you others, but I am passing blood."

Saying, "Fourteen days it is your time, and this I will give down
Until your trial is finished, you'll stay in Sligo Town. Now!"[18]

After all that, it came to the time that the MacDonaghs joined the Cauleys, and within a week after the fight they were the best of friends, everything was made up. Then the Stokeses joint the Cauleys and they were all one. But still, the Stokeses fall out with MacDonaghs, MacDonaghs fall out with Stokeses. The Cauleys do fall out with the Stokeses and the Stokeses fall out with the Cauleys. Cauleys fall out with the MacDonaghs and the MacDonaghs fall out with the Cauleys, and make it up again. So it goes on: good blood, bad blood; vinegar, wine.

Well, MacDonagh lost that time and Cauley won. And I'll tell you one thing, if that Old Cauley fought out in the open he'd beat six men with the horse. His horse was as clever as himself. He'd drive the horse a-top of any man he'd see, and every time he'd be passing them out, the horse galloping, he'd hit them a wallop with his sweeping-stick. And if a man ran from him, he'd catch him with the horse. That was always his ways of fighting, since he was a gossoon. That was his belief, the proper way to fight, and he never stopped it.

He's an old man of seventy years of age today and that's the first thing he'll grab, is a horse. You see, the horse, it'd rear up and fight himself. If a horse knows that you're in trouble when you're on his back, he gets excited with the roaring and the shouting and he'll fight for ya. The horse gets mad himself. Therefore, if you see a man come riding a horse ya better look out for it.

As I said, after my sister was married I felt I was me own man again, and it come along then that I got sick-up of filing, of tinking, tinking, tinking one day to the next. I got sick of looking at the one place, the one country, the whole time, and I got tired of my trade. Me mother never would axe me to leave the one place, Lord have mercy on her. She'd stop there forever if she had her ways. I was only after getting married meself and I hadn't very much money, but, says I, "I'd like to go to England and start a different life, never to join the road again, like." I said to the wife, "When I go over I'll get you a house, and I'll send back for you and you can come over."

"Right," she said to me, "bring the camera and take the photo so I'll really know you're telling me the truth.

Said I, "Fair enough." So I did.

I went to England and when I went to Liverpool, natural enough, I had no money, but I had the old camera that me cousin give me. "What'll I do?" I said. I looked across this road and I seen this house. A car comes up and a parson came out and he walked into the house. "That could be as good a man as any," I said. I crossed the road and I opened the gate and I knocked. "Good day, Your Reverence," I said.

"Good day," he said.

"Well, Your Reverence," I said, "I'm a very poor man. I'm after coming over from Ireland this morning and I've got no money. I'm down and out. Would you help me with me digs?"

"Oh, listen," he said, "I'm just about browned-off with people coming and telling me that yarn everyday. Why don't you go to the Labour Exchange or the National Assistance?"

"Well, begod," says I, "today is Saturday and it's closed. But if you could give me as much as'll keep me up until Monday, I'll be sound."

"Ah," he said, "what religion are ya?"

I said, "I'm a Protestant." (Of course, I'm a Catholic. I'd tell lies to the pope at the same time, you know. Anything to get the money.)

"Well," he said, "when you're that ways I'll help you." And he handed me a pound.

So I went down along and I inquired for where there was a priest living. I found out, and in I goes to the priest. I axed him could he help me.

"Oh, poor man," he said, "we're getting it very hard ourself, and it's begging we are ourself."

"Well," says I, "I was at the parson and I axed him, so he said to me that he'd help me if I was of his religion."

"Well, what did you tell him?" said the priest.

"I told him I was a Catholic. I wouldn't tell no lies, Father," I said.

"Oh, fair enough," says he, and he handed me another pound.

There was a priest and a parson one time and they were great mates. So the two of them walked out the road together and they meets a young fella. "Oh, good day," said the young fella.

"Good day," they said.

"There's a shilling," the priest said to the young fella. And the parson handed him two shillings.

"Will ya tell me," says the priest, "which one, me or the parson, is the Devil most after?"

"Oh, the Devil is after you, Father," the boy said. And the parson started to laugh.

"I knew that," says the parson.

"Well, I'll give ya another shilling now," says the priest, "if ya tell me the meaning of that."

"Well, of course, Father," the boy said. "The Devil has the parson already, but he's after you, to try and get you."

The parson got mad. "Oooo, ah," said the parson, "that's a very cheeky young fella!"

But 'twas a Friday, and the priest and parson goes along and they went up to the parson's place. The parson he said he had a goose and a turkey for their dinner. So the priest looked. "Well," he said, "to tell you the truth, I don't eat meat today."

"Ahhh, oh, come on," said the parson, "eat it today."

"Oh, no," said the priest. "But I'll tell ya what I will do. Put a little cover over that there for a minute," says the priest to the parson's girl. So she put the lid over the meat. Then the priest took off his roll and put it round his neck and he starts to pray. "Now," he says to the girl, "rise the lid of that." So when she ruz it, it was fish.

Now, the parson loved fish and he'd traveled about fifty miles looking for fish the day before and couldn't get it. "Oh, my goodness," says the parson. "Put the cover on mine." So they did. The parson takes out his roll and he starts to pray, but if he was praying yet 'twouldn't turn to fish. When the lid was ruz, 'twas still meat. "How is that?" said the parson, "that mine won't turn?"

"I don't know," says the priest. But they ate their dinner anyway and enjoyed it. "Come to my house tomorrow," said the priest.

So the priest goes home. The next day he said to his boy, "I want a goose and a turkey for the dinner today." So the boy went out and got the goose and turkey and plucked 'em and was putting 'em down, ready for the dinner.

And the boy said to the serving girl, "It's an awful thing," he said, "we're putting down the goose and turkey and we cannot get one bit o' them ourself."

"'Tis true enough," says the girl.

"Well, I'll get a bit o' them," says the boy.

"Alright," says the girl, "how'll ya do it?"

"Well, wait and see," he said.

In comes the parson, and the boy goes up to him. "Parson," he says, "I'm a decent man, and I have got to tell ya, do you know that the priest is going to take out one of your eyes today?"

"One of my eyes!" says the parson. "He will not!"

"He will," the boy said, "so it's up to yourself now."

The goose and turkey were cooked now and readied and all. So along comes the priest and the parson, in to the table. "You better run for it," says the boy in the parson's ear. So the parson did run.

"Oh," said the priest, "what's he running for?"

"He's after stealing the goose and turkey, Father," says the boy.

Well, they were mates for months before, but away goes the priest after the parson.

"Come back," says the priest.

"I won't," says the parson.

"Oh, come back," says he, "and I'll only take one of them."

"Oh, a-fair," the parson said, "I will not." He thought the priest was saying he was only going to take one of the eyes out.

So the boy got 'em gone, and he rolled up the goose and the turkey and he put them into a bag. And he said, "You'll both get none, for I'll have it all."[19]

I was getting on good now, but not good enough. I comes and I walked along to a pub at the corner. I had nothing left, now, but me camera and me two pound. "Begod," I said, "if I wait 'til Monday I'll get money in the Assistance, and if I go into the pub I could get a few bob in it." I tossed a penny anyway, head or harp. Head to go into the pub or harp to keep walking. Head it came, and into the pub I went.

I was drinking a pint of bitter and in comes this hairy man, a black man, and up he comes to me.

"Oh," he said, "Paddy, would you know where I'd get a job?"

"Oh," I said, "you just come in the right time. I'm a ganger and I'm the man can get you a job. When did you come over to England?"

"Today," says he.

"I can even fix you with digs and all," I said.

"Very good," he said, "and what countryman are you?"

"Ah," I said, "I'm Irish."

"Oh, a good type of people comes from there," he said.

"Well," I said, "I think you're a very nice-looking man yourself, and I think I'll take your picture."

"Fair enough," he said.

So I took him outside, up again the back of the pub, and I took his picture with the camera. I said, "Smile." He smiled. "Now," I said, "that'll cost you ten shillings, and I'll leave your pictures in this pub, or where do you want them?"

"Oh, it's alright, Paddy," he said, "wherever you say. You're an honest man."

"Of course I am," said I, "you give me ten shillings." And he did.

Well, I took a few more snaps outside the pub, of other fellas, and I got soft, handy money. Doing well now. Begod, I was taking this one fella anyway and the camera fell and got broke. "Begod," says I, "what am I going to do at all, me ways of living is broke! I'll tell you what I'll do, I'll close it and flog it altogether."

So in I goes to this man was sitting in the pub, he was an Englishman, of course. "Excuse me, Sir," I said, "there's a camera that I gave seven pound ten for and I'm very badly stuck for money. Would you be able to help me out, to buy this little camera, and I'll sell it to you at half price?"

"Well," he said, "it's a very good camera, to look at it now." And there was the black man looking over at me, looking, looking. He wouldn't take his two eyes from me.

"What do you want for it?" the Englishman said.

"I'll take a pound for it," says I.

"What? Ah no!" he said, "let me have a look at it." He couldn't open it. He said, "It's broken!"

"Here," says I, "is it worth ten shillings to ya?"

The black man jumped over a-top me. "What are you doing?" he said. "You took two of me photos, charged me ten shillings and now you sell the camera, my photo, and all for ten shillings! What am I going to do with ya?" And he grips his hands on me neck.

"You'll do nothing with me, Mate," says I. "I'll get the guards after you if you go trying anything with me." I've got the wind up now, and helter-skelter I runs, out the door of the pub.

Begod, I walked along anyway and I was in a bad state over the camera. The worst of all I never twisted the wheel. I should have twisted the wheel everytime that I took a snap. I had them all in a heap. I comes along and I meets a man, this'd be about five o'clock in the evening now, and I said to him, "Is the pawn open?"

"Why?" he said, "What have you to sell?"

"I was going to pawn me camera," I said.

"God, it's a grand-looking camera," says he. "How do you open it, how do you work it?"

Well, I didn't open it at all now, you know. I took it the way that it stood. Said I, "This way."

"Well," he said, "I don't understand about it."

"Well," I said, "your friend would, will you buy it?" So, begod, I sells him the camera for thirty bob. So, that I never met the man since, how would you think I'd got on then?

> Oh, me name is Dick Daglen, the cobbler.
> I served me full time out in Kent.
> Some call me an old fornicator,
> But I've got no cause to lament.

>> With me haw-baw-bawl-dadaladdy
>> Haw-baw-bawl-da-daw-lee
>> With me haw-baw-baw-bawl-dadaladdy,
>> The hammer and lobstone for me!

When I got you first, I really thought it was a robin with a red breast I got. Faith, and it wasn't. 'Twas a wee water wagtail I took.

"When you got me first I was a well-reared little girl. There was always three full dishes on my Da's table."

The while I was looking at 'em there were two of 'em empty, and nothing at all in the other one.

I don't know what way a woman's tongue is held in her mouth. I could give some idea of a man's. For the minute my woman's tongue hits her upper lip it goes click-clack, click-clack 'til I'm fairly bothered with her. If I hit her with the last she'll run out in the street and she'll roar, "Peelers, Peelers, Peelers! Look at the lump this old shoemaker's after putting on me with the last!" And I've got so used to her now I don't mind her. And it's eight o'clock and I must have those soled again nine.

> Oh, me name is Dick Daglen the cobbler.
> I served me full time out in Kent.
> Some call me an old fornicator,
> But I've got no cause to lament.

>> With me haw-baw-baw-bawl-dadaladdy,
>> The hammer and lobstone for me![20]
>> With me haw-baw-baw-bawl-dadaladdy,
>> The hammer and lobstone for me!

I was lucky that time, but me luck wouldn't hold.

I got a job in the works in England, and I stopped there three months, but I missed the old folks then. Didn't get the house now, but I come back anyways, back to Ireland, and I started in at the trade again in Roscommon. Me youngest brother, John, come with me. He was working the trade now, and sometimes we'd be Traveling together from place to place. When we come along to make tins in our own country we don't go to a different country, like, for to scatter. As much as I knew there'd be about a hundred and twenty families doing the tin in County Roscommon. You never have a country better for tins. There's about six hundred tradesmen, maybe in the one county. And no matter what day you go out in tin trade you'll always make from four to five quid, the worst day. I often seen six different men of us working the one village of houses, each of us, like, with the same sort of tins, and still sell our tins. Twenty tradesmen can stop together in the one little parish and still each man makes his own living!

I'd work houses today and sell some cans, basins, and all kind of things. And maybe the brother'd be stopped five miles from me and he wouldn't know that I worked that village and he'd work them the next day and every house he'd go into he'd sell something anyway. Or maybe I'd work a village of houses such as that I'd have a terrible day now, I wouldn't do no good at all. And the brother'd come along tomorrow and he'd sell.

If I sell a good tin can, well, the woman of the house'll always buy one when I come again. But if I make it too good, it'll stand too long and that does me no good either. There's good tradesmen and bad tradesmen, and just to make a can without soldering it now, that's no job. The seams'll bust and the can'll leak and a leaking can is no good to a farmer, no good to meself. So you have to solder your can and put some wire in the top of it and complete it out. Another fella comes along and he shakes his shoulders and he says, "Oh, you're going to too much bother with them cans altogether. I can go in in a fortnight's time and she'll give me more for my bad can than she give for your good can."

I'll say, "No matter. I still always respect and hold me trade."

Well, then it comes along that I'd sell a good can in a house, no such thing as a leak, and maybe a cow'd give it a kicking. Well, that was their fault, that wasn't my fault. But the woman'd come along and she'd say, "I'm never going to buy a can from you again. The can fell with a kid going to the well, and look what happened! Bad tin!"

Well, I'd say anything to get friends again, I'd say, "Well, I'll make you another one."

Then a fella'd come along, maybe me brother, with a can not half finished and there'd be a pound of dirt in the bottom of it to stop the water from coming out, 'til he get going. "Ohhh," he says, "oh listen, Missus, if ever you want a good can always wait for me to come along. That other fella's tin is no good, but mine is very good. I send for that tin to Dublin." And he wouldn't, you know, 'cause he'd be after getting it maybe in the same place as I got mine.

"Ohhh," she'd say, "you're a very decent fella."

"Well," he'd say to her, "what did me brother charge you for your can?"

"Well, he charged me seventeen and six pence."

"Well, I'll charge you only a pound for my can and it tries better'n his can."

And she'd say, "Ohhh, it's a bargain." And then, just as we'd be gone, she might be after milking the cow and having this can full of milk when the two lugs'd fall off, and of course the milk'd get spilt. She'd say, "Ohhh, Goddamn that pup anyway, he has me robbed. My cream is spilt!"

The brother might come back then on a few days after and she'd say, "What sort of can did you sell me? The handle's fallen out of it!"

"That wasn't my fault, that was your fault," he'd say.

And she'd say, "Well, why didn't you replace me one like your brother done when the cow give it a kick?"

"Well," he says, "you're an old liar. You told him that can fell of a kid going to the well."

"Well, I had to make up some excuse," she said. "But your can is not worth tuppence," says she.

So it come along that he'd keep burking, messing, and messing about. He'd find out that he come along into this house and that house and nobody'd buy a can from him. He'd be in a bad state now. He could make them good, but he wanted quick sale and light profit. I'd come along after him and I'd sell my cans in the houses that he'd be put out of and I'd say to him, "Make four cans less in the day and make them better." He learned the trade properly then.

Well, there was a farmer's house one time, and there was an old parrot there, was kept by the farmer and his wife. There was a boy and a girl working for that farmer, and it came to the time that anything they'd do or anything they'd say, the old parrot'd tell about it after.

The boy was in a bad state about this parrot. "There isn't half we're doing," he said to his girlfriend, "but that old parrot is telling."

As soon as the missus of the house come in the parrot'd say, "Ohhh, Mr. So-and-so kissed the girl," or something.

"You're a rotten old liar," says the boy. "I did not."

"You did," says the parrot, "I seen ya." So then the missus'd give the boy an extra job he had to do. Well, it was going on for a long time like that.

So the boy says to the girl this day, "I'll fix that parrot up now! I'll cut his tongue out and he canna talk."

"Don't cut the tongue out," says the girl, "burn it out of 'im."

So the boy reddens a file and puts it to the parrot's tongue and roasted it. The parrot couldn't talk now.

Back comes the old man and the missus. "Any news today?" she said to the parrot. But no talk from the parrot.

"Well, that's one blessing," says the boy. "No talk at all."

That night the old woman axed him again, "Have you anything to say?" But the parrot could not talk. He put his claw into his mouth where his tongue was burned and then he pointed over at the boy. "What's he trying to say?" says the woman to the boy.

"Oh," says the boy, "that parrot took a sworn oath with me today that he never would talk again and tell lies."

"Well, could be," said the woman, "otherwise, maybe there's something stuck in his throat." So she looked in, anyway, and she see the tongue burned of the parrot. "Who done it?" says the woman.

"Well, I didn't," says the boy. And the girl says she didn't do it.

But it comes along that she got the doctor to come and look at the parrot's tongue, and didn't he cure him and the parrot got his talk back. He ups and he started to tell the woman what happened, "He reddened a file and he stuck in the file and he burned the tongue out of me," says he. So didn't the boy get sacked!

129

So off the boy goes and he came to another house where there was another parrot, and he gets the job there, working around the place. So one day he was telling the woman of the house about what the first parrot done, told lies about him and all, the why he was sacked.

"You're wrong," says this other parrot. "A parrot doesn't tell lies, for he knows what he's seen and he's sworn not to tell a lie about nobody."

"Well, the Devil'll go with you," said the boy. "Maybe you're as bad as him."

"Sack him," said the parrot. "He's no good. Him and me won't agree."

"Alright," says the boy. "I promise I'll say nothing out of the way if you'll give me this chance."

"Alright," said the parrot. And the woman kept him on.

But the next, anyway, the woman left a pound in the dresser and the boy went and he takes it. Course, when the woman came in, the parrot said, "Missus, your change! That man took it!"

"Oh," the boy said, "I burned the last fella's tongue, but I'll cut yours out."

"Oh, Missus," said the parrot, "he burned the last parrot's tongue and he's going to cut mine out! Get rid of him."

So she did. She sacked him.

So the boy comes along, looking for work, and here he come to this other farmer's house and there he seen a parrot having a bit of sunshine. Out in the yard sitting on a stick. "Oh," he said, and he up with a big stone and he give it to the parrot a-top of the head, and kilt him. Then he goes in to the house. "Isn't that a grand parrot you have out there, Missus," he said. "Isn't it a pity he's dead!"

"Oh, not at all," she said, "he's out there to have a bit of tan in the sunshine."

"And does he talk?" said the boy.

"Oh, he did," she said, "but some man cut his tongue one time."

"Oh," said the boy, "if I'd ha' knowed that I'd never have kilt him. I'm after getting the sack," he said, "in two houses over the same sort of animal as that. And I promised," he said, "I won't get the sack no more."[21]

It come along then that we'd meet other Travelers from another county and they'd sit down making tins. Well, that's when you'd want to be a good tradesman then. They'll come up chatting you when you'll be working, and you wouldn't like for your tins to be worse than theirs.

So it come then that me brother was going on well and making his own ways in the world, and I had me own family now. We had the little girl, Margaret here, and Maureen was a young baby. We parted me brother then, for that time anyway, and me self and the wife got up and we came to a place outside Athlone called Cornafulla.

The wife was going out one side selling the tins and I was going out the other, making 'em. I used to send her out to it, you know, on the foot of the cart. And I'd say, "Here, I'll mind the child, the way you can sell quicker," 'cause she had another new one in her arms.

Margaret, she was about two years that time. I'd be sitting down at the fire and Margaret beside me, and everytime I'd look for a tool to make something she had it gone. So this day come when I had enough. "Oh," I said, "I'm not going to have this." Then didn't she go crying? She went crying! So, what am I going to do? I takes a-hold of the child and I puts her on my back, and I did a half mile of road, helter-skelter, as far as I could go. I left her on the side of the road and back I come and sit down working again. Aye, she was only about eighteen months, but she was walking.

She had half a mile to come back to the camp, and everytime I'd hit a tip on the stake I'd look out the door. "Ah, that'll chastise her," I said in me own mind. "She won't be dogging me no more." I was banging the things and I look out and I see her, still coming in her way, nice old walk. "Well," I said, "God, that's a hard one!" Now, I really was too fond of her, as I couldn't bear the smoke of the fire on her. "If she comes up this time I will not do anything with her," says I. "I'll stick her inside the wall," says I. "She won't get out then." So, anyway, it comes after a long time I felt real lonesome. And everytime I'd put a tip I'd look out. "Well," I said, "I shouldn't have do that." Threw the things in my hand down and up I goes to her. "I'm very sorry. Ah," I said to her, "'Twon't happen again." Well, I comes back along and brings her back. I was making the tins and she was sitting down beside me, happy again. Made food for her and give it to her and all. "Now," I said, "very sorry. I didn't mean that. But that's learning you a bit of sense."

Now, sure, I had to get some more fire. Well, I looks up. "I shall go for sticks now," I said. So I brings her with me and I went up and there was a corner of sticks inside a wall in a field beyond. And when I seen them I said, "I'll take so much and I'll bring the rest again." But as I starts for it a young fella come up to me.

"You leave down them sticks," he said, "or I'll tell so-and-so about them."

"Ara, the hell with you," says I, "and so-and-so."

So I was picking out the thick ones and leaving the light ones back, and the next I seen this man coming riding a bike out of the four houses above, a-top the hill. And I thought I seen an iron sticking in the front of the bike. He was coming very very fast. So I whip the bundle of sticks and hasten across the wall. Here comes a man with a gun!

Up he comes then. "Leave the sticks back where you took them from," he said, "or else I'll shoot you where you stand."

I said, "Would you!"

"I will," he said.

"I wouldn't think you would," I said. "Anyways, sure, they're no good to you."

"Well, they're on my land," he said. "The young fella told you not to take them, and you told him the hell with him and the man that ownded them."

"I won't go across that wall," says I, "if you're going to shoot me, but I'll throw them sticks in."

"Throw them in," he said.

So I done it. And I went back to the camp very unhappy. I kicked the cans around the road when I couldn't argue it with the man with the gun. "No fire and no more work today," says I.

Sure, the next morning I got up and the pony was gone. It was the one bad luck on another. The wife couldn't go out on the cart, now, without her, so I started looking to find the pony. Looking, looking, but I was afraid to go in this road what I left, where a man charged me with a gun. "But," says I, "I must look that road, wherever I go."

I came to the road now, went in a bit, and I got the tracks of the pony, in along, in along, 'til I come to the house. Says I, "She's gone now. What'll I do?"

So, just then, out your man come, and he shouted at me from across the ditch, "Oh, you left down there did you?"

"I did," says I to him.

"What is it?" he said.

Said I, "I'm looking for a pony."

"What color is she?" he says. And I told him. "Well, she's out on my land." he said, "and I'll give you a hand to catch her."

"He's going to shoot me now," says I, "when he gets me in along be the house." 'Twas four brothers of them in it and I seen three more of the brothers coming out the door.

One of them says, "You the *dravy shan* down there?"

"I am," I said.

"There's Tommy here," he said, "that went down to shoot you."

"Ah, but musha," says I (like that, you know, I had the wind up), "the man didn't mean it at all."

"Begod, I didn't," he said. So he came along and he got the pony 'til he caught her, and he give her to me then. "Come in and have tea," he said to me.

"Alright," says I to him. In we goes and we sits at the table and has our tea.

"Well, one thing I like about you and your wife," he said, "anything ever you've got to do down there of jobs, you brought them back and you done them right. And one thing I like about you," says he, "you're six weeks down there and every Sunday that ever came you tackled your pony and yourself and your wife and kiddies went to church. So," he says, "you mind your own business. 'Twas only be the way of having a joke of you, I was, with the gun. But when me and you got to have hot words," he said, "I got serious too. You give me as much back-cheek as I give you. But just the same, it was really loaded. So you saved your life and saved mine. Now, here's the pony," says he, "and the best of luck to you. You're always welcome of Cornafulla." So back I comes, safe and sound, to the camps that time anyway.

I tackled the pony and the wife went out with the car. "Now," says I, "I have me two days back to do." And I sits down and started working again. And the child, she started to nagging me, benighting me again. "Now," I said, "I'm not going to have this! Haste within the wall," I said, "and you won't get out this time." So I listened and she was crying into the wall. "Terrible!" I said, "but a bit of ease has hit the work anyways. You won't be denying me. And," I says, "there's nothing wrong."

So, I was going along working and the next anyways I hear a lot of galloping inside the wall, and what was it but cattle. "Oh," I says, "wild cattle!" Up I jumps and I went inside the field, but I couldn't find neither trace nor trice of her. I tried inside, outside, upside, downside and I roared and I cried and I couldn't know what her done. Then I said, "Well!" And there she was, stuck in the middle of a heap of whins and nothing up but her two heels. So I settled down then, as I knew she was sound.

So, there she is today, and a big girl, and I give her a very hard time, but she's none the worse for it, thank God. 'Twas just like the man that had two cats one time and they never could fight and what did he do? He tied their tails together and threw them across a branch. They nearly kilt one another 'cause one cat thought 'twas the other cat drawed at his tail.[22]

Me older brother got a house then in Ballinasloe. He left the road altogether, and he was the first of me own that done so. He stayed two years in it, and he went to England to work there. He left the wife at home. She'd set in her mind to go with him, as a lot of them that goes over never comes back. But he went without her that time.

For 'tis green grows the rushes and the tops of 'em small,
For 'tis love it is able for to gain my downfall.
Wouldn't I work while I'm able? It's me own clothes I'd wear.
Wouldn't I work while I'm able, for to gain my love's share.

He come under my window three long hours before day,
Saying, "It's rise, lovely Betsy, and with me come away."
Saying, "It's rise, lovely Betsy, for you know me right well.
I'm the bright star of Old Ireland, and the pride of Snow Hill."

For to go 'long with you, Jimmy dear, it's a thing I'll ne'er do,
To leave Daddy and Mammy, and to go 'long with you,
To leave friends and relations, for it's vain for to say,
To leave me Daddy and my Mammy, and to go with a rake.

"For there's some said I am foolish, and there's more says I'm wise,
But there's more said I'm guilty of a queer many crime.
But to make 'em all liars, will you come with me?
And we'll both sail far together, far across the blue sea."

For if I was a good scholar and could handle my pen
It is one private letter to my Jimmy I'd send.
I would write to my darling, with me grief, sad and woe.
Wouldn't I follow my Jimmy dear, if I knew where to go.

I am here in close harbor, and I am nearly romind,
Every night now and morning I've a trouble on me mind.
Every night now and morning I've a torment in mind,
For to tell yous the plain truth he left me behind.[23]

He sent for the wife then, to come out of Ireland. He said to himself that it was as easy to rear the lot in England, if he'd be sending money back weekly. So they all went over there, about six years ago, and they never come back here again. All his family now today, they're all educated, and he's married to a very respectable woman. He said to himself that he'd feel ashamed now to go and start the same job as he was at seventeen years ago.

Another brother, then, that was living in the County Roscommon, he was in a house in Elphin. He left the house, but he was going to go back to it again, and then a little kid of his got burned.

He had a caravan, my brother, and a camp and he was over fifteen months stopping in this place. There were nine in it, and five little boys. They put all the little brothers together lying in the little camp. About five o'clock of a summer's morning he looked out'n the back windy of the caravan and he seen the camp on fire. He jumps out, himself and the wife. All the kids ran out of the camp, pants on fire, couldn't ha' stopped. And the wife says, "Is all the childer out?"

The eldest boy said, "They are." But in about fifteen minutes after, the young fella walked out and nothing on him, but all skin and face and head burned. He only lived from that to the hospital. He died. He'd be about eight years old.

There was a man with a coat and a hat seen about a hour before passing by the road, and maybe he thrown a piece of cigarette or something. 'Twas from the top of the tent came the fire, you see, wasn't it funny? It puts me in mind of the unvisible man what used to be walking those lonesome roads at night, and he had a lot of harm done, and he never could be found after. It could ha' been him.

This man, he used to go around this country here a few years ago. He had the unvisible ring, but he was a plain man as soon as he take the ring off. Ye'd be just as near to him as I am to you, and he'd put on the ring and he'd disappear then. All girls he'd kilt, and women, and he used to come along and rob people of their money and they wouldn't know it. You'd see him, aye, always in woods and on the roads, but 'twas nothing you could do to him, you see. He'd run from a man, but he'd kill a woman.

One time we were stopped in Cuson and he came to Cuson and I seen him walking up the road. We followed him, me and Jim, to see where he was going and, there, he just disappeared. It was about six o'clock in the evening. Well, that night he came to the camps.

There was a woman in bed above in the caravan, one of them roundabout caravans, and she was going to have a lovely sleep. The next thing she seen a man in the front part of the wagon, looking in the door at her. So she axed was it her husband. It wasn't. Her husband was card playing now with me brothers. So she seen it was a different man, with a hat on him and a coat. He started laughing in at her, and she roared for the husband and the husband came. She said, "There's a man on the front boards." And he looked and he couldn't see no man. He was no sooner gone than the man hopped on the boards again and kept looking in at her. She roared for the husband again and he came. They tried all round the caravan then.

"Ah, you're dreaming," says her husband.

But she warn't. She really seen him, you see, he was an enchanted man. She was uneasy. She gets up anyway and sits down on the fire, 'twas a little stove there. She puts her two toes on top of the stove and she couldn't stop looking at the door. And the next thing he came again at the door. He laugh and wink his eye in at her. (He was a fine man, I heard them saying.) And the next he made a dive straight in on top of her. Well, the roars of her then!

They tried fields and everywhere then to see could they find him, and they seen him running through the field, but then he was gone. If he'd e'er the gold ring on his finger, as soon as he'd tip the ring he was disappeared again. That was three times he came to them, and she didn't sleep in that caravan yet, I think.

There is really a place here in Dublin where you come along and give about three thousand pound, maybe twenty thousand pound, for to get yourself changed, unvisibled. It really can be done. You can get your soul damned. Through injections, or you get this ring that change you, that you're not the same person at all, you know. If I had five, ten thousand like that, wouldn't I do it? And wouldn't I have that money back the next day? I'd go through every bank and take every shilling they'd have out of it! Oh, but it must take a lot of thousands to be done, because there is a lot of rich people who'd have it otherways.

Your man was caught anyway. He was caught in Athlone. He was shaving and the ring was on the table, and he couldn't get time to get to it. The police took the ring and it was never known what they done with it. And he was sentenced away.

They took him to jail for life, and I never heard nothing more of him. Seven days I got, one time, in jail and if I'd do seven more, I'd come out in the box, that's the truth. I'd die. But they took him for life because of the harm he done to all them people, not for the money he robbed.[24]

Sure, money is nothing and money is everything. A man that has a little and his health, he's everything, as they say. And about the life of the Traveling people, now: they've softer ways to make money than anybody in the world because they could do what a farmer couldn't do. They could stick their hand into any trade. There's money coming in every side if you wanted to look for it. A fair is a great place for the money, for one start. There was some days there that likes of our people have gone into a fair and they'd make maybe thirty quid in just the one day. Every game in the world, just to make the money. There was those women'd make them flowers and sell 'em, and maybe some combs and delft and tiepins and things. Or with the horses, they do sell 'em to one another, back and forward, and that's a trade of their own. I sold horses a few times, meat horses for England. They do make cornbeef out of them, all sort of stuff. They buy the old fat ones for that, when they're right for the knifes. Well, if our people do make all that money, they set no value in it, and they spend it when they meet their own people then. They might spend five hundred pounds in a week where that farmer wouldn't spend it in his life. And they might spend it in the fair itself. You see, he'd hold onto it, but they'd spend it and lavish it.

I was about nine years going to Ballinasloe Fair, and now I'm five year gone from it, never went back to it. But I loved it, every inch of it. I was too fond of it, and I got in the ways that I wouldn't leave it. I used to have great mates in it and there was a picture-house then for only four pence. There was a pub there, Ryans' was the name of it. I'd say to myself, "I'll go in there and have a game of darts with the lads there." It was a great pub for a singsong and there was a microphone. In Ballinasloe there were a trotting match of the horses and all one time, I remember, five pound for the winner and three pound second. And there was a bicycle race in it, and I remember when there was a boxing match in it. They boxed on the fair green. I'd all life and sport in it and I'd never stay home. The women, they usen't to have a real good time otherways, but it was all in a night with me. I'd go out to the country and earn some money and come back into Ballinasloe, into the pictures. But it's lonesome when the fair's not there now, it's a lonesome place.

I went to a fair in Ballygar one time and, you know, there was all the pigeens in little crates. There was three fellas and they bought three little penknifes in the stands. The little pigs had all their tails sticking out through the yokes and those fellas cut the tails straight from them. Well, here comes your man what ownded the pigs down the street and he was well drunk; he was flashing all of his bonhams. The next he seen this, the tails cut, and he axed this fella, "What happened to the pigs?"

"I seen a sow around here," your man says, "sucking the tails of them." And your man believes him, and he gone off looking for that sow.

A fair is a place where everything and anything does happen, and where all people meet that maybe didn't meet before, for a year, two years running. Well, say it were to be a horse fair, maybe in a month's time, two months' time, I know some Traveling men that makes a challenge for that fair. This man he'd send a message with Mr. So-and-so to tell me to meet him in that fair, that he sent a challenge. So I'd go down to meet him and we'd box, fight to finish, one to beat the other, 'til the other gives up. A fair do, like, only all hands. And if he's bet, then he didn't fight me no more: I'm a better man than him. We shake hands before the fight and we shake hands after the fight. But at a fair, likewise, there is often rows that starts out of nothing, only some little thing that maybe one fella might say, or didn't say. Not a challenge, now, but all-out, an argument, you see. And there does be great drinking at the fair, natural enough. Maybe sometimes fellas'd start a row in drink. Maybe it'd happen that one'd leave the other in hospital, what they wouldn't do for a thousand pound next morning.

Well, I know people that had a fight and was summonsed for the court. Again the courts'd be up they'd be friends again and they'd go back a difference. Saying, "I'm sorry. It was more of my fault than it was of his." Well then, they'd both have a fine to pay, the one thing, no presents.

It's just the same as two cocks fighting: you'd like to see your own winning. But I often seen a draw. One couldn't get the other and they'd separate them. That'd leave that they were as fresh as ever. I was as good a man as you. You were as good a man as me. I didn't give two damns for you, nor you didn't for me. So me and you never would like to fight again, barring that you couldn't help it. You'd say to yourself, like, "Well, he'd either kill me or I'll have to kill him, unless we're separated."

It'd been in September, 'twas late in the evening,
As we were leaving Belturbet town,
Around the corner was MacMahon's window,
And Ellen Heaney had broke it down.

Out runs old Duffy in uniform,
And he came grinning with an ugly daj.
He left his hand on Ellen's shoulder,
It's just because that he wore the badge.

He marched her off to a civvy station,
And he locked her up, she was closely bound.
In a few moments after, down runs a motor,
And brings her over to Dublin town.

They took her in, in the best of pleasure,
And then they axed her, what was the crime?
They took her in, all as a prisoner,
And kept her three days waiting on trial.

For when her trial, it was past and over,
They brought her back to Belturbet Street,
Into the courthouse to stand up lonely,
The stuttering justice she had to meet.

Well, he took the book, sure, up of the table,
And he looked at Ellen with a murdering down,
"Three months I'll give you for window breaking,
And the damage you've done'll cost fifty pound."

For when poor Ellen, she heard her sentence,
She looked at Bernie with a murdering down,
"It is bad luck, drink, it is misfortune
That I'm going for three months to Dublin town.

"Sure, take good care of yourself and family,
Oh, this thing never happened to us before,
And I'll give up, sure, the auld window breaking,
And we'll live happy for evermore."

For now the three months is past and over,
I never felt it, going near or far.

I met her again, sure, all in Belturbet,
And I brought her down to the auld cozy bar.

For now auld Duffy, he is still in motion,
That the Lord may curse him, both night and day.
For we'll keep cursing, but ne'er a blessing,
Until auld Duffy decades away.

But now she's back and we're living happy,
Sure, quite contented every day.
God's curse on auld Duffy and auld MacMahon
That nearly swore Ellen's life away.[25]

As I said, I loved it one time. Today, now, I wouldn't like to go to Ballinasloe at all, in the fair or otherways. The last time I was in it I had all me friends, but the majority of them is all dead now, gone, and I'd think Ballinasloe'd be a different place altogether now, in fact. I don't give no interest to the horses now, as I have no money for them, nor no car of me own. The mates have gone the same as the horses, and I have left that country. A few years makes a change, isn't it?

That country used to be like me own, me own place, and I had all friends in the houses along too. But when I come to the nuns, now, I'd keep walking. If you know Ballinasloe, you know the Ballinasloe road then. I used to stop there, and there's a convent in there to the right. Only all nuns is living in it, and they have over three hundred acres of land. And they have four bulls of their own. (The worksmen looks after them, but still they're the owners.) I often put a horse into the nuns' fields, you know, when it'd get dark at night. Open the gate and stick maybe two horses into it, and if the Sister seen them in the morning she'd get her man to bring up the horses and stable them. And she'd make you pay for them, for the feeding, before you could take them out, and she'd bring out the police. Oh, they were tight and mean, the same as any other person.

Well, I'll tell you one thing: if I was the headman over the priests, I'd give a priest leave for only the car and a small little bungalow. And if I was headwoman of the nuns I wouldn't give them no estate. Why should a priest get a four-story house? I'd give 'em no land or no stock. A priest is here today for to pray and, we'll say, to keep the peace. But some of them should help the poor is taking from the poor. Don't give a priest a hundred acres of land.

There was a priest lived in Dunnanon. He's not there now, he's gone. It's a big castle and he had a priest's house there, he had all the farms around him. He had four big race horses and his own jumping field. He'd ride his own horses and he'd make them jump. Well, I know that priest had over ninety head of cattle and race hounds too. And do you know what he wouldn't do? If you done twenty pounds of work or do a job for him, he put his hand in his pocket and he'd take up a shilling!

Me father was going out through that country one time. Me father, you know, he used to sweep the chimbleys. And the priest had a four-story house. "Hi! Stokes lad," he said, "go down and knock the crows' nest out of my chimbleys; there are three."

"Oh, fair enough," said me father. ("That'll be three pound," he said in his own mind.)

The priest said, "I'll pay now, 'fore you go down." He takes up three shillings. "Here," he said.

"What's that for?" said me father.

"That's for knocking 'em," he said.

"Ahhh," said me father, "it's a long time since I started eating ice cream. I don't work for three shillings, Father."

"Are you refusing three shillings?" he said.

"Tothan, I will," says me father, "and I'll refuse a pound from ya."

But the priest wouldn't give no more, so he sent to Roscommon for a man called Costello, an electric sweeper. "Now," says he to Costello, "what do you charge to do this?"

"Three pound, Father," Costello said.

"How!" he said, "I'll give you three shillings."

"Well," says he, "whether I do them or I don't, Father, it'll cost ya three pound for me coming, ya sent for me. This is electric that I'm working, so if you don't get your nest knocked, you'll still give me three pound."

"I won't," said the priest.

"If ya don't," Costello says, "I'll go to my parish priest in Roscommon and I'll show him your handwriting. He'll pay me then so you'll have to pay him."

"Go on and knock them," the priest said.

Oh, if he axed me to do a job for him I used to say, "Ahhh, I don't know how, Father. I don't know how."

A vicar came one time and he lived in this house. He had a big place, and at the end of the avenue there was a gatehouse, and a man and his wife was living in it. That man was the herd for the vicar, and he'd come along every day and look after the cattle and do everything the vicar'd axe him. The wife, she was a good-looking girl, about nineteen, and wasn't she expecting a baby.

Well, this day the herd was out and the wife was in the house and in comes the vicar. "Ohhhh, tch, tch, tch, my goodness," says the vicar to the woman, "what's wrong with you?"

"I'm expecting a baby, Your Reverence," she said.

"Oh, well," he said, "I've a good notion of sacking your husband."

"Now why is that?" she said.

"Do you know, my good woman," he said, "that you're going to have a baby without a nose?"

"Oh," she said, "what?"

"Yes," he said, "you're going to have a baby without a nose."

"Well, what am I going to do at all?" says the woman.

"Ah, well," he said, "just as long as I got here in time, that's good enough. I can put one in it."

"Good enough," says she.

So, anyway, he blackguarded the wife. "Now!" he said, and off he goes. He forgot to tell her not to tell her husband.

But she was crying, and back comes the herd. "What's wrong?" says he.

"Ohhh," she said, "you're a nice man anyway!"

"What did I ever do?" he said. "I never insulted you in my life!"

"I'm going to have a baby of you," she said, "and it has no nose. The vicar," says she, "had to come down and put a nose on it."

"Oh, he had, had he!" says the husband. "'Twas very good of the vicar!"

So then out the herd goes and started sharpening his knife, and his knife was of that length. "Now," he said, "I won't be back for about five hours."

This vicar had two hundred heads of cattle. Well, your man didn't leave a tail on one of the cattle, but he cut every one off.

And here comes the vicar, like the red roaring Devil, down the avenue in his motorcar. He come to the gatehouse. "Are you there? Are you there? Are you there?" says he.

"I am," said the herd, "what's wrong?"

"There isn't a tail on one of me cows," said the vicar, "and where were you that time?"

"Is there not?" said the herd. "Ah, but that's no harm. When you're able to put noses on childer," he said, "you're well able to put tails on cattle."[26]

You can get a doctor fiddler too, you know. It's just the same as I'm a doctor and you're a patient and I come to your house and I know this house, that there's thousands of pounds in it. "Well, now," say I to meself, "this man is going to do no good, this man shouldn't live three months more. But I'll see that he will live as long as he has a pound in his pocket." Well, that doctor'll keep you alive in pains. Everytime he's coming that's five or ten pound. And he'll say, "Well, now, the next time I come to you I'm going to bring you something for particular, but it'll cost you twenty-five pound. But I don't want you to tell this to nobody because I'm giving this three times under value."

Well, of course, you'll tell nobody, 'cause you says, "Oh, isn't that a gentleman!" He keeps coming to you, coming to you and you'll say then, "Well, I have no more money, Doctor."

And he'll say, "Well, you're no more good to me."

And the priests going now, they're all for money, all for money. Don't give a priest a hundred acres of land.

The time there was men, rich men, that had thousands and thousands of acres, big landlords; the people'd have to carry the rocks and stones in their back and the women'd have to work like the men. The people living on that land would have to pay him everything they had. And when the lord came along to collect his rent, say, there was a woman and her daughter now, a nice daughter, if the woman hadn't the two and six, he'd take the daughter. It came along then that those big lords died and all the land was divided, everybody got their share then. But still, the man that ownded that land or this land, really, he might never get it. They took your land and my land and all the land and you couldn't say no. And them was the poor times, of course.

'Twas a lord outside of Roscommon, Lord Caghton. He was a real gentleman. I knew him very well. He was about twenty-seven years of age, but his father was the boss until the day he died. He had seventy thousand acres of land, for twenty-six miles square of Roscommon he had the land. And when the father died and he was buried in his own land, "Well, me father is dead now," the lord said, "and I don't own one bit o' it from today. That's everyman's land," he said, "that my father and grandfather took." He went to the Land Commission and he said, "Here's all this land. I want all this give back to the people, here and there, to everybody that needs it. So I'm going back," he said, "where we're belonging, to England."

> Come listen a while my countrymen, and hear my latest news.
> Although my song is sorrowful, it's me yous will excuse.
> I left my peaceful residence, some foreign land to see,
> I bid farewell to Donegal, likewise to Lensfalee.
>
> Brave stalwart men around me stood, my comrades loyal and true,
> And as I grasped each well-known hand to bid my last adieu,
> I said, "My fellows, my countrymen, I hope you'll soon be free,
> 'Til we wave the green flag proudly over the hills of Lensfalee."
>
> No more among the sackymor will I hear the blackbird sing.
> No more for me the blue cuckoo will welcome in the Spring.
> No more I'll plough your fertile fields, a cusha geal mo chroí.
> On the foreign soil I mean to toil, far, far from Lensfalee.
>
> On the bright November morning, in the dawning of the day,
> I left my peaceful happy home to wander far away,
> And though it may lie three thousand miles between those hills and me,
> I'm a poor forlorn exile, far away from Lensfalee.[27]

He was a grand man and as good a countryman as anybody. You told him a tale now, that you were in the army, he'd say to you, "English army?" ('cause they were the headmen over the English army). He said, "Have you the English papers?"

"Oh, begad, no, Sir. I have got them and lost them."

"Well, right." If he'd never seen you afore he'd hand you a five-pound note, for just being in the army. But show your papers, well! He'd buy you a suit of clothes, pony and car maybe, and he might hand you maybe fifty quid, maybe a hundred quid. Them has all left the country now, the real gentlemen.

I joined up with me younger brother again now, and we did go where we were able and done what we could. Me family was growing and growing and I had nothing to do but work for 'em, you know. Well, me brother used to learn,

learn, learn himself then 'til he started to make tins for the wholesalers who supplied the country. No one of us could work like him. He could draw anything out like a machine, and today, where he keeps around, we have to leave that country. He took all the contract to it.

Well, we often got a hundred pound out of an order in a shop that time, to make some cans, leaden hoops, quart saucepans, the mugs, as you call 'em, and pint saucepans, three-quart cans, long cans, and buckets. The shops started selling those cans and things, what they hadn't done before. The shopkeeper he'd supply you with tin, rivets, and rosin, and as he buy them from ya he's selling 'em. He only makes a very small profit in them, again what you're making with him, like. Say, you'll sell him cans at fifteen bob a can, well he's selling them at fifteen and sixpence. Well, if you'd sell him a leaking can, say, he gets it back, of course. And you have to be good enough to make another for him. If he testes them cans, you know, with water, well then his cans get black, dark, you know. They lose that lovely shiny color and the people comes in they looks, and they says, "Oh, no. Them is no good." He won't sell them then. And I cannot see my customer losing either. Well, then I'll take the bad cans from him and I'll sell them into the country.

When it comes to the fall of the year then, if the shopkeeper he has maybe five dozen cans left, he might be selling 'em maybe for fifteen bob, cheap. They're hanging up there in the shop and he puts a price on the bottom of every can, like. Well, it might come along that I'd walk into another shop where I'd get an awful bargain of tin. The barman would say, "I have two hundred of tin there. Say, one hundred of tin costs twenty quid, but I'll sell the two hundred to you for ten pound. I'm getting out of that tin trade." Well I could a-well afford to sell my can five bob cheaper than the shopkeeper then. Well then, ten of us would come into that town and sell around that tin. We had him ruined, do you see? Why would you give fifteen bob for a can when you could get one outside the door from me for ten? You wouldn't do it. You'd buy the one outside of course. And the shopkeeper'd go mad, of course!

But he know the bad can and the good can. And if you sold him them bad cans, he'll buy that year from you, but he'll finish the next year. You come next year and say, "Well, Mr. So-and-so, what do you want this year?"

He looks at you and says, "Ah, nothing from you. You done me last year!"

We come along then and we came back to Roscommon, and times got hard and you'd have to change your ways of living, it doesn't matter if you'd agree to it. Since the plastic came out, the tinsmiths give up making the tins. Well, you could always mend tin, or even sometimes you could mend metal or copper and that, but you never could mend plastic anyway. So it just knocked us off the job. Bit by bit it just took away our trade, and a lot of them give up entirely.

For it's been here the other evening in Kilkenny Street,
A band of the Tinkers I happened to meet.
There was some from Kilkenny and more from Kildare.
There was more from Ballyhaunis and the Devil know where.

There was Rashigans, Quilligans, Caseys, and Bells,
There was that many Tinkers as I couldn't tell.
When them all got together, they crowded the hall,
And "The best good whiskey," the old Tinker did call.

There was one man amongst them and he run out of dough,
Put his box in his shoulder, to the pawn he did go.
And three weeks before it his wife had confined,
And 'twas into the budget he hammered the child.

"For I hear, Mr. Dempsey, you've money to spare.
I'll leave you my budget, my hammer and shear,
If you give me the price of one gallon of beer."

For he took in the budget so close be the wall,
He was not far gone 'til the child let a bawl.
Sure, out runs Mr. Dempsey and he called in his wife,
"There's a child in the budget, I bet you my life."

For he opened the budget and he made no delay,
And he got the child rolled in a small wisp of hay.
For he laughed and he laughed, 'til he nearly dropped dead,
For to see the trick that the Tinker he played.

For the town it was searched and the Tinker was found,
Settled with the pawnbroker to give him one pound.

So, whenever you come into Kilkenny Street,
Found your pockets is empty and is all taken short,
Let you never bring your budget to the pawnbroker's shop.[28]

Ah, well, I'll tell you the truth: I never knew that I'd come down. I never thought about the days before me. When I was sixteen years of age I always had two good horses and a nice new trap and was well fixed up, keeping myself lovely and dressed and respectable. And I'd plenty of money always, never thought about drink or smoking. And if I seen a man with a donkey and car I'd say, "Well, you're stupid. You can be as good as any man, it's only just simple." I always thought that if I seen a man crying or a woman crying, they shouldn't cry. I understood that they shouldn't cry.

If I came along to me sister's and I seen her just going to cook a dinner and the kids in bed, like, I'd beg to give them a slap in the jaw or something to make them cry. She'd say, "For God's sake, stop, leave them alone." And I'd enjoy that; I'd laugh at it. And I'd go on maybe to the next place and I'd do the same thing. I thought, like, that life couldn't be nicer! Now, today, I'd imagine that life cannot be harder.

Anyways, back in Roscommon now, and me old folks, what there was of them, was all in those parts, what wasn't in England or gone, the Lord have mercy. And we had to go on the dole. You wouldn't give no thought to it if you was on your own, you see. But those kids need it, to keep 'em going.

One day I was stopped outside Athleague, in aside of the main road, and my namesake, he comes along, a cousin of mine. He's Patrick Stokes and I'm Patrick Stokes, and he was stopped there with us. I was talking to him this day and this woman come down from a house and she said, "Would ya give us a cigarette? Me son was to come out from town with them fags," she said, "and he hasn't come and I'm in a bad way for a smoke."

"Oh, why wouldn't I give ya one, Ma'm?" says me cousin. So he hands her ten Players, that was never opened.

"Oh," she said, "I only want one."

"Ahhh, keep the ten, Ma'm," says he. "I have enough."

"Begod," I said, and I start laughing at him.

"Ah, well, God help us," he said. "That poor woman was in need of a smoke."

She was a big farmer in this part, but there was no shop in it. Her son wasn't living there, but he used to bring out the messages to her when he'd be finished in the evening, coming from town. And the son was the supervisor for the dole, but we didn't know it that time. The woman, she knew me cousin was Stokes, but she didn't know his full name. So she said, "Thank you very much, and I won't forget that."

So, here comes the son to the mother that night, at about twelve o'clock. He brings out the fags. "Well," she said to him, "that Stokes man give me ten. I went up and axed him for one," she said, "and he give me ten."

"What sort of fella was he?" says the son.

"A tall boy," she said, "with a cap. He's in a-below at the caravan."

"Well, that's Pat Stokes," says the son.

So we went in to the town the next day, about fifteen of us, to sign for the dole. This man, the supervisor, the headman that give out the dole, said, "You have to wait your turns." He was a real cross man, ya see. So when he looked out Patrick, me cousin, is about the twelfth man back. "Ah, Patrick Stokes?" he said. And I went in, of course. "Not you! Out!" he said to me. (Me and him used to be always arguing.) "You be the last," he said to me.

"You! That gentleman out there," he said to the cousin. "You've something else to do, Patrick, besides hanging around the door. Come up and sign now." Patrick looked at him. He thought it was to make a laugh of him that he was calling him. But up he goes.

"You give," the head said, "a packet of Players to me mother last night, that I hadn't forgotten you."

"Ahhh, thank you, Sir," said Patrick. "Thanks."

"Don't thank me," he said, "I thank you. Go off now and call back at two o'clock," he said.

"Alright," says Patrick. So Patrick come out and didn't make us none the wiser, but walked off about his business. Didn't say nothing, you see, thinking we might go in and get him finished off. He couldn't think of the turn he done for the head's mother.

Now Pat was getting two pound nine and sixpence in dole and I was getting three pound nine and six. He had a child more than me, yet he was getting smaller pay. He comes back at two o'clock and the head said, "Two pound nine and sixpence you're getting, that's bad dole! Well, there's something extra offered you next week."

In comes the bold Pat the following week and four pound nineteen and sixpence he gets. And if he was the last man that came in, from that day to this, he's the first man that's got his pay. Over that little turn for the mother now! Isn't that a funny thing?

One time there was Paddy Irishman, Paddy Scotchman, and Paddy Englishman, and the three of them met in Dublin. But, begad, no one of them had nothing, not a shilling.

So Paddy Irishman came along and he seen the Englishman. "Ahhh, good day, Sir," says Paddy, "what brought you over here?"

"The boat," says the Englishman.

"Ohhh, I see," says Paddy.

And the next he seen is the Scotchman. He said, "Oh, hello Jock. How're ya fixed?"

"Bad," says Jock.

"Well, now," says Paddy, "it's the three of us is three different countrymen, but, sure, we better not part as we met." So off on the road together with Paddy, Jock, and the Englishman.

"Begad," says Paddy, "I'm starved with hunger. What will we do at all? Ara, wait a minute," says he, "I'll go on into this shop to buy a pound of steak, and I'll say to the butcher that it's a pound of bacon, and we'll go arguing a point about it. Then you pass by," Paddy says to Jock, "and we'll see if we canna get the steak for nothing."

"I'll do that," says Jock, "anything you tell me."

Now Paddy was as smart as the smartest man at this trick. So off goes me bold Paddy into the butcher's shop. "Oh, good day, Sir," says Paddy.

"Good day," says the butcher, "what can I do for ya?"

"Well, begad, I want a pound of the best steak you have in the house."

"Oh, that's what you'll get," says the butcher, and he cut it and got it and weighed it. Paddy looked. "A pound of steak, I said," says Paddy.

"That's a pound of steak," says your man.

"That's a pound of bacon," says Paddy. "Do you think I never bought steak in my life before? I'm saying it's bacon."

"No, it's steak," said the butcher.

"Well, I'll tell you what I'll do," says Paddy. "How much is it?"

"Three and six."

"Well, I'll give ya seven bob for it," says Paddy, "if it's steak, or you'll give it to me for nothing if it's bacon."

"How'll we prove it?" says the butcher.

"The first man or woman that's coming down the street," says Paddy, "we'll axe him."

And here comes Jock. "Hi, Boss, come here, I want ya," says Paddy. "Tell me," says he, "what's that there? Is it bacon or steak?"

"Well," said Jock, "you wouldn't want to be a fool to know that. Doesn't God and man know," says he, "that it's bacon."

"Oh, my goodness," says the butcher, "maybe it is bacon! You won it. Go on, go off with it!"

"Oh, but," says Paddy, "give me the directions, now, on how to cook it."

So the butcher wrote him out the directions on a paper and Paddy took it.

"That's good enough," says Paddy. "Now we have the meat."

"But what about the bread?" says the Scotchman.

"Oh, I don't know," said the Englishman.

"I'll rook it," says Paddy.

Well, they come down the road and there was a bread van outside a shop and there was a baker going into the shop. Paddy goes to the van and took up a loaf.

"Oh, hi," says the baker, "what're you doing there?"

"Oh, I'm after buying a loaf down the street, Sir," said Paddy, "and to prove are they cheating or not I'm after measuring it beside your loaf, and one is as long as another."

"Get going with it," says the bread man, and that left Paddy with the loaf.

Anyway, they went down the road, the three together, going along. And after a while me Paddy said, "I have to go inside the ditch to loose the button."

"Alright," says the Scotchman and the Englishman. But they was that tired as they went asleep while they was waiting and here comes a dog and takes the pound of steak. Ah, the Scotchman wake and he runs over to Paddy.

"Paddy, Paddy, Paddy, Paddy, Paddy," he says, "we're done."

"What?" says Paddy.

"A dog," says Jock, "took the pound of steak."

"Fair enough," says Paddy, "it'll be no good to him anyway."

"Why?" says the Englishman.

"'Cause," says Paddy, "I've the directions in me pocket, and he doesn't know how to cook it."

So they went along again and they came to a cock of hay. They were starving, but they had the loaf the whole time, and now they must sleep. "Now," says Paddy, "whoever have the best dream tonight eats the loaf in the morning."

"Right," says the Scotchman and the Englishman, and they all lies down in the hay.

Now when Paddy get the two other boys asleep, he wakens up and he eats the whole loaf himself. Then he settle himself off, and sleeps the night. When the morning come they all gets up.

"Now," says Paddy, "what dream had you last night?"

"Well, I dreamed," said the Scotchman, "I lay beside a cock of hay."

"Oh, very, very good!" says Paddy.

"And what dream had you?" he says to the Englishman.

"Well, I dreamed," he said, "that I was lying in my clothes."

"Oh, a very good dream!" says Paddy.

"And what dream had you Paddy?" they says.

"Well, I dreamed," he said, "when I got the two of ye asleep that I wokened up and I ate the loaf." Ohh, that was the truest dream of course: the loaf was et.

"Very good," they said.

Off they goes and they seen this big house and there was a grand girl in it; they seen her in the windy. "Hi," says Paddy, "Wait a minute! Go up there," says he, "and axe the girl for some bread!"

"Oh, no, Paddy," they says, "we won't."

"I'll go then," says he. So up goes Paddy, and he gets down on his hands before the door of the house and started eating the grass. The girl looked out the windy.

"What're you doing down there?" she said.

"Ah, I'm starving with hunger, me lady," says he, and he started defending himself.

"Oh, come in," she said, and she brought him into the house and she give him anything and everything to eat.

Out he goes then and tells the Englishman and the Scotchman, so up goes those two boys and started eating grass too. And the girl looked out.

"What're you doing there?" she said.

"Oh, eating grass," said they.

"Oh," she said, "that's very rough. But there's a good off-the-grass field at the back of the house." Says she, "Ye can go there and eat enough."

"Ohhh, Paddy," they said, "curse ya now. She's making a fool of us!"

So they come along and it come that they got very itchy. They had not washed themself at all. They seen another house and, says Paddy, "I'm going in here to look for a clean shirt."

In goes Paddy to the avenue. He takes off his shirt and put it on the stone wall, and he picks up some stones and started firing them at the shirt. And here comes two ladies, down from the house.

"What're ya doing?" they says.

"Well," he said, "I'm firing away vermin."

"Oh, God help him," they says. "Come on up to the house." They brought him up to the house and they give him a wash, new clothes, and a shirt. So he goes down and tells the boys.

Ohhh, helter-skelter then with the two boys up the avenue. They takes off their two shirts and puts them on the wall and started firing stones, same as Paddy. And here comes the two ladies down again, about an hour after.

"What're you onto there?" says the ladies.

"Well, we're looking for vermin, me ladies," says Jock.

"Well, if you had been here an hour ago," says one lady, "there was a man throwing them away, and you could have all them too."[29]

That supervisor, he was a head officer in the army and me and him, we used to be always arguing. No matter what he'd do for me, I'd always say he was wrong, and he couldn't bear to be told that, ya know. This man, he'd take no talk. Says I, "Do you want me to go down and kiss your boots? Ara," says I, "to Hell with ya. If you were an officer and made better men than yourself salute you, remember, them days is gone. Them men today," I said, "'d break your neck. Because," I said, "some people that go down and polish your boots in the ways that you could see your face in it was better reared and better kept than you." Says I, "Do you fancy yourself a good man?" And what did I axe him? Didn't I axe him out to the back!

"Well," he said, "I'd be afraid to go out with ya. Ya'd kill me," he says, and he started laughing.

Well, later this day I went into a pub and I met another fella and told him about it. And he started telling me about the supervisor: wasn't he a professional boxer and a weight lifter! That was the why he laughed at me. Every morning when he come in he'd go down to the bars and keep at it, going up and down, for half an hour. But I didn't know it 'til after I challenged him.

In I comes the next week for me dole: no money. He had it but he wouldn't give it to me, and he calls me back to apologize to him. Says I, "Well, I'll have to go now and apologize."

"Well, Sir," says I to him, "is me old doler gone astray? I'm sorry. I apologize for the bloody argument I had."

"Well," he said, "what'd you do that for? There's one thing," he said, "you've a little bit of respect about ya now. There's it now," he said, and he give me me pay.

Well, I cursed him then and I cursed him 'til I got tired of cursing him. I said, "Transfer this to Athlone for me! And if ya don't the supervisor in Athlone'll do it for me."

"Oh," he said, "you're very funny." What did he do then? He stopped me week's pay, and that went down in his own pockets. "I'll twist ya out of that, and anyone I don't like," he said. "That goes down in my pocket for my pocket money." He was the meanest man that ever come from a mother. A man who looked forty-five years, but could be over fifty-five. Ah musha, a hardy looking fella, a raw-boned man.

"Listen," says I to him, "I was in the English army, I was in the Free State army, and I was in armies, but I never see a dog like you!" (And I wasn't in none of the armies.)

"Don't you tell me," he said, "about army. Do you want me to go over across the road and call the guards?" But he usen't to say "guards" at all but "the gawds, the gods."

"Gods here," says I, "or gods there. Neither you nor the gods is any good to me now! Ara," says I, "the gods has nothing to do with it at all!" And I went up to report him to the guards meself one time, and the sergeant laugh at me.

"I cannot go down to that man," the sergeant says, "for if I went down he'd strike myself!"

He was the man that wouldn't take chat from the justice. You ever see that sort of a man? He was too highly educated. He wanted to be saluted the whole time. He hated me.

It wasn't me alone. The poor people that lived in the town, he cut money off their dole. Do you know what they'd do at the finish? They'd break in a-top of him and kill him in a minute, ya know, that he was cutting them off the dole and everything. So people that was there had no money or no nothing that'd just as leave be above in Mountjoy as to be stuck with him! Oh, I was hoping for it every time that I'd go in and see him!

On me way to Dungarven in search of some fowl
Near Barleytown corner a pistol I found.
The first man that I met, a postman with a bag,
I presented my pistol and made him stand back.

Rol-de-fol-lo, Oh-rol-da-fee,
It's a long way from Bangor to Donaghadee.

"Oh mercy, oh mercy," the postman did cry,
"For that is the way that I earn my hire,
To support an auld woman, a wife, and one child.
Sure, I'll leave you me bag, if you spare me life."

I told him stand back to the wood that was by,
I told him stand back 'til his bag I would try.
In one of those letters was a fifty-pound bill,
All directed to Wexford, to one Michael Flynn.

I give him his bag and I bid him good-by.
I said, "I'll go further more vengeance to try."
The next man that I met was a mountain sogru,
I presented my pistol and made him stand stone.

His belt and his britches I tied round me waist.
I bid him good-by and I then walked away,
"If your captain is angry, as I know he will,
You can tell him you lend 'em to one Michael Flynn."

I went on to Carrick, I slept there that night,
'Twas early next morning I got a big fright.
Six armed mountain men they broke in the door,
And I left 'em all bleeding, lying dead on the floor.

I went on a bit further to a place called Delfinn,
I met Mickey Shure, the hangman, he had a drop in.
He looked at me face and he said to me then,
"Are you the one man they call Michael Flynn?"

He challenged me out to the yard was outside.
He challenged me out to the yard for a fight.
The first clatter I hit him I put him in gore,

"If I hit you another, my arm'll tell
That I'll send your old body and bones down to hell."

Rol-de-fol-lo, Oh-rol-da-fee,
It's along way from Bangor to Donaghadee.[30]

"God here or god there," says I, "I'll god ya now." And he started laughing at me, cause if ya struck him, definitely, like, he's the man'd be able to kill ya back. And then he'd get the best of ya at law.

The likes of him has been in the world since the world was made, and the world has never been rid of them yet. It seems that the hard ones has their ways of getting all they might want; fair or foul, they wouldn't be bothered. And there can be no one to stop 'em. Just the same as, today now, the farmers, they'll try to get rid of them crows. They'll come along and put out that carbine stuff, for making shots, to keep the crows away. Well, the funny thing: they canna do away with the crows. I think some things in the world must always stay the same though there's other things changes. And the differs'll be here forever, and was meant to be.

I know a man one time down outside French Park and he had an orchard of apples and he used to sell his apples to all the places around. But the birds was playing hokey-pokey with his apples, but not too bad now. Begad, he paid another man to cover the whole orchard in with netty-wire, 'twas gone for three miles. He covered all of it, and every bird that was taken in it was taken out of it. Well, as big a loss as he was at before, he was at seven times as big a one the next year with the insects of the ground. The worms, snails, and insects came up and moved all his apples, 'cause the birds wasn't taking them away. So he had to take the nets off again and let the birds back. That's the truth. Funny thing, when you do it to a little creature like that, you know, it's not wise.

Just the same as we're chasing the foxes, say, or chasing the hare. Now, they have got a father and mother the same as us, and the mother reared them just the same as our mother reared us, like. She looked for a bit for them, and she robbed and she stole. She did everything for their help, for the family. It's the same ways with the little animals is going. Their little heart goes crossways when you chase them you know, when you follow them and do that to them. It's not right, you know. Just the same as the time the Black and Tans was over here. They'd kill you for nothing, just if they didn't like ya. Now, still, you didn't like to die, nor nobody belonging to you liked to see ya going.

So I left Ireland again then and I went to England, meself and the wife and the family. I thought I'd find a happier life over there, and lots of our people was taking the boat, and still is today. That time I wasn't terrible fond of drink, and I was great at work and get plenty of money. But after I gone over in Birmingham it was hard to get a place. So meself and the wife and the kids, and me sister and the husband and one kid, we gets the one room together for the night. Well, begad, we started to go out to the pub, the two of us, no women. We started to drink 'til we drank our money and says I, "Here's now for to take the pledge, and we'll start the right way now." (Funny thing to tell, maybe you wouldn't understand much about it, to take a pledge. Well, I was stopping drinking.)

Off with us up the street. "Now," I said, "we have but a pound apiece, 'cause the black-and-tan was about three bob a pint, and a pound apiece is no good. There's a church above, we'll go to the rosary." So we did, and there was a priest's house there.

Says the brother-in-law, "We'll find out is there many priests living here, and we'll get a couple of pound around from each of them." So, up to the priests' house and we meets a boy at the door.

"Who's living here?" we says.

"Aw," he says, "there's Father So-and-so, and Father So-and-so, Father So-and-so, Father So-and-so, and Father O'Donnell."

"Oh," I says, "where does Father O'Donnell come from?"

"Roscommon," says he.

"Right! We want to see Father O'Donnell." (O'Donnell was my brother-in-law's name and he came from the same county, Roscommon.) Out comes Father O'Donnell. Oh, he was a grand man.

"Oh, good day, Father," we says.

"Good day," says he.

"We want to go to confession and we wants to take the pledge, Father."

"Oh, where do ye come from?" says he.

"We are Stokes and O'Donnell from Roscommon."

"Roscommon!"

"That's right, Father," we said.

"Do ye live in a house there?" says the priest.

"Aye, we do," we says. (We didn't, of course.)

"We came over today, Father, and to tell you the truth all the money I had, I lost it," says I. "I lost ten pound. We're after getting a room and we got a job, but we have no money to keep us going over the week." And we had a bit of a note we got from the gaffer, to start the job in the morning, and we showed it to him.

"Ohhh," he said, "where are you living?"

"Now," says I to the brother-in-law, "make sure and tell him that we're living in his district, 'cause if you didn't he'd put us to the other church."

"Well, it's Stoner Lane we're living in, Father," says he.

"Well," he said, "of course I'm the headman here and I'm to help the man that comes here."

"Ahhh, we know that, Father, but we don't like to axe you, maybe ya couldn't do it."

"Ahhh, I will," he said, "and anyways I'm O'Donnell too." He shook hands with the brother-in-law.

('Twas about six o'clock now, and half six the pub opened. We hadn't much time to be talking now.)

"Well, what could I do for ye?" he says.

"Well, Father, we got two rooms but we didn't pay for them, and he's charging us thirty bob apiece for the rooms."

"And why didn't ye get the one room for the two of ye?" says he.

"Ah, no," says I, "there was only single beds in each room, and we have to keep ourself going on grub."

He said, "What can I give ye?"

"Well, it's up to yourself, Father," we says.

"Well, sure, you're good lads and you're getting a job," says the priest. "I'll give ye ten pound 'twixt two of ye."

"Alright," we says, "ah, that's lovely. Now, we wants to take the pledge."

"Right, how long do you want it for?" says Father O'Donnell.

"Six months, that'll be enough," says I.

"Well," he says, "why don't you take it for a week?"

"What're you talking about," says I, "a week! I wouldn't have enough of money saved in a week."

"Well," he said, "you know I do take a drink myself."

Says I, "Do you!"

"I do," he said, "and I do get off it for a week and a fortnight. I thought that ye might do the same thing."

"Ah," says I, "I wouldn't take it at all if I took it for a week."

"Right," he said.

Now this is the gospel truth that I'm telling you: we took the pledge, the two of us together, for six months.

"Now," he said, "let me not catch ye in a pub."

"Ohhh, Father," said I, "we don't drink. All we take is two drinks" ('cause we thought that he'd smell the drink on us). "And a man give us them two drinks down the street, a decent man and an Irishman," I said.

This man was going to be hung, one time. And the judge told him if he could make a song in ten minutes that'd be all lies, he'd let him clear. But it would have to be all in lies, ne'er a word of the truth. But he got his ten minutes and he started:

> *I see Dublin fair city without either porter or ale.*
> *I see Clochan Hill in the bill of a small bantam hen,*
> *And the Mountain of Forth going down in a boat to Athlone,*
> *And a wooden-legged tailor and he driving a nail in the moon,*
> *And a goat making hay and she wielding a leather ding-dong.*
> *I seen a milk cow and her horns eleven foot long.*
> *I seen a buck-flea making hay for the Lord of Kilrone.*
> *Without any coddin' or maddin' or buggin' or tellin' a lie,*
> *Was there ever a man born has seen as much wonders as I?*

And the judge let him go free; he done it. [31]

Well, wait'll ya see. We went along anyway and there I'm looking behind me. And there I seen Father O'Donnell coming down after me. Say I, "The priest is after us." He was going to get us, you know, lifted. "We'll go into a shop," says I, "and we'll buy two pounds of grub apiece. That'll leave us still with six pound."

"Alright," says your man.

We went into a shop anyway and when the priest comes in after us, we buys the grub. "You're great lads," he said. He believed in it now. "I followed ye," says he, "past about four pubs."

"Ohhhhh, Father, listen," says I, "we're the last in the world to tell a lie to a priest." And when he's gone, off with us then to the pub. Well, I'll tell you one thing: we got drunk that day! We have about two pound apiece the next day!

This is the truth now I'm telling ya. You see, I might tell the lies to the priest, tell him something he wouldn't understand, but I'm a person that doesn't tell a lie about a priest, or about a parson or a minister. If I meet a minister or a parson in the street, I'll salute them the same way as I'd salute a priest. Certainly they are clergymen same as any man. Well, now, you must know yourself that one time ago 'twasn't the clothes that made a Catholic or a Protestant of you, 'twas just to go to church, no matter what religion you were. But, one thing, before a man can get to be a priest the seventy-seven generations before him has to be genuine. Now, therefore, if his great-grandfather's son kilt a man, something like that, he wouldn't get to be a priest. And the missioners has to be genuine too. The missioners have as much power as the Almighty God if they want to.

I know a place at Ballinaenglish where a dead girl come into a priest's house one time. This girl, anyway, come into this priest looking for a job. "I have no job, no vacancy for thee," says the priest.

But the other girl that was there working in the priest's house said to him, "Why not take her for slop-girl anyway? Wouldn't she be handy for washing the potatoes and delft and things? After all, she's only a poor girl."

"I'll call her back," says the priest. So he did.

So, she was about three months in it, and she wouldn't be here until she'd be there, and she'd have everything done inside of ten minutes. So one day the missioners came in. (The mission was in the church and the missioners they were all sitting down at the table.) There was this one missioner and he looks at the girl and he said to the priest, "Do you see that girl going out there? Is she long working here?"

"Three months here," said the priest, "and I wasn't going to give her a start. But," he said, "I never in my life had anything as good a worker as her."

"Nor you never will again," said the missioner. "That girl is dead."

"How do you mean," says the priest, "she's dead?"

"I'll question her now," says the missioner, "when she comes in." She was coming in with the dinner now. "Look at that girl's eyes," he says to the priest, "and she will never wink her eye." Dead persons never winks their eyes I heard. (Course, how could they when they're dead, I suppose.) The priest looked at her. No, he couldn't see no winks.

"Any harm if I axe you a question?" said the missioner.

"No, Father," she said.

"Are you dead or alive?" says he.

"I'm dead, Father."

"How long are you dead?" he says.

"I'm dead two years now," she said.

"Well," he said, "is there anything I could do for ya now, that could relieve ya?"

"Well, there is something you could do for me," she said. "A friend of mine sent me out for a pound of sugar," she said, "and I got the sugar, on me word, and I got the worth of the copper of sweets. But I died before I brought the sugar home again, and I owe the price of that pound of sugar, and I canna get to Heaven with it."

So the priest swore to pay for it and the girl got to Heaven. "Well," said the priest, "dead or alive, I'm not starting no more of them girls!"

So, you see, you may sometimes cod the priest but you canna cod the missioner, to save yourself.[32]

Anyways, as I was telling ya, up I goes again the next day to another priest there in Birmingham and I takes the pledge again, for six months again. I started working then, you know, and got twenty-one pound a week. The wife, she was getting ten pound, and my sister minded the kids for her. We were bringing thirty-one pound a week into the house every Friday night. We were putting over twenty-two pound a week in the post office and plenty of everything, grub and all, and we usen't to be drinking. Maybe me and the wife and the brother-in-law'd go out one night, myself and the sister'd go another night, but just only drinking lemonade or something.

We went up then and paid the ten pound back to Father O'Donnell and tell him everything we done with it. "Father," I said, "everything we told you was all lies. He is O'Donnell and he comes from Roscommon, but that's the only truth we told ya. The next time ever I come to tell ya a fairy tale, don't believe it," I said.

I stood in England for about three years then, without coming back, kleaping our money and thinking on what would come the next.

There was one time, in the County Roscommon, a very bad parish for to make a collection. Ara, as much as they put into it was a penny or tuppence. Well, the priest, Father Kane, he was tired 'til he was tired preaching, but a church had to be building and that's that. "Ara, nice fellas have we got," he says, "where am I going to get the price of it? I have nothing myself!"

And there was another priest there, Father Fleming was his name. "What are we going to do with this church?" said Father Kane to Father Fleming. "I don't know what to do, but Americay is as good a country as any."

"'Tis," says Father Fleming, "but what are ya talking about Americay for?"

"Oh," said Father Kane, "what about the two of us going to it and making a collection?"

"Begod, I don't mind, but sure we won't get going for nothing," says Father Fleming. So the two of them heads for the road and from that to America.

They went to America and told a few priests around there how they were situated and all. "Fair enough, Fathers," says the Yanks, "we'll do our best for ye."

"At the meantime," says Father Kane, "we won't give up. We'll go around streets and houses and all."

And they did. Oh, but they were getting loads of money then, 'cause in America is an awful lot of Irish and Catholics. They were going, going along, and they were well loaded. "Ah," says Father Kane to Father Fleming, "I think since I a-being harder than you, I'll carry the notes, and you carry the silver." Father Kane was a great boxer, a champ of a boxer.

"Alright," says Father Fleming.

But they were going along and they meets this fella coming that they didn't like the look of. "Here," says Father Kane, "take back the notes, here's the big money to you, and give me the silver." So he did.

Here comes the gangster anyway, a crook. "Hands up!" says the gangster.

"Oh, begod," says Father Kane, "we're only two priests came from Ireland to make a collection for a church. And we need it very badly."

"Church here or church there," says the fella, "I didn't axe ya where ya come from, nor you won't know where you're going to, so. The money I want!"

Father Kane gave the eye to Father Fleming for to go with the notes. Ah, but it was lovely holding anyway, so Father Fleming get going. "Now, whatever money there is," says Father Kane, "I have it and here it is to ya."

"Right," says your man, "and I wisht I had met a couple of more fellas like ye."

But Father Kane didn't like it. "Now," says Father Kane, "as you did take the money, to know that you're a good man: there's my auld hat, and put an old bullet hole a-through it, to prove that I met a gangster in Americay."

"Right," says your man, and he up and he gets the revolver and puts one bullet hole a-through it.

"Good man," says the priest.

"Ara, now put another one through it," says he, "to let me know I was in a bit of trouble with ya."

"Right," says the gangster. He up with the revolver and he puts another one.

"Go on," says Father Kane, "bore another one. That'll be three, the Father, Son, and the Holy Ghost."

"Right," says your man, and he did.

"Another one," says Father Kane.

"Well, I have no more," he said.

"How do you mean you have no more?" says Father Kane. "Well, take it off, Mate!"

"Ohhh," said the gangster, "what are you doing?"

And Father Kane, he up with the hand and he bet the brains of the gangster and thrown his gun away.

So here comes Father Fleming back. "Are ya alright, Father?" says he.

"Oh, indeed I am," says Father Kane.

"Have you the money?"

"I have," he said. "He used all his bullets on my hat and I used my hands on his face."

So, off goes the two of them, but they collected and collected and back they comes *to Ireland. There was three holes in Father Kane's hat, of course, but still he had the price of one in his pockets.*

He come back home and he thought that everything was going to be alright. But there, the next morning he got up and he looked for his works boy, and the works boy was dead late. And here he seen the boy coming along walking.

"Well, you're welcome back, Father Kane. We missed ya terrible since ya left," says the boy.

"Ohhh, I'm very lucky to be back," says Father Kane. "I was only going to be shot."

"Ah, ya weren't!"

"I was," he said, "look at that hat!"

"Ohhh, dear me, you must have great power," says he. "God was a-praying for ya."

"If I hadn't had the use of me tongue and the use of my hands," said the priest, "there'd be no praying for me. But, begod," he said, "I see you're lame, John. What's wrong with ya?"

"Well," he said, "I'm after coming near about three miles with a stone in me boot, and I hadn't time to take it off."

"Ya hadn't! Well, John," he said, "when you hadn't time, after three miles, to take a stone out of your boot, it's hard to say you'd take a stone out of my horse's hoof if it went into it. I'll give you the sack," said the priest. So he sacked the boy then.[33]

I come back here to Ireland afterward, and I come back changed, you know. I ha' got sorry, then, for telling bad things. I owed a hundred and twenty pound, now, to a friend of mine in Ireland, so I paid him what was his, and the next I come to Cherry Orchard, outside of Dublin here, with the wife and family. We stopped in that big camp, and there was other friends of me own in it, all come from the country to see could they get on. And when I did there was an SOS out for me on the radio, for to come, that me mother was dying. So I did go then, and that's what left me so poor, like, all that we held was gone. I seen my mother and I went down and buried my mother, the Lord ha' mercy on her. We had the funeral there in Roscommon.

One time ago when there was a funeral four women'd get shawls on them, the longest hair you could get, and they'd cry for seven miles after the corpse. There'd be four of those women in every parish, same in your parish and in my parish in Galway. Well, every funeral they'd be sent for. 'Twould be a pound apiece for them. They had to cry from the chapel to the graveyard after every funeral, that might be six times in the one day. Crying, crying, crying, you could hear them for miles crying. Well then, when those woman die they turn into a banshee, do you see. And if a banshee comes down to your place and cries there's somebody belonging to you very ill. They don't come for nothing.

But a banshee, she'll do you no harm if you're not meant to die. A banshee'd run from you. I could come along or you can come along, if you have the nerve, and you can pull that stick there and follow her. She'll run as fast as ever she can, the same as any woman, until she gets into a corner. But she whisht of a corner, when she canna get out of it. And you say to yourself, "I ran you. Well, now, why did you deny me? I'm going to kill you." But you're not going to kill her, she's going to kill you. If she could get through that stone, that corner, she'd run as far or more, but when she canna get no further, she's cornered up, she'll fight you within and you'll be done.

There was a woman in Kilcerran in the County Galway and the banshee came to her shop. She had the biggest shop, and has yet, Mrs. Glynn, 'least Dublin supplies her with all her stuff and she supplies all the County Galway. The banshee came along and when she woken in the morning her husband was dead. "Alright," she said. But in a month after, here the banshee comes again. Well, you know sweeping sticken, for sweeping chimbleys? Mrs. Glynn was selling them. She pulls one of them and they fought for two hours in the streets of Kilcerran, the banshee and the woman. "If you took my husband," the woman said, "you're not going to take my son. I've only got one! Or you won't take me!" she said. Murder! 'Til cocks crew in the morning! And the banshee didn't take her son, because she fought again her, and she broke the charm. Aye, thanks be to God, whatever I done, whoever I hurt, I never hurt them, the banshee.[34]

> When I was but a youngster bold I thought I'd like to roam,
> Like many another foolish lad I had no thought for home.
> The kind old friends around there, they thought so much of me,
> Sure, I left my dear old homestead and I went away to sea.
>
> At length I started o'er the sea, to lands far, far away,
> And toiled beneath the burning sun for many a dreary day.
> And as I gained the wish for home, the thoughts ran in my ear,
> The last kind words I heard from home was from my mother dear.
>
> I landed, alas, too late, my parents they were dead.
> My friends they had no charm for me, then, all my joys were fled.
> I longed to see the old ones, from whom I went away.
> Now often in my dreams I hear my dear old mother say:
>
> Oh good-by, God bless you, darling son, wherever you may roam.
> Let no false pride make you forget your loving ones at home.
> Good-by, God bless you, darling son, so sadly did she cry,
> While I have life I'll not forget my mother's last good-by.[35]

After me mother's funeral anyways I comes back up here to Dublin, and I'm here since. I give up the trade when I come to Dublin, but me younger brother, he's still around Castlerea, in the same place. And me cousin, Pat Stokes, he's a first-class tradesman today. It came to the time that he'd lose me and find me in trade, as he's that good. He's a man over six foot, fine man, and has everything that a man ever owned in value: new caravans and everything. And he learned without a father. When my father died he missed him more, cried more after him, than I did. Thought more about him. Still, today he's the richest that's ever carried my name and the best tradesman of my name in the regards of making big cans. But not in small ones. He was a faster tradesman making the big ones, but you know them little churns now? He could never make them.

I found the County Dublin here as good a county as any. I suppose it's up to yourself, no matter where you go. There's just the people that you needs and you like that keep you in it. And there's a man from every county in Ireland in Dublin today. Well, if one man didn't make nice company, you can always go along and find the other man 'til you find the right one. You might have got a-hold of the wrong one you see, you wouldn't know, like. There's a man from every county down in the Sites now. There's Connaught men and Leinster men, and Ulster and Munster.

There's a lots of changes in Travelers in different counties. For one start, there's Travelers now and one Traveler meets another on the street and they don't talk to one another. Fancies theirself that they're better than the others, you know. Just the same as you now: somebody'd meet you in the street and pass you by and wouldn't talk to you, and you'd meet some other boy'd be standing there and love to talk to you. It's the same way with Travelers.

And cant is a peculiar sort of a thing now. Therefore the Connaught people has different cant than the Leinster people now for one start. Our cant is only a dry cant, you know. Ours is, so-called, badly broken language. The right cant, you'll get it in a cant book, but then the cant you learn in the cant book, it'll be no good to us. Some people calls meat *carnish*, but we call it *fee*. And do you know what *weed* is? *Weed* is tea, and *animo* is milk. Well, sure, I'm not learning you at all. I'd call a horse a *corry*, now; I'd call a hare a *garrier*, that's the proper name for a hare. Isn't that funny? I'd call a dog a *comeragh*. I'd call a guard a *shade*, and I'd call a car a *lorc*. I'd call a man a *gloc*, and I'd call a woman a *buer*. I'd call a fire a *cherry*. I'd call a fag a *steamer*, and I'd call a bag a *lamper*. I'd call my money *gared*.

Now if you were a bad man and I didn't like you I'd say, "He's a *gammy gloc*," that you were no good. But a decent man is a *burra gloc*, that means you're good. A field is a *sark*, a house, a *cena*. A barrack, a *sharrack*. A settled person, you could call them a country *sham*, a *feen*, or a *gloc*. What's *lush mers*? It's steal, you should well know it because I'm always at it. And what would you call the canting talk? *Minkers' torry!*

Me father, he couldn't bear ya to speak about it. If you came now to our place and me father was making cans with that little *gurrup* and I said, "Ohhh, some big *gloc* is coming, Daddy," or something like that, he'd get stiff and upright.

He'd say, "Ah, whisht!" He wouldn't like ya to go talking about it. If ya spoke in a pub, in a shop, to him, he'd walk out of it. 'Cause he'd always tell ya, "Two knows that game." It was our own talk, like, and he wanted to keep it so.

The childer now, up here in the Sites, they'd be up to seven years of age before some of them'd know it. But not me own. I've a little girl there, Kathleen, is four, she knows it. And my little Bridget there, the little *swalleen*, she knows it right enough.

I was one day here and there was a guard coming down. I said to a couple of sisters of mine, "*Lackeen, laubra*, the *comeraghs*." That was, "Woman, go hide the dogs." So the guard said, "Ah, don't *subli*, I *soona* them." He said back to me in cant, "Don't, I see them."

When that guard'd come here he'd bring a dogeen with him, and we'd hide the dogs that we had not paid for. When all the dogs'd hear his little dogeen barking they'd all bark and run out. And he'd take all their names, of every dog. Them dogs all talked their same language too.

Do you remember what old Martin MacDonagh did once, when the guard come along the road? All them MacDonaghs were all stopping in Drogheda, and the old Martin MacDonagh used to live there for a farmer. So they seed a policeman coming up through it and they all hide the dogs in the tents, but they left Martin's two dogs out. So when the guard come up and he axed who owned those two dogs Martin said, "I do."

So the guard axed him, "Is there any more dogs here?"

"Aye," Martin said, "there's a couple here." He puts his two fingers in his mouth and all the dogs come out of the tents right 'round him, you know. He looks and then he counts the dogs. "How many is there now, Sergeant?" says he.

"Seven," said the guard.

"There's two more missing now," Martin said, and he goes up to the father's tent and goes in and loosens the two dogs is tied there. "That's them all now, Sergeant," he said. So the policeman he start laughing and walked off and never summonsed any of them.

There was Paddy the Scotchman and Paddy the Englishman and Paddy the Irishman one time, three mates going along together on the open road, and they wanted a place to sleep the night.

They looked and they seen this old mansion up on the hill, so they said, "We'll go up there."

So Paddy the Scotchman said, "I'll go up to bed first, and yous'll take the first watch. When I get out I'll take the next watch and yous can go up to bed."

"Fair enough," they says.

So up the Scotchman goes, finds the bed in the house, and he sits down and takes off his two shoes. And along comes a ghost, up to him. "It's no one here but me and you," says the ghost, and Paddy Scotchman flies out the door and down the hill.

So, Paddy Englishman said, "It's my turn. I'll go up and sleep now."

He goes up, finds the bed, and he takes off his two shoes, and the ghost comes in. "There's no one here but me and you," says the ghost. And Paddy Englishman flies out, down the stairs, and back downhill, he's that nervous of it.

So Paddy Irishman says, "Now, I'll go up."

He went up and he come to the bed, sit down, and he took off one of his shoes and left one on, and he sit there. The ghost comes along and he says, "There's no one here but me and you."

"Ah," said Paddy Irishman, "there'll be no one here in a minute, you effer, when I get me other shoe put on."[36]

But them dogs is for your sport, and the likes of our people'll always keep the dogs, least, when they can, they does. Up here in the Sites now you'll see as many dogs as you'd see down in the country 'round the camps. Just the same as the farmer keeps his dogs: for your sport and for protection, like, to let you know is anyone coming. And you can enjoy your own dogs more than when you go to the racecourse, like the big coursing hounds. Say, you have two hounds and maybe you're not stopped with me but you're stopped ten mile from me. We meet in a town and I'd say to you, "Do you chase the hares?"

And you'd say, "Well, begod, I do."

"Well, have you any dogs?"

"Well, begod, I have the two best hounds that ever ran in the County Dublin," you'd say.

And I'd say, "I have the two as good as ones that ever ran in the County Meath."

And you'd say, "What about us meeting on Sunday and we'll have a bit of a hunt?"

Well, now, that might be some day through the week, and I'd be telling a few lads that you were coming on Sunday, and, of course, you'd be telling a few lads. So all the lads'd gather up all the hounds and come. Now you were mad to see your dog winning and that was it. Although that you had no bet down on it, but still you'd love to have the title come back. Well, that's how it was.

What I used to do with me dogs when I had two, I'd feed them with roasted spuds and buttermilk and a little grain of oatmeal a-through it. It'd give your dog good wind, then, you know. You'd feel very much ashamed if people was praising your dog and maybe you'd give your dog a soft meal that morning and she didn't run well. She might be the best dog in the field, but she was no good, that time. Well, we wouldn't feed our dogs in the morning. No feeding at all, and that way they were hunted. We'd feed them well that night.

Of course, there's better hares in one county than there is in another, you understand that. There's the County Cavan now, for one start: a good terrier'd catch a hare there because the grass is high, the meadows is plenty of grass, which makes your hare soft. Say, in the County Dublin here now, where the good farms of land is and the grass is bare, the hare is good. He has a harder time of it and he's ran oftener. He has the good land to run and he has the hard grass, the food, to eat. Well, it's just the same as a man getting soft feeding: he's just good to look at but he's no good to work.

Well, your man brings his dogs from the County Cavan and he'll be all the way bumbling and bragging what he is, "I've the best dog in the County Cavan. She'll kill every hare she meets." For he's not thinking about coming to the plains of Dublin where there's no grass at all, where you rise a hare in the pure clay. He says, "Well, I think there's no difference in that hare than the ones I'm chasing." Well, there is, because in the County Cavan the grass is about four feet high in the middle of summer. The auld Cavan hare is soft, he's too happy and he's too fat. But the hare that's in the bare ground, he's only just getting enough to keep him going, well, he's bred for it. Well, your dog is going to make a cod out of that Cavan hound.

'Tis a great thing to go arguing about in a pub, with two men with hounds. I love to hear it, you know, about which county is the best. But definite, there is great hares in the County Dublin. But let you get that hare in the bare ground, let him be chased and chased and chased, and when he beats the dog he'll still come back to the same ground where he eats his grass before. The good hare, like, sort of fancies himself, that he's there for sport. There is differs, of course, in hares as there is in men.

It's like this: what you are you are, and you canna deny it. I'd go into a pub and I'd meet a farmer or somebody and I'd have an argument with him. And he'd say to me, "Well, you bloody Tinker, you bloody Gypsy!" or something like that. But, after all I'd dare with that man, still he was right, wasn't he?

There was a market one time in Dublin and this young fella came in to it from the country, and he was very, very poor. He had an ass and a car and a creel of turf to sell in it. So this smart guy as owned a shop there (he thought he was smart) walks over as far as the young fella and he said, "What're ya charging for the turf?"

And says the young fella back to him, "Twenty-five bob for the whole lot."

"Right," says the shopkeeper. So he pays him twenty-five bob and he takes the turf, the donkey, harness, and car. "You said, 'the whole lot,'" says he. And the young fella started crying.

Now there was two men witness that the young fella said, "Twenty-five bob for the lot," so there was nothing he could do. The guards came and took down the statement.

"We can do nothing for you," said the guards. That time there wasn't much law in the country, and the young fella started saying that he'd be kilt when he got home, and 'twas the only thing they were living on was the donkey and car.

So, who's coming, walking along the street, nice and easy, eating an apple for himself, but Dan O'Connell. "Aye," he said, "what're you crying for young fella? You're a bit too big to be crying."

"Ah, well, Sir," says the boy, "I sold a creel of turf to a man and I said, 'twenty-five bob for the whole lot,' and he takes me ass, harness, and car and turf for twenty-five bob. And the guards couldn't do anything about it because there was two more men there when I said it."

"Did you say it?" says Dan O'Connell.

"I did," says the young fella.

"Well, be a man to stand to it," says Dan. "When you said it you must stand to it. But don't worry," he says, "give me half an hour."

So Dan goes off down the street and who did he meet but this fella with bad boots on. The tops of the boots was all gone the way you could see his two feet within. And wasn't the top of his right toe gone as well, cut away.

"What happened to your toe?" says Dan.

"Well," said the fella, "my toe got cut in Mayo."

"And what did you do with it?"

"I buried it in Belmullet."

"Oh, my goodness," says Dan, "could I not buy you a pair of boots for that?" So he buys him the new boots.

"Oh, thank you very much, Sir," says the fella.

"Well," says Dan, "now will you come with me for a bit of a walk?"

"I will," says the man. He took Dan to be a fool.

So down they goes to the shop, what the smart guy ownded.

"Oh, good day," says Dan to the shopkeeper.

"Good day," he said, "what can I do for ya?"

"Would you be able to give us an ounce of tobacco, Sir?" says Dan.

"Oh, an ounce ain't nothing," he said, "I'd give you yards of it."

"Well, would you?" says Dan.

"I would," he said.

"Well, I bet you wouldn't," says Dan.

"I bet you I would," says the shopkeeper.

"That's a nice donkey and car you have outside," says Dan.

"'Tis," says your man.

"Well, I'll bet you thirty pounds again that donkey and car and ten pound that you won't have as much tabaccy as'd go from this man's right toe to his left ear."

"Oh ho!" says the shopkeeper. "You are stupid, you fool!"

"I bet you haven't," says Dan.

"There's a bet," says your man.

"Right," says Dan. "We'll bring a policeman on the job."

"Right," says your man. And he went to the door and called the policeman. "A bit of an argument here," he says, "this man says he has thirty pound betted again that ass and car and ten pound with me that I haven't as much tobacco as'd go from this fella's right toe to the top of his left ear."

"Stupid," says the policeman. And the smart guy takes out a tin of tabaccy.

"Well, now," says Dan, "this man's right toe is buried in Belmullet, that's in the County Mayo, and we're here in Dublin. Have you as much that'd go from here to there?"

"Ara, not at all," says your man.

The poor fella took off his shoe and there was no toe. "Yes," he said, "it is in Belmullet."

"Well, give me ten pound and me donkey and car," says Dan.

"Give it to him," says the policeman."

So back goes Dan to the young fella and he said, "Here's your donkey and car and here're ten pound for the time you lost. Go home now," says he, "and have your tea."

Well, Dan O'Connell was a very smart man and he was the best natured man in the country. And there was only one man that ever tricked Dan O'Connell, and that was a Dublin man. So, therefore, I often heard it said that a Dublin man is smarter than the smartest man going.

Well, Dan was a great man, but none of the big shots liked 'im, and they put it out that there was so much for any man could trick or kill Dan. You couldn't shoot him but had to get him in a trick or in an accident, you know. And if you did kill him you got the money.

Now, there's a hotel in Dublin here called the Tinkers' Hotel. Did you ever hear tell of it? Well, there is, and it was Dan O'Connell that done it, it didn't used to be called by that name.

One time Dan was walking along the street and he went in to this hotel. When he walked in the door this man, the clerk I suppose, was there. "Oh, good day, Sir," he said.

"Good day," says Dan.

"You know, Dan," he said, "I'm after getting two lovely hats today, and I'll give one to you and one to me."

"Oh, thank you," says Dan.

"Try it on you, Dan," he said, "to see how does it suit." And he give him the hat.

"Alright," says Dan, "but let me try it on you first." So he puts the hat on your man's head, tries it on him, and he stuck it on top to fit it down and wasn't there a *curra*, a screwdriver, in it that went down in through your man's head. Well, Dan kilt him, the same as he would be kilt.

So, when he did, he went up the stairs in the hotel to have his tea with about fifteen other men that was there. They axed him to come to tea. There was a serving woman in this hotel and she could sing Irish, talk Irish, and she had the seven languages. And didn't those men come along and they tells her to put poison in Dan's cup, do you see. So, fair enough, Dan don't know it.

So, when this woman was coming up with the tea she was to give the cups around, like that, but the cup that had the poison a-brew in it was in a certain place, for to give to Dan. So as she was coming up the stairs she started singing a song in Irish: "There's as much in your cup that'd poison a hundred! Dan, there's as much in your cup that'd poison a hundred!"

And of course Dan heard it, so he started humming to himself. He sung it back in his own language: "O.K. O.K."

So anyway, she give out the cups and then Dan, he ups and he looks out the window and he sees all those lovely little kids playing in the street. "Oh, my goodness," he said to all these men, "look out at all those grand kids playing." And he filled up his hat with silver, all half-crowns and two-shilling pieces, and he throws it out the window. "Come on," he said, "we'll have a look."

When he got the men looking at the kids running for the change, he put back his hand, behind his back and the changed the cups.

The crooks, they weren't interested in the kids at all. They comes back and sit down and drink the tea, and this one drinks the poisony cup. When he had it well drank, it wouldn't work for about a minute. "Now," says Dan, "you're a goner. 'Twas my cup of tea you drank." So when he said that, out Dan goes and he left them there.

He goes away and he comes back then as a common man, that he couldn't be known, put on all different clothes. "I'll do one thing," he said, "I'll get the boss of this hotel." In he comes and he axed to see the headman and the headman come out. "I'm going to have a party here of gentry," Dan said, "and I'm buying this hotel for one week. One week I'll own it, and I can do anything I like with it. But I'll not break one thing in it, nor do any damage on it, but that I am responsible," he said, "to pay for everything."

"Oh, fair enough," says the headman. "That's good enough."

Well, Dan got the hotel, and what did he do? He didn't leave a Tinker in the County Dublin, or in any county. Everywhere he could get one he axed them all to come to the hotel, the worst he could get: bags, baggages, toolboxes, and budgets and stakes and tin and everything come with 'em. "In here, ye are welcome," Dan said.

"Oh, no, no, no, no!" says the auld manager. "You can't take them Tinkers in here!"

But Dan says, "I bought it for the week, so I can do what I like with it."

So, anyway, the Tinkers started hammering, hammering, hammering all over the place. But Dan anyway, he was putting them up to everything, giving them the worst of drink, whiskey, and everything that'd make them worser. So they was dunking one another in the drink and was tearing the place down.

"Now," says Dan to the manager, "I'm putting it in the paper that the Tinkers ownded the hotel for a week." And he did. The manager like to died and it was wrote over his door, "Tinkers' Hotel."

But Dan comes along then, anyway, and who did he meet in the street but the Lord Mayor of Dublin, was a woman that time. Now, everyone that'd meet her they ought to salute her, but Dan passed her by a few times.

"Hi," she said, "you! You never saluted me anytime you passed me by. Do you not know," she said, "that I'm the Lord Mayor of Dublin?"

"Oh, no," he said, "do you not know that I'm the Full Stallion of England?"

So he went along and there was a skin of an orange in the street. Sure, didn't Dan walk on it and slip and fell on his backside!

"Oh, ho," she said, "that's one thing, the streets of Dublin is too smart for ya!"

"As smart as they are," he said, "I made them kiss me arse!"[37]

I ha' stayed in Dublin, good times and bad. When I come up here to Ballyfermot from Cherry Orchard, I come up and made my camp beside the Sites. I was hoping I could get a place in the Sites. I made this timber hut here and there's seven of us in it, the wife and five childer. This place, as bad as it is now, if you were left in it, it's a home isn't it, like?

The rats they're in thousands here. They hate this time of year; there's a lot of wet ground. And it's just the same as everything else, when they get hungry they come up for food. Rats always draws to where there's babies sucking bottles or anything like that. The young ones is all this time of year now, and they love the old cars. They always hide in the old wrecks. I wouldn't like to get one running up my toe.

There was a rat one time, now this is the truth, and he come into this house. And when he come in, just the same as a baby, he took a woman's breast. To get rid of the rat they couldn't do anything. The woman went to England and the rat followed her to the boat, got on the boat, and followed her to England. Well, of course, it was a serpent you know. This was two years going on now, and the woman's husband, he made a cartridge and filed up a two-shilling piece and put it into it. And he blew the rat off the woman with that, and that kilt him. Wasn't she a great woman to stick it out now? I often heard it said that you can listen to thunder but you canna see it, you know.[38] Well, I do feel very nervous at night in the auld place here, 'specially if I had a few drinks taken before.

I'd like to be sleeping 'fore twelve o'clock every night, 'cause after all, it's at twelve o'clock the ghosteses appear, like, they show theirself. But if I was sleep before twelve o'clock I was happy. I'd be looking at the clock and I said, "I'll be sleeping before it sticks twelve."

Well, there was one night here and these lads started coming in and out, in and out, chatting us 'til it was about one o'clock. And I says, "That's good enough, but I want to go to bed."

But the wife said, "Musha, don't go at all. Time enough going 'til morning."

Well, you see, the wife'll stay up 'til four o'clock in the morning and she'll sleep 'til the cows'll be coming home the next day, until I throw her out of it.

"Well," says I, "listen! 'Tis alright talking, but remember: this is an awful hour of the night to be staying up."

Well, around half past one the people was a-going. "Ah," she said, "why don't you wait for another while. *Ara*, Patrick," she said, "put down another drop of water and make it another sup of tea."

"*Cuttayer zee, Sraina*," says I.

"*Ara*," they said, "we don't want to wait for no tea, Missus, tonight."

"*Ara*," musha, you're grand company," she said. "Wait another while yet."

Well, now, from twelve o'clock 'til four the ghostes is out, you know, anything and anyone. She give them the tea and they drank it. I said, "Why don't you stay until morning now?"

"*Ara*, go on home now," she said to them, "sure, it's time for everybody to be in bed."

I had enough now. I said, "There's going to be trouble in the house tonight!"

But in I goes to bed anyway, and in I stayed for a while. She went to bed and the childer was in bed. Everything was very silent, it was drop a match on the floor you'd hear it. "Oh," says I, "I don't like that at all. Well," I said, "as true as I'm going to bed tonight, if I canna sleep, you won't sleep." And as I was saying my prayers I looked and she was snoring.

Now, I was ashamed to give in to her that I was afraid of a ghost. Says I, "I'm finished." The sweat, sure, that poured off me, and it poured off until it run out in kettles! I looked out of the window there and I thought I could see a face looking in every minute. "There it is," I said, "and, sure, it's snowing again. Well," says I, "what am I going to do? Ah, here's for it." I gets out of bed and I runs the clothes off the *lackeen's* arse and I give her two decent slaps on it. Oh-a, musha, sure she cried and she cried. "Now, good girleen," says I, and I goes back in the bed again. "Now," says I, "there'll be two waked in a minute."

Says I, over to the wife, "Get up, the child is crying and you have the good of a night!" She didn't waken. Says I, "Get up, the child is waking me."

Ahhh, up she gets and she did go over to the child. "Oh," she said, "I won't sleep a wink tonight."

"Musha," I said, "thank God."

"Oh," she says, "I'm dying for a sleep, Patrick."

"Oh," I said, "bad luck to you! You didn't think that a while ago when you were keeping the people to make tea." But in me own mind I says, "An' you're awake with me I'll think nothing of them ghosts no more."

'Twas early, early in the month of May,
When the green grass it was growing,
When 'twas young John Brown from the north country town
Came to court young Barbry Allen.

He sent his servants one by one,
Oh, to see if she was coming,
Saying, "My master, he wants one word from you,
If your name it is Barbry Allen."

"One word from me he never shall hear,
It's he or no man breathing."
Saying, "The better of me he never would be
If I heard his death bell ringing."

"Come round, come round to my bedroom
And it's there you'll find me hanging.
It's a silvery brooch and a gold locket chain
I bestow to you, Barbry Allen."

The very first town as I passed through,
Sure, I seen his funeral coming.
"Oh, leave down, leave down, that wearisome corpse
'Til I gaze one while upon him."

The more she gazed, the more she cried,
'Til all her friends, they gathered 'round her,
"Oh, to see this young man in such a state,
I'm ashamed of you, Barbry Allen."

As he was buried one side of the church,
And she was buried the other,
Oh, it was out of her breast they grew a red rose.
And it's out of his breast grew a briar.

Oh, those two trees grew so tall,
'Til they could grow no higher,
'Til they twisted into a true lovers' knot,
For all you men to admire. [39]

I do get a bit nervous of those things is unnatural, but the wife, she canna understand.

It'd be about twelve months ago, meself and the wife were going to the High

Mass over at Inniscomet and coming home again didn't we have a long road to go. It was night and we'd no ways but to walk. But, begad, I've a sister a widow woman and she has a great pony and cart and didn't me sister give us a lift.

Well, we were just coming to this wood, about twelve o'clock in the night, and whatever I said to my sister, I said something to her. It was nothing to insult her but, says she, "Get down out of the car." She puts me down, me sister!

"Sure, alright," says I.

"Well," says the wife here, "if he gets down I'll get down." So she did.

Now we'd have about fourteen miles to walk it from there, and it was about five mile of road closed on each side, where you couldn't see your hand in the day. It's outside Roscommon and they call it Black's Wood, and I was in an awful state with it. We had that kid and the wife had a lot of groceries. Down gets the two of us and me sister never pullt the reins 'til she landed home, never stood but she left us in this dead wood and enchanted wood.

"I'll carry the child," says the wife, "and you got the groceries." So we did. And I starts to tell her the story of what happened to me father, going along. Me father seen a ghost in this wood.

Now there was no house at all for six mile but one, but I knew that house, where I used to go to school with the boy. Says I, "When I get as far as this house this boy'll drive me home." It's be about quarter past one and we come to the boy's house. So, begad, I went up a bit of an avenue and I knocks at the door and the woman, she come out. Says I, "Is John in?"

"Oh, is that you Patrick?" she said. "What's wrong?"

So I tells her.

"Well," she says, "he's gone to the carnival and he won't be back 'til four o'clock in the morning." She axed me why I'd be out so late, but I didn't make her know the whys, but I made an excuse. So, helter-skelter, with the two of us along this road again.

I'd a few drinks taken and I was the man; I wasn't afraid. But now, wasn't the few drinks dying away in it, and I was getting the wind up now. Thanks be to God the wife never got a bit nervous because she didn't realize 'twas an enchanted wood. Every time I'd tell her one of them yarns about all the ghostes along she'd say, "God speed them, and I going home."

She had, you know, a shawl around her and the child was very heavy. And I said then, "Will you give me the child?"

She said, "No, I'll hold the child." But, sure, she couldn't keep step with me 'cause I was going like every step I'd get a half a mile.

Well, the next I hears a horse coming behind me. Now, I'd have a good ten miles there to walk still. And I heard that a ghost horse used to travel through this wood too. Says I, "A horse! This is it! This is it!" says I, and here he was coming along.

But who was it but the brother-in-law! Hadn't I a brother-in-law and wasn't he at the Inniscomet mass? But, lucky enough, didn't he meet company and stay there 'til about one o'clock, and here he was coming home late. He had a big black and white mare, a great mare to go. "Oh," I said, "thanks be to God, it's you!"

"Sit up," he said. We sat up.

Well, you could say that I'd have a nice journey to go, for it was two o'clock in the morning when we got home with the horse, and it'd be a quare hour when we'd get home with the walking. My two feet was as big as a boiler. It was delving rain. I think that's what saved us: it was delving rain the whole time.

Well, now, Sir, I didn't speak to my sister for six months after, over doing it to me. She forgot all about us. I said, "I never will go with you again, the long as you's ever to live." But she stood a bigger danger than me, me sister. If she had to be met on the road with only herself, she was only a woman too, see, I wasn't much help, but she could be torn asunder. We could be kilt in the woods, you see, not with a ghost maybe but with some people in a car or something. As the fella said, 'twas the night of the carnival and there was people come from every country and I was drunk.

There is women, of course, that could take care of theirself as good as any man. And there is women that is stronger than a man in their ways. I often went to a picture and seen women abroad in the foreign carrying childer on their back going working. Well, I've seen women of our people carrying childer on their back and one in their arms and have to walk from house to house. Therefore I says, "The man that runs down his wife is a bad man." I'd say to him, "I ain't giving ya no soot nor no respect for running down your wife." It's the main thing though, if they have no respect for the wife, why should they have it for any other body, to go and letting out their mind? It's the same as one night there I was at the mission, and the missioner started to tell about this man and he was very fond of drink. Every night he'd get drunk, he'd beat the wife to death.

"Well, what am I going to do at all with this man?" she said. "He won't stop the drink and he won't stop fighting."

Begad, she went to the missioners. "Father," she said, "I'm married to a man and he's worse than the Devil. He's drinking, he's fighting, and he clouts me every night he comes home."

"Aw, I'll quieten him," said the missioner. "Is there a butcher in the town?"

"There is," she said.

"Buy a cow's head," says he, "one with two horns. And when you know he's coming, singing and shouting, sit at the gate and put the cow's head over yours. When he says, 'Good night,' you say, 'I'm the Devil.'"

So she did, and there the husband comes this night and he was roaring and shouting what he was going to do when he come home. Here she was sitting at the gate anyway and she had the cow's head a-top of her head, and the two horns.

"Good night," she said.

"Oh, good night," he said.

"I'm the Devil," she said.

"An tothan," he said, "you're welcome. I'm married to your sister."[40]

Well, I'd love to work hard and stop drink if I really could do it. I'd just love to do it. But some side of the world just doesn't know how the other side is living, do you know? Just the same as you see two brothers there, and one hasn't a smoke and the other has thousands, a bit of luck.

Oftentimes I've got up of here and, you know, I didn't care what I'd do. I'd just feel like going down to the river and throw myself into it. I often come along to twenty quid, and I'd know I needed it very badly, need it for some purpose. But I'd go down in that town and I'd spend in a foolish way, with people that wouldn't give me no respect for it. I'd know in the morning that I done wrong, but I wouldn't admit it. I'd go off then and I'd say, "Well, I wisht I was dead and drownded. The kids'd be better if I was gone. They'd have somebody to look after them better, you know."

Then when I'd go on a study again, I'd feel real happy. I'd say, "I'm going to come up now and I will do it." So maybe everything was going on well then, when I'd meet some person and I'd love to have one drink with him and spend me money again. I'd say then, "Well, that wasn't a man in it. That was the Devil." I could not bear looking at that man then. I'd say, "He drew me that 'er bad luck."

This world is not my home, I'm just passing through,
My home is 'way up high, somewhere beyond the blue.
The angels beckon me from Heaven's open door,
And I can't stay at home in this world anymore.

Oh Lord, you know, I have no friend like you.
If Heaven is not my home, then, Lord what will I do?
Tha angels beckon me from Heaven's open door,
And I can't stay at home in the world anymore.

I have a loving mother, way over in Glory Land.
I don't expect to stop until I shake her hand.
She's waiting there for me in Heaven's open door,
And I can't stay at home in the world anymore.

Just over in Glory Land, we'll live eternally,
The saints on every hand, a-shouting victory,
The angels beckon me into Heaven's door,
And I can't stay at home in this world anymore. [41]

About a month ago, Tom McCann, he had about twenty-five sups of stout taken in a pub with himself and his brother and his wife and me sister-in-law, the four of them. So, they were trying to get him home after and he was well drunk. He said, "Do you think I'm drunk?"

"Oh," they said, "yeah."

"Well, here's for it!" says he, and straight he dive into the canal. Old Paddy McCann, the brother, nearly got himself drownded. He throwed himself in after him, shoes, boots, clothes, and all into it. He got wet inside and outside. And

Tom, he swum to the far side of the river and came out. "Now," says he, "am I drunk?"

He wasn't drunk when he come out, for definite.

I have got brothers and cousins that didn't believe in spending money foolish, drinking, or keeping yourself with bad company. If I knew my cousins were coming and seen me here, do you know where I'd go? I'd go under the bed hiding, and I'd tell the kids to say I wasn't there. I'd feel that much ashamed. Down in our country they never seen the likes of us. In our country, where I come from, I seen a cow with a better barn than this, or hens with better. I never was without a pony and car before in my life until now. I'm trying to get as far as a few quid to buy a caravan, when I used to have the price of five or six in me pocket. It came along that I let myself down that low as I feel I'd never like to see one of me own people again. If they came here they'd just say, "Well, what came over ya, or what have ya done to yourself?"

Of course, they say, money is nothing and money is everything. And you can't get nowhere without it. So, life is only how you make it, you know, like. If a man was steady he could be as well off as any other man. There's Travelers here in this place that's very well-off, but they had to work for to try and get that way too. They could be as poor as what I am if they didn't mind their business, you know.

I seen a young fella there now that come back from England. He's one of them new Ford lorries and a new trailer. I suppose his trailer's a few thousand pound if anything and his lorry's another thousand more. And he's only about twenty years of age. And how is it, like, that young fella left out his mind to do that? Well, he done it somehow, so the best of luck to him!

They say life is all the same, rich and poor. You just put it to a farmer, for one start now. He works hard all his life. Well, still he has the money to keep him going, hasn't he? And he has his family fixed up and you can see him going here and there with his family. You'd say, "What a nice car, for one start, and a nice home to go home to." Well, he'd work hard to get that. Well, you would see another man of the same class of people that started off young and was going from pub to pub and drinking all he was getting. Well, still, that man looked a rake and a fool, that was twenty years older, say, than that man that was working harder. And he ended up and nobody liked him, or nobody had nothing for him.

Meself, I've a very bad chance of getting the place in the Sites. It seems that only the rich people have got in, and there's some now only a-dreaming. The corporation man came down this morning and he said to me, "Well, you'll have to get out of here."

I said, "For what?"

He said, "This has to get bulldozed." And here's the bulldozer and a *shubrig* in it waiting just to give the word.

"Begad," said I, "you won't bulldoze this."

"It's not my fault," he said, "there is another higher man than me. I wouldn't do it to you," he said. "And, tell me anyways, how're you let to come in this field at all?"

Said I, "The ganger gave me permission to come in here." We were a-below at another yard when they bulldozed it. The flood came in then, you see, so the ganger he told us to come up here in the dry ground.

"Take them kids," he said, "out of the muck."

So when he hears that, didn't the corporation man go up then and play hell with the ganger over letting us in?

Now, the ganger, he's a very nice man, real small. "The hell with yous to be sure," says the ganger. "What're ya shouting about? Sure, I go down there in the muck and clavver meself, and, after all, if you want to get that bulldozed why didn't you get them people a hut, you have builded in there on the Sites? Didn't you build them for the poor?" he says. "It isn't to the poor you're giving at all, it's to the rich you're giving. And," he says, "if I knew there was a better place I'd have let them into that too. They're Christian," he said, "you can't treat them like an animal!"

> As I walked out one evening, the moon begin to rise.
> I seen the image in yon ditch that took me by surprise,
> His old ears was lobbed down to the ground, aye, flogged all o'er with hair.
> Aye, he'll bark and growl and get damn-well south of Pat from Bolaneer.
>
> Oh, they took me out to sell me onct I did go in foal,
> And a halter they slapped on me head and tied me to a pole.
> The master, aye, who owned me, marched me to Kilkenny fair,
> And sold me to a ragman called Pat from Bolaneer.
>
> Old rags and bones and other stuff was generally all me load.
> When I get tired from working, I lie down on the road.
> Big Pat come out, he jumped about, and he shook the ground with fear,
> "Oh, you'll carry that noble carcass for Pat from Bolaneer."
>
> Oh, but now I'm in sweet Timahoe, I'm all among me friends.
> The old feeding that they give me, it was a cap of skins,
> And they hunted me out on a winter's night to pick the bushes bare,
> And me curse I give, that as I live, to Pat from Bolaneer.
>
> Oh, but now I'm dead with hunger, I suppose they'll sell me skin.
> They won't get nothing for it, they have it bet so thin.
> But when the dog, he will find out and see me bones so bare,
> Aye, he'll bark and growl and damn the soul of Pat from Bolaneer. [42]

But the corporation man said to me, anyways, "This camp is to come down this morning."

"If you take this down," I said, "you'll bulldoze myself and the wife and five kids, 'cause I'm not leaving." But, aye, would you stay in a house and the bulldozer coming too a-near it? I'd get out of it.

Sure, the headwoman, the social worker come along, and she said to me,

"Don't you leave. You'll be fixed up with a place one way or the other." But if I settled down in the Sites, now, there's a lot more that wouldn't like to settle down there, you know, if they could find the ways. They'd rather, like, keep going back over the green grass. That's the way it is, like you go up and yoke an old horse there and rather live in an old caravan and go off on the old green roads. You'd see sport there, anyhow.

Well, now, I'd leave that tomorrow morning, aye, if I got a place. I'd never start going from camp to camp and bush to bush and house to house, and camp then under a canvas cover. It's not no life for no man; it's not much like the life of a dog.

One time ago, of course, 'twas water that used to leave a horse's hoof, now it is fire. You know, you see sparks leaving a horse's hoof, won't you? Well, the last world was drownded and this world's going to be burnt. That's the truth. That's in the prophecy. Well, matter of fact, a cover went on fire on myself in Cherry Orchard about six months ago, and me five kids within, in bed. I had a canvas shed over the fire and a green sheet over my camp. We had the fire down and the smoke goes up through the canvas.

Begad, I was over rambling and the wife here she was after leaving the hospital the same day with the new baby. And this other woman said to her, "Bring the baby over for a chat." The wife she wasn't usually used to go rambling and leave the kids there, but she did, and the tent took on fire. Well, the little eldest one was there anyway and she got all the kids taken out. When I come back there was nothing in it but just the burnt sticks. It was about eight o'clock in the evening.

We had very good friends there then, all the lads that was stopped around me, and they done anything and everything. Again I was there they'd saved everything they could. A man there called MacDonagh he got a bad burning in the hand doing his best to save it. He thought the kids was inside still. It was so dry, you know, and all the wind was getting at it. That social worker came along then and she gave me a new green sheet.

In Sligo a couple of months ago, there, three kids died and the mother died, of Sweeneys in Sligo. That woman she had a young baby too, three months old, and she had the candle lighting all night, probably on top of a box, like that there now. So when the candle wore down probably something took on fire, burning back along the whole tent. She was the first that woke up, the Lord have mercy on her, so she started to save the kids then, and that's how she got so badly burned. Two of the kids is living yet. Oh, God help us. It's very simple, you see, for a place to go on fire, especially in summertime.

So, here I was, sitting down one evening, feeling sorry for meself, and the wife said to me, "Go down and take the pledge, and we won't need them camps no more."

"Aye," I said, "I'll go down to the parish priest, begod, and when I'm right, I'll have a word about the Sites." So in I goes to the French father.

"Didn't you ever take a pledge before?" says he.

"I did," says I.

"Did you hold it?" says he.

"No, I broke them, Father," says I.

"Well, how long do you want it for?"

"I want it for a month," I says.

"Alright," said he, "I'll give it to ya for a month. You won't break this now?"

"Oh," I says, "No, Father, I will not."

"Well, don't," he says, "and you could be very well-off."

Begod, the following week came and I didn't go nowhere. "Awww," says I, "everything is going on grand now. I'll hold the pledge." Well, now, the following week after, I held it that week too. I was going on grand! So I was walking up along and I was very weak and weary and tired. "Now," says I, "down I goes to the nuns about the Sites." In I goes and I axed the headwoman.

"Well," she said, "you won't get in here."

Said I, "What? I won't get in where?"

"You won't get in the Sites," she said, "without a caravan, sure, that's impossible."

"Well," says I, "when you're no good to me, I'll be no good to ye. So," I said, "every man for himself!"

Helter-skelter for the pub I goes, and didn't I get drunk that night!

The following Sunday, "Ah," I said, "here's for it again." I takes the pledge again.

I was five Sundays hammering at it. I went five Sundays and took the pledge and the five Thursdays, hand-running, I broke it. But the huts, the Sites is for the first people coming in from the country, and you have to have a caravan to get in there. They're not for the likes of us.

Last Monday three cousins of mine came up from the County Cavan with antiques. Well, that morning I wasn't able to make the tins: I felt sick, I felt sorry, I felt helpless, that I didn't care if the sky fell, when the car pulled up. I knew those lads when I used to go off to the football match with them, to the pictures with them, to a bowl-alley, to fishing, to hunting with them, everywhere together. So they comes and says to the little girl, "Is your father in?"

And I said, "Who is that?" I was rough and ready and careless.

I came out and he shook hands with me and he said, "How are ya, Patrick? You're looking well." And I knew I was looking bad. Did ya ever get that way? Well, I could invite that man in for tea, now, but I never even axed him, after him coming from the County Cavan! I never axed him about his friends or relations! I knew that he found it very stupid of me.

"Well," he said, "I have a load of antiques here. Show me where Store Street is, could ya?" says he. I know Store Street, now, the same as I know you, but "I never heard tell of it," I said. And I knew that 'twas five pound from those lads for me if I only went with them, you know.

Then they said, "What's that in there?"

"Ahhh," I said, "an auld hut, and if it's fair enough, lads, I'd rather that ye didn't talk about it."

"Well, will you come," they said, "and have a drink?"

"No," I said, "I won't."

I sets down here and I felt real lousy, that I could be having a good caravan, respectable looking and as good as any man, and meet them lads and say, "Come and have tea." Wash and clean and shave myself and say, "The journey's so far for you tonight home, you can stop with me."

I knew how them lads felt, they felt horrible. They were like three gentlemen and you see what I done, that I let meself so low. So, therefore, a man can be worth ten thousand pound today and if he doesn't mind his business, that day twelve months he won't be worth ten ha' pence. There's a ways a man lives and keeps himself, but a man can let himself down too far that he cannot come up. That's the truth.

One time ago there was those two brothers living in a house, Jack and Bill. Of course, Bill was the fool and Jack was the wise man. But it came to the time that Jack got married and the wife didn't like to have Bill there, and she forced Jack to put Bill going. So, Bill didn't like that, as he had to go from house to house, working here and there with people, and he was very poor.

And it came to the time, in a couple of years after, that Jack's wife had a baby. "Begod," says Bill, "I'll go and I'll see the kid." So here comes Bill and he knocked at the door and out comes Jack.

"What do you want, Bill?" he said.

"Well," Bill said, "I came to see the baby."

"Well," Jack said, "you will not. You canna come in."

"Well, after all Jack," he said, "I'm the baby's uncle."

"Ah, that'll do," says Jack, "come in then."

So, when Bill came into the house there was a party and a gambling school, card-playing, of course. So Bill sat down and they started card-playing around the table, the whole crowd, and in a while all the money that Bill had, Jack won it.

"Well, you've all me money won, Jack," Bill said. "What about me suit of clothes?"

"Fair enough," says Jack, "put them down again a price." So he did and Jack won them too.

"Well, I've nothing left now," says Bill, "only me two eyes. I'll bet them."

"Fair enough," says Jack, "put them down." So Bill puts down the two eyes on a bet, and Jack won them, and when he own them he takes the two eyes out of Bill.

Away goes Bill, anyway, out the door, without nothing, poor and dizzy: no money, no clothes, nor no eyes.

So he was going along the road and what was coming but a flock of sheep and a herd, and Bill was walking in the very center of the road.

"Get in, you blind fool!" says the herd. "You're driving the sheep mad." The sheep was going everyways, of course, across the walls and all.

"I am blind," says Bill.

"Oh, I'm very sorry," said the herd, "very sorry about that altogether. I didn't know that. Wait there a minute," he said, "until I have the sheep fixed up, and I'll have a chat with ya. I'll see what I can do for ya."

"Fair enough," says Bill, and he stopped there.

Back comes the herd then and he said, "Me poor man, I'm sorry about that, and you're only a young man!"

"Ah, well," said Bill, "I went to see my brother's child tonight and there was a party card-playing. And my brother won my money and me clothes, and I had nothing else to bet with, only me eyes, and he won them too."

"Your brother took your eyes!" said the herd. "Ahhh, Lord, he must be a mean man. It's a wonder," he said, "you wouldn't go up to the little house a-below at the brink of the bog. The cats have great scenes there," he said, "and great yarn-spinning there. You could hear a lot there, and you could be very lucky."

"I don't know where it is," says Bill.

"Ah, sure, I'll take you," says the herd.

"Very good," says Bill, "I'm very thankful to you."

So the herd brings him down to the old house at the brink of the bog, and he opens the door, and he locks Bill into a press was there. "Now," he said, "don't make one bit of sound when the cats comes here tonight," says he. "They'll have a great yarn and you could be a man in this yarn that'd be very important."

"I hope so," says Bill.

"I'll be down in the morning very early," said the herd, "around seven. I'll see how'd you get on."

"Fair enough," says Bill. "I'll see you in the morning so."

So it comes along and here comes all the cats, and the auld mother cat, of course, she was there. "Ara," she said, "put down the fire, boys, and we'll have a good chat." (One time ago, you know, the cats could talk.) So the other cats made up the fire.

"Wasn't that shocking," says the auld mother cat, "what happened about that man, and his brother winning his clothes, his money, and his eyes? That was a shame!"

"Well," says the other cat, "if that man only knew, there's a little well in the bog, at a rock. If he went down there and get three drops of water, and if he thrown those three drops of water, one after the other, up in his eyes, he'd get two lovely blue eyes."

"Ah, musha, sure, there you are," says another cat. "Look at the lord's daughter where I live. She's not well, and any man that could cure her, her father'd give herself and the ranch, all his place, and all the money.

"I'm the cat out of that house and she's the only daughter, and she used to leave a glass of milk in the window stool. And one morning I jumped in where the window was up, over the glass of milk, and three of my ribs flew into the glass, and now they're three young kittens within her. And if that person only knew it, to go to that little well and get a little bottle of water and go in and see that girl, and order for her a basin of boiling water, and throw three drops of the water into it, the three kittens'd come out, and she'd be cured."

"Ah, good enough," says Bill in his own mind. "That's an idee anyway."

So, now, morning come and, "Rake the fire now," says the auld mother cat, "and we'll call it a night. We'll head for our home." So they did.

And here comes the herd in the morning, "Good morning, Bill," he says.

"Oh, good morning, Sir," he said.

"Well, what's the good news?" says the herd.

"Oh, a very good news it is," says Bill. "Do you know any little well in the bog at a rock?"

"I do, of course," says the herd, 'cause the herd, of course, used to travel everywhere with the sheep.

"Could you take me to it?" says Bill.

"I will, of course," says the herd. So he did, took him to it.

"You go now," says Bill, "and I'll see you later."

"Fair enough," says the herd, and he went off.

So Bill gets the three little drops of water, like that, and throws it up to his face, and he gets two lovely blue eyes. Had his small little bottle in his pocket and he fills it with water, and he heads for the road.

So when he did, he comes along and he sees this big place and he thought about himself. "Oh," he said, "I must go up and cure this girl."

So, as he went up along the avenue and up the lawn to the big place, he seen all those fancy big cars outside, of everybody coming, trying to cure her. So, Bill of course looked like a tramp. He knocked at the door and out comes a man. He said, "What do you want?"

Bill said, "I came to cure the lord's daughter."

"Clear off," said this doctor, "ya tramp. How dare you come around here and specialists and surgeons and all kinds of experts here, yet you'd come along! Get going," he said, "or you'll be shot!"

So then the lord looked out. "Let him in," he said, "If that man canna do any better, he won't do anything worse."

"Well, alright," said the doctor, and he let him in.

So in comes Bill and he comes to the lady's room. "I want every doctor and everybody out of this room," he said, "and I want a basin of boiling water."

"He wants to roast her alive," says the surgeons, "when he gets her all on her own."

"Well," says the lord, "if he is the cause of losing my daughter's life, he'll lose his, so give him the basin of water."

So, in he goes and gets the basin of boiling water and he puts down the three little drops of water out of his bottle. Then he catches a-hold of the girl and he puts her head down over it, and the three kittens jumped into the boiling water and got roasted, of course, alive. They couldn't jump out. Out comes Bill with the basin, like that, out the door, and he says, "There's the cause of your daughter's trouble."

"Oh, my goodness," says the doctors. They didn't like it, you know. The lord started to laugh.

"So, good day," says Bill.

"Oh, you're not going that way!" says the lord. "You'll have to marry my daughter," he said, "and you own all the place you're standing in and all the money, and this building."

"No," says Bill, "a tramp like me wouldn't be good enough for your daughter."

"Well, halt!" says the lord. "Bring him up here."

'Course, Bill was a good-looking man when he'd be dressed, but with bad clothes he wasn't the same man at all. They brings Bill up, dresses him with a new suit, and cleans him up, made him like a gentleman. You wouldn't know Bill when he came down, he was that lovely looking.

So the daughter come out smiling. "Oh," she said, "thank you, Sir, you saved my life." Bill was beautiful looking. The lord give him a big Jag. The daughter sits in one side and Bill sits in behind the wheel and they start to drive down along the avenue.

Well, now, they gets out on the road and who did they meet but Jack. He was driving a few cattle along. Bill beeped, of course, for him to get in on the road. He knew it was Jack that was coming, that Jack'd get a surprise. "Hello, Jack," he said.

"Bill!" he said. "What happened?"

"Ah, times has changed, Jack, since me and you was seen last."

"I see that," he said, "you've eyes! And the car, the Jag! Oh, and the lord's daughter!" (Bill's still with the lord's daughter. Of course, he'd had to do it.) "Well, tell me Bill," he said, "where'd you get the lovely eyes?"

"Well," Bill said, "do you remember the night I left your house, when you won me eyes?"

"Oh, I do Bill," said Jack, "I'm very, very, sorry for it."

"Well," said Bill, "as I was walking along the middle of the road a herd came along and he called me a blind fool, that I was putting the sheep mad. So I told him I was blind. He felt very sorry for me and he brought me to a little house at the brink of the bog, and he locked me into a press. The cats came then," says he, "and told me about the little well in the bog at the rock, to get those three drops of water and throw them up on my face and I'd get two lovely eyes. And to get a little bottle of water and throw three drops of it into a basin of boiling water and I'd cure the lord's daughter, to get her."

"Will you show me where it is?" says Jack to Bill.

"Well, now," says Bill, "it's very hard for me to show you where it is after all that you done to me."

"Ah, well, don't you know, Bill," he said, "that I've two very ugly eyes, they're very red now, and something like yours I'd want."

"Right," says Bill, "come on."

Ah musha, helter-skelter, with the two of them anyway. "That's where it is now," says Bill, "but you'll wait 'til tonight."

"Will you come down in the morning and see me?" says Jack.

"I will," says Bill.

"Ah, musha, away goes Jack that night on the secret, and here comes the cats. "Ara," says the auld mother cat, "fix the fire, boys, and we'll have a chat. Wasn't that comical last night, when we were talking about the two brothers, and that man did go to the bog," she said, "and he threw three drops of water up in his face and he got his two eyes?"

"And he brings the bottle of water to my place," says the other cat, "and he cures the lord's daughter."

"There must ha' been somebody listening," says the auld mother cat.

"No," says the other cats, "'cause we looked around."

"Look around again," says the mother cat. So they did and they looked upside, downside, and they said, "There's nothing now."

"Ara! Look in the press!" says the mother cat. So they looked and there was Jack within it. And didn't they take the two eyes out of him now, as he'd been listening to 'em!

But here comes Bill in the morning. "Good morning, Jack," says he. "What's wrong?"

"Owww, musha," says Jack, "when I get out to you I'll let you know that! I'd two red eyes yesterday, but I've none at all today! What am I going to do at all?"

'Course, poor Bill was harmless and he didn't like to see it happening to the brother. "I'm very sorry for you," says Bill. But the best that Bill could do was to bring Jack back to his house.

He brings him back and Jack's wife said, "Ohhh, what's wrong?"

"Jack," says he, "went where I got the eyes the other night, and the cats took his out altogether."

"Well, he wasn't much good first," she said, "but he's no good at all to me now. So you can keep Jack," she said, "and you can put down the kettle and make the tea and if I don't live happy that you may."[43]

Well, when I come to Dublin I give up the trade, as I said, and none of the lads here does the tins. Anyways, they thought nobody in Dublin had tools, you see. I was crazy about it enough, I shouldn't have spake about the tools, but I said, "I have a whole kit. I have everything and anything." And I'll tell you what I had now, and I had it coming here, a whole half pound of it: a half pound of rosin! A half pound of rosin'll do a man for his lifetime, let him live for a hundred years. But I had about, well, a quarter pound, that'd be fifty years' using. But do you remember the man who was living here, Bill Connors? We start to arguing then, who was the best tinsmith.

"But," he said, "have you got rosin and solder?"

"I have," I said, "I'll show you. I'll show you all the solder that I have here. There's two pound of solder there, and that solder'll do a man for the next thirty years." I gave him some of the solder. You can see there where I cut off summat for the fellas.

And he said to me, "Can I get the rosin?"

Well, in the night he left the whole packet of rosin out here and the little kids didn't know what it was and they stuck it all in the fire. So I was looking today was there any left, but none.

You canna solder without rosin or flux. Flux, now mind ya, is the best; you can solder galvanized now with flux, but you couldn't solder it with rosin. But I'd rather the rosin, your solder runs nicer in the rosin.

Well, I'd love to make them tins for you as you axed me. I'd make one of everything.

You see that can there? That can was really made for when we were in the County Cavan, where we'd gone through the houses. The wife'd have that for getting milk, you get from the farmers. But since ever we came to Dublin the wife never went out for that and the milk comes to the people's door from the dairy. So all our cans they're all gone rusty. So it's just the same as everything else: if that was down in the country that'd be new as a pin because we would look after it. Now, today, even if we do look after it, there's no purpose for it. That's no good for nothing. But that can isn't what we'd call well made now, that was for ourself. But if I had to make them for such as the likes of you, that you might be going around the country, maybe showing some other body, I'd want to show me trade. I'll do my best on them then.

I'll make those tins, and if I make those tins, I'll put them again any tinsmith in Ireland, but he won't best them. But that he might get one out of twenty to make one as good, he won't best it, for taste, style, and appearance.

And I'll tell you one thing now, it's like this: I'd just be delighted if you came here to me every night in the week. You're the only ones that I can chat here, you know. Even if you don't come here now, you know, meself and the wife here canna chat as good as I can chat a friend.

I don't mix or make with them people down there at all. I don't go around there now, because, the matter of fact, there's not one man in this place think that I take a drink. But I do take a few drinks, but never in their company, like. It's just the same as that, if you weren't here now a while ago and any man came to me door now, I wouldn't let them in. 'Cause a sober man is no good to talk to a drunken man. I wouldn't let them in no matter what, if they were drunk. You couldn't blame me, you know. Because I don't know them.

A house is lonely when you're not used to it, you see. It's alright if you have some friends around you, but if you have none it's very lonesome. If you're in a house and you see some of your old folk coming along, you get lonesome again, to see them leaving you. You sort of pack up and go with them. We're always used to plenty of company and meeting strange faces every day. I think we were Traveling since the world was made, from the seven generations back.

It's just the same as when we were staying outside Castlestrange one night and I seen one cat go up one of those hedges. And he said, "Oh, the wary, wary, wary, wary, wary! Go back! Go back! Go home! Go home!" He was, you know, putting the cats home.

Cats could talk one time ago, cats could talk and birds could talk, as I said. And you know yourself that a cat can cry like a baby.

Johnny Cassidy and Old Flynn, the father of Johnny's son-in-law.

Johnny Cassidy

STORYTELLER[1]

I'll tell you the stories and I'll tell you the history now: the stories is in me generation. The stories is in the Cassidy generation, in the seven generations and they was true one time.

I don't be like me father, now, going from house to house, stopping months in this house, months and months in the next one, but I do have the stories yet, or I have some of them. And those stories is worth me remembrance. It was where me life lain.

I was only a year and eight months when me mother died, and me father, he reared five of us, two brothers and three sisters, without a mother. I was the youngest one of them all and he carried me from house to house, carried me in his arms. And that's how I used to be listening to the stories more. You know, I'd have to listen to 'em 'cause I wasn't able to go any farther on me own. We'd go in in the nighttime to the house and he'd tell those stories over the big fire. We used to be sitting down alongside of him, and maybe I'd be sitting down on the hearth between his legs. Every night. And it come so that any of the family could tell the stories—me sisters could tell 'em.

When I was a child they'd be big gentlemen's houses where we was stopping, now, and we'd be lodging in them houses, sleeping in the loft of the barn maybe or the shed, the five of us and me father. Me mother died when I was little and I wouldn't go to bed without me father. When I was growed bigger, meself and me brother'd be working with the farmer of that house, and with the rest of the farmers around as well. We'd be helping at the thrashings for him, and so on like that. And me father'd be going around, now, doing his jobs in all them houses, have his run with the tin.

Well, when we'd be done there, we'd go about fourteen or fifteen mile to the next place, the next big house, and stay there as long more, two or three months maybe. We'd go 'round the coast of Wexford then, and maybe it'd take us twelve months 'til we'd be back at the same place again. That's the way it was in the old time, like, from place to place.

But me father was constantly telling stories, like, every night, from house to house where we'd go. And those neighboring men, from other farms around, they'd come to the house we was lodging in to hear him telling the stories, and they'd tell more of 'em. Well, he'd be learning the stories off of them and they'd be learning 'em off of him. That's the way it was. And he was a great storyteller, oh, different to me altogether.

He learned it from his father, and I learned it from me father. But I forgot the best part of the stories me father had. Just, they're only in history yet. But if I was going, like him now, through the houses again, I'd be telling 'em constantlier. The same as I'm telling 'em for you now, I'd be telling 'em constantlier, and they'd come back in me memories again, all complete, you see. But he was more used to the job, and he followed it up more. In them days, some years ago, that was the whole go: storytelling through the houses. But now it's all over.

So, with me father, we never used to go and Travel, Travel all through the country in all weathers. We hadn't the need of it. 'Twas only for about the last thirty year now, since I got married, that I went that road. I started Traveling mortally then!

The wife's people, they had a house in Wexford town, and they stopped there all the wintertime. But they might go out Traveling, now, in the summer, when they'd go. In the summer they'd go to the houses where the tourists used to stop, and the mother and the uncle'd go in. The mother'd sing and the uncle'd play the box, the accordion. He'd go in and play the box the same as me father was telling the stories, do you see: they were able to introduce theirself through the houses and they were able to get respect. Not like the people's going out now.

The young people's going out now can't get respect. They wouldn't be able to leave that out for theirself, because they wouldn't have the right ways to go through the houses, and they wouldn't have the manners for the country. See, they wasn't reared up in it, and you want to be reared up in that job. You must be learned the manners and the way to show yourself.

When we was childer, if I said a wrong word in a house I wouldn't say one the next time, I'm telling you. Me father, he'd kill you when you'd go out in the loft after. He'd kill you stone dead. You'd think of what you'd be saying the next time. You'd weigh the word good on your mouth the next time afore you'd speak it. You learned 'til you'd think, 'til you wouldn't make no more foolish mistakes. Ah, Lord have mercy on his soul, for e'er what he did give me, he didn't do me any harm. He done it for me good! 'Cause your father won't hit you if you're not going wrong. You'd have to be going wrong before your father'd hit you or your mother either. You might think bad of 'em for the time being, but they're only doing it for your help.

But the young people now, they won't chastise their family, do you see, and that's where the bad point is. They think the childer'll turn again 'em, but they'd rather have 'em tomorrow than the next day. Them childer wouldn't be going to jails and places if they'd chastise 'em, they'd keep 'em out of them places. See, they gets uncivilized.

You have to go according to the way you're reared. If I be owning a dog, there, to hunt, and I send him to hunt up a ditch. Well, that dog he may go wild up be the ditch, onct he's from me side. That dog could have every rabbit in Ireland riz afore I reached to him. He'd go wild, do you see, for the excitement. Well, I'll have to hit that dog with a stick, for to make him come back and hunt alongside of me. Well, that's just the same as with the childer: I must keep 'em under correction, in the way they could hunt alongside of me, and I'll know what they're doing. I'd say to 'em then, "'Tis the way with the world. But I'm not going to leave you to the way with the world. I bethinks of what ya done and I thinks on what maybe could happen." The dog, he'll take his time then and mate along with me, do you see, and it's just the same with a child: they have to get education.

There was a lot of ghost stories on me father, you see, in the old times. One time, this woman, was just a friend of his, got a pair of boots at a house, for a man's soul. You see, the man died and they give all the things away for his soul, his clothes and all, and she got the boots—they were new. Anything you get for a soul you're not supposed to sell it; you can give it away but not sell it. But she sold these boots to me father and he didn't know.

So, they were Sunday boots and he had the boots on him and he was drinking. He got drunk this night but it got too late and he couldn't get home, and he fell asleep in the ditch. When he woke up, he didn't know what time it was, but he looked up and there was a man standing over him in his bare feet.

Me father was only a low size but this man was a big man, about six or seven foot. The father never done nothing. He blessed himself and he got up and walked along for the house where we was lodging. So the big man kept walking with him, and everytime that me father's boots'd creak, the man'd look down at his feet. So he went on to the house, the Lord have mercy on him. I was only a little child then and waiting in the night for me father. I run out to the gate when I heard the gate opening, and I looked then and I seed the man. Me father never looked back but come up to the house, and when he come in he took off the boots and thrown them out the door. So when the next morning come, the boots was still there in the yard but the man was gone.

That dead man followed me father for those boots, and me father knew it was the boots when he seed the bare feet. Those boots were sold, do you see, and the things of the dead should not be sold. But that corpse wouldn't go in a-past the gate, that wasn't his home.

183

Yes, I often heard me father saying, "There's some born to see and more born not to see." And, says me father to me that time, "There must be woeful good stuff in ya. Ya didn't cry."

Well, I come into a shop to get a drink a month ago, in Wexford again, and there was great crowd of the countrymen there, and I didn't have the acquaintance o' none of 'em. But I come up on the floor anyhow and I started this recitation. And when I started, the man of the shop, Mr. Sutton, looked at me. "Is it any harm to axe you," says he, "if you're Willy Cassidy's son?"

"I am, Sir," says I to him.

"I was thinking," says he, "you're Willy Cassidy's son when I heard the recitation. 'Tis thirty years ago now since I heard it, and I never heard it with another man," says he. "But your father read it there a thousand times on the floor, and I know you the very minute you come out with the recitation. But I didn't know ya 'til then."

He shook hands with me. "God be good to your father's soul," says he. "He was the only man for the stories in the lot."

Hearts, Livers, and Lights and All

There was this widow woman one time lived outside of Wexford, and she had this fool of a boy, was her only son. But she fell sick anyhow and she wasn't able to go out. "Ah," says she, "if I had a good son that'd go to Wexford and get me a bit of meat for to make a sup of soup I'd be alright."

"Oh, Mother," says he, "I'll go to Wexford for you. But what sort of meat would you want?"

"Well, a liver," says she, "and a light."

"I'll never remember it, Mother," says he.

"Well, the way you won't forget it," says she, "keep saying 'hearts, livers and lights and all' to yourself and you won't forget it."

Off he started anyhow, in for Wexford. "Hearts-livers-and-lights-and-all. Hearts-livers-and-lights-and-all. Hearts-livers-and-lights-and-all. Hearts-livers-and-lights-and-all," says he.

But it was in the corning season anyhow and the boy was passing this public house when a man come out had been drinking. This man been out all night drawing corn with a horse and car, but begod, didn't his stomach get sick. And he was outside the shop retching up of his stomach. And the big fool looked up in his face, "Hearts-livers-and-lights-and-all. Hearts-livers-and-lights-and-all. Hearts-livers-and-lights-and-all."

"Go away!" says the man. "God to Eternity blast you! Are you praying," says he, "for me heart, liver, and lights to come up?"

"Well, what'll I say?" says the boy.

"Say, 'they're down that they may never come up,'" says the man.

The boy went on. "They're-down-that-they-may-never-come-up. They're-down-that-they-may-never-come-up. They're-down-that-they-may-never-come-up. They're-down-that-they-may-never-come-up." And he gone on to where there was a man sowing an acre of land with potatoes. He looked over the ditch at the man anyhow, saying, "They're-down-that-they-may-never-come-up. They're-down-that-they-may-never-come-up. They're-down-that-they-may-never-come-up."

"If I could get out to you," says the man says he, "I'd put you where you'd never come up!"

"Well, what'll I say?" says the fool.

"Say," says the man, "'they're putting thousands of them in the ground this year and they'll put ten thousand next year with the help of God."

Off the boy went, still talking to himself, "They're-putting-thousands-of-them-in-the-ground-this-year-and-they'll-put-ten-thousand-next-year-with-the-help-of-God. They're-putting-thousands-of-them-in-the-ground-this-year-and-they'll-put-ten-thousand-next-year-with-the-help-of-God." He went until he went to the graveyard, and there was a funeral in it. He looked in over the graveyard wall. Says he, "They're-putting-thousands-of-them-in-the-ground-this-year-and-they'll-put-ten-thousand-next-year-with-the-help-of-God. They're-putting-thousands-of-them-in-the-ground-this-year-and-they'll-put-ten-thousand-next-year-with-the-help-of-God."

"If I was out," says one of the men belonging to the corpse, "I'd put you in the ground!"

"Well, what'll I say?" says the fool. "Say 'The Lord have mercy on their soul,'" says the man.

So the boy goes on, "The-Lord-have-mercy-on-their-soul. The-Lord-have-mercy-on-their-soul. The-Lord-have-mercy-on-their-soul." But he was still running away and he went to where there was a man hanging a dog and a bitch that was after killing a sheep. The boy looks at 'em, "The-Lord-have-mercy-on-their-soul. The-Lord-have-mercy-on-their-soul. The-Lord-have-mercy-on-their-soul."

"Ah, you dirty ignorant bugger!" says the man. "What're you saying, the Lord have mercy on a dog and a bitch!"

"Well, what'll I say?" says the fool.

"Say 'They're a dog and a bitch tied together,'" says he.

So the poor fool began, "A-dog-and-a-bitch-tied-together. A-dog-and-a-bitch-tied-together. A-dog-and-a-bitch-tied-together. A-dog-and-a-bitch-tied-together." But he was still going for Wexford anyway and he met this boy and girl walking out the road. The two of them was linking one another. He looked up in their face anyhow, "A-dog-and-a-bitch-tied-together. A-dog-and-a-bitch-tied-together. A-dog-and-a-bitch-tied-together." The man made a box at him anyhow, to strike him.

"What'll I say?" says the fool to him.

"Ah, say," says he, "'I wish yous the greater joy together.'"

So on goes the fool. All the time saying, "I-wish-you-the-greater-joy-together. I-wish-you-the-greater-joy-together. I-wish-you-the-greater-joy-together." Until he went to where there were a poor man had two bullocks after being sunk in a marble hole. The man got one out and he couldn't get out the other, and the poor man was as far down in the hole as the bullock, trying to pull it up. But the fool looked in at the man, "I-wish-you-the-greater-joy-together. I-wish-you-the-greater-joy-together. I-wish-you-the-greater-joy-together."

"Oh, God," says the man, "if I could get out near you, I'd wish you the greater joy!"

"Well, what'll I say!" says the fool.

"Say 'There's one of them out now and the other'll be out by and by with the help of God.'"

But the boy forgot the 'hearts, livers, and lights and all' and he turned home saying, "There's-one-of-them-out-now-and-the-other'll-be-out-by-and-by-with-the-help-of-God. There's-one-of-them-out-now-and-the-other'll-be-out-by-and-by-with-the-help-of-God." And he was coming back past Friends of the Mountain, another pub, and there was a row after happening there with two men. They fought and one fella put the eye out of another fella with a bottle, and this fella was bleeding to death. And the fool looked up in his face, "One-of-them's-out-now-and-the-other'll-be-out-by-and-by-with-the-help-of-God. One-of-them's-out-now-and-the-other'll-be-out-by-and-by-with-the-help-of-God." The man made a dive at him and had him asleep in a box.

"What'll I say?" says the fool to him.

"Go home," says the man, "and never speak a word while you're alive. Go home," says he.

Home he went. No one could ever get a word out of him until the day he died. So put down the kettle and make the tea and if you live happy I may.[2]

Jack the Giant-Killer

Well, there was a widow woman one time and she had two sons. The eldest was a good lad, but the youngest was a sort of a soft harmless boy, and his name was Jack.

It was in the poor time then and the wages were getting too small. And this eldest boy says, "I'll go, Mother, and I'll try to get higher wages."

"Well, Son," says she, "maybe you wouldn't get any better wherever you go."

"Well, Mother," says he, "I'll try, and every penny I get I'll send it back to you."

So, begod, the first brother goes off in the morning and he went farther than you or I could tell 'til he was passing be this stile, and he met this old man. "Ho, fine young fella," says the old man, "you looks like a fella is wanting work."

"I do, Sir," says he.

"Well, I know where you'll get a job."

"If you do, Sir," says the boy, "I'll work."

"I don't know," says he. "There's several young fellas after going up there, but they couldn't agree on it."

"Well, I can do any work, Sir," says the boy.

"Come on up, so," says the old man, "and I'll show you the house."

He brought the boy up and brought him in to this farmer and the farmer hired him. It was sixteen pound a year and his grub and his bed. And he'd get his sixteen pound when and if he heard the cuckoo, whether he was one, two, or three months in it; that was the bargain.

The next morning the boy got up. "Now," says the farmer, "throw three buckets of slop to the pigs." And the chap throwed the three buckets of slop. "Get down now," says the farmer, "and eat your breakfast."

"Ah, Sir," says the boy, "I never et me breakfast with pigs."

"Well, that's all the breakfast you're going to get here," says he. "So, come in here 'til I show you the work."

He brought the boy into the barn and he showed him this corn and he give him a flail. Says he, "You'll have to have two barrels and a half of that thrashed for me again dinner time."

So the boy started thrashing away, but the poor fella was too hungry as he couldn't work. He got bet. He sat down and started to crying and your man come out. "Well," he says to him, "you haven't that two barrels and a half thrashed for me!"

"Well, Sir," he says, "I'm too weak. I'm not able."

"Are you sorry for hiring with me?" says the farmer.

"I am, Sir," says he.

"Alright," says the farmer, "turn around here." The boy turned and the farmer took a strip of skin from the top of the boy's head to the sole of his foot, and sent him home, bleeding to death.

The boy goes home anyway, never stopped running and bleeding 'til he got home. And when the mother seen him she got weak. "Ah," says she, "I was looking to view this!" And the fool in the corner looked at him.

"Brother," says the fool boy to his brother, "you're feeding me since I was a child, and I'm going off now to feed you. What road did you go? I want to go back, Brother, to the same man you work with."

"Go away, you fool, that never left that there corner in your life!" says the mother.

"Well, I'm the man that that farmer wants," says the fool. "I'll cure him!"

Good and best to him. The fool goes on and he inquired of others, and, the same as the brother was leaded, he was leaded to the same stile. And he met the old man. "Ho, me fine young fella," says the man, "where're you off to?"

"Ah, musha, Sir," says he, "I'm going to look for work."

"Well," says he, "I know where you'll get work if you'd agree with the farmer. But there're several men after going up to him and they wouldn't stay any longer nor twenty-four hours with him."

"Aye, that's the man I'd like to be with," says the Jack. "I'd agree with any man and I'd work with any man."

"Alright," says the old man. Up they goes anyway and under the same circumstances he hired with the farmer, the same as the brother. But the farmer didn't know, like, 'twas the brother of the other boy.

The next morning come as usual. Says the farmer, "Throw three buckets of slop to the pigs." And the boy thrown it. "Get down now," says the farmer, "and eat your breakfast."

"Ah, no," says the boy, "'twouldn't do. I never et me breakfast with a pig."

"Well, that's the only breakfast you're going to get here."

"So, alright," says the fool. "But would you tell me, are there e'er a shop around here where a man could buy his supper if he wanted it?"

"Come out here," says the farmer, and he opened the back door of the barn. "Do you see that tree above? There's a shop there in the hollow. We never goes any farther to sell whatever we have, but sells it there, corn, eggs or butter. It's a store and all," says he.

"It's the very place I'm looking for," says the boy.

"Well, come in," says the farmer, "'til I show you the work." He brought him into the barn and told him he must have two barrels and a half thrashed again dinner time.

"Alright," says the boy. When the farmer gone the boy got two wheels and an axle in the barn. He never done anything only took the two linchpins out of the axle and started thrashing the corn with the axle. There was a winnowing machine in the barn and when he had a barrel of corn thrashed he put it into the winnowing machine and winned it. He put it into a sack and up on his back. He opened the back door and lept through the field and up to the shop. Sold the corn at the shop and got his dinner and a new pipe and tobacco, come down back and started thrashing away again.

Now the farmer comes out and, says he, "You haven't the two barrels and a half thrashed yet?"

"I have," says the Jack, "and more. I went up with a half barrel for me dinner and there's another half barrel for me supper. I'm just now going to put it in the winnowing machine."

"What!" says the farmer, "If you don't get the best supper was ever et be a man!" And in the farmer goes to the old wife. "We're done," says he.

"Didn't I tell you he was like the other boy?" says she. "This boy's the other one's brother and he come to get satisfaction off you, and get it he will. Begorra," says she, "I'll tell you what we'll do. We'll boil a good supper for this boy and we'll give him a good breakfast, but we'll get the giant to kill him tomorrow."

Now the next morning, oh, he had the best breakfast he ever got!

"Now, Jack," says the farmer, "I have great work for you today."

"Ah, I don't mind, Sir," says the boy, "light or heavy."

"Well, I want you to graze cows now for me." And he sent him right down to the giant's meadow.

It was a warm summer's day anyway and Jack was laying up on the ditch, looking at the cows grazing, but he dozed asleep. And here comes the giant. "Fee, fie, foe, fum, I smells the blood of an Irishman. I'll have his bones for me stepping-stones and his blood for me morning dram."

This woke Jack up. "What are you blutting about?" says Jack. "And which will I put you: down through the ground with a poke of me toe or up through the air with a clout of me thumb?"

"Stop, Jack!" says the giant. "Thou excuse me, old Jack. I didn't think that you were an Irish giant!"

"Well, I am," says Jack.

"Well," says the giant, "I'll tell you, we'll forget all about it, what I said. But come down tomorrow and me and you'll go and gather a few sticks for an old widow is a friend of mine. We'll go to the wood, and whichever of us'll bring the biggest load out of the wood'll be the strongest man. And if I'm a stronger man nor you, I'll kill you."

"Oh, very good," says Jack.

That night Jack goes for his supper. "Well, Jack, did you see anyone at grazing?" says the old wife.

"I did," says he. "I seen a little fellow, he come up to me in the meadow. He said he'd have me bones for stepping-stones and me blood for his morning dram. I told him," says Jack, "I'd put him down through the ground with a poke of me toe or up through the air with a clout of me thumb, and he come and apologized to me."

"Well, Jack, Jack," says she, "you must be an awful man!"

The next morning come anyhow and says the fool, "I must go down to the little fella today. We must go to the wood for a load of firing for an old widow with no land."

"Alright, Jack," says the farmer's wife. "The giant's going to kill him today," says she.

Down Jack goes and, says he, "Good morning."

"Good morning, Jack," says the giant. "Come on now, Jack, we'll get the ropes." In they goes to the barn and Jack got the loom of ropes. Begod, the giant knotted up six or seven yards of rope, that he thought'd bring an awful load of firing. But Jack kept knotting away and knotting away and knotting away and knotting away. "Jack," says the giant, "what are you going to do with all the rope?"

"I'm going to tear up the wood," says Jack. "That widow'll never want a bit of a stick while she's alive. I'm going to tear up the whole wood."

"That'll do, Jack!" says the giant. "Let that there! Me great-grandfather planted that wood and I wouldn't wish it tore up for thousands of pounds."

"Alright," says Jack, "what do you want me to do?"

"Lookit," says the giant, "come down tomorrow and we'll have another bit of exercise. We'll have a bit of weight throwing tomorrow. Whichever of us'll throw the weight the farthest'll kill the other."

"Right," says Jack, "we'll agree on it."

Begorra, Jack come up to supper that night and they says, "Well, Jack, how'd you get on?"

"Oh, I got on alright. What way did you want me to get on? I was going to bid up the wood," says he, "and the giant wouldn't let me."

"Oh, God bless us, Jack," says the old wife, "you must be a terrible strong man!"

"You'll know how strong I am," says he, "when you're done me."

Now the next morning come, and down Jack goes again. He was out in the haggard and up come the giant. "Now, Jack," says he, "would you be able to fire that weight, that half-hundred weight, over them two links?" And the two links was about forty foot in height.

"You take it over first," said Jack.

The giant caught the weight and flung it over the two links. But Jack had an old tin whistle that he used to be in mind of whistling, and he put the whistle to his mouth and blowed. "What's up with you, Jack?" says the giant.

"Well, I have two little brothers at home in Ireland," says Jack. "And they'd give their liver and lights for this weight to play with. I'm whistling to tell them to come in out of the yard so I can peg it over to 'em."

"Stop, Jack!" says the giant. "Drop that weight. That's belonging to me seven generations, don't get rid of that in Ireland. You're an awful man altogether, Jack."

"Listen," says the giant, "I'll tell you what we'll do now, Jack, and we'll finish the argument. Come down tomorrow and I'll have a calf boiled for dinner. If you're able to eat more nor me, you'll kill me. And if I ate more than you, I can kill you."

"Right," says Jack, "it's a bargain."

So Jack went up to his supper. "Well, Jack, how'd you get on?" they says.

"I got on well," says Jack.

"God, Jack, you're a great man," says the farmer's wife.

"You'll know what I am," says the fool, "when you're done with me."

That night, anyhow, Jack goes up to the shop and he bought three yards of calico and a needle and thread and elastic. He stayed up in the bed and he made a white bag. He put a runner-string in the bag and put it on his neck and he left the mouth of the bag open in his bosom.

Down he goes to the giant the next morning, and the giant says, "Now, Jack, we'll have some dinner."

"Alright," says Jack.

They sat down to the dinner and the old wife brought 'em down two side dishes, cabbage, and fresh tomato paste: Jack kept eating away as much as he could 'til he was well bet. But, when he was well bet, he started filling the bag was around his neck, eating with his hands, you see. And the old woman kept coming with the dishes of meat and cabbage. "Oh, Jack, Jack, Jack," says the giant, "how can you eat so much?"

"Whoo!" says Jack, "is that all you know? I could eat as much more."

"Oh, Jack," says he, "how could you?"

"Sure, I could release meself," says Jack, "and eat as much more."

"You couldn't, Jack!"

"I could," says Jack. And Jack got the bread knife off of the table and ripped up the bag and all the meat and jelly fell on the floor!

"Oh, Jack, Jack," says the giant, "give me one lend of the knife." So the giant did the same with the knife and fell dead on the ground. His guts fell out.

Now Jack goes up to the old wife and the farmer and he got one of them be one ear and the other be the other. "Come down now," he says, "'til I show you the little fellow you started to get me killed." And he showed 'em the giant.

"Oh, Jack, Jack, you're an awful man entirely. We'll give you ten pounds more on your wages, Jack, when you're such a good man, and go home about your business tomorrow morning."

"I will not," says Jack, "I can't go that way, I'll finish me year's contract up."

Now that night the old wife says to the farmer, "I'll tell you what we'll do. This boy come to get satisfaction for his brother, and you're after punishing a lot of boys, but he's going to punish you. Put him out to plough tomorrow, and I'll get up in the ivy tree when he's coming to his dinner. When I cry 'cuckoo, cuckoo,' then just clap your hands and say, 'Jack, you're in luck! There's the cuckoo!' And give him his sixteen pound and let him go, in the name of God!"

Now Jack went out to plough the next day and he was coming in at dinner time. "Ho, Jack," the old wife said, "Cuckoo! Cuckoo! Cuckoo!"

"Jack, Jack, Jack," says the farmer, "do you hear the cuckoo? You're the luckiest man, for you're not anymore than a week here yet."

"Well, it's a rare thing to hear," says Jack, "a cuckoo this day of the year. I never see one of them this day of the year before." Jack started peeping around and he seed the old wife up in the tree. He cotched up a brick, unknown to the farmer. "Wait'll I see," says Jack, "is it a cuckoo." Jack up with the brick, fired it and hit her on the back of the head and down she fell.

"Ah, Jack, Jack, Jack," says the farmer, "you're after killing me wife."

"Oh," says Jack, "I thought it was the cuckoo. Are you sorry for hiring with me?" says he.

"I am, Jack. I am, Jack."

"Come turn around," says Jack. And Jack took a strip of the farmer's skin from the top of his head to the sole of his foot. "Well, now," says he, "You can bring me out me sixteen pound."

"My brother earned my lifetime," says Jack, "and kept me going. I had to come here for him. So," says he, "you'll never do anything else to any other chaps'll be looking for work."

And put down the kettle and make the tea and if you live happy I may.[3]

The Hen-woman's Daughter

Now there was this hen-woman one time and she lived in the gate lodge at a gentleman's gate. She used to rear the fowl and them fresh eggs for the big house. Anyhow, she wasn't married. She had no man, but she had a young daughter. And she reared this daughter in a chest, a big chest, in the way no one'd know she had any baby. And this girl, now, she come to twenty-one years of age and no one ever seen her but the mother.

But today the old mother fell sick, and she should go down with those fowl and fresh eggs to the lord's place. "I'm done," she says. "I'm not able to get up."

"Well, Mother," says the girl, "would you let me go down with 'em for you?"

"Ah," says the mother, "sure I couldn't. Where would they think you'd be after coming out of? They don't know that I ever reared a child."

"Oh, sure, Mother," says the girl, "if anything ever happen to you, what will I do? I'll have to make meself known," she says, "first or last. I'll go down, Mother, with the fowl and fresh eggs and I'll tell 'em."

"Well, alright Daughter," says the old woman, "but I'll tell you this: In the way that they'd know that you are me daughter, that you were reared in a chest and that you have no sense: anything they'd ever ask you to do, tell 'em you won't do it 'cept if you're asked a second time. Then they'll know," says she, "that you're innocent."

"Alright, Mother," says the girl.

Down she goes, anyhow, with the fowl and fresh eggs, down to the gentleman's house. The butler come out and says he, "Miss, who're you?"

"Oh, I'm the hen-woman's daughter," she says, "from the gate-lodge."

"Ah, no," he said. "The hen-woman never had a daughter."

"She had me, Sir," she says, "and you often sat, Sir, on top of me, on the big chest, and I couldn't breathe, 'cause it was in the chest I was kept. I'm telling you, Sir, I often heard you talking thousands and thousands and thousands of times, while I was in the chest below."

"Alright," he says, "wait 'll I go in to the boss."

There was a dance going on within, of course, in the big place, and the lord was there. "Well," says the lord to the butler, "did the hen-woman come yet?"

"No," says the butler, "but there's a girl abroad says she's her daughter. And she's the prettiest girl that ever the eyes of man seen. She says she's the hen-woman's daughter but I can't believe it."

"The hen-woman never had a daughter," says the lord.

"Well," says the butler, "she said I was often sitting on top of the chest where she was reared."

"Begod, it could happen maybe," says the gentleman. "Tell her to come in."

Out the butler goes. "The gentleman," he says, "want you to come in."

"Oh, tell him I won't go in, Sir," says she, "'cept he ask me the second time."

Back in goes the butler. "She says she won't come in here," says he, "except you ask her the second time."

"Oh," says the lord, "then she was reared in the chest! Tell her I did ask her the second time."

Out the butler goes. "Yes, Miss," says he, "he asked you in again."

"Alright," she says, "I'll go in."

When the young gentleman seen her he wouldn't dance with no other girl in the whole place, she was so good-looking. And they danced and danced, but now it come late after the dance and says he, "'Tis very late for you, Girl, to go home."

"What can I do, Sir?" says she. "I have to go home."

"You should stay with meself tonight," he says.

"You'd have to ask me again, Sir," she says.

"Well, I will ask you again," he says. And she stayed with him that night anyway.

The next morning she goes home and when the old mother seen her coming in she says, "I'm done! I knew well this'd finish me up! Was it with the butler, was it with the coachman, or who were you with last night!"

"Faith, Mother," says the girl, "I was with himself."

"Oh, worse and worse," says the mother. "I'll never get to show me face again. Worse and worse!"

"Faith, I'll show meself again, Mother," says the girl, "and I'll have him yet."

"You'd have the lord, the young lord!" says the old woman.

"I will, Mother," says she.

"You will not," says the mother. "Go away out of that, you dirty, indecent slummy."

"Ah, Mother," says the girl, "I'll have him yet!"

Begod, it come on anyway, rolled along, until the girl had this young baby boy. And it come 'til the baby boy was about six or seven months old. And at this time the young gentleman was going to get married to a lady. "Now," says the old woman, "look at the way you are!"

"I'll have him yet, Mother," says the girl.

"Go you out of that! He's going to get married on Wednesday!"

"He's not married yet, Mother," says she.

"You dirty so-and-so," says the mother.

Now, Wednesday come, and on Wednesday morning the bride went down, the lady, on a horse and saddle to the church. There was no motorcars in them times. "Now," says the mother, "there's the lady going down."

"Ah, but he's not married yet, Mother," says the girl. "I'll have him yet."

"The bride's going down and you'll have him yet, a hen-woman's daughter!" says the old woman.

"Well, I will," she says.

The girl went in anyhow and she dressed the baby in as good a dressing as she could. And she goes on to the church then and she sat down within, herself and her child. On comes the lady and the gentleman to be married, and when the girl seen 'em coming she stabbed the baby with a pin to make it cry. And then the girl start to sing:

> "Oh then hold your voice, Honey, you will never want for bread,
> Although your poor Daddy is going to be wed."

Then the young gentleman looked over:

> With that the young Squire, he commenced for to smile
> When he see this fine country girl and her child.

Now the other one, the lady bride, says to him:

> "Now me dear Love and Honey, is that what make you smile,
> When you see that poor country girl and her child?
> I have two at nursing, I have two at nursing,
> I had one for the butler and another for the groom.
> And I'll have another for the coachman,
> Ah, 'tis here in full bloom."

With that this young Squire he commenced for to swear:

> "There's no coachman's baby will ever be my heir."

He gripped his fine country girl by the hand, saying:

> "Me own Love and Honey, no longer you'll stand.
> I'm sure 'tis I owned it, I'm sure 'tis I owned it
> I am surely and certain no man owns it but me."

> Now he brought home his fine wife and young son.
> There's no time he'll look on her but he'll think on that one.

> "Oh, Lord, if I had of take the other one,
> Oh Lord if I had of take the other one,
> Oh, if I had take the other one wouldn't I be undone!"[4]

The White Gallows

Well, there was a big farmer one time and he was broken down drinking. He had four sons and he says to those four boys, "Now, Sons, I have nothing, only the place. And it'd be no use giving it to any of yous, because yous'd have nothing along with it. But what I'll do," says he, "is let the four of yous go search your fortune for a year and a day. And I'll give the place to the best-off man after the year and a day," says he.

So those four brothers went on the road, and they went farther than you or I could tell. One of them took to the County Tipperary. The other one took to the County Waterford. The other one went to the County Kilkenny. The other one went to the County Carlow. And they all got work.

But now, at the end of the year and a day, this one boy was leaving the County Carlow, and the man who worked him says to him, "Well, now, you're going home today, and you have your yearly's pay to get."

"Yes, Sir," says the boy.

"But would you rather," says the man, "be the best fortune-teller in the world, or have your seventeen pound in pay?"

"I'd rather be the best fortune-teller, Sir," says he, "in the world."

"Alright," says the man, "you're the best fortune-teller in the world."

Now the other boy was leaving the County Kilkenny, and the man what give him a job says to him, "Well, thee're going home today."

"I am, Sir," says the boy.

"Well, which would you rather," the man says, "have your seventeen pound pay or be the best marksman that ever caught a gun in his hand?"

"I'd rather be the best marksman, Sir, ever caught a gun in his hand."

"Alright," says the man, "you're the best marksman."

The other chap was leaving the County Waterford, and the same thing happened there. The man asked him, "Which would you rather be, the best robber that ever went out on two feet, or have your seventeen pound?"

"I'd rather be the best robber, Sir," says the chap. "I wouldn't be long getting the money back."

"Well, you're the best robber," says the man.

The other boy was leaving the County Tipperary and the man there asked him, "Which would you rather now, to be the best Tinker that ever caught an iron in his hand, 'tis nothing that you won't do, or your seventeen pound?"

"I'd rather be the best Tinker," says the boy.

"You're the best Tinker," the man says, "that ever caught an iron in his hand. 'Tis nothing'll stop you, that you won't do."

"Alright, Sir," says he to him.

But the four brothers came along and they met at the crossroads as usual, and went up along home to the father.

"Well, Sons," says the father, "how did it pass, the year and a day?"

"Alright, Father."

"How much of money have you?" says he to the youngest boy.

"I have nothing, Father," says he, "but I'm the best marksman ever cotch a gun."

"Well, go travel 'til you get something to shoot," says the father.

"What have you?" says he to the second eldest boy.

"I'm the best robber, Father, that ever lived," says he.

"Ah, you're no good to me either," says the father.

"What have you?" says he to the eldest fellow.

"I'm the best fortune-teller, Father, in Ireland," says he.

"You're no good either," says he.

"What have you?" he says to the fourth boy.

"Well, Father," says the boy, "I have no money no more than any of them, but I have another trade as well as them."

"What trade have you?"

"I'm the best tinsmith ever caught an iron," says he.

"Alright," says the father, "go until you get some job."

But the four poor chaps went off again, and they went farther than you or I could tell. They went 'til the night was falling on them and they got hungry and wet and cold and everything. They come into this wood and lit a big fire. "Well," says the marksman, "that's wonderful! Now we don't know whether we have the trade off or no!"

"Well, if I'm the best fortune-teller in the world," says the fortune-teller, "there's a nest in the fork of that tree yonder, and there's an egg in it. And if you're the best robber in the world," says he to the robber, "you'll go up and take it out of the nest and bring it down without breaking it."

He done it. The egg was above and the robber went up and brought it down. "Now," says he to the marksman, "if you're the best marksman that ever caught a gun, you'll blow the top off of that egg at fifty yards without spilling it."

The marksman done it. "Now," says he to the Tinker, "if you're the best Tinker that ever caught an iron, you'll solder back the egg the same as you'd never think it was broke." And he done it.

"Yes," they says, "we have our trade off. We're four good tradesmen." And they fell asleep at the fire.

In the morning they gets up and the fortune-teller says, "I'm after dreaming last night, and I dreamed a fortune is true. 'Tis a gentleman in such a place and he had a daughter, his one only daughter, and she was took from him seven year ago, stole. He didn't see her with seven years, but I know where she is," says the fortune-teller. "And there's seven hundred pound to be got for bringing her back, to anyone can get her."

"We'll go," says the robber. "Do you know where the gentleman's place is?"

"I do," says the fortune-teller. So on they goes until they got to this gentleman's house. Up they goes to the hall door and the gentleman come out.

"Sir," says the boy, "haven't you a daughter missing seven year?"

"I have," says the gentleman, "how did you know that?"

"I'm a fortune-teller, Sir," says he. "I can tell fortunes. And haven't you seven hundred pound reward for anyone would bring her back safe to you?"

"Yes," says the gentleman, "but the man that'll bring her back safe, instead of giving him seven hundred pound I'll give him the whole place and marriage along with her, if he'll let me see my daughter again."

"Well, yes, Sir," says the boy, "we're going tomorrow to where she is, meself and me three brothers, and we'll bring her back. She's on such an island, it's an enchanted island, with such a giant. And onct every seven years they be in a sleep for a week. Tomorrow," says the fortune-teller, "is the day of sleep, and she'll be asleep tomorrow and so will the giant. But we'll bring her back safe to you, Sir."

"Well, I hope," says the gentleman, "you do."

The next morning down they goes and got in this boat and they sailed across to the island. And they went on to the garden, where the giant and the lady was, and they seen them there. "Now," says the fortune-teller to the robber, "there're joy-bells on the gate of that garden, and if you ring those bells or tip the gate we're devoured with the giant," says he. "If you're the best robber in the world you're to lep that gate and cut the sheets from under her and over her, and don't waken the giant. Leap out over that gate with the lady in your arms."

"And I'll keep the gun on you," says the marksman, "and I'll blow the head off of the giant if he waken or stir."

So the robber lept the gate under cover, and he cut the sheets from under and over the lady, and he lept out the gate again with the lady in his arms and never rung the bell. They went down to the boat and sailed away and she never woken 'til she was halfways out in the channel, going back.

"Ah, Men, Men," she says, "I know yous are a-coming to bring me back to me father, and I'm delighted with yous. But we'll never reach home," says she. "The giant'll waken and he'll miss me gone. He'll drown yous four and he'll sink the boat, but he'll bring me back safe."

"He won't," said the marksman. "I'm the best marksman that ever cotch a gun. Would there be any chance for me to kill him?"

"There is," she says, "one chance. There's a little mark that ye could hardly deserve in his forehead. If you could fire and get him there, right in the center of that mark, he'd be finished," says she. "But there's no other way. You wouldn't kill him with a hundred shots if you didn't get him there."

Now they were only a long ways out on the channel and the lady looks up. "Here he is," she says. "He's in the appearance of this cloud now that's coming! Here he is! Make sure now," she says to the marksman, "for the sake of yous four and your people!"

"If I fire and hit him in the mark," says he, "are you sure 'tis alright?"

"Oh, yes," says she, "that's his life."

He took steady aim and fired and got him. But he let the giant come too much over the boat, and in falling the giant hit the boat and he cracked it. The boat started leaking. "Well done!" says the lady. "We'll never get back now, the boat is leaking too hard."

"Well, if I'm the best Tinker," the other boy says, "that ever cotch an iron, we'll be safe." He put the iron in the fire was in the boat and he soldered up the boat again, as quick as usual. "Sail on," says he, "everything is right."

They sailed on and got out on the land and they brought the lady up home.

Now, of course, the lady was to marry whichever of the four that she'd think was the best man that saved her. "Well, now, Daughter," says the gentleman, "which of those men would you rather have?"

"Father," says she, "I likes the four of them. They'd have been all drowned and I'd be took back again by the giant and a hundred men wouldn't clear me," she says, "but for the marksman."

"Yes," says he, "marry the marksman."

"Well, what about the fortune-teller?" says she. "There's no one'd ever know where I was only for the fortune-teller."

"Yes," the gentleman says, "he's the best man. Marry him."

"No," she says, "what about the robber that lept in and cut the sheets from under me and over me and I asleep. He lept out and there were joy-bells on the gate that'd be heard for seven mile, and he never tipped them, nor woken the giant."

"That's the best man," the father says. "Marry him."

"No, Father," she says. "We were all drowned only for the Tinker. The giant, he fell on the boat and the boat, she was sinking. The Tinker put the iron in the fire and he soldered up the boat as good as usual again and brought the five of us home safe. I'll marry the Tinker," she says.

"Alright, Daughter," says the gentleman.

Now in the morning, when the wedding and all was over, the other poor three chaps they took their own road. They got a good sum of money, of course, from the gentleman, and they took their own way. But they went farther than you nor I could tell and they were passing this big place, and the advertisement was on the gate that 'twas a hotel. Down they goes to the hotel and ordered their dinner and ordered some drink as well.

Now, of course, when they were after eating their dinner and after the drink, they were having a bit of a chat. And one chap says, "Well, if I'm not making a mistake there's a smell and the taste of dog flesh off of that meat we et!"

"Well, if I'm not making a mistake," says the other brother, "there's a taste of horse flesh off of the drink!"

"Well, if I'm not making a great mistake," said the last brother, "there's a taste of Christian's flesh off of the bread!"

Now, the cook of that hotel heard them talking so, that they insulted her, and she sent for the police. The guards come and those three brothers was arrested and they was brought before the justice to make their excuse. And the farmer that sold the wheat for the bread was got. He had to give his detail about the wheat, for to know whether that boy was guilty or unguilty of the lie. "Well, Sir," says the farmer to the justice, "that what the chap said of Christian's flesh on the bread could stand to reason. Where that wheat was sowed, 'twas a churchyard, in former days, I heard the old people saying," says he. So that boy was clear.

Now, the brewery man that made the drink was brought there. "Well, Sir," says the brewery man, "the time we made that drink the strainer was broke. We had no strainer and we punched a horse skin, and we strained the drink a-through it." Says he, "It could stand to reason the taste of the horse could be off of the drink." And the other brother was clear.

Now it come to the chap with the case of the taste of dog flesh off of the meat, and the farmer that reared the pig was sent for. The justice says, "What've you to say?"

"Well, I'll tell you now, Sir," says the farmer. "We were very poor, and the sow had only two bunions and then the sow died. We had a great big setter bitch after *having pups, and we put the two bunions on the bitch, and the bitch reared them. Yes,"* says he, *"that could stand to reason, the taste of dog flesh could be off of the meat."* And the other brother was clear.

Now the three boys was let go, and they come along up to the end of the lane and they lay down in a quiet place and fell asleep. But when they woken they saw this man coming along on a horse and saddle, and he come up to them. He says, *"What's your names?"*

"My name," says one chap, *"is such-and-such."*

"Well," says the man on horseback, *"you're going to be Lord Mayor of London."*

Then the other boy told him his name.

"Well, you're going to be Lord Mayor of England," says he to the boy. *"But I've no job for you,"* says the man to the last boy, the youngest.

"Ah, 'tis no different to me, Sir," says he. *"I was dreaming last night, Sir, that I was going to get the white gallows at twenty-one years of age."*

"Well, it must be true," says the other brother, *"'cause I was dreaming that I was going to be Lord Mayor of London."*

"And I was dreaming," says the other chap, *"that I was going to be Lord Mayor of England."*

"Ah, well, it must all be the truth," says the youngest brother, and they bid God be with each other and away they started on their own roads.

But the youngest brother, he felt lonesome now, and with everything as it was. As he was the best marksman, he said he'd join the army. He joined the army and when he come to twenty years of age he was out of love with the army again. But this night he was coming this road and he come to a crossroads, and this old woman met him there. *"Hello, Soldier,"* she says to him.

"Hello Ma'm," he says.

"You look like a poor soldier is benighted," says she.

"Oh, I am, Ma'm," he says.

"Well, I'll show you now," she says, *"where you'll get a grand stop 'til morning."*

"I'd be very thankful, Ma'm," says he.

"Do ya see the fork of that tree?" says she. 'Twas a big old tree, forked in the middle and the root cut out of it.

"I do, Ma'm," says the boy.

"Well, you'll go up and go down through that tree, and when you go down in the bottom of it, 'tis a door there," she says. *"You open that door and when you go in you'll see there's a dog with eyes as big as teacups within. Now there's a hankercher."* (And she give it to him.) *"Throw that on the floor and the dog'll know that you're a chum of mine. He'll lay on the hankercher and he won't mind you. Then you go to the next room,"* says she, *"and there's a dog there with eyes as big as millwheels. Throw the hankercher on the ground again and that dog won't mind you. Then you'll go to the next room,"* she says, *"and there's a dog with eyes as big as towers. Throw the hankercher on the ground again and he won't give you no trouble."*

"Now," says she, *"in that first room there's a million of copper. In the room where the dog with eyes as big as millwheels is, there's a million of silver. And in the room where the dog with eyes as big as towers is, there's gold. There's also a bed, bedclothes, and all provisions, and you've everything you want.*

"But in the cupboard in that room there's a little box, and bring that little box up to me when you're coming in the morning. Take any money you want, all you're able to carry for pocket money, but make sure," she says, "and bring up the little box to me."

"I will, Ma'm," he says, "and I'm very grateful to you."

Down he goes in the tree and he seen the three dogs as the woman told him. He spread out the hankercher and the dogs lain on it and give him no trouble 'til morning. In the morning, of course, he got whatever money he wanted from the three rooms. Got the little box from the cupboard. He locked the doors and come up the tree and down to the cross, and he met the old woman again.

"Now, Soldier," she says, "how did you enjoy the night?"

"Well, Ma'm," says he, "and I'm very thankful."

"Did you get the little box?" she says.

"I did, Ma'm," says the boy.

"Give me the little box," says she.

"Well, I will, Ma'm," says he, "but would you tell me what you want it for?"

"Oh, now," says she, "'tis no differ to ya what I want it for. But give me the little box, I done a great turn for you last night. Give me me box."

"I will, Ma'm," says he, "if you tell me what you want it for."

But she wouldn't tell him what she wanted the box for and he wouldn't give the box.

"If you tell me, Ma'm," says he, "I'll give you the box."

"No," says she, "it's a secret. I want the little box and give me the little box!" But she got into an argument with him anyhow and he shot her. And he kept the little box and he walked on.

He was a long time walking, and now he comes into this town, and he went up to this house where there was an old man and an old woman living and he got lodging in it. "I'll pay you Ma'm, for me lodging," says he.

"Ah, 'tis alright," says the old woman, "'tis only meself and the old bossman in it."

"No, Ma'm," says he, "I'll pay you whatever it'll be."

"Alright," the old woman said to him, "but don't leave us now. We're very taken up with you."

"No, Ma'm," he says, "I won't. And anyways I've no place to go."

"Well, you can stay here," she says, "as long as you like."

Now of course they got very fond of the boy in the house. And he still had his gun the whole time.

There was a landlord in this town and he had this pig used to come around through all those houses for her dinner. The people must have a dinner for the pig; the landlord made 'em do it. But one day the boy says, "Mother" (he used to call her 'Mother'), "who own the sow that you're getting ready the dinner for?"

"Well," says she, "that sow is belonging to the landlord, and we're living under the landlord. He owns all those houses that must have a dinner for her. If not," she says, "it wouldn't do."

"Well, don't get that dinner, Mother!" says he. "She'll never go back with the tale, Mother, to know whether we gave her the dinner or no."

"Oh, don't do anything with that pig!" says the old woman.

But, when the pig come to the house, he up with the hatchet and hit her in the head and split it in two halves. He sent out the old woman for salt and he cut up the pig and salted the pig and put her in a barrel and buried her in the garden. "Now," he says, "we won't be without meat, Mother, for the winter."

"We'll all be shot!" the old woman says.

"No, Mother, we won't," says he. "We'll be clear."

Now the pig was missing from home and that night the landlord says, "Me pig is held up, and I'd like to know where she is." But no account of the pig could be got no way. "I'll tell you," says the landlord, "I'm going to send out men, now, for to get their dinner in every house belonging to me. And if they get a bit of the fresh pork in any house," says he, "that's where the pig is kilt. Then," says he, "we'll behead the man that kilt her."

The men was implaced in every house and the dinner was got for 'em. But one man was in the old woman's house eating his dinner, and the boy kept watching him, and the man slipped a bit of pork down in his pocket. The minute he did the boy shot him. "You won't go back with the tale either," the chap says.

"Oh, murder!" says the old woman, "we're done!"

"No, Mother," says he, "we're not. We'll be alright." And he buried the man in the garden.

Now the man was missing and no account of him. And the landlord went to the old witch of that town, to find help. "It's the one man," the witch says, "kilt the pig and kilt the man too and I'll tell you what you'll do now," says she. "Set a trap tonight. In the shop window in the main street put two crocks of gold and also a trap of boiling tar. The man that kilt the pig and the man that kilt the man, he'll come there for that gold," says the witch, "and he'll be caught in the trap. Then ye can do away with him in the morning."

"Right," says the landlord. So he done it, put the trap in the town and this young boy he come by and he seen the gold, of course. Home he comes, and he says to the old man, "Did you see the gold in the window?"

"I did, but it's set there for a trap," says the old man.

"No differ," says the boy, "we'll go get it."

"No," says the old man, "we won't."

"We will," says the boy, "and you'll have to come with me."

'Course, after hours he bested the old man, and the old man had to go with him and they went that night. "Now," says he to the old man, "you go in the window. Lift out that gold to me and I'll take it from you." The old man lifted him out the crock of gold alright, but he got caught in the boiling tar and the boy couldn't shake him nor he couldn't get him out of it. So he shot the old man in it. "You won't tell the tale either!" the boy says.

Back he come home. "Where's the old boss?" says the old woman. And he up and told her. "Ah, murder, murder!" says she.

"Don't have a word, Mother," says he. "There was nothing we could do, we'd be all done away with. You'll never want for nothing now, Mother," says he. "I'll see you alright." But he peacified the old woman, of course, when she was done crying.

So the landlord went to the witch again. "The one man done it all," says the witch.

"Well, how are we going to make him out?"

"Well, that's to be told," says she. "You may send out now an advertisement, to big, little, and small, for a big dance. And if he's in the city he'll come to the dance. (He must be a sportsman when he's after doing away with so much.) Let your daughter make free with every man in the crowd," says she, "and I bet you she'll find him out."

The lord sent out for big, little, and small for to come to this dance, and they all come. And this boy went up to the dance, and of course he was knowed as a bit of a stranger among them all. The girl got on him, and got talking to him, and the while she was talking she cut a little bit of a mark out of the back of his coat.

"Well, Daughter," says the lord in the morning, "did you do any good?"

"I'm thinking I did," she says. "I put a mark on this man and I think he's the man guilty for all."

The lord went on to the old witch, to view her story. "Yes," says the witch, "that's the man. He's kilt the pig and he kilt the first man and he's shot the old man."

The lord and his men they goes down then and examined every man in the town and got the mark on the boy's coat. He was the man and they took him.

Now this boy was sentenced to be executed and got his day. "Well," he says, "yous'll have to give me a time for to make me soul."

"Yes," they says.

"Now, Mother," says he, "my time is run, but you'll never be poor. You have money enough to keep you going. But I don't care anyhow, Mother, because me lifetime is coming up." (Now, do you see, he was to get the white gallows at twenty-one years of age and 'twas still coming to him.) "But, Mother," says he, "where I got the first of my money was at such a crossroads." He told her of the first of his story. "Now I must look at this little box," says he, "afore I go, for to see what did that old woman want it for."

He caught the little box from under his head and he looked at it. He opened it, first time he ever opened it, and there was a little hammer and a little bit of flint in it. Says the boy, "What was this for?" He tipped the bit of flint with the hammer and out lept the dog with eyes as big as teacups.

"What's your command, Soldier? What's your command, Soldier?" says the dog.

Ah, he tipped it again and out leps the dog with eyes as big as millwheels. "What's your command, Soldier? What's your command, Soldier?"

He tipped it again and out leps the dog with eyes as big as towers. "What's your command, Soldier? What's your command, Soldier?"

"My command is," says the boy, "for you to have three sacks of gold here inside of a half an hour. And you have three sacks of silver. And you have three sacks of copper."

"Yes, Soldier," they says, "we'll have that." And they did. The money was secured.

"I'm right, Mother," says the chap, "there's a chance for me yet!"

"Ah, you're going to be done in," she says, "on Wednesday."

"Well, maybe I would and maybe I wouldn't. But I'm thinking," says he, "there's a good chance for me, when I'm after going so far."

Now, of course, there was an awful nobility sent for, for to see the execution. A big fire was made and the boy was put up on the burning flames, to be kilt. "Well, gentlemen and jury," says the boy, "afore I be executed will yous give a man preference, for to get one smoke out of his own pipe?" Everyone said they would, afore they'd see him burned.

He got out the little box. He opened the box and he struck the flint and out lept the dog with eyes as big as teacups. "What's your command, Soldier? What's your command, Soldier?"

He struck it again and out lept the dog with eyes as big as millwheels. "What's your command, Soldier? What's your command, Soldier?"

He struck it again and out lept the dog with eyes as big as towers! "What's your command, Soldier? What's your command, Soldier?"

"My command is," says he, "to have that old landlord and his lady pegged up in the sky, in the way every child in the city'd be running for their bones for sugar stick!"

All the nobility kneeled on their bended knees and said, "Mercy! Ah, mercy, Soldier! Spare everyone their life! Put the dogs back, and spare everyone their life!"

The old lord says, "Soldier! Put back them animals! I never seed the like of them animals before. Put 'em back! Spare meself and me lady our life, and I'll give ya me youngest daughter in marriage and the whole place!"

"Sign your hand to it," says the boy, "afore I put back those dogs."

The lord had to sign his hand, that he'd give him his youngest daughter and the whole place. That was done so, and the boy put back the dogs and put the little box under his arm.

Now, the next day the chap was married to the young lady and they lived in the big place. And it came that they used to be always out driving, everyday, with a six-horse carriage and a coach. But 'twas coming to the day of his twenty-one years, and he was in aloneness. "Father," the young lady says, "I can't get no talk out of him whatsoever."

So the lord says to him, "What's wrong with ya?" And he called him be name. "There's no cheer-up with you!"

"Ah no, Sir," says the boy, "'tisn't worth me while."

"Why," the lord says, "ain't you a happy man? Did you ever think that a private soldier would get married to a lord's daughter and own the estate?"

"Ah, well, alright, Sir," says the chap, "'tis too much for me. Sure, it's all no good to me. My lifetime is over."

"Why," says the lord, "what trouble is on your mind?"

"Well, I'll tell you, Sir," says the boy. "We dreamt one night, meself and me two brothers, a dream about ourself. One of them dreamt he was going to be Lord Mayor of London. The other dreamt he was going to be Lord Mayor of England. And I dreamt I was going to get the white gallows at twenty-one years of age."

"Sure, ya have already got her," the lord says. "My daughter was christened 'The White Gallows.' You're married to The White Gallows," says he, "you won't wait on her no more."

So the boy lived happy, and put down the kettle and make the tea and if you live happy I may.[5]

Dickie Milburn

Well, there was a man one time and he was a harmless man and his name was Dickie Milburn. But he was married to a woman, anyhow, and this woman, of course, she'd as leave have another husband as Dickie! But there was a minister used to come be this house and he used to get talking to this woman, and poor Dickie didn't know anything about it. Says the minister one day, "Would there be any chance we'd get Dickie away for a while? We'd have a grand bit of fun and diversions and we'd have our week's holidays."

"Well, I'll tell you what we'll do now," she says. "Dickie'll do anything that ever lies in his power, when I tell him. I'll let on to be sick tonight. And I'll tell him there's no cure for me if he don't go for a bottle of the World's Well Water. And when he'll go for the bottle of the World's Well Water ('tis exactly in the center of Ireland), he won't be back for a week anyhow, maybe longer."

Now that night when poor Dickie come back from his work she was moaning and groaning, you'd think there were a sack of fleas on her back.

"Musha," says Dickie, "what's wrong with you at all in the name of God?"

"Ah, musha," says she, "I'm dying."

"Ah, God help us," says he, "would there be any cure for you in the wide earthly world?"

"Ah, there would," says she, "if you were a loyal faithful husband."

"Well, I'll do anything ever lies in me power for you," says he.

"Well," says she, "there's no cure for me only you have to go to the center of Ireland, for a bottle of the World's Well Water, to a blessed well."

"But, sure, I never was in the center of Ireland, or Athlone," says Dickie. "But if you give me 'til daylight in the morning," says he, "I'll go."

She kept moaning and groaning all night, anyway, but poor Dickie got up in the morning and he started away early for Athlone, for a bottle of the World's Well Water.

Well, begod, he was going, after going a long journey when he met this brewery man with a horse and car. ('Twas in old times.) "Musha," says he, "bag o' bones, would it be Dickie Milburn I have! Is it out of your mind, Dickie, or where are you going?"

"I don't know whether I'm out of me mind," says Dickie, "but I'm going to Athlone, in the center of Ireland, to a blessed well, for a bottle of the World's Well Water for me wife. She have a pain all night that'd kill a bull!"

"Dickie," says the brewery man, "I know the bottle of water your wife want! Come back with me."

"Oh, not at all," says Dickie. "You're wrong."

"Here, Dickie," says he, "drink that bottle of ale." He pulled a couple of bottles of ale for Dickie and a couple of bottles for himself, and, of course, he made Dickie believe him anyhow, at the end of it.

"Oh begod, very well," says Dickie. "I'll go back with you."

"And Dickie," says he, "the way you'll find it all out, get down in that sack, now, on the car, and I'll tie the mouth of it."

Dickie got down in the sack anyhow and the brewery man tied the mouth of it, and they were going, going along the road 'til they was passing Dickie's house again. But as they were passing out runs the minister and he says, "Brewery man, come here, I want you! Bring in three dozen of stout," says he, *"and three dozen of ale."*

"Alright, Sir," says he. *Brought in three dozen of stout and three dozen of ale.*

"Now, Brewery man," says the minister, *"have drink with us afore you go."*

"I will, Sir, gladly," says he, *"but there's a sack, a parcel, I have left on the car, going to such a gentleman, and I'm a-feared it might be whipped off of the car. I'd have to bring it in and leave it inside the door."*

"Alright," says they, *"go get it."*

So the brewery man goes out and he's carrying in Dickie, and left the sack down inside the door. So, begod, they drank anyhow. And after they had some bottles drunk, says the minister, "Brewery man, will you give us a verse of a song?"

"Well," says the brewery man, *"I never sung a song 'til I hear one sung first."*

"Ah, well," says the minister, *"it wouldn't become a man of my coat for to sing 'til I hear one sung first."*

"Oh, well," says the wife, *"I'll sing first." And off she started anyhow:*

> *"Oh then, Dickie Milburn, you're gone from home*
> *For a bottle of water, down to Athlone,*
> *And I'll be with the minister 'til you come home.*
> *We're over a bottle of ale, more ale;*
> *We're all 'round a bottle of ale."*

"Now," says the minister, *"I'll give yous my verse:*

> Ah then, Dickie Milburn, 'tis little you think,
> I ate of your meat and I'll drink of your drink.
> If I have life, I'll be with your wife.
> *We're over a bottle of ale, more ale.*
> *We're all 'round a bottle of ale."*

The brewery man went over and he put the sack standing up and he cut the mouth of it. "Now," says the brewery man, *"I'll give yous my verse:*

> Oh then, Dickie Milburn, you are very near,
> Out of your knapsack now quickly devere!
> If you are slack I'll be at your back!
> *We're over a bottle of ale, more ale*
> *We're all 'round a bottle of ale.*

Dickie lept out of the sack and he gripped his blackthorn stick. "Wait now," says *Dickie, "and I'll give yous my verse:*

> Ah then, set yous all merry, genteel in a row
> Some of your secrets as well as you know,
> But I'll put a hump on the minister before that he'll go!
> *And we're over a bottle of ale, more ale*
> *We're all round a bottle of ale!"* [6]

Paying the Storyteller

There was this young gentleman one time and he was out to get the stories, and he met this old man that knew 'em. He says, "Will you tell me a story now, old man?"

"I will," he says, "tell you a story." And he told him this great story anyway. "Now," he says to the young gentleman, "pay me for me story."

"How much do you want?" says the chap. "'Twas a great story."

"Oh, no," says the old man, "I don't want any money, but you have to pay me for me story."

"Oh sure, I couldn't pay you if you won't take money for it. But 'twas a wonderful great story and I'll give you any money you'll ask."

"Well, when you'll pay me for that story," says the old man, "I'll tell you another one. But you have to pay me for it."

"I'm not able, Sir," says the young gentleman, "if you don't take money."

"Well, I won't take money," says he, "but I'll tell you what I'll do with you. If you don't pay me for me story I'll put you a bird in the air for a year and a day."

So he did. He changed the boy, like, into a swallow in the air for a year and a day. And after the year and a day was over the old man called him up again. "Did you get any account," says he, "how to pay me for me story?"

"No, Sir," says the young chap, "I didn't if you don't take money."

"No," he says, "money wouldn't pay me. So I'll put you a fish now in the main ocean for another year and a day."

And he done so, and after another year and a day he called him up again. "Now," says the old man, "can you pay me?"

"No, Sir," says he, "I can't if you don't take money."

"No," says the old man, "money wouldn't pay me. Right, I'll put you a jackdaw for another year and a day, so." And he did, the young chap become a jackdaw then.

But it was in cold wintry time and this jackdaw, that was the chap, went this night to a chimney for to roost. There was a wedding after being in this big house where the chimney was, and the old men was telling those stories to one another over the fire. One old man, he was finished with a story, and another old man says, "We better pay you for it."

"Ah, please," says the first old man.

"Well, for your storytelling that Heaven may be your dwelling," says the other, and the jackdaw was listening.

"I'm right," says the jackdaw, "if he ever call me up again, I'm right."

After the year and a day the old man called up the jackdaw again. "Well," he says, "could you pay me for me story yet?"

"Well, I think I can, Sir."

"Well, let us hear it," says he.

"Well, for your storytelling that Heaven may be your dwelling," says the jackdaw.

"That's right!" says the old man. "Where'd you get that?"

"Well, I was a long lonesome time going afore I got that answer," says the young chap, "and when I got it I had to get it from another the likes of you."[7]

NOTES

Introduction

1. Of the belief in "blood" among English farmers George Ewart Evans wrote that in regions "where most men's forebears are known for generations back, this rough guide has been elevated into a principle and a man's blood—the stock he stems from—is accounted a better indication of his real worth than his overt character which is assumed to be more or less an accidental acquisition." In this context, "to say that a man has gypsy blood in him is . . . to place him beyond the pale of the true village community," and if such a man shows, for example, erratic work habits his "blood" provides satisfactory explanation. He is "someone to whom normal rules do not apply; and for that reason no sleep need be lost over him" (AFH pp. 207–208).

2. Tinkers called their opposites "settled" and other more figurative names. One of these, "buffer," which is a mildly contemptuous slang word meaning "fellow" (OED, p. 1158), became popular in the mid-1970s although we had heard it seldom before then. The Gypsies of Britain have used a variety of names for settled or non-Gypsy folk—such as "gentile," *gadjo,* and *gorgio*—some of which are Romany (the Gypsies' language) or Romany derivations. To the best of my knowledge Ireland's Tinkers have no comparably definitive or venerable terms for non-Tinkers. *Sham, feen,* and *gloc,* the names for "a settled man" listed by Patrick Stokes in his discussion of the Tinkers' secret language, all mean "man" in general use, and none can be taken to mean "settled" outside of its active context or without qualification.

3. This kind of economic understanding can be likened to that which prevailed in certain levels of settled society in earlier stages of Western industrial and technological development. For example, E. P. Thompson observed that "the wages of the skilled craftsman at the beginning of the nineteenth century were often determined less by 'supply and demand' in the labor market than by notions of social prestige, or 'custom.' Customary wage-regulation may cover many things, from the status accorded by tradition to the rural craftsman to intricate institutional regulation in urban centres . . . Custom rather than costing (which was rarely understood) governed prices in many village industries especially where local materials—timber or stone—were used. The blacksmith might work for so much a pound for rough work, a little more for fine" (EWC, p. 235).

4. Houses, villages, government, and other features of settlement were not simply physically defensive, of course, but spiritually so: expressions of settled ideology that safeguarded the settled individual's spiritual well-being. For example, Ireland possessed— and in many instances still honored—a body of prescribed or customary architectural practice designed to foster human life within architectural bounds and protect it from harmful supernatural influences. Houses had to be built in auspicious ways and objects such as a horse's skull, certain stones, or coins incorporated in their foundations or masonry. Eggs under the roof, elder bushes by the door, and other talismans of various kinds warded off disease and misfortune. On specified days and hours certain things should or ought not be thrown out a house door (for example, foot-washing water and floor sweepings) because that would either please or displease supernatural beings. Bound-

aries of fields, farms, churchyards, and other holdings, the walls that delineated them, and the stiles or openings that breached them figured in ceremonies of blessing and could or could not be crossed on certain occasions, depending on the supernatural elements involved. Water from boundaries often had magical properties. Perhaps a greater proportion of Tinkers than settled folk subscribed to the beliefs that justified these customs. Johnny's anecdote about his father's throwing a dead man's boots out a door and the otherworldly helper who perches on a stile in his story "Jack the Giant Killer" show belief of this kind active in life and literature. Since Tinkers spent little of their time in houses, however, they were deprived of the spiritual security that steady observance of some such customs offered and often felt especially vulnerable to supernatural malevolence. For example, most feared being on the road without the family band during those night hours when supernatural beings were abroad.

5. Like many unlettered peoples, Tinkers developed prodigious retentive powers and often performed feats of memorization that seemingly had the main purpose of exercising and exhibiting those powers. Padraig MacGreine remarked on "one young fellow of 24, an army reservist, who can repeat by rote every instruction he ever received from a drill instructor. He proudly claims that illiterate travelers of whom there were many in the army were always better at answering questions than those who could read or write" (B 3:170 ff.). And one of Johnny Cassidy's sons was fond of reciting a memorized play-by-play radio broadcast of a football match.

6. MRC, p. 45.

7. MacGreine said that for Tinkers "things lucky or unlucky do not seem to exist . . . save [and here he quotes a Tinker informant] 'there's no day unlucky only the day you don't get enough to eat'" (B 3:170 ff.). Contrary to MacGreine, I am inclined to interpret this informant's words as an assertion that luck is always present and possible so long as one lives and has the strength to receive it.

8. Perhaps equally applicable to Tinkers was Anne Sutherland's observation that "one of the most apparent characteristics of the Rom [Gypsies] is that they are almost constantly involved in conflict with each other, a factor that masks their equally intense solidarity as a group. Although their expression of solidarity may be less obvious than their expression of conflict, the solidarity of the Rom is proportionally as intense as the degree of infighting" (Anne Sutherland, "Gypsies, the Hidden Americans," Society 12,2 [Jan./Feb., 1975]: 29).

9. Of the Gypsies of England and Wales in the 1800s it was "deemed . . . rather creditable . . . that so few of them had ever been imprisoned for heavier crimes than fortune-telling or stopping in the midst of sticks and grass" (IGT, p. 242). Similarly, the chief causes for Tinkers' imprisonment in the early 1960s were drunkenness, begging, malicious damage (largely to farm holdings, as mentioned), and assault (mostly of other Tinkers) (RCI, p. 157). Often reality did not seem to bear out the Tinker and Gypsy reputation for being seriously antisocial. It is undeniable, however, that some Tinker acts that may appear only nominally offensive to the modern citified observer have done serious injury to farming folk in the recent past. The loosing of animals where they could and did destroy whole crops, for example, and the breaking of essential boundaries had—besides practical consequences—profound psychological and cultural implications for the farmer. Such acts violated the orderly progression that was the sine qua non of agrarian settlement.

10. Many modern-day Gypsies have shared the Tinkers' incomprehension or disregard of the active purpose of clocks. E. P. Thompson points out that before the maturity of industrial capitalism such disregard was general among settled, independent craftsmen, farmers, and laborers for whom "the notation of time . . . has been described as task oriented." Where task-oriented timing prevailed "the peasant or laborer appeared to attend upon what is an observed necessity" and his community "appears to show least demarcation between 'work' and 'life.' Social intercourse and labor are intermingled—the working-day lengthens or contracts according to the task—and there is not a great sense of conflict between labor and 'passing the time of day.'" But "to men accustomed to labor timed by the clock, this attitude . . . appears to be wasteful and lacking in urgency." The Tinker attitude toward timed schedules was doubtless conditioned by the general truth that "attention to time in labor depends in large degree upon the need for the synchronization of labor . . . [so in] industry . . . conducted upon a domestic or small workshop scale, without intricate subdivision of processes, the degree of synchronization was slight and task-orientation was still prevalent."

Many Tinkers and Gypsies (e.g., the German rope dancer wearing two gold watches, [IGT, p. 45]) who did not read clocks nonetheless owned and cherished them, probably in remembrance of the eighteenth- and nineteenth-century status of "the timepiece [as] . . . the poor man's bank, an investment . . . [that] could, in bad times, be sold or put in hock" (E. P. Thompson, "Time, Work-discipline, and Industrial Capitalism," *Past and Present*, 38 [December 1967]: 57–71).

For some Tinkers the active clock symbolized not measurability and control but infiniteness and impotence, as in their tradition of "a clock in Hell which ticks 'forever, forever' without ceasing. The fear of Hell, through the medium of this story, is instilled into their children at an early age" (B 3:170 ff.).

11. A comparable loss of personal power had been endured by settled populations affected by industrialization in the nineteenth century when, as Stewart Ewen summarizes, "much of the impulse behind working class struggles . . . came not around the issue of obtaining and maintaining a fit wage, but against the wage process itself . . . [for it was] assumed that the wage, regardless of its amount, was a means of oppression that robbed working people of the possibility of self-determination: hence the common labor definition of the wage as 'wage-slavery'" (CC, pp. 8–9).

12. Gypsies resented this obtuseness. When Francis Hindes Groome asked a Gypsy friend why settled folk "take for Gipsies the Nailers, Potters, Besom-makers, all the tag, rag, and bobtail traveling on the roads," he was answered: "Easy enough, for what should low-bred people know but lowness? Show a mongrel a mongrel, and he's bound to call it a greyhound" (IGT, p. 102).

13. References to "Tinklers" and "Tinkler-Gypsies" abound in Scottish contexts where these were common terms for Traveling folk of, probably, Gypsy and/or Irish background.

14. In many instances it has been the Tinker's occupation that has warranted his inclusion in literary works. For example, one type of English-language ballad popular in the seventeenth and eighteenth centuries described sundry craftsmen and tradesmen (such as a tinker, a tailor, and a miller) in erotic encounters with their women customers. The typical duties of each craft (hammering, sewing a gown, and grinding) served as metaphors for the sexual act (e.g., CM pp. 279–281, 404–410). In other instances the Tinker in literature has represented outcasteness, strangeness, or animal-like otherness,

as he does in the counting rhyme *Eenie, Meenie, Miney, Moe.* Traditionally, in Britain and Ireland the rhyme ended with the injunction to "catch a Tinker [or sometimes a chicken] by the toe." By the 1950s the comparable American term "nigger" had supplanted "Tinker" in English children's versions (ODNR, p. 156), but Irish children continue to say "Tinker."

15. Genealogical issues have been central to the social status and functions of various groups of commercial nomads in the modern era. While some European Gypsies have kept detailed oral genealogical records that sustain a sense of their families' coherence and continuance independent of the settled community, certain Gypsies in India apparently possess no genealogy of their own but have been the important guardians and recounters of the genealogy of settled families. David Nemeth, a geographer currently studying Korean nomadism, has pointed out that the lack of proper genealogy is a decisive factor in the outcasteness of Korean nomad bands of entertainers, basketmakers, and butchers some of whose traditional tasks are proscribed for folk of higher, genealogically determined rank.

16. EIS, p. 84.

17. Ibid, p. 85.

18. Ibid.

19. Ibid.

20. CH, p. 113.

21. Ibid, p. 127.

22. EIS, p. 69.

23. Fox identifies "trade" and "commerce" societies as "the two models [that] describe the principal types of advanced social-economic organization known to the pre-industrial world," the "critical distinction" between the two being "the geographical range of their operations." The trade society is rooted in agricultural society that has "territorial or areal extent"; "the commercial society, by contrast . . . existed primarily in the linear dimension" and was characterized not by local territorial dynamics but by settlements devoted to "shipping or receiving goods in bulk to and from distant points of intensive production or wholesale distribution." Observing the coexistence of these two types of societies within France, around the ancient Aegean, and elsewhere, Fox remarks, "More important than the precise nature of these characteristics within either of the two major types . . . is their mutual independence. Even as they evolved into increasingly complex structures, they manifested no tendency to lose their separate identities, at least not until the transportation revolution threatened to destroy and replace them both" (HGP, pp. 19–53).

24. EIS, p. 56.

25. In antiquity each of Ireland's five provinces was associated with certain occupations and hence a certain level of the social hierarchy. The associations of Ulster,

Munster, and Leinster are named in the text; Connacht (Connaught) was deemed the seat of learning and Meath the seat of kingship (CH, p. 123).

26. FL, p. 289.

27. HMI, pp. 104–105.

28. JGLS 2:60–61.

29. Macalister states that "the right name is 'Sheldru' . . . 'Shelta' being a corruption due to imperfect speech or hearing. Other variants are 'Shelter' or 'Shelterox'—all being perversions of the Irish *belra* or *berla* . . . meaning 'speech, language, jargon,' and now most commonly . . . used in the sense of 'English.' It may also be heard of under the names *Minkers tari* or *Minker-taral* ('tinker-speech'), or in Gaelic *Caint cheard* ('craftsmen's speech') or *Laidionn nan ceard* ('craftsmen's Latin'). It is also called *Gam* (or *Gamox*) cant, which would seem to mean 'Bad Talk.' . . . Other names are 'Bog Latin' . . . and 'The Ould Thing'" (SLI, p. 137).

30. The Shelta lexicon compiled by Macalister from the collections of Sampson and others includes words that the collectors took for Shelta but which Macalister suggests may be derived from Yiddish, such as *finnif* (five-pound note), *horer* (clock), and *pi* (mouth) (SLI, pp. 183, 193, 209). In some cases both Yiddish and Romany derivations for the same word seem possible to Macalister. This situation evokes the complexity of the street argot of the period and the diverse cultures of which it partook.

31. This statement of purpose appeared in the inaugural volume of the *Journal of the Gypsy Lore Society* in 1889. "The final solution" mentioned is the discovery of truths of Gypsy origins, history, and culture, not the elimination of Gypsies.

32. The wide variety of uses of the term *cant*, as verb and substantive, elaborate the sense it conveys of obliquity and secrecy as well as persuasiveness or cajolery (OED, pp. 77–79).

33. In fact, Hugh T. Crofton first pointed out that "Shelta was formed by the application of 'back slang' to Irish" (SLI, p. 132). Meyer's subsequent work, however, greatly enlarged on the observation.

34. SLI, p. 164.

35. Gypsies in western Europe and their settled supporters who have worked to stimulate Gypsy "nationalism" and achieve improved status and rights for Gypsies have latterly adopted the word *drom* to indicate "way" or cultural style. An information sheet published by the Association of Gypsy Organisations in Britain, for example, called attention to the 1968 opening of "Romano Drom [Gypsy Way] schools on encampments by the roadside" in Bedfordshire.

36. Although individual British and continental Gypsies have often sought to avoid military conscription by such methods as disguise in women's dress and self-mutilation (burning the finger-tips with lime, for example [IGT, pp. 15–16]), there is ample historical evidence that Gypsies, like Tinkers, were able impromptu fighters and that

they were often pressed into soldiering in centuries past. MacRitchie has pointed out those who served in Hungarian regiments and a Swedish company of Gypsies that fought in the Thirty Years War (JGLS 3:228–232). And according to Lucas, at the time of the American Revolution "the [British] Government was in need of soldiers, and the tinkers were apprehended all over the country and forced into American service. This kidnapping system was, according to the testimony of persons of intelligence living at the time . . . the means of greatly breaking up and dispersing the Gypsy bands in Scotland. From this blow they never recovered" (YG, p. 132). Thus, meaningful numbers of British Gypsies may conceivably have been conscripted to serve in Ireland in the past and remained there.

Regarding the commonplace form of punishment—transportation—Macalister's "Continuous Specimens" of Shelta include the phrase *Solt, skait, and surt,* or "Arrested, transported and hanged" (SLI, p. 143), which is curious for its proverblike articulation and for the absence (to my knowledge) of any period of systematic transportation of Tinkers *from* Ireland.

37. SLI, p. 161.

38. Strictly speaking, by the time Leland, Sampson, and its other first students encountered Shelta in Britain, it was not exclusive to Tinkers there. Some Gypsies knew it and, like Romany, it had contributed words and phrases to the argot of the roads and slums spoken by people of neither Gypsy nor Tinker heritage. Some Shelta words are common in settled slang use today, such as *gammy* (bad), *lush* (drunk, or drink), and *bug* (take, get away), as are some Romany words, *pal* (friend), for instance. In Ireland in the 1960s and 1970s Shelta fluency was generally confined to Tinkers and those settled people who had occupational reason and opportunity to learn it: policemen and publicans.

39. SLI, p. 153.

40. For example, the Irish folklorist Sean O'Sullivan maintained that a list of Tinker surnames "shows, if proof were needed, that almost all of our itinerants are of common Irish stock and are in no way related by blood or derivation to the exotic gipsies of other lands. Their family names are a cross-section of those found all over Ireland" (FRW, p. 507). Although Tinkers' names may form the least part of the argument for their exclusively Irish origin, it should be pointed out that for a century at least Britain's most prominently identifiable Romany-speaking families have also used commonplace English, Scottish, Welsh, or Irish surnames, such as Beckett, Kennedy, Lee, Bailey, Herne, Stanley, Smith, and Boswell. Many American and European Gypsies make a policy of using different names in different social situations.

41. Although there is no record of major Gypsy immigration into Ireland, tradition attests to early invasions of Scotland by Gypsies coming from Ireland. One episode that has particularly piqued scholars was reported in 1865 by Walter Simson thus: "In the reign of James II . . . it happened that a company of Saracens or Gypsies from Ireland infested the county of Galloway, whereupon the king intimated a proclamation . . . that whoever should disperse them and bring in their captain, dead or alive, should have the Barony of Bombie for his reward. It chanced that . . . the laird of Bombie's son [of the McLellan family] fortunated to kill the person for which the reward was promised and he brought his head on the point of his sword to the king and thereupon he was immediately seized in the Barony of Bombie and to perpetuate the memory of that brave

. . . action he took for his crest a Moor's head and 'Think on' for his motto." Simson notes that the invading Gypsies "would very naturally be called Saracens by the natives of Scotland, to whom any black people at that time would appear as Saracens" and that "almost all Scottish Gypsies assert that their ancestors came by way of Ireland to Scotland." The presence of Gypsies in Ireland then Simson attributes to "the edict of Ferdinand of Spain of 1492" causing flight to Ireland among other places (HG, pp. 98–99).

In the late 1800s much was written to confirm the "Moor's head" as a representation of a Gypsy. Joseph Lucas further interpreted the McLellan motto as evidence of the Saracens' Gypsy identity: "'Think on' means 'remember.' How would that commemorate the slaughter of this particular tribe? For this reason, *that it was their name.* Zincano, pl. Zincani, or Zincan, in which the 'Z' is pronounced like TH. Thus the motto has a double sense, being a pun or a play upon the name of the conquered" (YG, p. 103). Zincano and variants thereof had long been names used for Gypsies in continental Europe, and Lucas presents an argument that from zincalo/zincaro derived "tinker" and "tinkler," "which occurs as early as in the charter of William the Lion (1165–1214)." The Oxford English Dictionary states that while "tinker" is of "origin uncertain," "Sc. *tinkler* and Eng. *tyncere* appear as trade names or sur-names in 1175 and 1265 respectively, and in many instances before 1300, long before any trace of *tink* or *tinkle* has been found," this in refutation of the verb *tink* ("to emit a metallic sound" or "to mend, solder, rivet . . . pots and pans") as the root of "tinker" (OED, p. 3329). Seemingly there is latitude for Lucas's conviction that tinkler/tinker developed from a Gypsy name, possibly a name that predated Gypsy European immigration. Lucas's interpretation of "Think on" was echoed in Patrick Stokes's habitual punning use of the verb *tink* to mean both "think, connive, plan" and "work, make things of metal," as in the first lines of his tale "The Tinker and the Crucifixion."

42. GB, p. 33.

43. In 1965 Tom Stanley, a king of the Gypsies in Detroit, stated that "Detroit is very good to Gypsies. . . . The men are very good as metal and coppersmiths and they can always find work in the factories. . . . They also trade in used cars." But Detroit's permanent Gypsy community was estimated at only about two hundred families (Rutha Blair Snowden, "Bearding the Gypsy King in His Detroit Castle," *Detroit Free Press* magazine, Feb. 7, 1965, pp. 6–9).

44. A recent documentary film by Eric Metzgar, "Gypsies: The Lost Americans," focuses on a Russian Gypsy family of the Kalderash (or cauldron maker) group living in Los Angeles and gives some glimpses of how such auto-body work is conducted.

45. The Scottish border village of Kirk Yetholm was from the late seventeenth through the nineteenth century known to be inhabited almost exclusively by Tinkler-Gypsies. According to a local tradition, village houses had been granted to Gypsies in the 1690s by a local laird out of gratitude to a Gypsy fellow soldier who had saved his life in battle. In the late nineteenth century the village gained notoriety as the home and seat of Gypsy Queen Esther Faa-Blyth. By then the actual Gypsy population had greatly declined and Queen Esther remarked that the villagers had become "mostly Irish," though if Irish Tinkers she did not say (YG, pp. 2–11). Landed Gypsy colonies founded by means other than grant are remembered in other parts of Britain. Legend held that in "the time of the Great Death 1348–9 . . . the village [of Blaxhall in Suffolk] was

deserted owing to the ravages of the plague [and] the Gypsies moved in and settled here and were never wholly displaced" (AFH, p. 207). I know of no tradition of comparable Gypsy or Tinker colonies in Ireland, which is not to say they have not existed.

46. In the 1960s one of the most prominent Irish of Tinker background was Bernadette Devlin, the Ulster politician and M.P., who wrote that her father's family "was of the clan known as the 'fighting Devlins' because that's all they ever did . . . but their earlier name was the 'hawker Devlins' because for years they had been travelers, selling china and pottery." Her paternal grandfather, she explained, had taken up a settled job and permanent housing when these were offered him as a wounded veteran of the British army (Bernadette Devlin, *The Price of My Soul* [New York: Alfred A. Knopf, 1969]).

47. PCSM 1:i–x.

48. Gypsy fads and fashions flourished in many parts of Europe from the eighteenth century until the twentieth. Pushkin and Tolstoy were but two of the prominent nineteenth-century Russians infatuated with Gypsy life who as young men spent much of their substance patronizing Gypsy gambling games, singers, and dancers. The habit was not confined to writers. An 1889 *Harper's Magazine* article reported that in Moscow "no fete is considered complete without the Bohemiennes; no prodigality in money or jewelry can satisfy their rapacity; reserved, disdainful, inaccessible to the enterprises of gallantry, these Gypsy women drive the gilded youth of Russia wild with enthusiasm, and stir their torpid souls" (JGLS 2:124–126).

49. This item from the *Morning Leader*, London, Jan. 16, 1912, is cited in the magazine *Romantishels, Didakais and Folklore Gazette*, vol. 1, no. 1, London, January 1912.

50. *The Gypsy and Folklore Gazette, Reflecting also the Opinions of Romantichels, Didakais, Tinkers, Trav'lers, Show-Folk, Poshrats and Ganjos*, London, 1912.

51. M. Bataillard offered this theory in his *Origines des Bohémiens*, 1875; *État de la Question de l'Ancienneté des Tsiganes en Europe*, 1877; *Les Zoltars*, 1878; and *La Question du Bronze et du Fer Aryens*, 1880 (IGT, p. 281).

52. Francis Hindes Groome championed and perhaps originated the theory that Gypsies brought to Europe the tales we now call Indo-European. He reasoned that "many of the survivals of dead savagery [in such tales] mentioned by Andrew Lang were still living realities in Gypsy tents," and "many stories collected in modern days from Gypsies in Europe were more perfect in literary form and detail than parallel stories among non-Gypsy peoples" (GF, pp. ix–lxxxiii).

53. JGLS 2:204–221.

54. GB, p. 42.

55. In time this situation was modified by a few works of fiction and ethnography. J. M. Synge's play *A Tinker Wedding* (1901) made perhaps the first imaginative inquiry into Tinker personality. That inquiry—as well as the broad portrayal of Tinker practical activity—was continued by some later Irish novelists, notably Maurice Walsh and Bryan MacMahon.

56. Cultivation of political arts, such as clique forming, making and breaking of useful alliances, and power jockeying, has been intrinsic to Gypsy—and Tinker—society. It is the masterful application and adaptation of these arts to settled power structures—while retaining cultural integrity—that has been difficult for these peoples. Various Gypsy groups, for example, in modern Hungary and Czechoslovakia, have zealously entered the settled political arena and failed to achieve the legal and administrative provisions for Gypsy welfare that they have sought.

57. In 1952 this questionnaire was sent by the Irish Folklore Commission to "its correspondents throughout Ireland." For the most part these were paraprofessional folklorists, many of them civil servants, who had been instructed in the methods and purpose of collection by the Commission and who reported on the localities where they lived and worked as schoolteachers, postmasters, and other functionaries. The questionnaire covered a wide range of topics, among them Tinker names, craft and trade, religion, social organization, and behavior. "One hundred and thirty-one replies were received . . . the only county from which no reply [came] was Louth." The replies have not been published in their entirety but remain in the archives of the (now) Department of Irish Folklore, University College, Dublin. The replies are cited several times in these notes.

58. In the 1930s MacGreine characterized the Irish Tinker's tent as semicircular, nine to twelve and a half feet long, and about four feet wide, made of canvas over "strong hazel rods" bent from a ridgepole to the ground (B 3:170 ff.). Some Tinker tents in the 1960s matched this description, but many were smaller. None were as commodious as the nineteenth-century British Gypsy tents Groome noted, which were twenty feet long, twelve feet wide, ten feet high, and "tilt-like in form . . . sheltered in winter by 'balks' or 'barricades,' a kind of fore-tent where stands the hearthstone or the charcoal brazier, and which sometimes connects two tents pitched front to front" (IGT, p. 55). The nomadic Gypsy groups of continental Europe have in recent decades used tents far larger than the ones Groome describes.

59. The Gypsy wagon was typically a flat or bow-roofed, box-shaped, four-wheeled conveyance that could be pulled by a single horse. It was frequently fitted inside with several bunks and storage compartments and decorated outside with red, green, black, or white paint and carved abstract designs as well as lucky emblems such as horseshoes, shamrocks, and horses' heads. Wagons like these were widely used by Gypsies in continental Europe, America, and Britain in the nineteenth and early twentieth century when the settled community used vehicles that were structurally nearly identical for commercial purposes and (in the mid-1800s) for travel. Such wagons were almost invariably built by settled firms for sale to Gypsies, and they may not have been used by Tinkers in Ireland before the first decades of this century. The best Irish wagons as well as harness and other horse gear were said by Tinkers to be made in Ulster.

60. "Tinker" was a commonplace surname in Britain, however (see note 41). The Irish-language word for a metal worker, tinker, or craftsman is *ceard*; other Irish words, such a *tincéiri*, were used regionally.

61. To the general settled community Tinkers seemed "a hardy race" who possessed superior bodily toughness, agility, and resilience; however, these attributes may have been more apparent than real. The Commission on Itineracy pointed out Tinkers' high infant mortality rate, the shorter average life span of Traveling adults, and the high

incidence of pulmonary disease and "digestive ailments" among them. In particular, Tinker men, "although in many cases of good physique and appearance, are generally not strong and the available evidence from employers and others indicates that they often lack stamina" (RCI, p. 46). A similar observation had been made a generation earlier: "Some of them [Tinkers] in the British Army in World War I had no resistance; they had no strength in them" (Q).

62. Although popular etymology held that *tinker* derived from the characteristic tinking noise of metal work—and thus I call tinsmithery the Tinkers "nominating trade"—in fact, *tinker* may have had quite a different history and an original meaning unrelated to "tin" or "tink" (see note 41).

63. Tin-plated sheet steel or iron was a relative novelty in the history of European sheet-metal crafts. Sheet gold and bronze, for example, had been worked since antiquity, and sheet lead was an important decorative component in medieval architecture. In Britain, where tin had been mined and smelted in the Bronze Age, tin plate only became a significant medium perhaps as late as the seventeenth century. Historians suppose that the craft of tin-plate work derived in part from the precepts of sheet-metal work developed by ancient armorers. Wire making—from which derived the craft of nail making, a specialty of some nineteenth- and twentieth-century Traveling smiths—was also historically associated with armory, which utilized wire in chain mail and other equipment. The possibility that Tinkers' and Gypsies' work with tin plate may have evolved from a historical involvement with armory or armed forces invites further investigation.

64. Itinerant Gypsy tinsmiths in many parts of modern Europe have used portable braziers for their fires whereas their Irish Tinker counterparts have characteristically worked from fires laid on the earth.

65. The eminently workable qualities of some weights of tin plate plus its glittering brightness when new (it was sometimes called "poor man's silver") often inspired the craftsman's fancy in Ireland and elsewhere. Some nineteenth-century American tinsmiths created realistic full-size articles of women's apparel out of tin, such as shoes or hats replete with lifelike feathers, ribbons, and flowers, to be presented as tenth wedding anniversary gifts (e.g., the collection displayed under the title "The Tinker and His Dam" at the Museum of American Folk Art, New York, Jan.–March, 1970).

66. CIM, p. 92, 97.

67. Certain groups of Irish Tinkers may have customarily assigned different phases of tinsmithery to different, individual smiths. A tinsmith of County Antrim reported to James Gow that his "tribe was made up of different craftsmen . . . 'makers' and 'menders.' The makers were fully trained tinkers and the menders were those who had just started to learn the trade" (UF, 1971, 17:90). Patrick Stokes began tin work as a mender.

68. CIM, p. 101.

69. Ibid.

70. In 1885, Groome gave the opinion that British Gypsies' habitual use of tents was a fairly recent innovation and that in his day "very few of the real Welsh" Gypsies

used tents but wintered in rented houses while "in the summer, they're all for stopping in barns" (IGT, p. 28). The Tinkers' avid interest in literary and firsthand stories (such as several told by Patrick Stokes) in which they or other wayfarers were subjected to natural or supernatural dangers while staying in barns or empty houses may have reflected earlier Traveling custom as well as their general fear of enclosure and entrapment in the settled realm.

71. The Tinker contribution to the violence at Irish fairs has given rise to a special, descriptive idiom, as when people arguing or brawling are said to be "cross as Puck Tinkers" or when a melee is called a "Donnybrook." Puck Fair in County Kerry in August and the October Horse Fair in Ballinasloe, County Galway, remain major Tinker convocations. Donnybrook Fair in County Dublin, formerly frequented by Tinkers, was terminated in the mid-nineteenth century for being the scene of general battle. While some settled folk kept their distance, for others "it was supposed to be a special treat at Puck Fair to watch the tinkers fighting" (Q). Tinkers also congregated at the sites of local "patrons" or religious pilgrimages to worship and to sell small wares and entertainments.

72. The heat and freedom of Tinker women in combat has long impressed settled observers, contrasting as it does with most settled women's avoidance of such strife. Simson described many instances of ferocity and bravery and the wielding of "cutlasses" and knives by Scottish Tinkler-Gypsy women in preceding centuries (HG). Gypsy women in other parts of Britain have not had a reputation for being warlike.

73. Funerals were generally of great importance to Tinkers; they spared neither crippling expense nor tremendous inconvenience to attend, often returning from England or America when a relative died. The funeral of any respected old person who had been a member of a large clan was likely to have hundreds of participants, and the funerals of kings have apparently been attended by thousands. Noting a comparable attitude among American Gypsies, Sutherland (in the work cited in note 8 above) stated that for them "solidarity is perhaps best manifest when death or a serious illness occurs" but that "death is not the only time when the Rom come together as a group. Any serious trouble . . . will unite everyone in a collective effort to help. . . . This cooperation is more than a method of self-protection as a group against outsiders, it is also a measure of the value that is placed on group membership." For Gypsies and Tinkers alike the burial of an old king and the election or coronation of a new one seem to have often occurred at the same convocation, lasting several days or longer.

74. The County Galway funeral of the eighty-four-year-old king John Ward and the coronation of his fifty-five-year-old nephew Martin Ward were reported in *The Ranger, a Journal for Connaught Rangers*, since both Martin Ward and his rival for the newly vacant office, "John Davis, an Englishman born at Otford, Kent," had served in that regiment of the British army. The magazine states that Martin Ward won the kingship because he was John Ward's nephew, he was head of the large Ward clan, he had won a drinking contest with John Davis and, finally, he "had a truly impressive record in street battles at rural fairs." He was crowned with a "heather wreath . . . made of three types symbolising the King's three powers: to speak for the tinkers, to settle any tribal disputes that may arise, and to preserve laws and customs," although which tribal disputes he would deal with, and how, and what laws and customs applied the writer did not say. Martin Ward's coronation oath was "by the grace of God and the strength of me fist" (*The Ranger, a Journal for Connaught Rangers*, 11, 52 [May 1946]: 28–30).

75. P, pp. 11–16, 23, 24.

76. The exposition of perceived antisocial behavior in the *Report of the Commission on Itineracy* refers often, albeit obliquely, to the sense of locality shared by Tinkers and police and the cooperation between them. It is interesting that the report implies that this local cooperation contributes to the lack of cohesion of Traveling and settled communities on a nationwide scale. Thus: "It must be accepted that itinerants are not unintelligent and a certain number of them may be expected to take advantage of lack of action or leniency by those whose duty it is to enforce the law. . . . If the law is not to fall into disrespect, a sustained effort must be made to . . . bring home to them the necessity for being law abiding. . . . The fact that a crime is of a petty nature and the wrongdoer has moved to another district should not be allowed to affect the pursuit of an offender or the prosecution of a case" (RCI, p. 100).

77. Doubtless one of the oldest and best known accounts of Gypsy seductiveness is the British ballad called "The Raggle Taggle Gypsies" or "Johnny Faa, the Gypsy Laddie" about a charismatic Scottish Gypsy chief (and leader of the Faa clan to which Queen Esther Faa-Blyth, of notes 45 and 82, later belonged). Faa had enjoyed the royal patronage of James V and then fell out of favor and was hanged. The ballad, probably composed after his death, tells of a noble married lady who is smitten with Gypsies' singing, sleeps with Johnny Faa their leader, and renounces her settled life: "Yestreen I lay in a well-made bed / And my good lord beside me: / This night I'll ly in a tenant's barn, / Whatever shall betide me" (ESPB, p. 483). A ballad on a similar theme "current in the [British] armed forces" in 1957 and called "The Highland Tinker" does not mention singing but emphasizes the monstrous sexuality and otherness of the Tinker: "The lady of the manor was dressing for a ball / When she saw a highland tinker p——g against a wall / With his dirty great kidney-wiper and b——s the size of three / And half a yard of parkin hanging down below his knee" (CM, p. 438, including dashes). The lasciviousness of many Tinkers and Gypsies of literature has not been observed in their modern-day, real-life models. In 1944 Vesey-Fitzgerald wrote that "up to quite recently" any British Gypsy girl guilty of prostitution "was invariably disowned by her family" and that there was a tradition that in the past she might have been buried alive (GB, pp. 59–60). Walter Scott suggested that the many reported abductions of settled women by Gypsy men were effected not by sexual attraction but by Gypsy "mesmeric power" or "glamour," which he defined as "the power of imposing on the eyesight of the spectators, so that the appearance of an object shall be totally different from the reality. . . . [For] besides the prophetic powers ascribed to gipsies in most European countries, the Scottish peasants believe them possessed of the power of throwing upon bystanders a spell to fascinate their eyes and cause them to see the thing that is not . . . in the old ballad of 'Johnnie Faa,' the elopement . . . is imputed to fascination" (JGLS 1:42).

78. Much more and precise information has been collected about marital arrangements among Gypsies than among Tinkers. Groups of British Gypsies had permitted trial marriage, divorce, and multiple marriages and, in some instances into the twentieth century, polygamy (GB, pp. 55–71). Settled nineteenth-century observers testified that Tinkers occasionally exchanged wives, who were often lumped together with horses or tools when their husbands negotiated a bargain. Most settled folk agreed with "an Irish lady" of Limerick who reported witnessing such transactions in 1887 and concluded that "tinkers are not very particular as to the means used to 'mate' them" (JGLS 1:350–357).

The very inclusion of property and other formal features of such exchanges, however, would seem to argue that Tinkers' mating arrangements were not casual but were governed by marriagelike strictures.

79. GB, p. 60. Some British Gypsies employed elaborate means such as a catskin chastity girdle to ensure an unmarried girl's virginity, which was also protected by a courtship (like Tinker courtship) so controlled that "the ordinary, uninitiated gorgio [settled person] might be forgiven for wondering how . . . man and maid even manage to communicate their desire to each other" (GB, pp. 63–64).

80. Tinkers were reputed to have observed—in the recent past at least—an arcane marriage ceremony known as "jumping the budget," and writers have speculated that the ceremony featured bride and groom stepping over a broomstick or budget (the box or bag in which a tinsmith kept his tools) witnessed by family members. Tinkers themselves were often quick to refute the existence of a special ceremony, perhaps for the same reason that they did not discuss earlier serial marriage: any suggestion that church and state had not solemnized a union could invite settled censure. In telling of their own or others' marriages several Tinkers mentioned that boy and girl had in some manner "run away" before taking part in a church ceremony or before their union was openly accepted by their parents.

Perhaps some Tinkers still followed a custom similar to that found among Gypsies (i.e., GB, pp. 64–65), and among settled Irish a century or more earlier in which young men "stole," abducted, or eloped with their intended brides and only after a specified period of time returned home to be married by priest and/or community. If this were the case, then "jumping the budget" could have referred literally to the girl's climbing over her father's tool box in her hasty exit from tent, camp, or caravan and metaphorically to the young couple's temporary flight from the rules and norms of family life.

81. Patrick's wife was known to him and to her friends as Mary Ellen Ward, not Stokes. The Irish-language tradition of being called, even after marriage, the daughter-of-one's-father persisted long in English-speaking Ireland where women identified themselves only secondarily by their husbands' names. Many Tinkers still kept the custom in the 1960s and 1970s, though most other Irish had abandoned it. That Bridget was widely although not invariably called Murphy, her married name, was perhaps another indication of her acceptance of contemporary settled manners.

82. YG, pp. 8–9.

83. Crockery, despite its bulk, fragility, and weight, was a specialty of Scottish Gypsy and Tinkler-Gypsy hawkers. In the 1800s Simson wrote that "almost all . . . individuals hawking earthenware through the country, with carts . . . are Gipsies" and that many who had recently ceased Traveling "now keep shops of earthenware, china and crystal. Some of them, I am informed on the best authority, have from one to eight thousand pounds invested in this line of business" (HG, pp. 347–348).

84. Sean O'Sullivan's partial but lengthy list of non-nutritive and nonindustrial uses of native plants, including groundsel, attests to the great interest in herbal remedies in Ireland in the past (HIF, pp. 285–288). British Gypsies apparently made little use of groundsel. The herbal practices of both Traveling women and Traveling men (see note 104) probably tended to substantiate the supernatural powers Travelers were said to

possess. That Tinkers and Gypsies included the use of herbal poisons (against animals and people, sometimes at settled commission) in their practical science doubtless enlarged the fear of those powers among settled folk (GB, pp. 138–160; IGT, p. 381).

85. According to Hindu sacred law, in the ideally realized fourth stage of a man's life he severs his connections with property and community and becomes a "homeless wanderer," thus gaining in religious enlightenment (WI, p. 158). The *sadhus*, or wandering holy men of modern India, are partly holy by virtue of their mobility, which signifies abandonment of worldly interests.

86. Some such Gypsies claimed to have descended from biblical figures—Cain and Noah, for example—whereas others presented letters of safe-conduct from sundry kings and popes attesting that the Gypsies were errant Christians traveling in expiation of their sins. The devout townsfolk of Germany and France thus gladly gave the wanderers shelter.

87. "The Tinker and the Crucifixion," a version of which is told by Patrick Stokes, is the closest thing to a legend of origin that has been found among Tinkers, and it establishes a fundamental and possibly magical sympathy between the Tinker and Christ. The same event, the crucifixion, puts an end to the ordinary human existence of each: Christ dies and is no longer a man; the Tinker loses his place in the settled community of men and is condemned to eternal wandering.

88. Q.

89. In 1890 Sampson wrote that Irish country folk were especially wary of a Tinker woman Traveling alone, for such a woman sometimes moved in advance of her band and, taking advantage of the householder's sympathy, was granted a night's lodging and protection. She would then be joined by a large, unruly crowd of other Tinkers (JGLS 2:204–221).

90. The Gypsy affection for the hedgehog—as food, remedy (see note 94), and mascot of Traveling life—contrasted with the superstitious aversion felt in some regions of Ireland for this animal, which was said to harm cows by sucking milk from their udders and which was thus promptly killed when discovered (GPST, p. 57).

91. Settled English greyhound breeders attempting to improve the qualities of their stock have sometimes crossed them with lurchers, as did Horace Walpole, whose successes inspired "the very start of the romance of coursing and the Greyhound world" (BTG, p. 57). In addition to a kind of dog, in cant *lurcher* meant "a glutton . . . a petty thief, swindler, rogue" (OED, p. 508). The swiftness, silence, and intelligence of lurcher dogs ideally suited them to poaching. Their name may derive from *lurks*, a nineteenth-century word for confidence games or styles of thievery (see IGT, p. 357).

92. In house-dwelling periods some Tinkers kept cats as well as dogs for pets and showed no sign of sharing the restrictive attitude of British Gypsies to whom "dogs and cats are *mochardi* [unclean] . . . because they lick themselves all over" (GB, p. 44).

93. Groome described one Gypsy man's splendid dress as consisting of "a high-crowned, ribbon-decked hat . . . a yellow silk handkerchief, brown velveteen coat with

crown-piece buttons, red waistcoat with spade guinea dittos, cord breeches, and leathern leggings . . . [while] his left hand wields a silver-headed whalebone whip." A Gypsy woman comparably attired wore "a gorgeous kerchief . . . [over] her coal-black, curiously plaited hair. Her ears are pierced by old-fashioned hoops of heavy gold; a necklace of amber, coral, and coins runs thrice about her neck; and her hands are bedizened with massy rings, one of them wrought . . . from a guinea welded upon three wedding rings. A parti-colored apron over a short blue woollen dress, and naily boots . . . with a cutty pipe . . . she has doffed the *monging-guno*, or alms cloth in which, as in some medicant friar's hood, are stowed the breadwinnings of her daily rounds" (IGT, pp. 2–4).

94. Several Tinker women in their forties and fifties explained that hair oiling prevented their turning grey. Ewart Evans wrote of Suffolk, England, in the 1950s that "an old lady called Black Mary . . . lived here a generation or two ago. Her hair was black as a raven's right up to her death . . . they say, she knew the gypsy's *hair patent* as she was herself descended from a traveling woman. The lotion was made from the grease of a hedgehog, soot from the chimney, a drop of eau de cologne or lavender water . . . and a few drops of olive oil. She used it regularly" (AFH, pp. 208–209).

95. Sovereigns and so-called half-sovereigns—large gold coins—were and are worn also by British Gypsy women in necklaces, pendants, and rings. Jewelry made of precious materials and coins traditionally constituted a Gypsy woman's wealth—wealth always carried on her person in public view and of a form suited to immediate use as currency—as does the jewelry of women in some regions of India. Sovereigns bearing the image of England's Queen Victoria and the large coins commemorating Austria's Empress Maria Theresa had both been popular with Gypsies, perhaps for their symbolic as well as their monetary value. Victoria's reign coincided with a period of relative ease for Britain's Gypsies, and Maria Theresa (like her son, Joseph II, see note 113) took an active interest in the improvement of her Gypsy subjects' lot.

96. Many settled Irish felt that Tinker involvement with smoke and soot was more than circumstantial. Although in general Irish tradition soot and smoke had various beneficial uses (e.g., soot for skin eruptions and cuts, smoke for preserving food and for "banishing evil spirits"), some comparable uses by Tinkers were remarked as idiosyncratic. The most commonly cited of these was that Tinker "health is good due to the practice, they say themselves, of giving youngsters generous doses of soot to swallow" (Q).

97. European Jews have been often described as "black" by their Christian country-men; neighboring but ethnically different European Gypsy groups have identified them-selves as "black" and "white"; and Irish Tinkers in Scotland called local Gypsies "blacks." In these instances and many others, differences in physical appearance or complexion have formed only a small part of the distinction being drawn.

98. Some such British Gypsy practices forbade men to eat or drink any food or from any vessel that a woman had stepped over, forbade women to comb their hair in the presence of man, and forbade a woman to walk in front of a seated man. Stringent measures were taken to isolate women from men at times of menstruation and childbirth (GB, pp. 43–54).

99. Sampson, Groome, and others quoted British Gypsies' disapproving remarks about the way "Irish Crinks" treated their wives, which was apparently less ceremonious

and more physically abusive than the Gypsies thought proper. Gypsies offered this difference as a reason why Gypsy girls should not marry Tinker boys (see, for example, IGT, pp. 30–36).

100. In the 1800s a Gypsy woman told Groome: "Everyone can tell fortunes these times. It isn't at all what it used to be. Even the lowest Irish tell fortunes now—for sixpence! and that's a thing ought to be put a stop to" (ICT, p. 377).

101. RCI, p. 34.

102. Some American and European Gypsies—notably Gypsies living in cities—have made a principle of keeping the locations where they practice trade distinct and far from locations where they dwell so that their trade relations with settled folk will not jeopardize their domestic relations with them, and vice versa.

103. Sampson remarked that "the strange inverted reverence between parents and children is one of the many strange features of gypsy life . . . a whole tentful of rough gypsies will hush . . . while a poor gypsy baby stammers out some little saying . . . [and] children are allowed to indulge in the freest open ridicule of their parents without rebuke" (JGLS 3:199–211).

104. In Britain and Ireland Travelers and other individuals who were exceptionally able in the management of horses were often said to possess "the horseman's word." The exact nature of "the word"—which was most often used to tame a wild horse, to quiet an unruly or frightened horse, to move a balking horse, or to make a horse stay in place—was a closely guarded secret, sometimes said to be passed down in given families. It brought prestige and some wealth to those who knew it, for they were called on by their less gifted neighbors to help with difficult animals and often paid for their services. In Ireland it was widely believed that he who had "the word" whispered some magic formula into an animal's ear and instantly got the desired result. Ewart Evans inquired into the phenomenon in England and concluded that "the word" designated a range of horseman's practices of ancient origin, many of them depending on intricate knowledge of the horse's sense of smell, which fact was hidden from uninitiated bystanders by whispering or other means. A horse coper with this secret knowledge would have used substances with distinct odors to stimulate, pacify, frighten, or attract horses, and "in the old days it is likely that the horsemen prepared their own mixtures and got most of their medicines from herbs and trees, as the gipsies do to this day." Fenugreek, for example, was used for a "drawing oil" (to attract a horse); vinegar, gin, milk, and cigarette smoke were pacifiers because they masked other, fear-inspiring aromas in stall or farmyard. Evans thought that Gypsies might have introduced some of this herbal horse lore to Britain but that much of it was probably older than their arrival and had been associated with the privileged craft of horsemanship in antiquity. "Apart from the necessity of keeping their secrets for their own advantage, the old horsemen probably realized however dimly that it was to the society's advantage that their knowledge should remain esoteric. For in irresponsible hands the real secrets of the Word were dangerous; and if they had become common knowledge, especially at a time when the horse was literally one of the motive forces of society, the result would have been anarchic" (HF, pp. 245–271).

We were told that a cousin of Old Tom Murphy (Bridget Murphy's father-in-law) had possessed "the word."

105. Gypsies too claimed that their personal animals found settled life intolerable and that settled folk could not command such animals' loyalty and obedience. One of Groome's informants said that "Romanis' animals are never like gorgios' [settled peoples']. . . . There was old Tinker, as I called my neddy [ass] after . . . my daddy sold him to a man to work down in a coal pit . . . [in] about three weeks . . . old Tinker got loose . . . and come straight down to the [Gypsy] place . . . and the fine gorgio had hard work to get him away. He'd kick like anything" (IGT, pp. 135–136).

106. An Irish Tinker in Liverpool told Sampson that an important Tinker activity was "trading in calves and asses" (SLI, p. 136), the only mention I know of Tinkers as cattle dealers.

107. An excellent firsthand account of the life of a nineteenth-century *spalpeen* can be read, in English, in Michael MacGowan, *The Hard Road to Klondike*, trans. Valentine Iremonger (London: Routledge & Kegan Paul, 1962).

108. Thomas Munnelly has observed that "cross-border smuggling played an important role in the life of many Irish Travelers during and after the Second World War when many commodities were rationed or scarce" and that a humorous contemporary song, "Smuggling the Tin," was written by a Traveler and can be currently heard sung by Liam Weldon on *Dark Horse on the Wind* (Mulligan Records no. Lun 006). Traveling smugglers in the late 1970s and the 1980s have dealt chiefly, Munnelly says, in "luxury items bought from bomb-damaged stores in that troubled area [Northern Ireland] and peddled in the Republic."

109. Jan Yoors wrote that his Dutch Gypsy friends seized the opportunity for black marketeering during World War II and that their eventual contribution to the Resistance was a result of their familiarity with underworld life and survival tactics and not of their political allegiances (G, pp. 251–256). Similarly, some Tinkers spoke of having sheltered Irish freedom fighters from British authorities during the upheavals of 1900–1916 and mentioned wartime profiteering. None ascribed these activities to conscious political motive.

It is not surprising that military and political conflict elicited from Gypsies and Tinkers the evasive and exploitative maneuvers in which they were well versed and not the desire to defend nations that effectively deprived them of nationality. Tinker enlistment in the British army may thus be justifiably viewed as a form of breadwinning. But the army probably represented other social opportunities. It seems that a good proportion of men who either became prominent leaders or kings within Tinker society or who successfully integrated into settled life (see notes 46 and 75) had had military experience, and this may have also been true of certain Gypsy groups. For example, Gypsy king Tom Stanley stated in the interview cited in note 43 that his grandparents had been English and that he himself was in the RAF as a flight leader and then (when the U.S. got into the war) a colonel in Intelligence. He explained, "I was valuable because I had contacts behind the lines in all the countries." The Scottish Gypsy chiefs mentioned in notes 45 and 77 had soldiered for settled monarchs. Tinker or Gypsy men may have learned in military life skills that later helped them become effective leaders. Living intimately with other, settled, soldiers under the surveillance of settled officers, some Tinkers must have come to appreciate the personal similarities between themselves and those from whom, in civilian life, they were estranged by class or caste differences. The Travelers' understanding of the nature of those differences and of the uses of regimentation and impersonal authority must also have improved. Such appreciation and understanding would have been of great value to the Traveling king's activities as liaison between Traveling and settled communities. Cross-cultural sophistication of this kind has made a path to prominence for underclass or subculture leaders in many societies. Jackie Robinson, for example, became the first black baseball player admitted to white games not only because of the excellence of his play but because he "had the college education, he had the exposure to the military. He had operated and functioned in formal systems" (Branch Rickey, Jr., in "Only the Ball Was White," produced by Ken Solarz, WTTW, Chicago).

110. *Live Like Pigs,* a play by John Arden, portrays the conflict arising between a Traveling family and its working-class neighbors in an English housing estate. Conflict grows from cultural differences belying the circumstantial similarities of the two groups. Arden stated that his Travelers are "the direct descendants of the [English] 'sturdy beggars' of the sixteenth century . . . put out of their fields by enclosing landlords," Travelers who have found that in contemporary Britain, "there is just no room for nomads." Their difficulties with house dwelling and settled values are comparable to those many Irish Tinkers have suffered.

Arden's play was controversial when first produced in 1958, and its English author was "accused by the Left of attacking the Welfare State." Arden subsequently lived for many years in Ireland, where he took an active interest in Tinkers (TP, pp. 100–189).

111. The Tinkers' mid-twentieth-century insistence on occupational self-determination, their pride in a nominating vocation (even when it had fallen into disuse), and their avoidance of long term wage-labor, as well as their persistent sense of alliance and status within occupational groupings (i.e., tinsmiths)—as opposed to identification with a cross-occupational economic stratum (e.g., labor, or management)—evokes the historical estrangement of settled artisan or craftsman and his laboring counterpart. As Thompson wrote of England: "Among such specialized artisans (i.e., as nail and chain makers) at the commencement of the nineteenth century . . . 'we have industrial society still divided vertically trade by trade, instead of horizontally between employers and wage-earners.'" And "the distinction between the artisan and the laborer—in terms of status, organization, and economic reward—remained as great, if not greater in . . . London of the late 1840s and 1850s as it was during the Napoleonic Wars" (EWC, p. 240). In the 1970s a County Antrim Tinker "speaking about his trade . . . explained how it was the tradition that no tinker should hire himself to a boss who would expect him to do unskilled labor as this would lower him in the eyes of his family and fellow-tinkers. 'Think,' he said, 'of a craftsman being a laboring man'" (UF 17:91).

112. This "trick" was but one of many examples of practical confidence artistry that drew upon and substantiated Tinkers' and Gypsies' reputations as masters of transformation and invocation. Both men and women practiced confidence artistry but seemingly with some specialization. Groome, for example, first had the "big trick" explained to him by a policeman, who said it was undertaken largely by Gypsy women who "gets in with ignorant servant-girls . . . under the stall of fortune-telling, and love-charms. . . . They'll get round some old farmer's wife . . . in an out-of-the-way place, when they knows there's money kept in the house,—for there's many of them farmers as wouldn't trust the Bank of England with a sovereign" (IGT, p. 357). Settled people's mistrust of banks was cited in the Irish press in the 1960s also as a motivation for Tinker con games. Some settled folk enjoyed meeting the challenge posed by Tinker duplicity and apparently always have done. The game is nicely reversed, for example, in an old story about

Tinkler-Gypsy Will Baillie, well-known brigand and leader of a gang of pickpockets in seventeenth-century Scotland: A prosperous farmer whose gold-filled purse was picked at a fair by one of Baillie's gang stuffed a second purse with stones, put in in his pocket, and went out again into the fair. There he seized the pickpocket in the act of taking the second purse. The farmer promised not to harm the thief if his gold were restored. He was led to a nearby house, the gang's rented headquarters, where Baillie himself appeared, went "to a concealment in the wall and brought out the very purse the farmer had lost with its contents untouched, which he returned to the farmer" (HG, pp. 107–108). It was my impression that far from being discountenanced when they were caught in their deceptions, some Tinkers seemed to relish such a development. Whatever object might have been lost by the uncovering of a ruse seemed compensated by the pleasure of a challenging, unexpected new twist in the game. As a County Kerry Folklore Commission correspondent said, "They are the greatest white liars in existence, but they enjoy being tripped up or caught out in their lies" (Q).

113. In 1980 Thomas Munnelly wrote to me that although most Travelers were still unlettered "and thus their story and song repertoire has not been greatly affected by print . . . like their settled peers young Travelers are [now] often a bit embarassed by the 'old-fashioned' songs and prefer pop music. This situation was aggravated by the introduction of the portable radio and a watershed in the decline of traditional singing was reached. Then came portable televisions—and I've seen color televisions recently in bow-tents!—and the decline accelerated greatly. . . . In the few years since the material for *Puck of the Droms* was collected people like Bridget Murphy, Patrick Stokes and Johnny Cassidy have become very scarce, and of those who still retain the old songs and stories: who will listen?"

114. RCI, p. 106.

115. The Site idea, though new to Ireland, was not a new one in the 1960s. Apart from the settlement of Gypsies by their enslavement and by grant of unsupervised lands, European Gypsies had from time to time been provided with means and encouragement to settle by supervisory, settled authorities who intended to convert them to settled attitudes. Territorial or architectural containment of Gypsies and other peoples unassimilated by or ill-adapted to a dominant culture had also often been associated with the idea that the children of the unassimilated could and should be divested of their cultural peculiarities. Containment lent itself to schemes of special education from which other family members—such as the parents of the Navajo children drafted into American schools in the early decades of this century—were excluded.

In the late 1700s, for example, Joseph II of Austria initiated reforms meant to better the lot of nomadic Gypsies. Housing was provided for adults while it was stipulated that Gypsy children should be "removed from all intercourse with the race" and given secular and religious schooling. Children were kidnapped and placed with settled foster parents who received payments from the state. The experiment reportedly failed; "when young Tziganes grew up . . . they had lost none of the instincts of their race, and took the first opportunity of escaping to rejoin their relations" (YG, 133–135). Some later similar and possibly more humane Site schemes may have come closer to achieving their object, such as the Gypsy colonies sponsored by princely patrons in late nineteenth-century German towns offering family cottages, local children's school, and alternative adult occupation (i.e., as "industrious workmen on the railroads") which had the desired effect of making resident Gypsies abandon their own language (JGLS 1:33).

In the pre-Stalinist Soviet Union, Gypsies briefly enjoyed the status of "nationals" and engaged in apparently self-directed settlement in the settled style. They "established cooperative workshops based on traditional skills . . . primary schools, with instruction in the Romani language . . . social clubs and evening classes . . . [and they] petitioned for free land and in many cases formed and ran collective farms" (Grattan Puxon, "Gypsies: Blacks of East Europe," *The Nation*, April 17, 1976, p. 461).

116. Some Sites required Tinker residents to own caravans or wagons, which were to be slept in.

117. Tinker apprehension of being confined behind closed doors amplified the horror many felt at the idea of being jailed, which in any case threatened an alarming separation from the trusted family-centered society.

118. Grattan Puxon continued his work outside of Ireland and became a leader of the developing international Gypsy civil rights movement. He was a member of the Geneva-based Comité International Rom until 1971 when he was elected secretary general of the World Romani Congress, based in Salonika, and he is the author of many papers on present-day Gypsy problems, including *Rom: Europe's Gypsies*, commissioned by the Minority Rights Group in London.

Notes on the stories, songs, and verses have been generously contributed by and are signed with the initials of several scholars who have brought to the task authoritative knowledge of their fields which are:

> *Irish folk song: Thomas Munnelly (T. M.)*
> *Irish folk tale: Dáithí Ó hOgáin (D. O.)*
> *Irish folk tale: Sean O'Sullivan (S. O.)*
> *American popular song: Robert K. Oermann (R. O.)*
> *Romany fortune-telling: Ruth E. Andersen (R. A.)*
> *Children's lore: Iona Opie (I. O.)*
> *(The signature A. C. marks my additional comments.)*

Bridget Murphy
Hawker and Housewife

1. Bridget Murphy: Hawker and Housewife consists of biographical materials recounted by Bridget Murphy in 1967 in County Wicklow. Avowedly literary materials included in this section are distinguished by typeface and credited to the individual Travelers from whom they were collected.

2. Sullivan John (sung by Mickey Murphy, in Co. Wicklow)
Usually called "Sullivan's John." Practically every Irish folk group performs or has recorded "Sullivan's John" and during the folksong fad of the 1960s and early 1970s it was one of the most widely and consistently heard. It first came to most people's notice when a Wexford Traveler and street singer began playing around the folk clubs. This Traveler, "Pecker" Dunne, claimed to have written the song himself and said he based

it on an actual happening. According to him this Sullivan eloped with a Tinker girl and went on the road making his living as an accordion player. "Tool box" in the first verse is frequently rendered "tootle box," that is, accordion. Pecker's claim to authorship is generally conceded, though a number of informants I have worked with, including Travelers, have vigorously contradicted it. Incidentally, Pecker got his nickname from the surname of a man he worked for in Wexford, and it does not have the same connotation in Ireland as it does in the United States. The Spancil Hill horse fair is still held on St. John's Day, June 25, and is itself the subject of a number of songs.—T. M.

3. Early, Early in the Spring (sung by Luke Wall, in Co. Wicklow)
Purely narrative songs in the Irish language are practically nonexistent. You could get the stanzas, shuffle them around in any order, and they would still make as much sense. Of course, purely lyrical songs are also common in the English-language tradition, and this song is a perfect example of the random adhesion of ubiquitous verses to form a song. The individual stanzas can be found in scores of other songs; for example: verse 1 is a standard opening to "The Croppy Boy," verse 2 is associated with "Love Is Pleasing," verse 3 with "Waly Waly," and verse 4 with "I Know My Love."—T. M.

4. Paddy MacInerny (sung by Patrick Stokes, in Co. Dublin)
This song is also known as "Old Caravee." "Carramee" or "Caravee" is most likely a corruption of Cahirmee, the site of one of the great annual horse fairs much frequented by Travelers in the county of Cork. This song does not seem to have any currency in the settled community. A version may be found on a record, "The Bonny Green Tree" (Topic 12t 359). The Traveler who sings it on this disc, John Reilly, sings: "And she *used* the black bottle on me." Guinness is the favorite tipple of the Irish Traveler, and the bottles, black in color, are often used as instruments of aggression.—T. M.

5. I Went into a Shiney's House (recited by anonymous child, in Co. Dublin)
The basic source of this rhyme seems to be the dipping (i.e., counting-out) rhyme given in Iona Opie and Peter Opie, *Children's Games in Street and Playground* (London: Oxford University Press, 1969).

> I went to a Chinese laundry, to buy a loaf of bread,
> They wrapped me up in a tablecloth and this is what they said:
> Eenie meenie mackeracka
> Rare-ri dominacka,
> Chickeracka lollipoppa om pom push.

Our surveys have been confined to England, Scotland, and Wales for the most part, and the oldest version we have in our files is dated 1943–1951. In recent years the verse has been adopted for hand clapping, for which there was a great craze in the 1960s continuing unabated to the present day. In the clapping version (collected 1969 onward) it is not a laundry but a restaurant that is visited for bread, and what "they" say is: "My name is Ooni poonie chickerie chickerie om pom alarie Chinese cheese." I would imagine the "shiney's house" is a corruption of "Chinese house." The last part of this Irish verse is more of a problem but could conceivably have grown from a song like this skipping song:

> There's somebody under the bed,
> Whoever can it be?

I feel so blooming nervous
I call _____ in with me.
_____ lights the candle.
_____ looks under the bed.
Get out, you fool, get out, you fool,
There's nobody under the bed.

It is amazing how these rhymes evolve, using bits of other rhymes by association until an almost new rhyme comes into being.—*I. O.*

6. The Man Who Caught the Mermaid (told by Patrick Stokes, in Co. Dublin)
The legend of the man who marries a mermaid or seal woman is found in the coastal area of northwest Europe (Ireland, Scotland, Iceland, and western Scandinavia). For references to the legend see Séamus Ó Duilearga, *Leabhar Sheáin Í Chonaill* (Dublin, 1948), pp. 438–439. It is listed as no. 4080 in Reidar Th. Christiansen, *The Migratory Legends* (Helsinki, 1968). Other versions and notes are in Seán Ó Súilleabháin, *The Folklore of Ireland* (London, 1974) no. 22, and NYT, no. 74.—*D. O.*

7. Carrickfergus (sung by anonymous woman, in Co. Dublin)
Also known as "Do Bhí Bean Uasal" (There Was a Lady). Until recently this was known almost exclusively as a macaronic or wholly Gaelic song, and as such many versions can be found in the manuscript collection of the Department of Irish Folklore, University College, Dublin. In the 1960s Seán Ó Ríada's influential musical group "Ceoltóirí Cualann" made a recording for the Gael Linn record company. This version (sung by Seán Ó Sé), like some of the macaronic versions, had all the verses in English, which were approximate translations of the Irish stanzas. Because of the popularity of this recording, many people who knew no Irish learned the English-language verses and sang them as a separate composition. It is likely that this is the source of the present informant's text. The two great nineteenth-century Irish collectors, Bunting and Petrie, give us copies of "Do Bhí Bean Uasal" in PPC and in BAMI, p. 52. The theme of this song is similar to that of the well-known Northumbrian song, "The Waters O' Tyne." Kilkenny is known as the "Marble City," marble being so plentiful in the area that it was used as an ordinary building material. Even footpaths were made from it.—*T. M.*

8. Billy Boy (sung by Kathleen Kiley, about age seven, in Co. Dublin)
I follow the example of Bronson and Sharp in considering this pleasant little ditty to be related to Child 12, "Lord Randal," but do not go as far as Baring Gould, who considered it to be a prototype. Bronson says (1:226), "It is clear, at any rate, that the records of the parody are of approximately equal age with those of the serious ballad" and "it is reported that the first appearance of the song was in *The Bee*, an Edinburgh magazine, in May 1791." Frank C. Brown collected no less than forty-seven versions in North Carolina and, in spite of the paucity of Irish texts in print, there are very few children in Ireland who could not furnish the collector with some fragment of "Billy Boy," for it remains a firm favorite in street and classroom.
Britain: JFSS 8:210 (Dorset), SFE 4:6 (Worcestershire); *North America*: BNC 3:166–169 (North Carolina), SKSA 1:39 (Virginia); *Ireland*: JIFSS 18:33 (Kerry). See also Bronson, under Child 12 (appendix).—*T. M.*

9. No Place to Lie Down (sung by Johnny Connors, in Co. Dublin)
"Can I Sleep in Your Barn Tonight Mister," its more common title, was collected by

Vance Randolph (*Ozark Folksongs,* vol. 4). He cites it as part of a nineteenth-century complex of songs sentimentalizing hobos. Evidently the earliest version recorded is Charlie Poole's of 1925 (Columbia 15038D). It was recorded by Vernon Dalhart in 1927 (Edison 51901), by Joe Reeve (real name: Miller Wikel) in 1928 (Conqueror 7254), and by Marvin Williams with a Hawaiian band in 1930 (Okeh 45467)—R. O.

Two versions from North Carolina are also found in BNC 3:420–423.—T. M.

Of the varieties of American popular and commercial song to which Travelers (through their settled contacts and through broadcasts) had been exposed by the 1960s, songs in the general tradition of country and western were most firmly established in their affections and repertoire, perhaps partly because the themes of songs such as this one seemed particularly sympathetic.—A. C.

10. Selling the Child
This account gives an interesting insight into condescending attitudes toward itinerants among certain sections of society in Ireland. The episode nevertheless represents an exaggerated attitude and must be an isolated instance. Motif D2071 (Evil Eye) is very strong in Irish folk belief.—D. O.

11. Wallflowers (sung by Biddy Donovan, about age nine, in Co. Dublin)
This is a well-known children's ring game in Ireland, comparable to the American "Ring Around the Rosie." A group of children join hands and circle round while singing. With each repetition of the verse the name of the youngest child facing center is called out, as "Mary" is here, and that child turns to face outward but remains a part of the circle. The game concludes when all the children are facing outward. The wallflowers referred to are those of a commonly cultivated and also feral plant that clings to walls and old buildings and has a distinctive scent. The term *wallflower* is also used in Ireland for a young woman who is outside the social whirl. In this game the association of climbing wallflowers with girl children who "do not like to die" and who are named in ascending order of age seems metaphorical. Wallflowers may have been associated with the deaths of children, thus Groome's account of a British Gypsy infant's funeral: ". . . men brought the little coffin down; and two little girls come dressed all in white, and they brought two great bunches of wallflowers and put them all over the child in the coffin" (IGT, p. 65). A longer version of "Wallflowers" is in E. Brady, *All In! All In!* (Dublin, 1975).—A. C.

12. A Fortune (told by an anonymous woman, in Co. Wicklow)
When Romany Gypsies left India about A.D. 900 they took with them their particular form of the art of fortune-telling, a convenient, profitable means of livelihood which proved uniquely suited to their continuing status as exotic outsiders. Both Tinkers and Gypsies have for several hundred years been fellow travelers on the byways of Britain, and much cultural borrowing has occurred. It is possible, then, that Tinkers learned this form of fortune-telling from the Gypsies, who have been present in the British Isles since the 1400s. Whether or not this is so, this Tinker fortune is quite similar to those told by Romany Gypsies in the United States and Britain and bears several formulaic hallmarks of the genre. First, the teller begins with a reference to the lines of the palm but never again mentions any configurations of the hand. Gypsy fortune-tellers in the United States often advertise themselves as palm readers, yet they make little or no reference to the hand in their presentations, simply holding it and looking at the customer's face, where they probably find much more information. They also liberally employ such endearments as "honey," "darling," and "sweetheart," as the teller here uses "dear." This text shows

the elements common to many forms of fortune-telling, including a blend of character analysis, general advice, and specific information about the life of the customer. The use of endearments emphasizes the role of the fortune-teller as adviser, increases the engaging personal quality of the event, and lends the teller an aura of kindly yet powerful wisdom. Also, the teller here employs questions as a means of involving her hearer in the situation. In every Romany fortune I have collected the seer uses a similar question (such as "Am I right or am I wrong?") repeated at intervals to hold the customer's attention and, if many responses are positive, to reinforce the impression of the fortune-teller's skill. As with any type of feedback between performer and audience, this question-and-answer technique allows the performer to gauge the appropriateness of what she has said and make necessary adjustments. Finally, the teller uses the type of paradoxic parallel construction identified by Graves in his model of the fortune-telling event (Graves and Andersen, unpubished paper, 1979). This good-but-bad structure (as in "You're a person is not fond of rows or arguments, but you've got a hasty temper when your temper's risen") is used in this case to qualify bald, definite statements and present a well-rounded total picture of the customer's life. The Tinker's actual predictions are quite specific, probably because she is performing at a fair and will thus be moving soon to a new location, where she will not be required to answer for her statements. Also, as C. G. Leland points out in his study *Gypsy Sorcery and Fortune Telling*, the telling predictions are usually noticed and remembered while the others are forgotten. The traditional insistence on silver has become part of the stereotype of fortune-telling, although I have never encountered it in the United States (where the going rate for a fortune is five dollars and up). It may be traced to the medieval science of astrology, which reached its height as a learned field in the fifteenth and sixteenth centuries and became part of popular culture in England in the later part of the seventeenth century. In the astrological symbolic world, the moon represents the area of dreams, illusions, and imaginations. Mediums and seers are thought to be especially influenced by the moon, the planet symbolized in the mineral kingdom by the metal silver.

The definitive modern study of fortune-telling as a form of folkloric performance has yet to be written.—R. A.

13. Avondale (sung by Bridget Murphy, in Co. Wicklow)
Revenant ballads in which a victim of drowning visits his true love are plentiful (e.g., "Lowlands Away"; "Willie Leonard," Laws Q 33; "Lost Jimmy Whelan," Laws C 8), but this example of the genre is completely unknown to me. It fits into the traditional mold well enough, but the twist in verse 4 makes it somewhat unusual. Whatever its genesis, it is a fine song and as moving as any I've come across in many a day. Avondale, Co. Wicklow, was the birthplace and home of the great political leader Charles Stewart Parnell (1846–1891), himself the subject of many songs, at least two of which are called "The Blackbird of Avondale." "Avondale" is also the title of a song on Parnell attributed to Dominic Behan. A short distance from the Parnell seat the Avonmore joins the Avonbeg River, and this junction was the inspiration for Thomas Moore's famous drawing-room song, "The Meeting of the Waters."—T. M.

Bridget Murphy reported that she learned this song from one Johnny Porter in Avon-dale itself.—A. C.

14. McCaffery Murder (sung by Patrick Stokes, in Co. Dublin)
"'McCafferty' has seldom appeared in print but there is hardly a regular soldier who does

not know a version of it," states A. L. Lloyd in his *Folk Song in England* (New York, 1970), p. 262. It is equally popular among the Irish singing public and particularly so among Travelers. Of nineteenth-century origin, the song cannot be ascribed to any particular incident. The story in our text is somewhat garbled. Usually, the soldier is merely ordered to take the names of the children's parents (verse 2). Verse 3 is a compilation of two verses and should run something like this:

> With a loaded rifle I did prepare
> To shoot my captain on the barracks square.
> 'Twas Captain Hamilton I meant to kill,
> But shot my colonel against my will.
>
> I done the deed, I shed the blood.
> At the Liverpool Assizes my trial I stood.
> Said the judge to me: "McCafferty,
> Prepare yourself for the gallows tree."

That, at least, is how my father, a Dublinman, sang it, and agrees with the versions Lloyd prints from Suffolk (*Folk Song in England*, pp. 263–264). The tune used is inevitably that of "The Croppy Boy" (Laws J 14).—*T. M.*

15. Young Tom Murphy (sung by Old Mick Murphy, in Co. Wicklow)
We have here an evocative picture of the life of a Traveler. Presumably a "jin" is a jennet, for the cross between a horse and donkey is colloquially referred to as a "jinnit." The beast in this song, like "Pat from Bolaneer," has a miserable existence, condemned as he is to survive on the furze bushes of the Wicklow Mountains. In the time I spent in Aughrim, Co. Wicklow, or over the Carlow border in Hackettstown I did not encounter Travelers, though such a song as this would be probable at the campfires of the families that wander these roads. To date I have not collected "Young Tom Murphy" in any part of Ireland. "Ballinaglen" is probably Ballinglen, Co. Wicklow.—*T. M.*

Old Mick Murphy said that he composed this song himself.—*A. C.*

16. The Little Bit (told by Martin Donovan, in Co. Dublin)
This humorous anecdote concerning alms from a priest is of a kind popular in Ireland. I have heard a version of this story in Co. Limerick in which the beggar is a drunkard who uses the money, unknown to the priest, to buy alcohol, the priest pretending all the while that the money appears miraculously each day at a statue of the Blessed Virgin while the drunkard carries on a novena to help him abstain. Motif used here is J2348 (dupe is persuaded that money will grow if he buries it), but in this case the dupe outwits the motif!—*D. O.*

A version of the Gypsy/Tinker confidence game described in the Introduction (see p. 52) is here enacted as a battle of wits between a priest and an "innocent fella," the "innocent" proving himself the greater trickster of the two.—*A. C.*

17. The Balty Mare (sung by Old Tom Murphy, in Co. Wicklow)
More commonly known as "The Galtee Farmer," this is a popular song and one that is a particular favorite among Travelers. There would of course be many among the

Traveling fraternity who would have carried out such cosmetic overhaul on a cheaply bought hack to resell it. Just add a little pepper under the horse's tail and it is almost possible that the original owner might not recognize the animal! In spite of its popularity "The Galtee Farmer" seems to have slipped through the net of the most prominent Irish collectors, for it does not appear in the indexes of Petrie, Joyce, Sam Henry, or others. Of the dozens of versions I have collected in the field, very few have been as complete as the text printed here.—T. M.

18. The Factory Girl (sung by Luke Wall, in Co. Wicklow)
According to Dr. Hugh Shields, "'The Factory Girl' enters an ancient tradition which first appears with the troubadours, and yet archaic even for the troubadours" (CSLP, p. 7). The *pastourelle* form, in which hero and heroine meet in a pastoral setting, was readily absorbed from French into Irish tradition and evolved from the Irish language into English as the latter gained acceptance in certain areas. A dramatic stage in its continuing evolution is found in "The Factory Girl," where the traditional shepherd and shepherdess stand in the shadow of the Industrial Revolution. Shields tells us that the song appeared on Waterford broadsheets of the mid-1800s and perhaps before. A strikingly beautiful version can be heard sung by Mrs. Makem of Armagh on Topic (no. 12 t 182).
    Britain: PWS, p. 29 (Hampshire); *Ireland*: SCL, pp. 8–10, 2 versions (Down and Derry), MSU, pp. 31–32 (Armagh).—T. M.

19. The Wren Song (sung by Patrick and Mary Ellen Stokes, in Co. Dublin)
The custom of "hunting the wren" is still widespread in Ireland, although it may not be as prevalent as in the past, and even a cursory examination of the collection of the archives of the Department of Irish Folklore in U.C.D. reveals scores of variants of this rhyme from practically every county. Nowadays the teams of so-called Wren Boys who sing this song while visiting house-to-house on St. Stephens' Day are more likely to have an effigy than a real bird to accompany their festivities. Rather than quote specific examples, I recommend the interested reader to refer to notes on the subject such as Kevin Danaher's entry in his *The Year in Ireland* (Cork, 1972), pp. 243–250; JFSS 18:78–79; or Estyn Evans, *Irish Folk Ways* (London, 1957), pp. 211–212.—T. M.

20. Prayer for Toothache (recited by Old Tom Murphy, in Co. Wicklow)
Such charm prayers were in great use in Ireland. For a fourteenth-century version see *Irisleabhar na Gaedhilge* 7 (1896): 116. Other published examples in B 3 (1932): 120, 126, 169; B 4 (1934): 56; B5 (1935): 215; B 6 (1936): 52, 103; and RSC, vol. 2, 58063, 382–3 390–1, 416–7.—D. O.

In her *Ancient Legends of Ireland* (London, 1888), Lady Wilde gives various cures for toothache, including a verse substantially the same as this one which "is to be sewn on the clothes" (p. 196).—A. C.

21. My Mary Dear (sung by Old Tom Murphy, in Co. Wicklow)
Often called "Here's a Health to All True Lovers" or "Willie-O"; cf. Child 248. Child reprints the ballad that David Herd called "The Grey Cock" in his *Ancient and Modern Scots Songs* (Edinburgh, 1766). This ballad is in the form of an *alba*, a medieval song type concerning lovers who must part with the dawn. The characters in the *alba* are

manifestly corporeal, and in "The Grey Cock" there is no suggestion that one of the lovers is from beyond the grave. It has been well argued that the supernatural elements found in this ballad are a later (nineteenth-century?) rationalization of the story, influenced by an age in which romantic poetry was endemic and it was much less offensive for a maiden to allow a ghost to enter her boudoir than a healthy youth! The form we have here is what is most commonly found in Ireland; a recording of a Traveler singing a version may be heard on Topic (no. 12T 359). Three relevant and totally engrossing studies have been published by Dr. Hugh Shields: "Une alba dans la poésie populaire anglaise:" *Revue des langues romanes* 89 (1971): 461–475; "The Dead Lover's Return in Modern English Ballad Tradition," *Jahrbuch für Volksliedforschung* (1972), pp. 98–114; and "The Grey Cock: Dawn Song or Revenant Ballad?" *Ballad Studies* (The Folklore Society, London, 1976), pp. 67–92.

    North America: KNF 100–102 (Newfoundland), SKSA 1, 259 (North Carolina); *Britain*: OBS, 89 (Scotland, exact area not specified), JEFDSS vol. 7, no. 2, p. 97 (Birmingham). Bronson and Coffin have many more versions under Child 248.— T. M.

22. The Cradle Song (sung by Mickey Murphy, in Co. Wicklow)
Very large families were considered desirable among most rural folk. Until they had reproduced, individuals were not considered whole adults, and impotent males were often the butt of cruel humor. Such black humor is particularly common among Travelers, for they still consider a man's social stature by the size of his family and would have very little sympathy for the narrator of "The Cradle Song." Though I have not come across the song before, I suggest that verse 6 is somewhat confused. Surely it would be the narrator, and not the visitor, who would be banished from the nuptial bed to the cradle? Therefore the last line should read: "And she lent *me* [sent me to] the blooming big cradle."—T. M.

23. Prayer to Stop Blood (recited by Old Tom Murphy, in Co. Wicklow)
This charm prayer, known in Irish as *Ortha na Fola*, was very much in use as a means of stopping bleeding. Some people still alive are credited with being able to cure bleeding with the prayer even at a distance, that is, by reciting it without visiting the afflicted person at all. Published versions in B 3 (1932): 356, 371, 427; B 6 (1936): 257; and RSC, 2: 380–383, 416.—D. O.

24. My Gentle Mother's Grave (sung by Bill Cassidy, in Co. Dublin)
Some suppose this song, also known in Ireland as "Gentle Mother," to be of American country and western origin; however, that may not be the case.—A. C.

My wife and I heard this song often in pubs in the years we lived in northern Ireland (1973–74), but I've never encountered it in the United States in all my years of involvement with popular music. So I believe it must be Irish or British in origin. The mother and death themes seem to indicate the Victorian period. Most Irish singers probably know the song from the version by the popular Irish showband Big Tom and the Mainliners which was a hit there in 1967–68. Big Tom's last name is McCormick. Although it shares a common title, this song is quite distinct from the American parlor song "My Gentle Mother's Grave."—R. O.

Patrick Stokes
Laborer and Tinsmith

1. Patrick Stokes: Laborer and Tinsmith consists of biographical materials recounted by Patrick Stokes from 1967 through 1969 in County Dublin. Avowedly literary materials included in this section are distinguished by typeface and credited to the individual Travelers from whom they were collected.

2. The Tinker and the Crucifixion (told by Patrick Stokes, in Co. Dublin) Such origin legends concerning the life of Our Lord were very popular in Ireland. For other versions of this particular legend see Seán Ó Súilleabháin, *Scéalta Cráibhtheacha* (Dublin, 1952), also B 21, no. 2, and NYT, no. 102.—D. O.

In early Gypsy studies there were many scholarly attempts made to search out reason for the then apparent similarities between Gypsies and Jews in Europe, to find a common origin and develop a history of Gypsy dispersal and migration rationalized by Judaic scripture. Gypsies were also linked with Jews in popular tradition, and Groome recounts an Alsatian legend (from Dr. G. Muhl's "Die Zigeuner in Elsass und in Deutschloth-ringen," *Der Salon*, 1874) that he supposes Gypsies "probably devised expressly to refute" responsibility for Christ's crucifixion, a responsibility often given them in stories similar to "The Tinker and the Crucifixion." The Alsatian legend says: ". . . there were two Jew brothers, Schmul and Rom-Schmul. The first of them exulted at the Crucifixion; the other would gladly have saved Our Lord from death, and, finding that impossible, did what he could, pilfered one of the nails. So it came about that Christ's feet must be placed one over the other and fastened with a single nail. And Schmul remained a Jew, but Rom-Schmul turned Christian and was the founder of the Romani race" (IGT, p. 279). The episode of the stolen nail (although told without the same Jewish compo-nent) was well known in Ireland, and some Tinkers believed that there was one day each year, often said to be Good Friday, when they could steal with impunity since it was a Tinker who had saved Christ from the fourth nail.—A. C.

3. Long Time A-Growing (sung by Mary Ellen Stokes, in Co. Dublin) Commonly known as "The Trees Are Growing Tall" or "The Bonny Boy," this venerable song is extremely popular in Irish and British tradition. Almost anyone with old songs will have a version of it. It is said that the song is about an actual marriage, that of an Urquhart of Craigston to Elizabeth, the daughter of the Laird of Innes. Young Urquhart died in 1634. This may indeed have been the origin of the song, but it is more probable that the facts become attached to the song than vice versa. Many will share the enthusiasm of Maude Karpeles, who described these poignant verses as "perhaps the most beautiful of all ballads outside the Child canon." One may be forgiven for wondering why in fact it was not included in that canon as its antiquity and ballad form, if slender, surpass a number of those texts given Child's imprimatur.

North America: KNF 120 (Newfoundland), FONE 196 (Connecticut); *Britain*: JFSS 11, 95 (Devon), OBS 112 (Scotland, exact area not specified); *Ireland*: KBI, pp. 473–474 (Co. Donegal).—T. M.

4. Pub Recitation (recited by Johnny Cassidy, in Co. Dublin) Commonly called "The Hap'orth of Lies," there are many texts of this little celebration

of the ridiculous in the MS collection of the Department of Irish Folklore, U.C.D.; another version of it, "The Song of Lies," is included in this collection.—T. M.

Johnny Cassidy explained that when he entered a likely pub and held an open book upside down in front of his eyes while reciting the "Pub Recitation" at a great speed (and thus gave the impression that he was a miraculous reader) his performance was greatly appreciated by the pub's patrons, who rewarded him with rounds of drinks.—A. C.

5. The Little Beggarman (sung by Joe Donohue, in Co. Dublin)
This is also known as "The Old Rigadoo" and "Johnny Doo." It is not uncommon to find songs celebrating the supposedly carefree life of the beggarman in the repertoire of the settled community, though it may be considered mildly surprising that this song is just as popular among Travelers, who are completely aware that such a life is anything but idyllic. Colum O'Lochlainn (OMSB, pp. 230–231) gives the text of a broadsheet, "The Old Settoo" (seettoo = surtout = overcoat), which is apparently the precursor of our song. Johnny Doo means "black-haired Johnny," from the Irish word *dubh*, meaning "black."
Ireland: KBI, pp. 772–773 (Belfast), OMSB, pp. 52–53 (Dublin).—T. M.

6. The Boy and the Banshee (told by Patrick Stokes, in Co. Dublin)
A legend of the banshee which was quite popular in Leinster and east Connaught. For other versions see Patricia Lysaght, "*An Bhean Chainte*: The Supernatural Woman in Irish Folklore," *Eire-Ireland*, Winter 1979, pp. 27–28, and Patricia Lysaght, "*An Bhean Sí*" in Breandán Ó Madagáin, *Gnéithe den Chaointeoireacht* (Dublin, 1978), pp. 62–63.—D. O.

Cf. AT 810 (The snares of the evil one).—S. O.

7. A Small Bit of Butter (sung by Tom and Mickey Murphy, in Co. Dublin)
Also known as "Gut-'ems Damnation Buck Fleas." There is a story told about a Donegal *spailpín* (itinerant farmworker) who was having his first supper in the house of the farmer who had just hired him. The farmer's wife spread some honey on his bread and passed it to him. Unimpressed by the miserly quantity he received, the laborer scrutinized the honey closely and commented: "Begob, ma'm, I see ya keep a bee!" This same tightness of rations is experienced by the hero in our song. With such a high proportion of *spailpíní* in the labor pool in the nineteenth and twentieth centuries, it is natural that there are myriad songs on the theme of the farmworker hired by miserly or cruel farmers. "The Bradys of Killann" and "The Galbally Farmer" are known throughout the country, and there are many with comparatively localized circulation such as "Snotty-nosed Nagel" and this song, which I myself have only heard in Co. Wexford. One is tempted to refer to these songs as a genre as "bothy songs," even though one usually restricts that description to songs of Scottish origin. Nevertheless, many an Irish laborer brought songs from the Scottish bothies (farmworkers' lodgings) and left as many behind him to be dispersed by the Scots *bothy chiel* (farm hand) on returning to his native village. The large quantity of songs that lampoon the farmers and bosses these men worked for can be gauged from even a cursory glance through Ord's collection (OBS). To the best of my knowledge, this song has not previously been published.—T. M.

The ravenous Goodham in this song calls to mind the "Cobham" or "Cob'em" who was "the greedy dog of Romani nursery lore, who 'gobbles his food without waiting to chew it'" (IGT, p. 88).—A. C.

8. The Giant Pike (told by Patrick Stokes, in Co. Dublin)
The story of the cats is the international folktale AT 113A (King of the cats is dead). See Irish versions in IT. The episode of the pike obviously springs from a real event.—D. O.

9. I'm a Rambler, I'm a Gambler (sung by Mary Ellen Stokes, in Co. Dublin)
Usually called "The Moonshiner," this is a curiously garbled fragment in which moonshine has become "sunshine." Delia Murphy sang the version, which can be found on the lips of almost every Irish person over thirty years of age. For thirty years, at least, it would be heard on Radio Eireann on the Saturday afternoon program sponsored by Walton's Music Saloon (a music store, not a pub). The program continues and the same recording is frequently heard. In a collection published by the Waltons, the song is attributed to the late Delia Murphy herself (WNT, p. 47). James N. Healy says no more than "traditional, 19th century" (HCS, p. 7). But on the recent record album of Delia Murphy's 78 rpm discs published by E. M. I. (Stal 1055) we are told on the liner notes that this is "an Amerian drinking song." This latter is much more likely, and it is perhaps a product of the days of Prohibition. For an excellent collection of songs on this genre see BNC 3:41–82.—T. M.

10. The Shaving Ghost
The teller here shows the tendency of many tellers of such stories to put his narrative material in the context of a personal experience. Cf. Motif F331.2 (Mortal wins fairies' gratitude by letting them cut his hair and shave him). The fairies and the dead continually swap traditions in Irish folklore.—D. O.

An Irish ecotype of AT 326 (The youth who wants to learn what fear is), Motif E 281.—S. O.

11. The Half-crown Song (sung by Bill Cassidy, in Co. Dublin)
This song is a satiric comment on the introduction of Children's Allowances, which began to be paid sometime in the early 1930s. Quite a number of songs and poems appeared at the time, suggesting, like our song, that many would try to revive or stimulate their reproductive powers in order to qualify for the payment of two shillings and sixpence for each child!—T. M.

This song seemed particularly popular among Travelers we met who had lived in the counties of Dublin, Wicklow, and Wexford.—A. C.

12. Killing a Swan
This is a particularly interesting memorate, for the teller has very neatly strung together episodes based on the strong Irish belief in the human traits of swans. Motifs D161.1 (Transformation: man to swan) and C841.5 (Tabu: killing a swan).—D. O.

The Irish tradition that it is unlucky to kill or molest a swan is rooted in the belief that swans are the incarnation of human souls, frequently those of nobility, a belief reflected in present-day swan protection laws. There are as well, widespread in Ireland, Britain, and northern Europe, a number of traditional tales of noble youths or maidens who are changed into swans and delivered back into human shape by the fulfilling of an obligation. One such Irish tale is "The Children of Lir" which some scholars believe contributed to the legend in Holinshed of King Leir, in turn the basis for Shakespeare's *The Tragedy of King Lear.*

MacGreine reported Tinkers telling him that cranes (herons) as well as swans ought to be left in peace, "for it might be their own grandfather or grandmother" (B3:170 ff).—A. C.

13. Molly Bawn (sung by anonymous man, in Co. Dublin)

Patrick Weston Joyce recalled hearing this song sung in the last century "in the streets of Dublin by a poor woman with a child on her arm." It is unfortunately true that the practice of street singing is now extinct, though the practice of begging is not. This is particularly true of Travelers who were until recently active in the business of selling and singing ballads at fairs and gatherings throughout the country. "Molly Bawn" was a frequent money spinner for the ballad singer, for this song is a favorite throughout the English-speaking world (Laws quotes thirty-six versions from recent tradition; Laws O 36). The song, as we know it today, is probably Irish, but the story of the ill-starred hunter goes back at least to the Greeks. They knew it as the tale of Procris and Cephalus.

> North America: CM, p. 66 (Michigan), KNF, pp. 113–114 (Newfoundland); Britain: JFSS 2:59 (Somerset), JFSS 7:17 (Norfolk, with interesting notes by Ann Gilchrist); Ireland: OISB, pp. 58–59 (Tyrone), JIFM, p. 220 (Limerick).—T. M.

14. The Pregnant Woman's Trick

This story is widely known in Ulster, according to Michael J. Murphy who published a version of it in 1967 under the title "A Long Night in the Spike." He had collected it from a south Co. Armagh man who "had been a pahvee-pedlar and tramp-navvy in England" but who, as the story's protagonist, identifies himself as a "melodeon musicianer." Murphy's version takes place in England and involves an Englishwoman. "'Spike' [is] a slang term formerly applied to the Workhouse and now given to Night Shelters" (UF 13:1–8).—A. C.

15. Oxford City (sung by Jeannie and Bridget Murphy, in Co. Wicklow)

Although this ballad is known in North America and has been reported frequently in Britain, it is quite a rarity in Irish tradition. The only man whom I heard singing it (John Reilly of Boyle) died before I recorded it from him. This singer was a Traveler; and a Waterford-born Traveler, Mary Doran, sings a similar version to our ballad on Topic (12T 195), recorded in Belfast and published in KBI. Kennedy also recorded a version from another famous Traveling family, the Stewarts of Blairgowrie. Fred Jordan, a Shropshireman, sings his version on Topic 12 T 150 and says that he got it "from traveling folk drifting through."

> North America: FBV, p. 92 (Vermont), GCM, p. 75 (Michigan); Britain: JFSS 7:41–42 (Dorset), PWS, p. 46 (Hampshire): Ireland: KBI, p. 715 (Belfast).—T. M.

16. The North Strand (sung by Kitty Flynn, in Co. Dublin)

Child 4, also known as "False Johnny," "The Parrot Song," and "Six Kings Daughters," this classic ballad is still popular with Traveling and settled singers alike. This particular ballad has not only excited the imagination of singers but scholars have for many years been equally animated about it. Scores of articles have appeared in the academic press and there are at least two books dealing exclusively with it: Iivar Kemppinen, *The Ballad of "Lady Isabel and the False Knight"* (Helsinki, 1954), and Holger Olof Nygard, *The Ballad of Heer Halewijn* (Knoxville, 1958). Child gives this ballad the title "Lady Isabel and the Elf-Knight," aptly demonstrating his uncanny knack of choosing for his master title the name least likely to be used by the traditional performer. More importantly, he devotes a longer introduction to this than any other ballad in his canon, some thirty-two large pages of Olympian scholarship. Bronson published no less than 142 versions in his sister canon. The first Irish version cited below I recorded from a Traveler and it resembles (if somewhat more complete) our text very closely.

    North America: FONE, pp. 129–131 (Maine), DBV, pp. 65–67 (Massachusetts); *Britain:* JFSS 30:300–302 (Isle of Man), BMCS, pp. 164–165 (Somerset); *Ireland:* FMJ 3(1): 17/19 (Roscommon), MSU, pp. 21–22 (Fermanagh). Also see Bronson and Coffin under Child 4.—*T. M.*

Male and female Gypsy brigands specializing in the theft of clothing were notorious in Scotland in preceding centuries. For example, Simson wrote that "it is common practice for old female Gipsies of authority to strip . . . defenseless individuals of their wearing apparel when they met them in sequestered places" (HG).—*A. C.*

17. Learning Flattery (told by Patrick Stokes, in Co. Dublin)
Humorous stories of misunderstanding of speech were very popular in Ireland, as elsewhere. A wide variety of such tales are cataloged in IT under AT numbers 1696–1700.—*D. O.*

18. The Stokeses, Cauleys, and MacDonaghs (sung by Patrick Stokes, in Co. Dublin)
Although I have collected quite a lot from Travelers in the Drumshanbo and general Leitrim area, I have not encountered this song before. The theme of interfamily feuds is a firm favorite among Traveler songwriters. The Cauleys referred to are the MacCauley family.—*T. M.*

19. The Goose and Turkey Tale (told by Patrick Stokes, in Co. Dublin)
AT 1747 (The priest's guest and the eaten chickens). For Irish versions see IT under same number.—*D. O.*

20. Dick Daglen the Cobbler (sung and recited by Johnny Cassidy, in Co. Dublin)
Usually called "Dick Darby the Cobbler." Should you ask an Irish singer today to tell you the source of this song (if he had it in his repertoire), you would be at least 99 percent certain that he would reply, "'The Clancy Brothers and Tommy Makem.'" Indeed, their recording of this song sold as plentifully as any pop song in Ireland in the early sixties. Tommy Makem learned his version from a neighbor, Mrs. Toner, in Keady, Co. Armagh, who told him it came from Scotland. Diane Hamilton, who published a recording of Makem singing this in 1956 (Tradition TLP 1004) says, "Aberdeenshire tinkers in Scotland sing a similar version." I have seen the song in a number of ephemeral songbooks but cannot locate a version in the collections I have to hand. Nevertheless, songs about cobblers abound, e.g., "The Cobbler" (HSP-M, no. 551), "Fagan The Cobbler" (KBI, p. 502), "The Bold Belfast Shoemaker" (OISB, pp. 50–51). The recited section of "Dick Daglen" here is most likely to be a personal (rather than traditional) addition by the singer.—*T. M.*

There is considerable Irish lore about the bird called the water wagtail, including a belief that "the willie wagtail . . . had three drops of the Devil's blood on its tail, and so could never stand still" (GPST, p. 53). In Europe it is also often identified with nomads. Groome stated that "to Gypsies all over England the water-wagtail is known as the '*Romano chiriklo*,' or 'Gipsy magpie,' and they believe that its appearance foretells a meeting with other Gipsies, kinsfolk or strangers, according as it flies or does not fly away; also that the Gipsy lad who kills one of these birds is sure to have a lady for his sweetheart. . . . It is a noteworthy fact that the Greeks had a saying, as old as at least the fifth century B.C., 'Poorer than a *kinklos*' (. . . water-wagtail), and that peasants in the third century A.D. called homeless vagabonds *kinkloi*" (IGT, p. 24).—A. C.

21. Parrots (told by Patrick Stokes, in Co. Dublin)
A finely wrought narrative based on Motifs such as B 131.3 (Bird betrays woman's infidelity) and J55.1 (Cocks who crow about mistress's adultery killed).—D. O.

In the 1800s John Sampson collected a song about a parrot from one of the Lees, a large and prominent English Gypsy family, and translated it thus from Romany into English:

> My mother's bird never told a lie.
> My mother's bird talks like a parson,
> It said yesterday I'd die in prison,
> I'll go home and wring its neck.
>
> If I choke it my father will beat me;
> If my father beats me I'll kill my father;
> If I kill my father I'll be taken to prison,
> And then the parrot's words will come true.
> (JGLS 2:80–93)

The particular style of entrapment the parrot threatens here is nearly identical to that effected by the birds in Patrick's "Parrots." Cf. AT 243 (The parrot pretends to be God).—A. C.

22. The Kilkenny Cats
Widely known in Ireland is the story about two cats in Kilkenny city (tail-tied, as here, in some accounts) who fought so viciously that there was nothing but their tails left, hence the phrase "to fight like Kilkenny cats."—T. M.

23. Green Grows the Rushes (sung by Kitty Flynn, in Co. Dublin)
Also called "The Pride of Snow Hill," the song more commonly associated with this title (also known as "The Red, White and Blue," "Green Grows the Laurel Lily," and in North Carolina "The Wild Olive") is difficult to classify as it is composed of ubiquitous "floating" stanzas. The present song is also textually unstable in tradition, though I have heard similar performances from a number of Travelers. Elements of this song can be found in another (unpublished) song heard at many a campfire, "The Town of Castle d'Oliver," and yet another song that O'Lochlainn calls "The Sporting Youth" (OISB, pp. 94–95) but which is usually known to singers as "The American Stranger." I cannot cite the exact geographical locations, but two Ulster versions of "Green Grows the Rushes" may be found in HSP, no. 165b, and JIFM 13:29.—T. M.

24. The Un-visible Man
This story represents a fine narrative development of Motif D1076 (Magic ring). The account of the establishment in Dublin where invisibility can be achieved through magic for a vast sum of money is a fine example of intimate group lore of the itinerant community.—D. O.

25. Ellen Heaney (sung by Patrick Stokes, in Co. Dublin)
Without stretching the bounds of speculation I think it probable that this Ellen Heaney is no distant relative to Peter Heaney, whose songs are very popular among the Travelers of the North Midlands. Two of his songs, "Willie Heaney" and "Peter Heaney," are autobiographical accounts that also concern brushes with the law. "Peter Heaney" can be heard on Topic Records no. 12T359. Belturbet is in Co. Cavan. It was here on September 5, 1975, that I recorded Bernie Reilly, a relative of the Heaneys. He sang me a song in gammon which was also on the smashing of a (pub?) window! I am almost certain there is a pub named "The Cosy Bar" in Belturbet.—T. M.

26. The Vicar and the Child's Nose (told by Patrick Stokes, in Co. Dublin)
This story represents a very smart development of Motifs such as J652.3 (Priest seduces man's wife), V465 (Clerical vices), and J1530 (One absurdity rebukes another). The servant who outwits his master is a very popular character in Irish folklore (see Irish versions of AT 785A, 875, 921 in IT). In many versions of these stories the master is Dean Swift (see Mackie L. Jarell, "Jack and the Dane: Swift Traditions in Ireland," JAF 77 (1964): 99–117).—D. O.

Cf. AT 1725 (The foolish parson in the trunk) through 1824 (The parody sermon).— S. O.

In the recent past, mutilation of farm animals such as that which takes place in this story and in the foregoing anecdote about piglets' tails was said to be a favorite way for Gypsies and Tinkers to avenge the wrongs or slights of farming folk.—A. C.

27. The Hills of Lensfalee (sung by Jeannie Murphy, in Co. Wicklow)
With its proper title, "The Hills of Glenswilly" or "Glenswilly," this song is attributed to Michael (and sometimes his sister, Bridgit) McGinley of Glenswilly, Co. Donegal. Its popularity, however, is by no means restricted to that county, and it may be heard at practically any gathering of singers, traditional or otherwise, today. Its dissemination was no doubt aided by its appearance in such highly popular songsters as the *Walton's Fireside Songs* (Dublin, 1954), where it can be found in 2: 19. In verse 3 the cuckoo is usually "blythe" rather than "blue."—T. M.

28. The Child in the Budget (sung by Patrick Stokes, Co. Dublin)
Also known as "Kilkenny Street," "Quare-Bungle-Rye," "Bum Your Eye," and "Mind-Your-Eye" (e.g., HSP 700), all tell of a girl who outwits a would-be seducer by offering to sell him an unspecified mysterious concoction concealed in her basket. Sometimes, as in the popular "Basket of Eggs" (e.g., JFSS 2:102), the seducer thinks he is buying farm produce. In all cases, however, the Don Juan of the piece finds he has been duped and discovers that he has just purchased an infant. He is left literally "holding the baby" after its mother has disappeared. "The Child in the Budget" is a successful variation on the same theme. I have heard it sung at a number of campfires and it can be found in the manuscript collection of the Department of Irish Folklore, U.C.D.

North America: PNF 895 (Newfoundland); *Britain*: LPP 416 (Scotland); *Ireland*: HSP 700, HSP-M 66 (Antrim).—T. M.

J.-P. Clébert tells an old story of "a Gypsy [who] stole a sheep near Roye in Picardy and wished to sell it for a hundred sous to a butcher, who refused to pay so much. The butcher went away, whereupon the Gypsy took the sheep from the sack . . . and instead put one of his little boys [in it]. Then he ran after the butcher and said: 'Give me so much more and you'll have the sack as well.' The butcher paid and went off. On arriving home he opened the sack and was highly astonished when he saw come out of it a little boy who . . . seized the sack and fled." Clébert observes that "the peasant mentality of the period was easily stretched to see in this a feat of witchcraft" (CG p. 52).—A. C.

29. The Three Paddys (told by Patrick Stokes, in Co. Dublin)
Paddy the Irishman, with his two comrades of other nationalities, is a favorite character in humorous tales in Ireland. Paddy always proves himself the smartest. One of the Motifs here is the well-known K44 (Dream bread: the most wonderful dream).—D. O.

In this story Paddy the Irishman, who eats the bread that others are dreaming to have, and his disappointed companions perfectly exemplify the differing Traveling and settled attitudes toward temporal development and personal gratification described in the Introduction, pp. 5, 52–53.—A. C.

30. It's a Long Way from Bangor to Donaghadee (sung by Patrick Stokes, in Co. Dublin)
Usually called "Brave Michael Power." Ballads concerning highwaymen are not numerous in Irish tradition. When they are to be found they frequently exhibit a quality as superior as anything to be found on the British mainland. Their scarcity may be explained in the context of the Irish political situation wherein deeds of outlawry are conventionally associated with political struggle rather than simple robbery—a situation that may be echoed in the many bank robberies taking place in contemporary Ireland. One is tempted to wonder if in some cases the robbery is for private gain if the thieves are not apprehended and for "the Cause" if they are. "Brennan on the Moor" (Laws L 7), "Whiskey in the Jar" (Laws L13 A), and "The Newry Highwayman" (OISB, pp. 70–71) are fine oft-encountered highwayman ballads; less well-known ballads may still be encountered in the field. Examples of this genre which I have recently come across include "The Newtownbarry Carman" and "Valentine O'Hara." The present song is not one I have ever collected from Travelers. Even among the settled community it is a rare song. The versions I have collected usually finish with the narrator promising he will go on to further adventures, as in the version to be published (on casette) by Sruthan Records, Dublin, which comes from a Co. Clare octogenarian. The present title of this song may be found misleading as in Ireland it usually applies to the humorous ballad "The Old Orange Flute," and outside Ireland it signifies that the tune belongs to the "Villikens and His Dinah" family, a family with ubiquitous progeny.
Donaghadee and Bangor are in Co. Down. Dungarven is in Co. Waterford, as is Carrick (on-Suir). There is another Carrick (on-Shannon), which is not too far from Elphin, Co. Roscommon. But then there is a Delvin (Delfinn?) in Co. Westmeath. Looking at the song from any geographical point of view, our hero covers a good many miles in the course of his adventures. "Mountain sogru," here, is usually "mounted dragoon," to rhyme with "stand soon."—T. M.

31. The Song of Lies (sung and told by Johnny Cassidy, in Co. Dublin)
This is an English-language version of "Amhrán na mBréag," a song composed without a word of truth in it. As here, the singer often gives as "authority" or basis of the text that a man was challenged to compose such a song on pain of death. Versions in Irish in *Irisleabhar na Gaedhilge* 12 (1902): 171, and *an Lóchrann* (June-August 1911), p. 5. Music and translation of another version are included in JIFSS 20 (1923). Ann Gilchrist treats the subject in *The Song of Marvels (or Lies)* in JFSS 5, 20: 277–296. Closely related are the "Tales of Lying," AT, nos. 1875–1965.—D. O. and T. M.

32. The Dead Girl
A good example of the teller's skill in employing conversation to present his story. Cf. Motif V42 (Masses release souls from purgatory). The idea of the returned dead having eyes continually open shows a keen development of narrative from observation. Irish variations on this theme, "The Dead Seek Help," are to be found in HIF, p. 247.—D. O. and T. M.

33. Father Kane and Father Fleming (told by Patrick Stokes, in Co. Dublin)
This is a variant of AT 1527a (Robber induced to waste his ammunition). For other Irish versions see IT. Priests are often regarded as having particularly keen insight, as well as magical powers, in Irish folk tradition.—D. O.

34. The Woman and the Banshee
This story seems to represent a confusion between belief concerning evil female spirits on the one hand and the banshee as presager of death on the other. Motif E452 (Ghost laid at cockcrow).—D. O.

The crying of professional women mourners (who, Patrick states here, become banshees after death) is "keening" (Ir. *caoine, caoineadh*: cry, lament). Keening for the dead goes back to ancient times in Ireland and has been commented on by native and visiting writers down through the centuries. Only in very recent times has the custom declined, although one is loathe to say with complete conviction that it is extinct. As late as 1956 Sidney Robertson Cowell recorded two examples of the *caoine* on Inishmore, one of the Aran Islands off the Galway coast. Both these examples, the only commercially available recordings of the *caoine*, may be heard on the Folkways album *Songs of Aran* (FM 4002). A collection of relevant essays in Irish has recently been edited by Brendán Ó Madagáin: *Gnéithe Den Chaointeoreacht* [Types of Laments] (Dublin, 1978).—T. M.

35. My Mother's Last Good-bye (sung by Mary Kiley, in Co. Dublin)
Obviously literary, and probably Victorian, in origin, this song owes some of its considerable popularity to broadsheets and popular songsters. Its main means of dissemination, however, is oral. This has been confirmed by the many informants who have sung this song for me throughout the country. It is not surprising that this song does not appear in any of the standard collections, for this is not the form of song editors to date have considered worthy of inclusion, a factor that must lead to a very unbalanced picture of the tradition their works seek to document.—T. M.

36. Paddy the Irishman and the Ghost (told by Patrick Stokes, in Co. Dublin)
Comparable to "Paddy the Irishman" in this collection. A similar popular anecdote to this one has Paddy the Irishman banishing a skunk (for a wager) by the overpowering smell of Paddy himself.—D. O.

37. Dan O'Connell (told by Patrick Stokes, in Co. Dublin)
Daniel O'Connell (orator, statesman, and lawyer, 1775–1847) is one of the most popular
hero figures in Irish tradition. Much of the lore concerning him has to do with his
smartness and repartee. He continually outwits the English and pompous Irish. The
legends here are among the most popular told about him and are widespread throughout
Ireland. For a discussion of Daniel in Irish folklore see Caoimhín Ó Danachair, "Dónall
Ó Conaill i mBéal na nDaoine," *Studia Hibernica* 14 (1974): 40–66. Other stories
concerning him can be found in NYT, nos. 52–56. Motifs used here include K195 (A
ribbon long enough to reach from ear to ear), H1515 (Attempt to kill hero by feeding
him poisoned food), B521.1 (Animal warns against poison), Q582.8 (Drinking poison
prepared for victim), and K1613 (Poisoner poisoned with his own poison).—D. O.

Several interesting customs are alluded to in this story, including the Irish practice of
giving severed or amputated body parts a proper churchyard burial. In the past many
instances were recorded of people journeying distances to bury an amputated limb
properly near other family graves in the home county and, too, of an amputee's friends
and relatives breaking into a doctor's house to obtain an amputated limb for this purpose
Folklore [London, 1907] 18, 1: 82). Singing a warning, as the serving woman does here
to O'Connell, was a means of disguising the warning's import, and Tinkers mentioned
to us the use of sung warnings in their own experience. Apparently Gypsies too used
this disguise. Sampson recorded and translated into English a Romany warning that was
sung by one Gypsy to a relative who was about to buy a bad horse at a fair: "Don't buy
that horse / He's a kicker—he'll kick you; / The Gentiles have been giving him /
Medicine all day" (JGLS 2: 80–93).
The "seven languages" the serving woman has here are referred to often in Irish
literature, and Groome quotes an English Gypsy as saying that "Romani . . . isn't one
of the Seven Languages." But the exact identity of these languages remains an enigma.
Munnelly suggests that "to say someone is possessed of the seven languages is to credit
[him] with extreme wisdom and such an ascription is common when the folk referred to
great [Irish] poets, e.g., Eoghan Rua Ó Súilleabháin." He also suggests that the symbolic
number seven emphasizes the magnitude of that wisdom. For an additional suggestion
see the glossary.—A. C.

38. The Woman and the Rat
Other examples of this narrative concerning a rat have been collected in various parts
of Ireland by the Irish Folklore Commission. Motifs included are A2435.6.2.1 (Snake
sucks from woman's breast) and D1385.4 (Silver bullet protects against giants, ghosts,
and witches).—D. O.

39. Barbry Allen (sung by Johnny Connors, in Co. Dublin)
Child, no. 94, "Barbara Allen," "Barbro Allen," etc. There can be little new to say on
this the most popular of all ballads. Bronson prints no less than 199 versions and even
this scarcely takes account of the scores of versions from Irish tradition. Of these, an
extremely interesting variant was recorded by Dr. Hugh Shields during fieldwork in Co.
Derry in July 1969. The singer sang 20 verses and the story contained therein included
the opposition of Barbry's parents to her consorting with her lover and thus a reason for
her reluctance to visit him on his deathbed. Dr. Shield's version is printed in *Folk Life:
The Journal of the Welsh Folklore Society* 10 (1972): 90–93, and can be heard on Leader
LP no. 4055, *Folk Ballads from Donegal and Derry*. This motif is also found in the HSP
text. The paucity of Irish versions of this ballad in print is an excellent gauge of the
sparsity of publication on the ballad tradition of Ireland.

North America: BNC 3:111–130 (North Carolina), PNF 3:652–659 (Newfoundland); *Britain*: JFSS 2:80 (Norfolk), OBS, pp. 476–477 (Scotland, exact area not specified); *Ireland*: HSP, no. 236 (Co. Derry), JAIM, p. 79 (Co. Limerick).—T. M.

40. The Woman with a Cow's Head
This anecdote is fairly popular in Ireland. For other versions see NYT, no. 92, and Ken Nixon, *Best Ulster Jokes* (London, 1970), pp. 34–35.—D. O. and T. M.

41. I Can't Stay at Home in This World Anymore (sung by Johnny Connors, in Co. Dublin)
The text given here is still a favorite with Irish Saturday-night cowboys and is featured by a majority of dance bands in country and town. Their source in all cases is the late Jim Reeves. Reeves died in 1964, but his records still sell extremely well on the Irish market.—T. M.

Also called "I Can't Feel at Home in This World Anymore," this song occurs quite late on Country recordings. J. E. Mainer's Mountaineers was the earliest group I could find doing it, in 1935 (Bluebird 6088), titled "This World Is Not My Home." All subsequent Country records have repeated this title. The Monroe Brothers did it in 1936 (Bluebird 6309) and Claude Sharpe and his Old Hickory Singers in 1949 (Columbia 20450). Sharpe also published it in one of his songbooks. None of the versions so much as hints at a composer's name. I assume it is a nineteenth-century revivalist or camp-meeting song spread by traveling evangelists.—R. O.

42. Pat from Bolaneer (sung by an anonymous man, in Co. Dublin)
Songs that purport to speak from the point of view of an animal, usually a horse, are not uncommon in Anglo-Irish tradition, and one of these, "Skewball," has not only entered the repertoire of singers in Britain and Ireland but is even found on the lips of such noted black American singers as Leadbelly. Some animal songs such as "The Papish Ass" or "The Old Grey Mare" have a politically allegorical sense while many others, including this song, do not. "Pat from Bolaneer" is merely the complaint of an ill-treated horse or donkey. "Pat of Mullingar" (OISB, pp. 178–179) is a song of praise for a jarveyman's favorite mare and was performed by Dan Lowrey, the owner of Dublin's most famous music hall. Maybe he was familiar with this song or perhaps its author was familiar with Lowrey's piece. There is a Timahoe in Co. Laois and another in Co. Kildare, but of Bolaneer I can find no trace.—T. M.

43. The Cats and the New Eyes (told by Patrick Stokes, in Co. Dublin)
Variant of the Irish ecotype of AT 613 (The two travelers). For other Irish examples see IT.—D. O.

Johnny Cassidy
Storyteller

1. Johnny Cassidy: Storyteller consists of biographical material recounted by Johnny Cassidy from 1967 through 1969 followed by six avowedly literary stories he told in the same period.

2. Hearts, Livers, and Lights and All (told by Johnny Cassidy, in Co. Dublin)
Cf. "Learning Flattery" in this collection. A wide variety of such tales are cataloged in
IT under AT, nos. 1696 (What should I have said/done?) through 1700 (I don't
know).—D. O.

3. Jack the Giant-killer (told by Johnny Cassidy, in Co. Dublin)
This is a composite story including AT, nos. 328 (The boy steals the giant's treasure),
1089 (Threshing contest), 1065 (Contest in chopping), 1062 (Throwing the stone), and
1149 (Children desire ogre's flesh). For Irish versions of these see IT. Irish storytellers
have a tendency to string together various tale types in this way, due to a desire for
stylized lengthening and elaboration.—D. O.

AT 1000 (Bargain not to become angry) plus 650 plus 1049 plus 1088 plus 1029.—S. O.

Some details of this version of "Jack the Giant-killer" seem to reflect conditions typical
of Ireland's spalpeenage system (see Introduction, p. 50), for example the prearranged
terms of Jack's employment, the manner in which he is boarded, the variety of his duties,
his sale of stolen farm produce, and the rapacity of his employer.—A. C.

4. The Hen-woman's Daughter (told by Johnny Cassidy, in Co. Dublin)
No point of reference in other collections or standard indexes has been found for this
interesting story-song in which the social degradation wrought by the illegitimacy of
both the hen-woman's daughter and her infant is repaired by the agency of other
illegitimate births to which the lady competitively confesses. The daughter, the lady,
and the lord all confess to their indiscretions in song. The comparable themes of a
discarded lover who sings at and destroys his sweetheart's wedding and an abducted bride
who is reunited with her brother by means of the message concealed in his song appear,
respectively, in no. 11 and no. 13 of the "Romantic Tales" Sean O'Sullivan lists as
common in Ireland (HIF, p. 625). Also, cf. AT 884 (The foresaken fiancée).—A. C.

5. The White Gallows (told by Johnny Cassidy, in Co. Dublin)
A composite tale including AT 653 (The four skillful brothers) plus AT 950 (Rhamp-
sinitus). For other Irish versions of both these types as well as other composite versions
including them, see IT.—D. O.

Whatever occupational titles they have in various versions of the tale, "the four skillful
brothers" are almost invariably one who hunts or shoots, one who prognosticates or is
farsighted (often an astronomer), one who steals, and one who mends (usually a tailor).
The fact that Tinkers have specialized in precisely the same group of activities (petty
thievery, hunting/poaching, foreseeing the future, and mending) may have inspired a
Tinker storyteller (either Johnny or some other) to make the mender a fellow craftsman,
thus giving the brotherhood the nice completeness it has here. In other versions the
princess chooses another brother; in choosing the Tinker here she chooses he who
epitomizes Traveling trade.
The Tinker would seem an improbable candidate for the task of boat mending required
of him in this tale. But there is a late nineteenth-century report from Scotland of a
Tinker band composed of three men, two women, and several children who were "sailing
from place to place on the West Coast and among the Islands, making and mending
pots and pans . . . [in a] good sized fishing smack" (JGLS 2:319–320). Other passing
references of the period also suggest that seafaring may have been an established way of
life for certain Tinker groups.

The exact significance of "White Gallows" as a name remains unclear. One figurative meaning is suggested in the glossary. And a principle like that stated in the English proverb "he that fears the gallows shall never be a good thief" may have contributed to the choice of this name for the tale's second ingenue.—A. C.

6. Dickie Milburn (told by Johnny Cassidy, in Co. Dublin)
"Dick Daglen," "The Song of Lies," "The Hen-woman's Daughter," and "Dickie Milburn" all utilize a prose section combined with verse. Of these, "Dickie Milburn" is the most developed example of the form, which is known as *cante fable*. As a tale, AT 1360C (Old Hildebrand), this piece has had a venerable existence and has been recorded all over Europe and beyond. In various forms it has appeared on British broadsheets since the eighteenth century. Klaus Roth prints a photograph of an early nineteenth-century broadsheet text in his *Ehbruchschwanke in Liedform* (Munich, 1978), p. 499, and quotes two other English texts, pp. 399–400.
    North America: JAF 55:134–136 (New Jersey); *Britain*: FMJ, vol. 1, part 4, p. 265 (Dorset); *Ireland*: B 7:71.—T. M.

7. Paying the Storyteller (told by Johnny Cassidy, in Co. Dublin)
A few stories about stories were popular in Ireland. The source for this narrative appears to be some variant of Motif H1382.2 (Quest for unknown story), which is found in medieval Irish literature. See Tom Peet Cross, *Motif-Index of Early Irish Literature* (Indiana, 1952), p. 353.—D. O.

GLOSSARY

The chief purpose of this glossary is to provide American readers with useful definitions of Tinker words and phrases that may be unfamiliar. Certain entries—such as Shelta and English street slang words and the names of Irish civic bodies—may be completely foreign to readers. Other entries have some but not universal currency in American speech, and yet others are merely peculiar spellings adopted to convey Tinker pronunciation. The definition given for each entry is not intended to be comprehensive but only to describe the active meaning of the word or phrase as it is used in this book. Further, while one word (e.g., "kilt") may be used in several different senses in the book's text, the glossary defines only the most unusual or idiomatic sense or senses of it (i.e., badly injured) and not the others (i.e., killed). Readers must therefore apply definitions with conscious discretion.

The glossary's secondary purpose is to call attention to features that distinguish the Tinkers' idiom overall. I have tried to point out some subtle differences and interesting parallels between this Irish idiom and a standard American one and to suggest possible derivations of words and phrases that I find provocative. Because Tinkers were not constrained by printed models, Tinker speech was exceptionally adaptable. Changes of pronunciation, for example, often changed or clouded word sense, and approximate homonyms might readily supplant traditional words in a song, adding new color and sometimes mystification. Tinker speech was rich with such "corruptions." Tinkers' innocence of print and other conditions also encouraged their retention of certain usages lost to other English-speaking Irish and often mistakenly interpreted by settled people as corruption. I have tried to recognize and vindicate these archaisms where they occur.

Apart from references to the book's bibliography, the abbreviations used here are

> I. — Irish
> S. — Shelta
> obsc. — obscure
> p.m. — possible meaning

abroad	outside, out-of-doors; out and moving around
a cush geal mo chroí	I., "bright pulse of my heart" (a term of endearment)
advertisement	announcement, notice (without commercial purpose)

a-fair	good; of course
afore	before
again	before; against the time that; after, afterward; another time; against, in opposition to
(to) agree	to be compatible; compliant, cooperative
(to) agree on it, to it	to find it agreeable
animo	S., milk
ara	I., "but, now, really, then, truly": used in an expostulatory or deprecating sense largely by speakers of English"—DD
arse	buttocks
ashamed	"reluctant through fear of shame"—OED
Assistance	financial assistance given by the state to small farmers and the unemployed in town and country
asleep in a box	knocked unconscious by a single blow
Athlone	a large town in Co. Westmeath on the River Shannon and an important market and military center; popular belief holds that Athlone lies in the exact center of Ireland and it has sometimes been called *Imleacan Eireann* (the navel of Ireland)
at the end of it	finally
atweenst	between
auld	old; "having the manners of sagacity of age" (OED) and being sentimentally respected for these traits; often an affectionate epithet
Auld Mammy	title of affectionate respect given an older woman (e.g., grandmother, mother-in-law) by members of her extended family
avenue	road that leads from a public thoroughfare across private lands to the door of a house; a driveway
awful	awesome, impressive; peculiar; unpleasant, oppressive; powerful
awful nobility	a great assembly of nobles or important people
(to) axe	to ask

B-man	one of the "B-Specials," a division of the Special Ulster Constabulary composed of part-time policemen who patrolled the northern side of the Republic of Ireland's border and who were reputed to have a strong dislike for the Catholic/nationalist section of the population
back-cheek	impertinence; mockery, sly insult
balty	obsc., p.m., corruption of Galtee
bank notes	paper money
banshee (*bean sidhe*)	I., fairy woman
barrage balloon	parachute silk
Battle of Waterloo	the 1815 battle in which Wellington defeated Napoleon and in which Irish regiments of the British army were importantly involved
barring	unless; in the event that
(the) bars	exercise bars
(the) bawn (*bán*)	I., "lea or grassland"—DD
be	by; beside
beating the hares up	beating bushes and grasses to flush hares for hunters
bedad	"by dad, or by God (cf. begad)"—OED
begad, begod	by God (exclamation)
begorra	obsc. (cf., I. "*goradh*—act of heating, warming, melting" and, perhaps irrelevantly, "*goradh an tinnceara*—tinker's solder"—DD)
(to have) belief in it	to be accustomed to it
belonging to	possessed by; related to (by family)
(to) benight	to trouble; to threaten
(to be) benighted	to have no place to stay at nightfall
(to) best	to overcome, triumph over; to be superior to
best-off	most prosperous

(the) best part	the larger part
(to) bet	to beat; to fight with
bet	beaten
(to) bethink	to consider deeply
(to) bid up	to take for one's own
big-a-boo	peek-a-boo
(the) big family	the whole number of children of a husband and wife
(the) big house	the residence of the owner of a large estate or farm
big, little, and small	all the various classes of local society
(the) big son	the eldest son
bit	coin (cf. American, "two bits")
bit of silver	silver coin (i.e., shilling, two-shilling, or half-crown piece)
bitter	bitter beer (usually English ale, never domestic Irish beer)
Black and Tans	a paramilitary force introduced into Ireland in 1920 by British authorities to act as a police force there; the Black and Tans were named after their mixed-color uniforms and were renowned for their extralegal and terrorist activities
black-and-tan	drink combining stout and ale
black bottle	black glass bottle in which Guinness, the favorite drink of Travelers and other Irish, is sold
Black Flu	a lethal strain of influenza epidemic in Ireland after World War I
(to) blackguard	to fool, trick, dupe; to betray
black man	any man whose coloring was darker than or whose features seemed exotic to the speaker (e.g., an African, Indian, Indo-Chinese); a man with dark hair
blessed candle	candle, obtained from the church, which has been consecrated for votive use and is attributed with curative powers
blessed well	natural well or spring associated with religious ritual and belief (often of pre-Christian origin) the waters of which have curative powers

(got) blind	wept (cf. American, "blinded by tears")
bloody	futile; cursed (corruption of the oath "by Our Lady")
blooming	awfully; "full-blown; often euphemistic for bloody"—*OED*
blue cabbage plants	a variety of edible cabbage with grayish or purplish-blue leaves, widely grown in gardens and farms
(to) blut about	to blubber about, complain about
bob	shilling
bog	wilderness wetlands, flat or low hills, where turf is cut; often thought to be the habitation of ancient and supernatural forces
boiler	a wide, shallow, open vessel
bones for sugar stick	bones broken into pieces like sugar candy
bonham	piglet (cf. I., *banbh*, piglet)
boreen (*bótharín*)	I., lane, little road
borna, borna	obsc., p.m., bang, bang (onomatopoeia for hammering) (cf. *OED*: "Borned, variant of *burned* a. *Obs.*, burnished" and "Burnished . . . to make [metal] shining by friction . . . with a hard smooth tool")
boss	person responsible for important decisions or management
boss-man	head of the household
(to) bottom	to solder a new bottom onto a metal vessel
(a) box	a blow of the hand
(the) box	accordion; concertina; coffin
brewery man	employee of a brewery where ale or beer is made
browned-off	exasperated; discouraged
buck flea	large, hungry flea
buckled	married
budget	leather bag or box in which a tinsmith kept his tools of trade; by extension, the tools themselves
buer	S., woman

(a) bugger	a perverse fool
buggered	spoiled, ruined; sodomized (although often used in a non-specific sense, the term always carries a sexual connotation)
bullock	young steer; bull calf
bull-wire	heavy wire or wire cable
bumbling	boasting
bunions	piglets (see *bonham*)
burking	deceiving, misleading (cf. *OED*: "Burking . . . a. The action of murdering in Burke's fashion," i.e., by smothering, "b. fig. The action of stifling or quietly but effectively suppressing")
burns	streams; springs
burra	S., good (*burra* or *burri* for "good, beautiful, great" appears provocatively in other contexts besides Shelta: in Anglo-Indian, "*burra*, adj. great, big; important, as *burra sahib*, chiefly in India: from ca. 1800" [DSUE] and in Gypsy speech, "Bare, or o . . . great, Bari . . . beautiful" [YG])
cake	loaf, usually of plain bread
camp	tent; shelter improvised of found materials such as boards, sheet metal (one of Groome's Gypsy mouthpieces described Tinkler-Gypsies as "mumply [half-breed] people . . . who called 'tents' camps and who could not stomach *hotchiwitchi* [hedgehog]"—IGT, p. 20)
cans	tinware
canna	cannot (emphatic negative)
cant	the secret language of Irish Tinkers (cf. *OED*: "the secret language or jargon used by gipsies, thieves, professional beggars, etc." and "trick, slight; illusion")
cant book	obsc., p.m., an informal written lexicon of the Tinkers' secret language (T. M. remarks: "I have been told by Travelers that such glossaries are kept by the police to aid them in keeping an eye on Travelers' affairs")
cap of skins	capful of potato skins
car	open cart, usually having two wheels and pulled by a horse or ass

carbine stuff	obsc., p.m., gunpowder; explosive
caravan	enclosed wagon or van, either horse or automobile drawn, fitted out as dwelling place
carnish	S., meat (according to other Traveling informants, *carnish* means unsalted meat, *féacha* means meat—RGW)
carnival	market, fair, or other gathering featuring games of chance, merry-go-rounds, exhibitions, and other amusements
case	suitcase
cash box	safe box, for holding money and other valuables
céilí house	I.–Eng., a house at which neighbors meet to sing, dance, and tell stories
cena	S., house
(to) chance	to risk
chap	young man, boy
chat	conversation
(to) chat	to engage socially, make contact; to talk persuasively
(to give) cheek	to speak discourteously or without observing social proprieties
cheeky	audacious, bold; impertinent
cherry	S., fire
Chert	obsc., p.m., tough (cf. OED: "Chert . . . App. a local term which has been taken into geological use . . . [for] a variety of quartz also called 'whinstone.'" Chert is said to derive from "chart . . . 'a rough common overrun with gorse'": Whinstone is said to be used figuratively to mean "hard, tough"); the fashion for naming dogs after ideal attributes (e.g., Fido, Swift) may have produced this name alluding to the toughness of gorse/furze/whins; a list of the sires of champion greyhounds in 1911–12 includes one "Whinstone Lad II"—BTG), p. 181
chesty	having a weak chest or symptoms of pulmonary disease
childer	children
chimbley	chimney

Christian Brothers	an Irish fraternity that is bound by religious commitment to educate the poor and that runs many grammar schools, generally believed to be superior to state-run schools
churchyard	yard of a church, usually a burial ground
churn	tin vessel, usually with two handles and of conical, waisted, or cylindrical shape, often with a fitted lid (not used for churning but resembling a wooden butter churn)
chum	friend
civvy station	police station (Irish police are often called "Civic Guards")
(in a) clap	suddenly
class	kind
clatter	heavy blow
clay pipe	slender pipe of white clay, until very recently one of the most popular modes of tobacco smoking for Irish of both sexes
(to) clear	to be cleared of charges; to be freed; to free
cloak of scale	mermaid's fishlike skin or garment
close harbor	sad confinement ("close-harbor, a harbor enclosed by break-waters or excavated in the shore," but this use of the phrase seems, additionally, figurative in the sense of "Close . . . shut up in prison . . . enclosed with clouds" and of "Harbor . . . place of sojourn . . . refuge"—OED)
cock of hay	mound of cut hay left in the field (cf. American, "haystack")
(to) cod	to lie; tell a half-truth; to playfully deceive
(a) cod	a fool; a dupe
coddin' or maddin' or buggin'	tricking or exaggerating or pretending
cold hair	artificial or vegetable fiber
(to) collar	to grasp, seize
comeragh	S., dog
Confirmation	ritual of the Roman Catholic church in which at the "age of reason" (about eleven years of age) a child's religious commitment is renewed and he/she takes a new, Christian name

Connack Rangers	Connaught Rangers, a highly regarded Irish regiment of the British army, prominent in the action at Talavera, Balaclava, the Dardanelles, and other sites; Connaught Rangers serving in India mutinied to protest atrocities committed in Ireland by the Black and Tans (see *Black and Tans*) and were widely admired for the act
Conny	Connemara man, thought to be hardy, hot-tempered, and self-reliant
constantlier	with greater regularity; more often
copper	penny
corn	grain (usually barley, oats, wheat, or rye)
corry	S., horse
corning season	harvest season
corporation man	official of the Dublin City Corporation, the primary municipal authority
(to) cotch	catch; hold
country	region characterized by family or cultural unities, not necessarily coinciding with county lines and not necessarily rural
countryman	regional or national identity; person with the same regional identity as oneself
County Home	main hospital in a given county, run by that county's "County Council"; a workhouse (see *workhouse*)
coursing hounds	greyhounds bred and trained to compete for speed and agility in chasing hares
cover	canvas sheet
cozy bar	public house with a section (often called "the snug") partitioned from its stand-up bar and furnished with chairs and tables, often reserved for the use of women or others who must be segregated from the majority of patrons
creel of turf	large basket of turf (see *turf*)
cross	crossroads
crow's nest	large, untidy nest of twigs built by a crow, often in a disused chimney

(to) cure	to change; to punish
(The) Curragh	a large plain in Co. Kildare, the site of horse races and gatherings since ancient times and the location of barracks and training facilities of the modern Irish army
curra	S.? obsc., p.m., metal spike, stiletto
cut him out	excluded him, shunned him
'cute	acute, sharp; clever, cunning
Cuttayer zee, Sraina!	S., Shut up, Mary!
cutting the cards	reading a fortune from a deck of playing cards
Da	Daddy
(the) Dail	the parliament of Ireland's central government, established in 1919 as an act of independence
daj	S.? obsc., p.m., look, grimace
deal ditch	ditch (see *ditch*) surmounted by a wooden barrier or fence of boards or sticks ("bog-deal," the trunks and limbs of trees found buried in bogs, was a commonly used timber on Irish farms)
dear	expensive
(to) decade away	obsc., p.m., to decay (a corruption)
decent	fair-minded, honorable; generous
delft	household dishes and vessels of ceramic clay, so-called after the popular ceramic wares formerly imported by Ireland and England from the manufacturing city of Delft in the Netherlands
delving rain	raining heavily
demesne	large estate or acreage, often enclosed by walls
(to) deserve	to discern; to see
despicions	suspiciousness
detail	account; explanation
De Valera	Eamon De Valera, Irish freedom fighter and leader of home-rule party; elected first president of the Dail in 1919

devere	obsc., p.m., appear
didideras	S.? Travelers; itinerants who are part Gypsy (cf. English Romany, *didikai*, half-breed)
differs	difference
digs	place to stay, usually a room in a rooming house
dindling away	dwindling away; disappearing
ding-dong	penis; bell
(to) dissemble	to have the appearance of
ditch	raised mound of earth, usually overgrown with grasses and hedges, dividing fields or running alongside a road
(to) do away with	to destroy, get rid of; to kill
do me endeavors	try my best
dogeen	little dog (the Irish diminutive suffix *een* is often attached to English words to give them a playful or affectionate sense)
(the) dole	the supplementary income provided by the state to those in need (cf. American, "welfare")
doler	dole payment
(to be) done	to be cheated, deceived
down the Swanee	lost forever; wasted
(to) draw	to attract; to cause
(to) draw down	to converse about; to give exaggerated praise to
drawing corn	hauling grain
(to) draw nice sceneries	to look attractive (cf. American, "make a pretty picture")
(to) draw out	to make; to produce
dravvy shan	S., Traveling man
drills	raised ridges of earth in which seeds or seedling are planted
(to) drink	to consume alcoholic drinks

(had a) drop in, taken	had imbibed a little alcohol, was a little drunk
dry cant	obsc., p.m., inferior, incomplete Shelta ("dry" often connotes incompleteness, failure, and the like, as in "dry run," "dried up," and "dry fist"—*DSUE*)
Dunlops	large English manufacturer of rubber goods, such as tires
dump pit	village or regional dump for garbage and refuse
(an) earth	a mound of earth, hillock
(to) eff	to curse; euphemism for "to fuck"
effer	fucker
effing	fucking
enchanted	empowered or inhabited by supernatural forces
engage this mare to do all work	claim this mare can do any kind of work
English papers	documents of discharge from the British army
et	ate; eaten
Evensong	Vespers, the evening church service of prayers, hymns, and lessons
(the) Exchange	(see *Labour Exchange*)
eyeglass pensioners	retired British army soldiers whose pensions included a stipend for the purchase of eyeglasses
fag(s)	cigarette(s)
(a) fair do	a fair or honorable fight
fair-green	common-field of a town, where markets, fairs, or other large gatherings are held
fairy tale	deceptive story, elaborate lie
(to) fall out	to disagree; to have bad relations
(a) falling out	a disagreement; a conflict
false courage	courage or confidence that springs from a false presumption of

	the nature of circumstances; bravado brought about by the consumption of alcohol
family	children
farms of land	fields used for grazing or cultivation
fee	S., meat (see *carnish*)
fee	money; personal wealth
feen	S., man; settled man
fiddler	cheater, trickster, confidence artist
fifty-fifty	on terms of equality
filing	working metal with a file
(to) fire	to throw with force
(the) fire it is rigged	the fire is raked, and properly banked so as to stay alive overnight
firing	kindling wood, fuel for a fire
firing away vermin	driving away fleas, lice, etc.
fiver	a five-pound note or bill
flail	wooden tool for threshing grain, consisting of a handle on a free-swinging paddle or rod with which the grain is beaten
(to) flash	to show off, boast about
(to) flog	to sell; to get rid of
flogged	densely covered
flux	paste used in soldering metal (it aids the flow of melted solder and inhibits the forming of oxides)
(to) follow	to chase, pursue; to hunt
forestry	plantation of trees
for one start	for instance
fortnight	two weeks

fortune	bridal gift of money or goods made to husband or bridal couple by the bride's parents; dowry
(your) fortune	the fulfillment of your destined role in life; a destiny
(the) Free State	the Irish Free State, established in 1922 following an act of the British parliament; consists of the twenty-six counties of the independent, present day Republic of Ireland (excluding those counties of Ulster ruled by Britain)
French father	priest who is a member of a French holy order (e.g., the Cistercians)
fret	flesh
front boards	curb or foot-board at the front of a horse-drawn caravan, where the driver mounts and sits
furze	prickly native shrub widely used as a food for animals and often chopped for this use, also called gorse or whins
gaffer	day-labor recruiter for construction and other manual labor jobs; overseer of such jobs
galvanize	zinc-plated sheet steel
gambling school	people gathered for the purpose of (illegal) gambling, usually on cards or "pitch and toss" (coin pitching)
gammy	S., bad
gammon	Shelta; talk, slang (cf. OED: "ridiculous nonsense used to deceive simple persons only")
ganger	foreman of a labor crew or gang
(the) Gap	Wicklow Gap, a desolate mountain pass
gared	S., money (cf. OED: "Goree . . . slang . . . Obs . . . money")
garrier	S., hare (cf. I., *giorria*, hare)
gate house, gate lodge	small house beside the gate of a large estate, where the one acting as gatekeeper lives
(me) generation	the family of which I am a part; my beginnings, personal origin
gentry	people of high rank, nobility

get me own back	take revenge; get back what I put into it
(to) get satisfaction	to take revenge or recompense
girleen	little girl
gloc	S., man; settled man
good and best to him	good luck to him (with an implication of irony and resignation)
good blood, bad blood, vinegar, wine	friendship can turn to animosity as readily as wine to vinegar
(the) good of a night	a night's sleep
go on a study	make a purposeful effort
Good night	Good evening (usually a salutation at meeting, not departing)
golden sovereign	British gold coin of high value
goldfrinch	goldfinch, a popular cage bird
gossoon (*garsún*)	I., youth, boy
go to the rosary	go to a devotional meeting featuring prayers counted on rosary beads and meditations
grain of	small amount of
grass field	field used for grazing
great action in me eye	good to look on
greeshuck (*gríosach*)	I., live coals from a fire, embers
grub	food
guard	policeman (the official name of the Irish police is *An Garda Síochana,* "The Civic Guard")
guinea	traditional monetary parcel used for large or formal purchases, consisting of one pound plus one shilling
Guinness	Guinness stout (beer)
gurrup	S.? small wooden board used for shaping tinware
Gypsy	person who is culturally, linguistically or by birth identified as Rom or a member of a related tribe

haggard	small farmyard in which hay or grain may be kept
half-crown	silver coin equal in value to two shillings and sixpence or (currently) one-eighth of one pound sterling
hall door	front entrance to a house
hames	rigid metal or wood curved structures of a horse collar
(to) hammer	to force; to work hard at
hankercher	handkerchief
hand-running	continuously
handstick	field anvil, a relatively light, small anvil that can be erected by driving its pointed base into the earth
hard	unyielding; tough, strong; adamant
hardware	tinware, crockery, and other goods offered for sale and distinguished from "software" such as lace and artificial flowers
harmless	ignorant, naive
hasty	threatening; alarming
(to) have him	to engage him, gain his commitment; to marry him
(to) hawk	to sell things, on the street in towns, or out in the countryside, from door to door or customer to customer
hawker	one who sells door to door, etc., usually a woman or child
head or harp	the signal to call a side for the flip of a coin, as Irish coins had the figure of a harp on one side (cf. American, "heads or tails")
headman	person in charge of an activity or an institution
hell for leather	fast; with energy and purpose
helter-skelter	running; hurrying as fast as possible
herd	one who cares for sheep, cattle, goats, pigs, or other animals; usually a man or boy
Hi	Wait, Stop (exclamation used to arrest or call attention, not a casual greeting)
High Mass	*missa solemnis,* one of the four types of Catholic mass, at which

	there is singing, use of incense, and additional clergymen to assist the celebrating priest
himself	the important one
(the) hob	the iron or stone lip or shelf of a fire grate on which vessels are placed to keep warm
hoist the black flag	declare war; take command
hokey-pokey	mischief
Holy Communion stage	the stage at which Catholic children prepare for and receive their First Holy Communion (partaking of the sacrament); about seven years of age
holy water	water that has been blessed in a special ritual by a priest and that has many sacramental and curative uses besides those acknowledged by the church
(the) Home	see County Home
horrible	painful, difficult; impressive
horse-car	horse-drawn cart or wagon
horse fair	fair held chiefly for the buying and selling of horses
idee	idea; plan
I'll see you alright	I'll provide for you, protect you
(to) implace	to station, position
in aloneness	psychologically isolated, in oneself
in it	taking part in it, involved; present
innocent	gullible
in the appearance of this cloud	in the form of a cloud
(an) iron	a gun, usually a shotgun; a tinsmith's hammer or anvil
ivy tree	large ivy plant, grown to the size of a bush
jackdaw	common corvine (black) bird that frequents human settlements

Jag	Jaguar, an expensive English automobile
jarred	mildly drunk, inebriated
Jew-man	Jew; Jewish trader
jin	jennet, the offspring of a male horse and a female ass, thought to be more intractible than either ass or mule
jobbing	doing jobs for pay based on the number of tasks or pieces completed
Jock	common sobriquet for a Scot (cf. Paddy or Mick for an Irishman, Taffy for a Welshman)
joy-bells	bells of celebration or announcement
justice	judge; magistrate
(to) keep the fire going	to sustain life and work
(to) kill	to punish; to beat
kilt	badly injured
(to) kleap	obsc., p.m., to keep, hold onto (cf. OED: "Cleek . . . to lay hold of, clutch, grasp, or seize firmly")
(to) knock the wall	to break a hole or an entrance through a wall
knocked	broken, destroyed, collapsed
Labour Exchange	the local employment office, which also authorizes individuals to receive National Assistance or the dole (see *Assistance* and *dole*); whenever work becomes available in the locality, recipients of Assistance or dole are obliged to renounce these payments and go out to work
lackeen	S., little girl
lads	boys or men (the term is occasionally used to describe a group of children of both sexes)
lapped	closely wrapped
lamper	S., bag
Land Commission	The Irish Land Commission, set up in 1881 under Gladstone to

	set rents fair to tenants and landlords, to arrange loans for tenant farmers who wished to buy their holdings, and to distribute the lands of the large estates among tenant farmers; after independence in 1921, the commission was chiefly concerned with dividing unoccupied farms among farmers who needed more land
laubra	S., hide, conceal
last	wooden form used by a cobbler to shape leather
(to) learn	to teach; to help someone learn
lemonade	any commercial soft drink, usually ginger-flavored
(a) lep	a leap; a sudden movement
(to) lep	to leap; to hasten
(to) let, leave out his mind	to become able to (i.e., do a particular thing)
(the) letter of an old hag's death	the authoritative document attesting to an old woman's death (cf. American, "death certificate")
(me) lifetime is coming up	the time allotted for my life is nearly ended (cf. American, "my time is up")
lifted	apprehended in a guilty act
lights	lungs of sheep, pigs, etc., which are eaten
linking one another	arm-in-arm
links	hillocks, hummocks of earth
lino	linoleum (synthetic flooring material)
Lipperpool 'sylum	Liverpool Asylum
(you can) listen to thunder but you canna see it	there are powerful forces that may be felt but not seen
live there for a farmer	live and work as a farmer
lobbed	dropped
lobstone	"Lapstone . . . A stone that shoemakers lay in their laps to beat their leather upon"—OED

lock of nails	handful of nails (OED: "Lock . . . A quantity, usually a small one, of any article")
loft	a half floor, a common feature of Irish cottages; often built above and around the chimney and hearth and used for sleeping and storage; the upper floor of a large barn
longer nor shorter	sooner or later
looking to view this	expecting this to happen
look sharp for 'em	take care of them
loom of ropes	coil of rope; quantity of rope
loose the button	urinate (euphemism)
lorc	S., horse-drawn or hand-drawn cart
lord	gentleman (the term is often used for any man conspicuous for his prosperity or polite manners)
lorry	large motor-driven truck; trailer truck
lose me and find me in trade	far exceed me in competence in the trade (cf. American, "run rings around me")
loub (*lúb*)	I., "loop, link, coil"—DD
low size	of small physical stature
(for) luck I'll give a pound	to bring luck to a transaction the seller often returns to the buyer a small part of his payment, in this case a pound; this return is called "giving the luck penny," regardless of its actual amount
lug	handle on the side or lid of a vessel, usually formed of a flat strip of steel and so called because of its resemblance to the human ear (OED: "Lug-ear")
lush mers	S., steal (*lush* has the additional meanings of "bite," "take," "drink," "smoke," and "eat"; *mers* is obscure)
linchpins	pins that secure wheels to an axle
mackintosh	raincoat
(the) main ocean	the open sea

magpie	common corvine (black and white) bird of fields and roadsides, thought to predict coming events by its behavior or numbers
(to) make free with	to freely socialize with; to flirt with or seduce
(to) make him out	to find him out, discover him
(to) make me soul	to make peace in my soul (i.e., prepare for death)
(a) man of my coat	a man with my religious office (cf. "a man of the cloth")
marble hole	quarry pit where marble has been excavated
mate	friend, companion
(to) mate along with	to act cooperatively with; to accompany
me	my (sometimes implying greater intimacy than the term *my*)
mean	ungenerous, tight-fisted
messages	light shopping; little necessities
minkers	S., Tinkers
missioner	missionary priest who makes the rounds of assorted Irish parishes holding "missions" consisting of talks and religious exercises intended to stimulate faithful Catholics and correct backsliders
Missus	ordinary term of respectful address used by Travelers toward a settled woman
Molly Bawn (*Mollaí Bán*)	I., fair Molly
morning dram	small drink of liquor taken in the morning as a restorative
morning dressing	morning-dress, a nineteenth-century woman's garment that was relatively light and informal
mortally	intensely, fervently
mountain men	men from the back country, hence backward or ignorant
Mountjoy	Mountjoy Prison, in Dublin
(to) move	to take

moving camp	dismantling shelters, packing gear, and Traveling to a new location
muck and clavver, muck and clobber	wet earth, mud, and stones
mumper(s)	"tramp(s) . . . among Gypsies it means a 'low-grade' Gypsy— one who has no van"—*DSUE*
murdering down	hostile, warning glance (cf., OED: "Down . . . *slang* . . . 'a down is a suspicion, alarm or discovery'")
musha (*muise*)	I., "indeed, well indeed"—*DD*
myxomatosis	infectious, usually fatal viral disease of rabbits intentionally introduced into Ireland in the 1950s as a means of controlling the rabbit population, which it decimated
nackers	S., rogues; Tinkers (cf. DSUE: "Nackers . . . the testicles")
National Assistance	see *Assistance*
National School	state-run school for free elementary education of children
nervous	frightened
netty-wire	wire netting (cf. American, "chicken wire")
never looked back	things went well from that point onward
nor	than
(the) North of Ireland	the section of the province of Ulster which remains part of the United Kingdom and participates in its parliament
oar boat	wooden boat propelled by oars (cf. American, "rowboat")
Odearest	trade name of an expensive mattress
off-the-grass-field	field used for grazing animals
oftimes	often
onct	once
(at the) one time	at the same time
only in history	confined to the past (i.e., not part of the present)

on the fair	at the fair ground
ornamental brown	obsc., p.m., corruption of "holland brown" (unbleached linen cloth)
out to the back	ouside; to have a fistfight
out of love with	separated from (similarly, in Ireland the phrase "to make love to" something can mean to borrow or steal it)
(to) overlook	to exert a supernatural and malicious influence upon (cf. American, "give the evil eye")
parson	any Protestant clergyman
(to) part	to part with, separate from
(for) particular	as a specific to cure disease; medicinal
passing blood	urinating blood
Peelers	policemen ("Peeler . . . a member of the Irish constabulary . . . Ex: Sir Robert Peel, Secretary for Ireland, 1812–1818"— DSUE)
(to) peacify	to calm, pacify
(to) peg	to throw; to aim
(to) pick at	to annoy
picture house	movie theater
pigeen	little pig
pig troughs	troughs to hold slops (food) for pigs
pint	pint of Guinness (see Guinness), an imperial pint (20 ounces) and the common measure of a single drink in a public house
plate	silver-plated metal, as in flatware and serving vessels
plattering	chattering, talking
Players	expensive English cigarettes sold (at the time) in packets of ten or twenty
playing on him	wearing him down, tiring him
(the) pledge	a vow to abstain from alcohol for a set period of time, extracted

from heavy drinkers by various Irish clergy; the Pioneer Total Abstinence Association, a large Irish teetotaling organization, also requires that its members (mostly settled) "take the pledge"

population	number of people
porter	dark, bitter-tasting beer
post-boy	letter carrier (cf. American, "mailman")
(in the) post office	Ireland's and England's postal systems maintained low-interest savings accounts for small depositors who were not (at that time) welcomed by other banks
presents	court-ordered monetary award to an injured plaintiff
press	large cupboard or wardrobe
press-bed	bed enclosed by walls (i.e., in a cupboardlike space in a caravan); bunk bed
priest's roll	stole or long cloth that the Roman Catholic priest wears around his neck when administering the sacraments
pub, public house	bar, an establishment licensed to sell alcoholic drinks to the public
puck of the droms	trickster of the roads ("Puck . . . a mischievous spirit or demon of popular superstition . . . in ME. a wicked man, a 'devil'; now, one given to mischievous tricks"—OED; and "Drum, Drom . . . a road . . . [a] Fly word in current use among . . . Gypsies" from Greek dromos, road.—YG)
pull that stick	take up a stick for a weapon
put a hump on	thrash, beat
(to be) put on remand	to be held in custody of the court while awaiting trial
put you a bird in the air	transform you into a bird
(to) queue	to line up, form a row
quack	medical practitioner or healer (not necessarily a fraudulent one)
quare	peculiar; extraordinary
quid	pound (monetary unit)

(on the) quiet	secretly
ragman	dealer in rags and other "soft" scrap
rake	wastrel, good-for-nothing
rake the fire	rake the ashes over the burning coals so as to preserve their fire until morning
(to) ramble	to move about paying social visits
rap you up	awaken you
reddens a file	heats a metal file until it is red hot
(to) reliver	"to give up again, restore"—OED
retching up of his stomach	vomiting
rigadoo	tramp's walking stick
(to be) right	to be adequate, competent, to be effective
(I'm) right	I'm ready, prepared
riz	arouse; aroused
road	direction (cf. American, "way")
(on the) road	involved in the Traveling way of life
(to) roar	to loudly lament, weep; to shout
(to) roast	to heat, burn; to cook (by any method)
rocking the cradle	becoming a parent
roldering and soldering	obsc., p.m., rosin or some other soldering aid and solder (early students of Shelta noted the use of "ordinary rhyming slang derived from English words, such as . . . *grawder* 'solder'"—SLI; perhaps this is another such example)
romind	obsc., p.m., mad with grief (cf. OED: "Romying," crying, lamenting)
(to) rook	to steal; to connive
rosin	substance derived from turpentine which is applied to metal surfaces to assist the flow of solder

roundabout, round-topped, roundy top caravan	horse-drawn caravan or wagon with a bowed top, usually of canvas over a wooden frame (also called a "barrel wagon" or caravan)
row	physical fight; brawl
run	path or accustomed route followed by a Traveling tradesman; habitual path of an animal
runner-string	drawstring
(to) run in ya	to be in your nature, by inheritance
ruz	lifted; risen
(to) sack, (to give the) sack	to dismiss from employment or participation
sacymore	sycamore tree
Salty Jack	obsc.
sark	S., field
saucepan	large tin cup with closed handle, used for scooping and serving; any pot with a rigid handle
scattering	separation and dispersal of family or friends, as when individuals go off to work and live in distant places
scaws	obsc., p.m., stains, spots (cf., OED: "the mod. Sc. *scaw* 'a faded or spoilt mark'")
(to) scour scaws	to scrub stains, possibly in cloth (cf. OED: "Scawe . . . some kind of defect in cloth")
scutches	rounded or slablike sticks of wood, used in shaping tin
(a), (the) serpent	evil incarnate, sometimes the Devil
serving woman	woman servant
settled	customarily residing in one place and participating in the vital institutions of that place; non-Traveling
(the) seven generations	obsc., references to this measurement of past time and/or family and the qualities that authenticate an individual or his enterprises are commonplace in Irish tales and lore; precisely what time-counting, kinship, or other system the "seven" here

	reflects is unknown; the number seven has widespread magical efficacy in Irish lore (e.g., a family's seventh son was often attributed with special powers)
(the) seven languages	obsc., p.m., Irish and English, plus the secret languages reviewed in SLI, namely, Shelta, Ogham, Bog Latin, Hisperic, and *Bearlagair na Saer* (secret language of masons)
(the) seventy-seven generations	obsc., probably an elaboration on "the seven generations" (see above) for purposes of emphasis
shade	S., policeman
sham	S., man; settled man
sharrack	S., barrack
sheet iron	sheet steel
(to) shift	to move by force
shimmies	sleeveless undergarments (cf. "chemise")
shiney's	obsc., p.m., corruption of "Chinese"
shook	in a bad way; without resources, enfeebled
shop	public house; general store
shower of an old hag's death	news of an old woman's death ("Shower . . . something which shows; an indicator"—*OED*)
shubrig	S.? obsc.
sick-up	impatient; exasperated (cf. American, "fed up")
sing-song	gathering at which there is general singing
(the) Site(s)	temporary housing and parking facilities for Travelers, authorized by the Dublin Corporation and other civic bodies, in or near Dublin and other towns
Sit up!	Get up into the car or wagon, so you may ride!
slated house	house with a slate roof (as opposed to thatch)
slop	edible waste (vegetable trimmings, soured milk, etc.) fed to animals
slop girl	kitchen maid

slummy	low, conniving character
smart	cunning, clever
(the) smoke of the fire	disadvantage, discomfort; ill fortune
snare	noose arranged so as to trap an animal
snips	heavy shears for cutting sheet metal
soft	without care, incautious(ly); foolish
soft money	money easily earned or got (cf. American, "easy money")
sogru	obsc. (cf. "Sugrue," a Co. Kerry surname)
solder	tin and lead alloy with a relatively low melting point, used for joining metals
some born to see and more born not to see	some people have the ability to perceive supernatural realities but the majority do not
soona	S., see
sooner	closer; shorter distance away (spatially)
(no) soot and no respect	obsc., p.m., no suit (i.e., honor, acknowledgment) and no respect (cf. OED: "*Suit and service*: attendance at court and personal service due from a tenant to his lord" and figurative uses of this and the comparable phrase "suit and homage")
Sork	S., Sir
SOS	urgent personal message
sound	able to survive; adequate
sportsman	man who takes risks, seeks adventure and gratification
spuds	potatoes
St. Stephens's Day	December 26, the day on which Wren Boys (local youths in costume) ceremonially hunt for and kill a wren (or an effigy) and then carry it from house to house, singing and accepting gifts of money, food, and drink from the householders
stauncher	stronger
steak	any large piece of edible beef, not necessarily a choice cut
steamcoach	railroad car

steamer	S., cigarette
steel rack	metal comb
(to) stick it	to endure it
stile	steps built over a wall or ditch, for easy crossing
(to) stir	to move gently, rhythmically
stone dead	severely; to the end of endurance
stone mad	completely outraged; violently distraught
stone weight	weight measured by stones (i.e., 14-pound units)
stood	remained inactive (with an implication of submissiveness)
(to) stop	to stay in one place
(a) store	a storage facility; a depository
stout	Guinness beer (cf., OED: "Stout . . . a cant name for strong beer")
strand	beach; sea's edge
stuttering justice	obsc., p.m., possibly a reference to the speech defect of a local district justice
subli	S., friend; boy
Subsistence	payment advanced against wages
summat	some of it
(a) sup	a modest quantity
swalleen	girl (i.e., possibly "little swallow" or corruption of I. *cailín*, colleen)
(to) swally	to swallow; to believe in; to regard as the truth
sweeping stick(en)	long, stout stick(s) and brush(es) used for cleaning chimneys
(to) tackle	to round up and harness
take chat from the justice	defer to the justice (judge), submit to the court and the law

taken up with	attracted to
(to) take the boat	to emigrate
tastier	more attractive; better looking
tenner	ten-pound note or bill
terrible	intensely; extraordinarily
thankful	grateful; relieved
thatch	thick straw or reed mat forming the roof of a house
(to) thrash	to thresh grain (i.e., separate the seeds from the stalks by beating)
three dozen of stout, ale	three dozen bottles of stout, ale
thrupence, thrupenny bit	coin worth three pennies, thus of little value, and often made of yellow brass (both Irish and English currencies are used in Ireland; the English thrupence was brass, the Irish was nickel)
tick	thick pad stuffed with feathers, fiber, or hair
tied together	locked in coitus
tights	underwear; swimming costume
timber	wooden (i.e., made of finished wood)
tin	tin-plated sheet steel
(to) tink	to hammer; to work tin; to think (a punning usage)
Tinker	outcaste; one who works as or is related to a tinsmith, an itinerant manufacturer of metal vessels and implements
tip	light blow
(to) tip	to bump; to give a light blow or push
'tis nothing that you won't do	you can make anything of tin; you can meet any exigency
(have the) title come back	regain a good reputation
topping	good, fine

torch	electric flashlight
torry	S., talk, conversation; language
(an) tothan	obsc., p.m., truth and . . . (an oath)
to their deadly cost of me	as they nearly cost me my life
(to) touch	to beg; to cajole
townland, townsland	smallest administrative unit into which the Irish countryside is divided, the sequence of division being townland, parish, barony, diocese, county; a townland can be wilderness, rural, or urban in nature
(no) trace nor trice	no evidence of (emphatic) ("trice . . . conjectured to be a variant or erroneous form of *trace*"—OED, cf. *roldering and soldering*)
trade	handcraft; business
(a) tradesman	one who has mastered a handcraft, usually tinsmithery
trailer	house-trailer, to be pulled by an automobile
transfer this to Athlone	arrange that payments be administered and collected from the office in another town, Athlone
trap	small, light, two-wheeled, horse-drawn vehicle
Traveler	Tinker (see *Tinker*); one who does not dwell or conduct life's business largely in one place and who does not participate fully in the society of the settled (see *settled*)
Traveling	way of life characteristic of Travelers and marked by constant or seasonal movement relating to occupation (not used to describe an occasional journey or the specific act of movement)
(to) try	to stand up to trial or use
turf	peat: decayed, compacted vegetation dug from bogs and dried for burning; for long the principal household fuel of modern rural Ireland
tuppence	two pennies
(a) turn	a favor; an act of assistance
(to) turn it to bad health	to say that it caused bad health

(to) turn money on it	to gain money by its use
(to) twist	to cheat, to contrive to rob
two toes	two sets of toes (i.e., both feet)
(a) twixt	between; shared by
two-and-six	two shillings and sixpence (or the coin called a "half-crown")
unvisible	invisible
van	procession; group of people and vehicles; motor-driven truck
vest	undergarment, usually a shirt with sleeves
vicar	a priest of the (Protestant) Church of Ireland; any Protestant clergyman
wagon	caravan; a covered, horse-drawn vehicle
wallflowers	common plant with yellow flowers which often climbs on masonry
(for the) want of	because of the lack, need of
(to) want	to need
wary, wary, wary	obsc., p.m., beware, beware, beware
wattle	slender stick of wood
wee water wagtail	wagtail: small black and white bird that wags its long tail up and down and that frequents farmyards, roadsides, and pastures
weed	S., tea
weigh the word	judge beforehand the effect of speaking
Western story	pulp magazine featuring adventure stories set in the American Wild West
(to) wheel	to push a wheeled vehicle by hand
(to) wheel turf	to bring in turf after it has been cut and dried
(neither) wheels nor meals	no means of livelihood (i.e., wheels to Travel a trade route, meals to sustain strength)

where me life lain	that part of my being that is the source of my aliveness (cf. "my heart")
whins	gorse bushes (see *furze*)
(to) whip	to punish, beat; to steal
whisht	"an utterance to enjoin silence"—*OED* (cf. American, "shush" and "hush")
whisht of a corner	obsc., p.m., becomes silent in a corner; hates being in a corner (cf. OED: "Wersh . . . Sc . . . b. Physically weak or sickly; squeamish")
(the) white gallows	obsc., p.m., fire; stake or apparatus at which victim is burned, here figurative (cf. "the black gallows," gibbet)
(the) why	the reason
(to) winn	to winnow, cause the chaff to be blown off the seeds of grain
winnowing machine	machine that tosses grain, separating chaff from seeds
window stool	window ledge or sill (cf. OED: "Stool . . . *Arch.* The sill of a window")
(to have the), (to get the) wind up	to become frightened
(the) wind is playing the harp	the wind is blowing hard (cf. American, "the wind is whistling") ("There is an Irish tale which tells how the inventor of the harp was inspired by listening to the wind play through the skeletal ribs of a whale or other creature"—*T.M.*)
windy	window
within	inside
woeful good stuff	great moral courage
wood	forest, grove
workhouse	charitable hostel for the sick, poor, or elderly, run by a fraternal, religious, or state organization
(the) works	the factory
works-boy	boy-of-all-work, hired to do odd jobs and run errands
works-men	hired hands, men employed for farm and maintenance work

world's well water	obsc. (many Irish tales set a hero the task of fetching special, miraculous water from "the Well at the World's End")
Yank	American
yarn	untrue story, lie; story
yarn-spinning	storytelling
ye	you (plural)
yoke	thing, device
your friend	an (undesignated) friend of yours
your man	the person referred to earlier; the person in question (cf. American, "the man," "my man")
yous	you (plural, emphatic)

REFERENCE
BIBLIOGRAPHY

AFH   Evans, George Ewart. *Ask the Fellows Who Cut the Hay*. London: Faber and Faber, 1965.

AT   Aarne, Antti, and Thompson, Stith. *The Types of the Folktale*. Folklore Fellows Communications no. 184. Helsinki, 1961.

B   The Folklore of Ireland Society. *Béaloideas*. Dublin, 1927 to present.

BAMI   Bunting, Edward. *The Ancient Music of Ireland*. Dublin, 1840.

BMCS   Broadwood, Lucy E., and Fuller Maitland, J. A. *English Country Songs*. London, 1893.

BNC   Brown, Frank C. *The Frank C. Brown Collection of North Carolina Folklore*. 7 vols. Durham, N.C., 1952–1964.

Bronson   Bronson, Bertrand Harris. *The Traditional Tunes of the Child Ballads with Their Texts, According to the Extant Records of Great Britain and America*. 4 vols. Princeton, 1959–1972.

BTG   Ash, Edward C. *The Book of the Greyhound*. London, 1933.

CC   Ewen, Stuart. *Captains of Consciousness*. New York: McGraw-Hill, 1977.

CG   Clébert, Jean-Paul. *The Gypsies*. London: Vista Books, 1963.

CH   Rees, Alwyn, and Rees, Brinley. *Celtic Heritage*. London, 1961.

Child   Child, Francis James. *The English and Scottish Ballads*. 5 vols. Boston and New York, 1882–1898. Reprint. New York, 1956 and 1965.

CIM   Lister, Raymond. *Craftsman in Metal*. Cranbury, N.J.: A. S. Barnes and Co., 1968.

CM   de Sola Pinto, V., and Rodway, A. E. *The Common Muse*. New York: Philosophical Library, 1957.

Coffin   Coffin, Tristam Potter, and Renwick, Roger de V. *The British Tradi-*

---

tional Ballad in North America. Rev. ed. Austin, Tex., and London, 1977.

DBV   Davis, Arthur Kyle. *Traditional Ballads of Virginia.* Cambridge, Mass., 1929.

DD   Davis, Arthur Kyle. *An Irish-English Dictionary.* Dublin, 1927. Reprint 1970.

DSUE   Patridge, Eric. *A Dictionary of Slang and Unconventional English.* New York, 1961.

EIS   Dillon, Myles. *Early Irish Society.* Reprint. Dublin, 1959.

ESPB   Child, Francis James. *English and Scottish Popular Ballads.* Cambridge, Mass.: The Riverside Press, 1904.

EWC   Thompson, E. P. *The Making of the English Working Class.* New York: Vintage Books, Random House, 1966.

FBV   Flanders, Helen Hartness, and Brown, George. *Vermont Folk-Songs and Ballads.* Brattleboro, Vt., 1932.

FL   MacNeill, Maire. *The Festival of Lughnasa.* London, 1962.

FMJ   Journal of the English Folk Dance and Song Society. *Folk Music Journal.* London, 1965–.

FRW   *Festschrift fur Robert Wildhaber.* Switzerland, 1972.

G   Yoors, Jan. *The Gypsies.* New York, 1967.

GB   Vesey, Fitzgerald, Brian. *Gypsies of Britain.* London, 1944.

GCM   Gardner, Emeylyn E., and Chickering, Geraldine J. *Ballads and Songs of Southern Michigan.* Ann Arbor, Mich., 1939.

GF   Groome, Francis Hindes. *Gypsy Folktales.* Reprint. Hatboro, Pa.: Folklore Associates, 1963.

GPST   Danaher, Kevin. *Gentle Places and Simple Things.* Cork: Mercier Press, 1964.

HCS   Healy, James N. *Comic Songs of Ireland.* Cork, 1978.

HF   Evans, George Ewart. *The Horse in the Furrow.* London: Faber and Faber, 1967.

HG   Simson, Walter. *A History of the Gipsies.* London, 1865.

HIF	O'Sullivan, Sean. *A Handbook of Irish Folklore.* Reprint. Hatboro, Pa.: Folklore Associates, 1963.
HMI	Costigan, Giovanni. *A History of Modern Ireland.* New York: Pegasus, 1970.
HSP	Henry, Sam. *Songs of the People.* A series of songs published in the *Northern Constitution* newspaper of Coleraine, Co. Derry, between the years 1923 and 1939.
HSP-M	Mouldern, John. *Selections from the Sam Henry Collection. Part One.* Belfast, 1979.
IGT	Groome, Francis Hindes. *In Gipsy Tents.* Edinburgh, 1880.
IT	Ó Súlleabhain, Seán (O'Sullivan, Sean) and Christiansen, Reidar Th. *The Types of the Irish Folktale.* Folklore Fellows Communications no. 188. Helsinki, 1967.
JAF	The American Folklore Society. *Journal of American Folklore.* Washington, D.C., 1888 to present.
JAIM	Joyce, Patrick Weston. *Ancient Irish Music.* Dublin, 1873.
JEFDSS	*Journal of the English Folk Dance and Song Society.* London, 1899–1931.
JFSS	*Journal of the Folk-Song Society.* London, 1899–1931.
JGLS	The Gypsy Lore Society. *Journal of the Gypsy Lore Society.* Old Series. 3 vols. Liverpool, 1888–1892.
JIFM	Joyce, Patrick Weston. *Old Irish Folk Music and Song.* Dublin, 1909.
JIFSS	*Journal of the Irish Folk-Song Society.* London, 1904–1937.
KBI	Kennedy, Peter. *Folksongs of Britain and Ireland.* London, 1975.
KNF	Karpeles, Maude. *Folk Songs from Newfoundland.* London, 1971.
Laws	Laws, G. Malcolm, Jr. *Native American Balladry.* Rev. ed. Philadelphia, 1964.
	American Balladry from British Broadsides. Philadelphia, 1957.
Motif	Thompson, Stith. *Motif-index of Folk Literature.* 6 vols. Copenhagen, 1955–1958.
MRC	Farb, Peter. *Man's Rise to Civilization.* New York: E. P. Dutton, 1978.
MSU	Morton, Robert. *Folksongs Sung in Ulster.* Cork, 1970.

NYT   Murphy, Michael J. *Now You're Talking*. Belfast, 1975.

OBS   Ord, John. *The Bothy Songs and Ballads of Aberdeen, Banff and Moray, Angus and the Mearns*. Paisley, 1930. A facsimile edition was published in Edinburgh by John Donald Ltd., no date, perhaps ca. 1974.

ODNR   Opie, Iona, and Opie, Peter. *The Oxford Dictionary of Nursery Rhymes*. London, 1952.

OED   *The Compact Edition of the Oxford English Dictionary*. 2 vols. New York, 1971.

OISB   O'Lochlainn, Colm. *Irish Street Ballads*. Dublin, 1935. Reprint, 1967.

OMSB   O'Lochlainn, Colm. *More Irish Street Ballads*. Dublin, 1965.

P   Binder, Pearl. *The Pearlies, a Social Record*. London, 1975.

PCSM   Dorson, Richard M., *Peasant Customs and Savage Myths*. London, 1968.

PNF   Peacock, Kenneth. *Songs of the Newfoundland Outports*. 3 vols. Ottawa, 1965.

PPC   Petrie, George. *The Petrie Collection of the Ancient Music of Ireland*. Dublin, 1855.

PWS   Purslow, Frank. *The Wanton Seed: A Selection from the Hammond and Gardiner Collection*. London, 1972.

Q   Responses to the Questionnaire about Tinkers, issued by the Irish Folklore Commission to its correspondents throughout Ireland in February 1952 (MS vols. 1255, 1256, 1379, 1540, 1565, 1669, Department of Irish Folklore, University College, Dublin).

RCI   The Commission on Itineracy. *Report of the Commission on Itineracy*. Dublin, 1963.

RGW   Maher, Sean. *The Road to God Knows Where*. Dublin, 1972.

RSC   Hyde, Douglas. *Religious Songs of Connacht*. Dublin, 1906.

SCL   Shields, Hugh. *A Latter Day Pastourelle*. In *Ceol: A Journal of Irish Music*, 1, 3: 5–10. Dublin, 1963.

SFE   Sharp, Cecil J. *Folk Songs of England*. 5 vols. London, 1908–1912.

SKSA   Sharp, Cecil J., and Karpeles, Maud. *English Folk Songs from the Southern Appalachians*. 2 vols. London, 1932.

SLI   Macalister, R. A. S. *The Secret Languages of Ireland.* London, 1937.

TP   Arden, John. *Three Plays.* Middlesex, England: Penguin, 1964.

UF   The Ulster Folk Museum. *Ulster Folklife.* Hollywood, Co. Down, 1955 to present.

WI   Basham, A. L. *The Wonder That Was India.* New York: Grove Press, 1959.

WNT   *Walton's New Treasury of Irish Songs and Ballads.* Dublin, 1966.

YG   Lucas, Joseph. *The Yetholm History of the Gipsies.* Kelso, Scotland, 1882.

INDEX

movement in, 16; institutions in, 13; isolation in, 9, 13; itinerancy in, 9, 10, 11, 14, 15–16, 17; land control in, 14–15; landlord system in, 15, 16; language in, 19, 20; law in, 14–15; migrant labor in, 50; Normans in, 13, 14; North of, 104, 105–106, 107; oral literature of, 1; outcastes in, 16; pastoralism in, 15; peasants of, 15–16; settlement in, 9, 13; slavery in, 11–12, 15; supernatural in, 38, 207–208 n. 4; surnames in, 28; tribes of, 9–10, 11, 13–14; turbulence in, 13–14, 21; Vikings in, 13

Irish Folklore Commission, 26
Irish Free State, 1, 104, 105, 106
Irish Tourist Board, 54
Itinerant/itinerancy, 14, 15–16, 17; horsemen, 12; metal-workers, 12, 30; performers, 9, 11, 12, 13; priests, 12–13; professionals, 9, 10–11; religious significance of, 38, 220 nn. 85, 86, 87; v. settled, 12; slaves, 11–12
"I Went into a Shiney's House," 62

Jackdaw, 206
"Jack the Giant-Killer," 187–191, 207–208 n. 4
Jail, 135, 208 n. 9, 226 n. 117
Jamaica, 18
James II, 212–213 n. 41
James V, 218 n. 77
Javis, John, 92
Jewelry, 41, 221 n. 95
Jews, 88, 89, 221 n. 97, 234 n. 2
Jigging, 49
"Johnny Faa, the Gypsy Laddie," 218 n. 77
Jordan, Fred, 237 n. 15
Joseph II, 221 n. 95, 225–226 n. 115
Journal of the Gypsy Lore Society, 24, 25
Joyce, Patrick Weston, 231–232 n. 17, 237 n. 13
Jumping the budget, 118–119, 120, 219 n. 80
Junk dealing, 51

Karpeles, Maude, 234 n. 3
Keady, 238–239 n. 20
Keegan, Paddy, 62
Keening, 242 n. 34

Kern (County), 217 n. 71
Kerry (County), 217 n. 71; Folklore Commission, 224–225 n. 112
Kilcerran, 157
Kildare, 142; County, 61, 71, 244 n. 42
Kilkenny, 64, 142, 228 n. 7; cats, 239 n. 22; County, 195; fair, 77, 171
Kings: coster, 33; funerals of, 217 n. 74; Tinker, 32–33, 217 n. 74, 223–224 n. 109; tribal, 9
Kinship, 3–4, 9–10, 11. See also Family/clan
Knocknatruss, 73
Knowledge, Tinkers on, 4, 208 n. 5

Labor: farm, xi, xii, xiii, 50, 53, 98–101, 182, 187–191; gypsy, 22–23; migrant, 50, 223 n. 107, 235–236 n. 7, 245 n. 3; skills, 3; slave, 11–12, 15; wage, 3, 22–23, 52, 207 n. 3, 209 n. 11, 224 n. 111
Labour Exchange, 33, 78, 124
Laminstown, 73
Land: control, 14–15; reform, 141
Land Commission, 141
Landlords, 15, 16, 140–141
Lang, Andrew, 214 n. 52
Language: English, 19, 20; gypsy, 18, 20 (see also Romany); Irish, 19, 20; secret, 19, 20, 207 n. 2; seven, 163, 243 n. 37; Tinker's, 18, 21, 62 (see also Shelta)
Laois (County), 244 n. 42
Laundresses, 50
Lavender, 37, 221 n. 94
Leadbelly, 244 n. 42
Lear/Leir, King, 236–237 n. 12
Leinster, 14, 158, 210–211 n. 25, 235 n. 36
Leland, Charles, 18, 19, 20, 212 n. 38, 229–230 n. 12
Lensfalee, 141
Letterfrack, 102
Lies/liars. See Lying/liars
Limerick (County), 231 n. 16
Liszt, Franz, 21
Literacy, xii, 5, 6, 71, 105, 106, 225 n. 113
Literature: gypsies in, 24, 25; oral, 1; Tinkers, 8, 9, 25; of Tinkers, xi
"The Little Beggarman," 94–95

Liverpool, 18, 27, 51, 123–124, 125–127
Lloyd, A. L., 230–231 n. 14
Lohan, Pat, 103–104
Loneliness, 7–8
Longford (County), 26
"Long Time A-Growing," 91
Lowrey, Dan, 244 n. 42
Lucas, Joseph, 212–213 n. 36, 213–214 n. 41
Luck, 5; swans and, 111–112
Lurchers, 40, 220 n. 91
Lying/liars, 87, 124; in songs, 152, 242 n. 31; to a priest, 151–153, 154

Macalister, R. A. S., 19, 20
"McCaffery Murder," 72
McCann, Paddy, 169
McCann, Tom, 169–170
McCormick, Big Tom, 233 n. 24
MacDonagh, Martin, 159
MacGreine, Padraig, 26, 208 nn. 5, 7, 215 n. 58, 236–237 n. 12
McLellan family, 212–213 n. 41
MacMahon, Bryan, 214 n. 55
MacNeill, Maire, 15
MacRitchie (of the Gypsy Lore Society), 24, 211–212 n. 36
MacWeeney, Alen, xi
Magical powers, 38
Magpies, 7, 68–69
Mainer, J. E., Mountaineers of, 244 n. 41
Makem, Tommy, 238–239 n. 20
Manchester, 27, 51, 78, 79, 80
Mandolin, 49
Mankam, John, 92
Maria Theresa, 221 n. 95
Marriage, 32, 117, 118; age at, 34; arranged, 34; endogamous, 21; gypsy, 35, 218–219 n. 78; Protestant-Catholic, 121; serial, 35, 219 n. 80; Tinker-settled, 34–35, 60–61
Mathis, Johnny, 6
Mattresses, 3, 50, 109–110
Mayo (County), 161, 162
Meath (County), 160, 210–211 n. 25
Merginstown, 63, 64
Mermaid, 63–64
Metal-working, 12, 17, 23, 24, 30, 216 nn. 63, 64. See also Blacksmith; Smithery; Tinsmithery; Whitesmith

Meyer, Kuno, 19
Missioners, 153–154, 168
"Molly Bawn," 112–113
Monasteries, 12
Money, 6, 75, 110, 135, 151–153, 154, 170
Monks, 20
Monroe Brothers, 244 n. 41
Moore, Thomas, 230 n. 13
Mortality, infant, 35, 215–216 n. 61
Mother, in songs, 85, 157
Mountain of Forth, 152
Mourners, 156, 242 n. 34
Moybalea, 109
Muhl, G., 234 n. 2
Mumpers, 87
Munnelly, Thomas, 223 n. 108, 225 n. 113, 243 n. 37
Munster, 14, 158, 210–211 n. 25
Murder: in songs, 72, 115; in stories, 201
Murphy, Bridget, xi, xiv, 7, 32, 59–85; ancestry of, 34–35, 60–61; crockery of, 36, 79; family relationships of, 47; goes to England, 78, 79, 80; as hawker, 76; on her mother, 62–63, 64, 65, 66, 67–69, 70, 72–73, 74, 80, 84–85; jobs of, 79, 81, 84; raises nephew, xii, 84; refused assistance, 33; settles, xii, 80, 81–83; on subsistence, 78; on traveling life, 70–71, 72–73, 74–77, 78, 79, 80, 84
Murphy, Delia, 236 n. 9
Murphy, Michael (Mickey), xii, 48, 74–77, 78, 79, 80, 81, 82
Murphy, Michael J., 237 n. 14
Murphy, Tom, 73–74, 222 n. 104
Music/musicians, 3, 6, 21, 48–49, 182
"My Gentle Mother's Grave," 85
"My Mary Dear," 82
"My Mother's Last Good-bye," 157
Myxomatosis, 96

Nails, 88, 89, 234 n. 2
Names. See Surnames
National Assistance, 124, 125
Nazis, 26
Nemeth, David, 210 n. 15
Newbridge, 109
Newcastle, 79
New England, 30
Newtown Mount Kennedy, 76

St. Peter, 81

Sampson, John, 18–19, 24, 212 n. 38, 220 n. 89, 221–222 n. 99, 222 n. 103, 239 n. 31, 243 n. 37

Schmul, 234 n. 2

Scotland, 18; gypsies in, 17, 212–213 n. 41, 213–214 n. 45; Tinkers in, 50, 209 n. 13

Scott, Walter, 218 n. 77

Scrap dealing, 42, 51, 75

Seduction: by priests, 139–140, 240 n. 26; in song, 142–143, 218 n. 77

Serpents, 164

Settled, xi, 172; gypsies become, 225–226 n. 115; as stable, 3; on success, 4; on time, 5; and Tinkers, 31, 32, 33–34, 37–38, 39, 40, 44–45, 53; compared to Tinkers, 2, 12, 131–132, 224 n. 110; on Tinkers, 5, 6, 26, 38, 42, 43; Tinkers become, xii, 2, 7–8, 52, 54–55, 80, 81–83, 133; Tinkers marry, 34–35, 60–61; Tinkers' services to, 37–38; as tradesmen/craftsmen, 30, 142

Sexual mores, 35, 218 n. 77

Shannon River, 28

Sharp, Cecil, 228 n. 8

Sharpe, Claude, 244 n. 41

Shaving, 108–109, 236 n. 10

Shelta, 18–20, 22, 25, 37, 47, 211 n. 29; Celtic sources of, 18, 19, 20; police and publicans know, 212 n. 38; and Romany, 19, 20; as secret, 19, 20; Yiddish in, 211 n. 30

Shields, Hugh, 232 n. 18, 232–233 n. 21, 243 n. 39

Shure, Mickey, 149

Simson, Walter, 212–213 n. 41, 217 n. 72, 219 n. 83

Singing, 36–37, 49, 60, 182; in pubs, 3; street, 237 n. 13; a warning, 163, 243 n. 37. See also Songs

Sites, xii, 54–55, 158, 160, 164, 170–171, 172, 173, 225–226 n. 115

"Skewball," 244 n. 42

Slavery, 11–12, 15, 17, 18

Sligo, 172

"A Small Bit of Butter," 100–101

Smithery, cold-metal, 3, 7, 22, 29. See also Blacksmith; Tinsmithery; Whitesmith

Smuggling, 50, 105, 223 n. 108

"Smuggling the Tin," 223 n. 108

"The Song of Lies," 152

Songs: begging in, 94–95; bothy, 235–236 n. 7; clothing in, 117–118; cobblers in, 127; courts in, 137; death in, 71, 85, 91, 230 n. 13; drinking, 236 n. 9; drowning in, 71; farm labor in, 100–101; ghosts in, 82, 113; hobos in, 67; horses in, 77, 171; lying in, 152, 242 n. 31; macaronic, 228 n. 7; mother in, 85, 157; murder in, 72, 115; parrots in, 118; quarrels in, 122–123; seduction in, 142–143, 218 n. 77; swans in, 112–113; warning in, 163, 243 n. 37

Soot, as medicinal, 221 n. 96

Spain, 23, 30

Spalpeenage, 50, 223 n. 107, 235–236 n. 7, 245 n. 3

Spancil Hill fair, 59–60, 226–227 n. 2

Spirits/supernatural, 38, 108–109; belief in, 207–208 n. 4; fear of, 165–166, 167. See also Banshees; Ghosts; Superstitions

Stanley, Tom, 213 n. 43, 223–224 n. 109

Statute of Kilkenny, 14

Stealing, 39–40, 48, 117–118, 234 n. 2, 237–238 n. 16

Stokes, Patrick, xi, 7, 30, 31, 34, 87–179, 207 n. 2, 212–213 n. 41, 216 n. 67; in army, 141, 148; begs, 94; children of, 130–131, 132–133, 158; on doctors, 140; on dole, 144–145, 148–149, 150; drinks, 112, 113, 114, 153, 167, 168–170, 173, 179; in Dublin, 157–158, 164, 178; on fairs, 135–136, 138; family of, 29, 90, 91; as farm laborer, 98–100; on foxes, 48, 150; goes to England, 123–127, 150–154; on hares, 48, 150; on his father, 89–90, 91, 92, 93, 94, 101, 102, 113, 116, 158; on his grandfather, 90; on his mother, 91, 92, 93, 94; in jail, 135; on landlords, 140–141; marries, 113, 114, 115; on missioners, 153–154, 168; on money/saving, 110, 135, 170; in North of Ireland, 104, 105–106, 107; on plastic, 142; on priests, 38, 99, 138–140, 151–154; on pubs, 136; sells horses, 135; sells mattresses, 3; on settling, 172; on Sites,

tents of, xii, 27, 46, 54, 76, 134, 172; on time, 5, 6–7, 146–147, 209 n. 10; and violence, 5, 39, 217 n. 71; vulnerability of, 3, 4, 39; on wage labor, 3, 52, 224 n. 111; wagons of, 27, 54, 215 n. 59, 226 n. 116; weddings of, 35, 117, 120–121; workmanship of, 30, 34, 128. *See also* Women

Tin plate, 29, 216 nn. 63, 65

Tinsmithery, xi, 2, 21, 29–31, 42, 50, 64, 75, 76; competitions in, 34; in Europe, 30; gypsies in, 216 nn. 63, 64; and itinerancy, 30; by settled, 30; Patrick Stokes does, xii, 47, 87, 89–90, 100, 101, 113, 127–128, 142, 178–179; tools in, 102, 178; World War II affects, 93–94, 109

Tipperary (County), 71, 195

Tiree, 18

Tobacco/smoking, 93–94

Tolstoy, Leo, 214 n. 48

Toothache, 81

Trade, 13; associations, 30–31; cycle/route, 31–32, 109, 182; societies, 210 n. 23

Trailers, 27, 170

Traveler. *See* Tinkers

Traveling life, xi, xii; Bridget Murphy on, 70–71, 72–73, 74–77, 78, 79, 80, 84

Trespass, 6, 39, 40, 96, 131, 208 n. 9

Tribes, 9–10, 11, 13–14

Trout, 96

Turf, 99, 161

Ulster, 14, 158, 210–211 n. 25, 215 n. 59

University College, Dublin, 26

Urquhart of Craigston, 234 n. 3

Valleymount, 73

Vesey-Fitzgerald, Brian, 22, 24, 218 n. 77

Victoria, Queen, 221 n. 95

Vikings, 13

Violence, 5, 39, 217 n. 71

Virginia, 18

Wagons, 27, 54, 215 n. 59, 226 n. 116

Wales, 17, 18

Wall, Johnny, 61

Wallflowers, 68

Walpole, Horace, 220 n. 91

Walsh, Maurice, 214 n. 55

Ward, John, 217 n. 74

Ward, Lawrence, 33

Ward, Martin, 217 n. 74

Ward, Mary Ellen, xii, 35, 114–115, 130, 165, 166–167, 172, 219 n. 81

Waterford, 13; County, 195, 241 n. 30

"The Waters O' Tyne," 228 n. 7

Water wagtails, 127, 238–239 n. 20

Weldon, Liam, 223 n. 108

Welfare. *See* Dole, on the; National Assistance

Westmeath (County), 241 n. 30

Wexford, 61, 149, 182, 184, 185, 186; County, xiii, 18, 236 n. 11

Whistle, 49

"The White Gallows," 195–203

White iron. *See* Tinsmithery

Whitesmith, 29, 30

Wicklow (County), xii, 62, 63, 71, 73, 76, 230 n. 13, 231 n. 15, 236 n. 11

William the Lion, 212–213 n. 41

Williams, Marvin, 228–229 n. 9

Windows, broken, 122, 137, 240 n. 25

Wintering over, 31–32, 182

Women, 38, 40, 168; beg, 43, 44–45; as dirty/unclean, 42, 43, 221 n. 98; economic role of, 34, 36, 39; do farm labor, 50; fight, 32, 217 n. 72; as fortune-tellers, 43–44; gypsy, 217 n. 72; as hawkers, 36, 37, 43, 45, 61–62, 73, 76, 130; as herbalists, 37; jobs of, 36, 42, 72–73, 90; modesty of, 35; as scrap dealers, 51; and settled, 39; singers, 60; status of, 43; surnames of, 219 n. 81; trade in clothes, 51

World Romani Congress, 226 n. 118

World War II, 1, 93–94, 109, 223 n. 108

Worshipful Company of Tin Plate Workers . . . , 30, 31

Wren Boys, 232 n. 19

Wrens, 79–80

"The Wren Song," 79–80

Yiddish, 211 n. 30

Yoors, Jan, 223–224 n. 109

"Young Tom Murphy," 73–74

Designer:	Carl Barile
Compositor:	Prestige Typography
Printer:	Vail-Ballou
Binder:	Vail-Ballou
Text:	10/11 Goudy Old Style
Display:	Caledonia/Memphis